Household and Class Relations

Household and Class Relations

Peasants and Landlords in Northern Peru

Carmen Diana Deere

UNIVERSITY OF CALIFORNIA PRESS

Berkeley • Los Angeles • Oxford

University of California Press
Berkeley and Los Angeles, California
University of California Press, Ltd.
Oxford, England
© 1990 by
The Regents of the University of California

**Library of Congress Cataloging-
in-Publication Data**

Deere, Carmen Diana.
  Household and class relations: peasants
and landlords in northern Peru/
Carmen Diana Deere.
    p. cm.
    Bibliography: p.
    Includes index.
    ISBN 0–520–06675–8 (alk. paper)
  1. Peasantry—Peru—Cajamarca (Dept.)
  2. Haciendas—Peru—Cajamarca (Dept.)
  3. Households—Peru—Cajamarca (Dept.)
  4. Cajamarca (Peru: Dept.)—Rural
conditions. I. Title. HD 1531. P4D44 1990
306.3'49'098515—dc 19—dc20   89–36110
                                            CIP

Printed in the United States of America

1   2   3   4   5   6   7   8   9

DATE			

For my grandparents
Wilma and O. U. Deere,
who nurtured my love for the land

CONTENTS

LIST OF TABLES AND MAPS / *ix*

PREFACE / *xiii*

INTRODUCTION / *1*

PART I • THE CAJAMARCAN HACIENDAS AND THE PEASANTRY, 1900–1940

1. The Political Economy of the First Four Decades:
   The Dominance of the Hacienda System / *23*
2. Class Relations on the Cajamarcan Haciendas / *59*
3. The Peasant Household on the Hacienda / *95*
4. The Peasant Household in the Independent Community / *121*

PART II • THE PROCESS OF CAPITALIST TRANSITION, 1940–1980

5. The Development of the Market in Milk, Land, and Labor / *147*
6. The Development of Agrarian Capitalism: Junker and Farmer Paths / *163*
7. The Peasant Household in the Transition / *187*
8. Structural Changes in the Provincial Economy / *210*
9. The Agrarian Reform in Cajamarca:
   State Intervention, Capital, Labor, and the Peasantry / *230*

PART III • THE CLASS ANALYTICS OF PEASANT HOUSEHOLD REPRODUCTION AND DIFFERENTIATION

10. The Generation of Household Income and Peasant Household
    Reproduction / *265*

11. The Family Life Cycle and Generational Reproduction / *292*
12. Epilogue: The Province in the 1980s / *316*

APPENDIX I: The 1876 and 1940 Peruvian Censuses / *327*
APPENDIX II: Estimating Peasant Household Income on the
Hacienda Combayo / *332*
APPENDIX III: The 1973 Cajamarca Income Survey / *336*
APPENDIX IV: The 1976 Peasant Family Survey / *338*

BIBLIOGRAPHY / *341*
INDEX / *355*

LIST OF TABLES AND MAPS

TABLES

1. Districts of the Province of Cajamarca, Ranked by the Concentration of Rural Population on Haciendas, 1940 / *25*
2. Average Annual Population Growth Rates, Province of Cajamarca, 1876–1940 / *30*
3. Estimated Person–Land Ratios, Province of Cajamarca, 1876 and 1940 / *32*
4. Arrendires of the Haciendas Santa Ursula and Porcón / *37*
5. Employment in the Peruvian Sugar and Rice Industries, 1912–1940 / *48*
6. Rental Arrangements on Haciendas in the Province of Cajamarca, 1920–1950 / *60*
7. Rental Rates for Grazing Rights on Haciendas, 1900–1944 / *66*
8. Labor Use on the Hacienda Combayo, Late 1920s / *80*
9. Daily Wage Rates on the Hacienda Combayo, 1917–1928 / *82*
10. Peasant Indebtedness on the Hacienda Combayo, 1928 and 1929 / *83*
11. Return per Hectare and per Labor Day Worked in Peasant Production on the Hacienda Combayo, 1917 / *113*
12. Average Amount of Landholdings, Animal Holdings, and Rental Payments by Resident Peasantry on the Hacienda Combayo, 1917 / *113*
13. Levels and Composition of Annual Household Income on the Hacienda Combayo, 1917 / *114*
14. Average Daily Wages Paid to Agricultural Field Hands in the Sugar Industry, 1912–1928 / *118*
15. PERULAC Suppliers, Daily Milk Collection, and Capacity Utilization, 1949–1978 / *152*

ix

16. Observations on Daily Agricultural Wages for Males, Province of Cajamarca, 1942–1976 / *160*

17. Registered Land Sales on Selected Haciendas / *176*

18. Purchases of Haciendas by Gonzalo Pajares / *182*

19. Land Sales by Gonzalo Pajares to the Resident Peasantry on Three Haciendas / *184*

20. Observations on Monthly Wages of Milkmaids on Provincial Dairy Farms, 1942–1976 / *190*

21. Distribution of Land Purchases by Size on Selected Haciendas / *194*

22. Price per Hectare, Land Sales on Selected Haciendas / *195*

23. Average Value of Land Purchase and Equivalency in Animal Stocks and Wage Labor on Selected Haciendas / *197*

24. Distribution of Land Purchases on Selected Haciendas According to Registered Owner / *200*

25. Estimated Average Annual Migration from the Department of Cajamarca to Selected Areas of Peru, 1952–1981 / *206*

26. Characteristics of the Dairy Industry, Province of Cajamarca, 1972 / *214*

27. Price of Milk Paid by PERULAC, 1944–1972 / *218*

28. Agricultural Enterprises Reporting to the Ministry of Labor, Department of Cajamarca, 1965–1981 / *222*

29. Participation of the Peasantry in the Sale and Purchase of Labor Power, Province of Cajamarca, 1973 / *224*

30. Cash Wages and the Payment of Labor in Kind, Province of Cajamarca, 1944 and 1976 / *227*

31. Agrarian Reform Adjudications, Province and Department of Cajamarca, December 31, 1980 / *239*

32. Associative Enterprises, Province of Cajamarca / *244–245*

33. Daily Wages Earned by Full-Time and Part-Time Wage Workers, Province of Cajamarca, 1973 and 1976 / *259*

34. The Class Analytics of the Composition of Peasant Household Income / *270*

35. Rates of Participation in Income-Generating Activities, by Land-Size Strata, 1973 / *273*

36. Sources of Income: Composition of Net Income, by Relative Importance of Source and Land-Size Strata, Province of Cajamarca, 1973 / *275*

37. Household Participation in Multiple Class Relations, by Land-Size Strata, Province of Cajamarca, 1973 / *277*

38. Levels of Household Reproduction, by Land-Size Strata, Province of Cajamarca, 1973 / *279*

39. Productivity and Surplus Appropriation in Agricultural Production, Province of Cajamarca, 1973 / *281*

40. Frequency Distribution of Activities of Peasant Households, by Principal Family Member Responsible, Province of Cajamarca, 1976 / *283*

41. Composition of Household Income, Province of Cajamarca, 1917 and 1973 / 290
42. Life History of María Rumay de Aguilár of Pariamarca / 293
43. Life History of Rosa Fernández de Sangay of La Succha / 294
44. Principal Activity of Children Who Have Left Home, by Sex and Land-Size Strata, Province of Cajamarca, 1976 / 308
A1. Concentration of Population on Haciendas, Department of Cajamarca, 1876 and 1940 / 328
A2. Concentration of Population on Haciendas, Province of Cajamarca, 1876 / 329

MAPS

1. Peru, Department of Cajamarca and Selected Departmental Capitals Highlighted / xii
2. Southern Provinces of Department of Cajamarca, Provincial Capitals, Province of Cajamarca and District Capitals Highlighted, 1970s / 26
3. Province of Cajamarca, District Capitals and Selected Haciendas, 1940s / 28

Map 1. Peru, Department of Cajamarca and Selected Departmental Capitals Highlighted

PREFACE

The Peruvian department of Cajamarca is known principally as the site where the conquistador Pizarro defeated the Inca Atahualpa, ushering in some three hundred years of Spanish colonial rule. But this northernmost highland department differs from the rest of the Peruvian highlands in other important ways. The kingdom of Cajamarca was the last major region conquered by the Incas, and the relatively brief fifty-seven years of Incan domination failed to completely transform the inherited socioeconomic and cultural structures. Nevertheless, for the Spanish, it proved to be the most easily acculturated highland region; by the late nineteenth century, the majority of the population of the department was categorized as white or mestizo and Spanish-speaking. Moreover, this was the most densely populated department of highland Peru. Most striking of all was that by 1940 in Cajamarca a higher proportion of the rural population resided on haciendas than in any other highland Peruvian department.

When I chose the province of Cajamarca as the field site for my dissertation research, my intent was to study the gender division of labor in peasant agricultural production and in the labor market. Cajamarca was appealing because, although it had been studied less than other regions of Peru, a major, three-year research effort, known as the Socio-Economic Study Program of the Cajamarca–La Libertad Pilot Project (PPCLL), was just being concluded there in 1975. Under the leadership of Ing. Efraín Franco, this program had conducted a household income survey of fifteen hundred farmers in the provinces of Cajamarca and Cajabamba, carried out twenty-six community case studies, and compiled case histories of four haciendas.

This book—an attempt to construct a regional economic history from the perspective of the peasant household—has been possible only because of the initial efforts of the researchers in the Socio-Economic Study Program. It was their work that led me to appreciate the importance of the hacienda system in Cajamarca. My greatest debt is to Efraín Franco, who arranged my affiliation in the Ministry of Agriculture in Cajamarca and who gave me access to the data generated by the Socio-Economic Study Program. He also provided critical guidance to the formulation of my research project. Two other members of the Socio-Economic Study Program, Françoise Chambeu and François Gorget, also contributed significantly to my understanding of Cajamarca's development process. Both were very generous in sharing the primary data they had collected on the hacienda system.

My other major debt is to Alain de Janvry, who directed my Ph.D. dissertation in the Department of Agricultural and Resource Economics at the University of California, Berkeley. My field research and dissertation, which formed the starting point for this work, bear the stamp of his intellectual guidance.

My field research methodology was quite interdisciplinary, reflecting my growing interest in the historical development of the region. I carried out my initial intention of executing a representative follow-up survey—focusing on the gender division of labor—of the 1973 Cajamarca Income Survey. In addition, my research methodology included participant observation and life histories of men and women in villages and former haciendas throughout the province, case studies of capitalist dairy enterprises and agrarian reform production cooperatives, and archival research. In a fifteen-month research project (September 1975 to December 1976) of this scale, spanning the province of Cajamarca, one naturally incurs a great many debts.

My community case studies included a number of villages initially studied by the researchers of the Socio-Economic Study Program: Hualqui, La Laimina, and La Succha in the district of Jesús; Quinoamayo and Michiquillay in La Encañada; La Laguna in San Marcos; and Pariamarca, Santa Barbara, and Tres Molinos in the district of Cajamarca. In most of these communities, I resided with the schoolteachers; I greatly appreciate their hospitality. In three of the villages, I conducted detailed household case studies, living and working with three families for several weeks. To them I owe a very special debt; regrettably, for the purposes of this study, they must remain anonymous.

I compiled life histories both in the independent peasant communities and in several villages made up of former haciendas, principally Combayo, Polloc, and Santa Ursula in the district of La Encañada. My case studies of capitalist dairy farms included the Hacienda Tres Molinos and the fundo Cristo Rey in the district of Cajamarca. The agrarian reform production cooperatives I studied included the CAPs Huacariz de San Antonio and Porcón in Cajamarca and the CAP Huayobamba in the district of San Marcos. I am most grateful to the management, to the members and workers of these enterprises, and to their families for the time they generously gave me.

I undertook the 1976 Peasant Family Survey after I had been in the field about nine months. I was assisted in carrying out the survey interviews by Ninfa A. de Figueroa, Juan Fernández Gonzales, Manuela Pajares, and Ilsen Rojas Fernández. Ilsen also served as my able research assistant throughout 1976 and again upon my return visit to Cajamarca in 1981. In addition, the survey was possible only because of the assistance of Bill Gibson and his brother, Charlie, who helped maintain a jeep.

In Cajamarca, I lived in the caserio Aranjuez, a community formed of recent immigrants just outside the city limits. My neighbors were extremely generous in sharing their skills as well as their histories and those of their communities of origin. I owe a special debt to my compadres Sebastiana and Samuel Briones, to Carmen and Marcelo Vásquez, and to the del Campo and Taico families.

Many of the propositions in this study were enriched by long conversations with Victor Bazán and Telmo Rojas during my stays in Cajamarca. I am also grateful to the Gómez Sánchez, Pajares, Rojas, and Rossell families of Cajamarca for sharing their histories with me. The friendship and assistance of Carmen Muñoz and Durman Franco, and Cecilia Barrantes, Socorro Barrantes, Nora Bonifáz, Haydée Quiroz, and the other members of the Women's Democratic Front of Cajamarca were also very important to me.

I discussed many of the ideas in this book with friends and colleagues in Lima during various visits. To Azril Bacal, Maruja Barrig, Heraclio Bonilla, José María Caballero, Blanca Fernández, Adolfo Figueroa, Efraín Gonzales, Gene Havens, Javier Iguiñiz, Susana Lastarria-Cornhiel, Hector Maletta, Rodrigo Montoya, Charlie Oman, and Virginia Vargas I am particularly indebted.

My research in Cajamarca was made possible by an International Doctoral Research Fellowship for Latin America and the Caribbean of the American Council of Learned Societies and the Social Science Research Council. I began the analysis of the primary historical data and the writing of the first drafts of this book while a faculty fellow at the Bunting Institute of Radcliffe College in 1981–1982. The Bunting fellowship, complemented by a grant from Sigma Xi, the Scientific Research Society, allowed me to return to Cajamarca province in December 1981 for a follow-up visit.

A faculty fellowship at the Kellogg Institute for International Studies at the University of Notre Dame in the fall of 1984 permitted me to complete the first draft of the manuscript. A number of people there, as well as other friends and colleagues, read and commented on various chapters. I am particularly grateful to Nelly Acevedo, Ron Berg, María de los Angeles Crummet, Nancy Folbre, Gillian Hart, Carol Heim, David Ruccio, Nola Reinhardt, Helen Safa, Marianne Schmink, Charles Wood, Diane Wolf, and Michael Zalkin.

The organization and arguments of the book were refined as a result of the careful reviews by Florencia Mallon, John Gitlitz, and an unidentified reviewer for the University of California Press. I have also learned a great deal about the Peruvian highlands from the research of Mallon and Gitlitz. Over the years, my collaborators on various studies of rural women have contributed in significant ways to my understanding of gender analysis. Particular thanks go to Magdalena León and to the women of the Rural Women's Studies Team at the Center for Research on the Agrarian Reform (CIERA) in Nicaragua and at the Center for Research for Feminist Action (CIPAF) in the Dominican Republic.

The moral support of my great-aunt Pilar García del Rosario, my cousin Pilar G. Campbell, and Marcia Rivera was crucial in maintaining my enthusiasm for the project as I revised the manuscript while on sabbatical in the spring of 1986 in my native Puerto Rico. In preparing this manuscript for publication, I was assisted by Larissa Costa, Judy Dietel, Hector Saez, and José Tavara. I am also indebted to Dr. Pauline Collins for advice on the bibliography and to Roy Doyan for his skillful cartographic work. The readability of the text is in large measure a result of the helpful assistance of John Stifler, James Leheny, and my editors at the University of California Press, particularly Naomi Schneider, Mary Lamprech, and Mary Renaud. Finally, the encouragement of my friends Carollee Benglesdorf and James Leheny ensured that this project would reach fruition.

Introduction

For the past several decades, debates in the field of peasant studies have centered on three issues: 1) the most appropriate concepts for the study of peasant economy; 2) the fate of the peasantry in capitalist social formations; and 3) the theoretical implications and class consequences of peasant participation in wage labor.

The first issue places peasant studies center-stage in the debates over the status of the concepts of historical materialism. Whether peasant economy can be thought of as a peasant mode of production, for example, largely depends on how one conceives of a mode of production. The difficulty of defining modes of production with any consistency has led many students of peasant studies to abandon this framework. The alternatives to analyses based on modes of production, however, have not proven to be totally satisfactory.

The second issue, the fate of the peasantry, has been the focus of the *campesinista/descampesinista* debate in Latin America.[1] This debate concerns the relevance of the Leninist hypothesis of peasant social differentiation to Third World social formations and whether social differentiation necessarily produces the two main classes of capitalism, proletarians and capitalists. In the descampesinista view, inequality in access to means of production among direct producers, in the context of growing commoditization of the rural economy, produces a growing concentration of means of production among the few while dispossessing the majority, providing the impetus for increased reliance on wage labor by poor peasants and the purchase of wage labor by rich peasants.

1. The campesinista/descampesinista debate has centered on Mexico but has been replicated throughout the Third World. Among the major contributors to the campesinista position in the Mexican case are Stavenhagen (1978), Warman (1980a, 1980b), Esteva (1978), and Díaz Polanco (1977). The descampesinista position is argued by Bartra (1974, 1982), Feder (1977, 1978), and Foladori (1981). See Meyers (1982) for a brief summary of the debate concerning Peru.

The campesinistas, in contrast, argue that the agrarian class structure generated by dependent, peripheral capitalism will not resemble that of the advanced capitalist countries because of the very nature of underdevelopment. In their view, complete proletarianization of the peasantry is precluded, either because the peasantry is functional to capital—as a source of cheap food production or cheap labor—or because peripheral capitalism cannot absorb a fully proletarian labor force. The campesinistas also question whether peasant social differentiation has taken place—citing factors intrinsic to peasant communities that mitigate inequalities—and highlight the factors that might explain the persistence of the peasantry.[2]

Nonetheless, the inverse relation between access to land and peasant participation in wage labor in Latin America has generally held empirically.[3] This trend has generated debate on the third issue: whether peasant participation in wage labor signals a process of proletarianization. Whereas most descampesinistas assume this by definition, campesinistas such as Arturo Warman (1980a, 202–208) argue that participation in wage labor might forestall complete dispossession of the peasantry through the contribution of wage income to the reproduction of peasant economy. This is an important insight. In the analysis offered here, I show how a focus on the multiple income-generating activities of peasant households helps explain the persistence of the peasantry in the midst of its often thorough social differentiation. I differ, however, from the campesinista position that one must always consider petty production as the primary objective of peasant households.

To resolve the stalemate in the debate over the fate of the Latin American peasantry, it is first necessary to reconsider the concepts of class analysis. The reformulation I employ here allows me to analyze the peasant household as the site of multiple class relations and then to show how peasant participation in multiple class relations serves to reproduce the peasant household as a unit of production and reproduction.

In the literature of peasant studies, relatively little attention has been given to the conditions that support the peasant household as both a unit of production and a unit of reproduction of labor power. All too often, relations within the peasant household are assumed to be unproblematic. My aim in this study is to analyze both the class relations in which peasant men and women participate and the relations between men and women within households. I explore how class relations impinge on and interact with the constitution and reproduction of peasant households and the social relations within them. I also

2. See Warman (1980b) for an in-depth analysis of the reciprocal relations within peasant communities that might mitigate the proletarianization process in its classic form, complete dispossession. See Reinhardt (1988) for a good summary of the factors intrinsic to the peasantry that might account for its persistence.

3. For evidence on this inverse relation, see Bartra (1974), Foladori (1981), and Deere and Wasserstrom (1981), a review of the major household income surveys undertaken in Latin America.

seek to illustrate how the constitution of households and the relations between men and women within them contribute to changes in—and the reproduction of—heterogeneous class relations.

This analysis of the interaction of household and class relations generates the central theme of the study: the subordination of women has high costs for the well-being of rural households, exacerbating peasant poverty. Moreover, the gender division of labor often sustains peasant household participation in multiple income-generating activities, explaining the persistence of the peasantry in the face of its growing impoverishment.

My focus on household and class relations also leads me to posit an interpretation of the Peruvian hacienda system, its dissolution, and the development of agrarian capitalism that differs from that of studies focusing on the transition from feudalism to capitalism, the articulation of modes of production, or the subsumption of noncapitalist units to capital. These other frameworks leave little room for human agency, for the role of rural men and women in shaping regional processes of socioeconomic change.

THE PROBLEM OF CONCEPTS IN PEASANT STUDIES

One of the central issues in peasant studies is whether peasant economy can be conceptualized as a mode of production, one whose theoretical status equals that of the concept of the capitalist mode of production. The answer to this question depends in part on how a mode of production is theoretically defined and how, specifically, the articulation of modes is theorized.

Through the 1960s, a mode of production had been defined within orthodox Marxist thought in terms of the base/superstructure dichotomy—the former encompassing the forces and relations of production, and the latter the corresponding ideological and political milieu. Dissatisfaction with the economic determinism inherent in the orthodox conceptual framework led to a number of alternative formulations of the concept of mode of production. Particularly influential was Louis Althusser's (1970) reformulation of the abstract concept of mode of production as comprising three levels—the economic, the political, and the ideological—each with relative autonomy. For others, however, mode of production remained an economic concept, defined in terms of the forces and relations of production or at the level of the enterprise.

Part of the controversy stems from the various ways Marx used the term *mode of production*, sometimes referring to the "mode of material production" (or how production is carried out) and at other times referring to an economic system or epoch of production.[4] Harold Wolpe (1980, 7–8), in his attempt to clarify the concept of mode of production, distinguishes between the "restricted" and the

4. One of the best summaries of this problem in the Marxist classics is provided by Montoya (1978, 145–156). The problem is also noted by Harnecker ([1969] 1985, 152–153).

"extended" use of the concept. The restricted form is used to encompass only the relations and forces of production at the level of the enterprise. The extended form takes into account not only the relations and forces of production but also the mechanisms by which enterprises are linked and the processes by which the relations and forces of production are reproduced, that is, its laws of motion. The extended form thus requires additional concepts—such as circulation, distribution, the state, and so on—to be specified as Marx specified them for the capitalist mode of production in the three volumes of *Capital.*

The debate over what constitutes a mode of production is part of an ongoing epistemological debate concerning the status and relation of abstract concepts in the production of theory and the problems of essentialism, rationalism, and empiricism.[5] For example, Barry Hindess and Paul Hirst (1975) argue for a restricted concept of mode of production in order to avoid the twin traps of teleology and idealism. They consider it possible to specify the mechanisms of reproduction of a mode of production (what they term the economic, political, and ideological "conditions of existence" of a mode of production) only at the concrete level of a given social formation.

There is general agreement that the concept of mode of production is abstract, whereas the term *social formation* refers to specific societies in history. But there is considerable disagreement about how the articulation of modes of production within given social formations should be conceptualized. Most prevalent in the literature has been the conceptualization of a social formation as the interrelation between a dominant extended mode and subordinated restricted modes (Wolpe 1980, 36–40). But unless this conceptualization is posited as a result of the transition from a social formation initially character-ized by two extended modes of production, one is left with the logical question of why some modes of production have laws of motion and others do not. In other words, it is not satisfactory to employ the concept of mode of production with two different meanings.

Another problem is a lack of agreement on how to specify the precapitalist or noncapitalist modes with which the capitalist mode may be articulated. Moreover, in much of the current Latin American agrarian literature, the noncapitalist mode is left undefined or vaguely specified to include all relations of production that are not capitalist. Others, often inspired by the work of A.V. Chayanov (1966), err in a different direction, in my opinion, by attempting to construct a specifically "peasant" mode of production. These attempts generally focus on constructing a peasant mode of production as a restricted concept, usually emphasizing the behavioral characteristics of the family-labor enterprise. This tendency is partly a result of the difficulty of specifying abstract political and ideological structures with which peasant enterprises

---

5. For a thorough discussion of these issues, see Resnick and Wolff (1987).

might be universally identified. It also is a result of the difficulty of conceptualizing the specific laws of motion of such a mode of production. Defining a peasant mode of production as a restricted concept does not solve all the problems, however.

Judith Ennew, Paul Hirst, and Keith Tribe (1977, 307–308) argue convincingly that the concept of a peasant mode of production is deficient because there is no one-to-one correspondence between a family-labor enterprise and a given set of relations of production. They illustrate how a family-labor enterprise is compatible with the relations of production of a number of modes of production, such as a simple commodity or a feudal mode. Moreover, they argue that the family-labor enterprise is not a unitary form, because it requires kinship relations as its condition of existence, relations that cannot be specified to allow construction of specific "peasant" relations of production.

Although they reject the concept of a peasant mode of production, Ennew, Hirst, and Tribe suggest that households that combine the functions of consumption and commodity production can best be analyzed as a simple commodity mode of production. The concept of this mode presupposes private property and a social division of labor engendering market exchange. What differentiates the simple commodity mode from what they consider ill-advised attempts to construct a peasant mode is that "the conditions of production are secured through the economic forms of private property in land ... and the production of commodities and their sale in the market. Hence the units of production are formed and maintained through *nonfamilial* conditions, conditions which do not depend on kinship or on communal sanction" (Ennew, Hirst, and Tribe 1977, 309).

I will subsequently challenge the proposition that simple commodity production based on household units can always be conceptualized independent of kinship. Here, I want to call attention to the fact that Ennew, Hirst, and Tribe remain strangely silent with respect to a key component of the relations of production: the specific mode of appropriation of surplus labor. Their construction of a simple commodity mode thus remains as unsatisfactory as they found the attempts to construct a peasant mode of production to be.

Other attempts to conceptualize peasant economy as a simple commodity mode of production suffer from a related deficiency: the need to posit the domination of this mode by another mode of production in order to account for the form of appropriation of surplus labor. Roger Bartra (1974), for example, considers the laws of motion of the simple commodity mode of production to be those of the dominant capitalist mode, and he locates the mode of appropriation of surplus labor from simple commodity producers in the articulation of the two modes rather than in the commodity mode's own relations of production. Bartra's formulation of the simple commodity mode of production is subject to the charge that it is an ahistorical mode of production, incapable of evolution except at the behest of capital (Foladori 1981, 133–137). No one, however, has yet satisfactorily constructed the laws of motion of a simple commodity mode of production, that is, constructed it as an extended mode.[6]

Dissatisfaction with the formalism of structuralism (Roseberry 1983; Smith 1984) or the implicit functionalism of positing the reproduction of a noncapitalist mode as a function of the logic of the dominant mode to which it is articulated has led many researchers to abandon an approach based on modes of production (Bernstein 1977; Zamósc 1979). Others, such as Hindess and Hirst (1977), now consider the concept of mode of production to be rationalist.[7] The problem of defining this concept in a consistent fashion has led me, and many other researchers, to search for alternative concepts for the analysis of peasant economy in capitalist social formations.

Forms of Production

Over the past decade, the concept of "form of production" has been increasingly used in the literature to describe variations of peasant economy. For some scholars, this concept is a way of sidestepping the debate over modes of production (Schejtman 1980, 117); for others, it allows the specification of enterprises with which no laws of motion can be identified or which would never be dominant within a social formation (Long and Roberts 1978, 326).

The most rigorous attempt to give theoretical content to the concept of form of production has been made by Harriet Friedmann, who argues that it should be defined by the double specification of the unit of production and the social formation: "The social formation provides the context for reproduction of units of production, and in combination with the internal structure of the unit, determines its conditions of reproduction, decomposition, or transformation" (1980, 160).

Friedmann's objective is to distinguish between a simple commodity form of production and specifically "peasant" forms in capitalist economies. Drawing on her work concerning the American plains, Friedmann clearly sees the simple commodity form as the capitalized family farm that does not rely on wage labor, in competition with capitalist firms that do. The conditions of reproduction of the simple commodity form are derived primarily from the capitalist economy: perfectly competitive product, input, credit, and labor

---

6. Foladori (1981, 133–137) proposes, somewhat problematically, that the law of motion of simple commodity production is the law of value (or competition), whether or not the capitalist mode of production is dominant. See de Janvry (1981, 97–98) for a critique of this position.

7. Rationalism became an issue partly because of the way Hindess and Hirst (1975) defined a mode of production, structured by the dominance of the relations of production. As they later note, the link between forces and relations of production implied a causal effect. Thus, in their 1977 work, they throw out the concept of mode of production and consider a social formation to be constituted by a plurality of relations of production and their conditions of existence, with no necessary structure. By this point, however, they have redefined the relations of production to consist of "the distribution of possession of and separation from the means of production" and the capacity to control their functioning (1977, 24). See Wolff and Resnick (1986) for criticism of this position.

markets, with a high degree of factor mobility. But the internal structure of the family farm, based on nonwage labor, also determines its conditions of reproduction; the farm will remain in production without earning a profit, in contrast to capitalist firms that must show profits. The only commonality between simple commodity production and various potential forms of peasant production, in Friedmann's analysis, is that household reproduction requires only the renewal of the means of production and of consumption. But although the aim of production in both forms is attaining subsistence (as historically defined within the social formation), in simple commodity production survival depends on adapting to changes in relative prices and continually increasing the level of output through technological change and a rising organic composition of capital (Friedmann 1980, 165).

Whereas the reproduction of the simple commodity form depends on its insertion into competitive market relations, the reproduction of peasant forms involves communal and noncommodity relations: horizontal and vertical reciprocal ties for renewal of means of production and subsistence (i.e., access to land, labor, credit, and products). The main dynamic force in Friedmann's formulation comes from the process of deepening commodity relations within the cycle of reproduction: "The transition from peasant to simple commodity production has as its underlying mechanism the individualization of productive enterprises. Personal ties for the mobilization of land, labor, means of production, and credit are replaced by market relations" (1980, 167).

Although Friedmann belabors the point that peasant production has no specific form but is defined by the particular conditions in which peasants exist, she reduces the concept of the simple commodity form to the particular historical conditions that allowed the development of capitalized family farms in advanced capitalism—market conditions that induced family farms to invest in capital rather than wage labor (Smith 1984). Specialized simple commodity producers, particularly artisans, have certainly existed in environments where capitalist relations were not yet dominant in the social formation. Another problem in Friedmann's attempt to develop a "classic" form of simple commodity production is that although product, input, and labor markets are well developed in Latin America, this has not led to the prevalence of capitalized family farms. Questions thus arise about the possibility of theoretically deriving a form of production from the double specification that Friedmann posits, viz., the characteristics of the social formation and the unit of production.

Whereas Friedmann and Carol Smith (1984) place primary emphasis on the external environment (commoditization or the phases of market development) to conceptualize forms of production, Jacques Chevalier (1983) and Alexander Schejtman (1980) highlight the internal logic and behavior of household-based production units to distinguish forms of production. Chevalier emphasizes how forms of simple commodity production may differ according to whether the valuation of labor and means of production is subject to market calculations, regardless of whether land and labor in fact constitute commodities. His main concern is discerning when simple commodity production may be considered a variant of capitalist production.

In contrast, Schejtman, heavily inspired by Chayanov, focuses on constructing a specific peasant form of production. He defines a peasant form of production in terms of "family-type units engaged in the process of [agricultural] production with the aim of ensuring from one cycle to another the reproduction of their living and working conditions" (1980, 117). The starting point for the organization of production is the available family labor force, and productive employment must be found for all family members. In addition, part of the family labor force is "nontransferable"; it has a zero opportunity cost in employment outside the farm. This consideration leads to the use of labor-intensive technology and invokes the Chayanovian law of labor intensity: there will be a tendency to intensify labor as the ratio of dependents to labor units rises. The employment of women, children, and the elderly within the family farm also provides the basis for the competitive edge of peasant units over capitalist forms of production: they can bring products to market at lower prices.

Schejtman argues against characterizing the peasant economy as an economy of petty commodity producers, because the internal logic of the unit of production is not purely market-oriented. Peasant households face the market principally as producers of use values (products that figure in the producers' own consumption); decisions about what to produce and what to sell are based on the role of a particular product in supplying the needs of the household. But Schejtman does allow for variability in the degree to which peasant households are integrated into the market. The more the household depends on purchased inputs and goods for its reproduction (i.e., the higher the degree of commoditization), the greater the role of market considerations in decisions regarding what and how to produce.

According to Schejtman (1980, 127–130), the articulation between peasant and capitalist forms takes place in both product and labor markets, leading to the "cheap food" and "cheap labor" functions of peasant economy that have been well described in the literature (de Janvry and Garramón 1977; de Janvry 1981; Astori 1983). The peasant form of production will produce cheap food because peasant households will produce at prices lower than those that capitalist firms, which must earn a profit to stay in business, would be willing to accept.[8] In the labor market, peasants provide cheap labor because they will accept a wage lower than the costs of reproduction of labor power. For

---

8. Caballero (1984) offers a rigorous analysis of the differences between unequal pricing, unequal exchange, and unequal competition and of how each is related to the organization of peasant and capitalist production.

Schejtman, both cheap food and cheap labor are based on the characteristics of the peasant economy, because the amount of labor and products supplied, as well as the wages and prices peasants are prepared to accept, is determined by production conditions and demographic characteristics of the peasant farm.

A major point of contention in the literature is the assumption that peasant or simple commodity producers aim only to meet subsistence needs. This assumption, held by many who follow the "forms" approach, seems tenable only if it is posited that subsistence is the *minimum* aim (Deere and de Janvry 1979; de Janvry 1981; Heynig 1982; Caballero 1984). It is particularly difficult to think of Friedmann's capitalized family farmers not acting at least as income maximizers, if not as profit maximizers, given that they must invest in expanded means of production to stay in business. There is a range of objectives consistent with the household as the basic unit of production, from generating subsistence to maximizing profit, and these will vary (although not necessarily in a linear fashion) with the degree of integration into markets. Moreover, it is important to recognize that simple reproduction may be the result of peasant integration into heterogeneous class relations and, thus, that the limitation on the possibilities for accumulation may result from exploitation or the transference of the peasant surplus to other social groups (Deere and de Janvry 1979; de Janvry 1981; Heynig 1982).

The Peasantry and Capital

As noted earlier, one of the main criticisms of the modes of production framework is that its application is often functionalist and teleological: whether the noncapitalist mode is reproduced or destroyed is seen as a function of the needs of the dominant capitalist mode. In a similar vein, world-systems theorists and others have fallen prey to "capital-logic," taking as their point of departure the notion that peasants are subsumed to capital and, at the extreme, that simple commodity producers embody capitalist social relations.

Samir Amin (1975, 54) was among the first to posit that petty commodity producers produced surplus value for capital. Applying Marx's concepts of "formal" and "real" subsumption, he argues that "the domination of the capitalist mode over petty commodity producers is expressed in the dispossession of the peasantry's *real* control over means of production, leaving it only with *formal* control. . . . Thus while the peasant retains the appearance of a petty commodity producer, in reality he is selling his labor power to capital" (1975, 40; my emphasis).

This line of analysis has been taken up by Jairus Banaji (1977) and Henry Bernstein (1977, 1979), who contend that once capital controls the conditions of peasant reproduction, it extracts surplus labor from peasant units in the form of absolute surplus value. In Bernstein's formulation, this comes about through the "simple reproduction squeeze": deteriorating terms of trade, capitalist competition, and vertical control over peasant production by different forms of capital (finance, merchant, the state, and so on) result in peasant units having to work longer hours and intensify the use of unpaid family labor. For Bernstein, petty commodity producers are reduced to "wage labor equivalents," whereas in Banaji's formulation peasants are proletarians.

Others who do not necessarily reach this conclusion concerning the class position of peasants but who do see absolute surplus value being extracted from petty commodity producers because of their lack of independence in input and product markets include Bartra (1974, 1982), Lehmann (1982), Goodman and Redclift (1982), Chevalier (1983), and Roseberry (1983).[9] In the most extreme application of this subsumption approach to the Latin American case, Claudia von Werlhof and Hanns-Peter Neuhoff (1982, 89) argue that the entire rural population (petty commodity producers, subsistence producers, and housewives) is subsumed to capital, enhancing capital accumulation, because contemporary production relations are the result of capitalist development.

Various Latin American scholars have taken issue with the subsumption framework, making an important distinction between market *subordination* and subsumption to capital at the level of production (Llambi 1981; Zamósc 1979; Foladori 1981). They argue that Marx's use of the concept of subsumption, whether formal or real, presupposed capitalist relations of production, the free wage worker. Labor must be a commodity for absolute surplus value to be appropriated, based on the distinction between necessary and surplus labor time and the sale of labor power for a wage less than the value of what labor produces.[10]

Those who see Marx's use of the concept of subsumption as first requiring capitalist relations of production argue that what must be theorized is *how* peasant units of production become subordinated to capital, producing formal subsumption in the extreme case (Foladori 1981, 127–139; Llambi 1981). For example, Luis Llambi defines different forms of market subordination of peasant units of production under capitalism in terms of the control that an external agent may have over a condition of reproduction of the peasant unit of production—an approach also followed by Rodrigo Montoya (1982, 75) and Danilo Astori (1983). If the result of these asymmetrical relations is the *absolute* control of peasant means of production by capitalist units, market subordina-

9. These authors differ, however, on how they see formal subsumption and the extraction of absolute surplus value. For Bartra (1974), absolute surplus value is extracted from simple commodity producers in the process of formation of prices of production, because these are based on capitalist conditions of production; he refers to this as unequal exchange. Goodman and Redclift (1982) place primary emphasis on Bernstein's simple reproduction squeeze.

10. The distinction between formal and real subsumption, on the one hand, and the appropriation of absolute versus relative surplus value, on the other, is based on the transformation of the labor process by capital that allows increases in productivity in the wage good industries to reduce necessary labor time. These authors argue that Marx's interest in employing the concept of subsumption was to demonstrate how capital revolutionized the productive process and had less to do with the relationship of petty commodity producers to capital.

tion has then produced subsumption at the level of production. This requires that peasant labor be remunerated at the market wage and, in my opinion, that the capitalist firm or its agent have effective control of the product of peasant labor (i.e., is the first appropriator). There seems to be general agreement that the concept of formal subsumption is most relevant to the case of complete peasant vertical integration into agro-industries.

The subordination approach is certainly preferable to simply positing that peasants surrender surplus value to capital once capitalism is dominant within a social formation. But focusing on peasant subordination or subsumption to capital provides few insights into how peasant households reproduce themselves as units of both production and reproduction over time. It also provides little space for taking into account that peasant households may participate in relations of production other than those with capital and that all of these relations may be the focus of struggle. An approach focusing on class relations tries to overcome these problems.

THE HOUSEHOLD AS THE SITE OF MULTIPLE
CLASS RELATIONS

It is increasingly recognized that Latin American peasant households often rely on a broad range of economic activities to generate income (Warman 1980b; Meyers 1982; Lehmann 1982; Roseberry 1983; Long and Roberts 1984; Collins 1988). These activities are sometimes referred to as the "polyvalent occupations" of rural household members (Feder 1971, 124). Besides working in agricultural or livestock production, combined with processing and transformation (i.e., farm activities), household members often are also petty merchants or artisans and engage in the service trades or wage work.

A number of years ago, Alain de Janvry and I developed a conceptual framework for the analysis of peasant households that takes into account their participation in multiple income-generating activities. Arguing that the analysis of peasantries under capitalism should be based on the multiple relations of production in which peasant households participate, we focused on the mechanisms of surplus extraction in production and circulation that might result in peasant households being able to attain only simple reproduction or that might produce social differentiation.[11] To further develop these insights, it is necessary to first draw upon recent innovations in Marxist class analysis.

11. In Deere and de Janvry (1979), we identify seven mechanisms of surplus extraction: three operate through rents that result from the private appropriation of land (rents in labor services, kind, and cash); three operate through the markets (for labor, products, and credit); and one operates through the state (taxes). However, we begged the question of whether each of these actually constitutes a relation of production or a class relation. Friedman (1984) has recently developed a similar conceptual framework, analyzing the income pooled by households as derived from a multiplicity of labor relations. But her analysis is also deficient in its class specification.

I have found the work of Stephen Resnick and Richard Wolff (1979, 1982; Wolff and Resnick 1986) particularly useful in rethinking the analysis of the class position of peasants. Resnick and Wolff draw attention to what was unique in Marx's analysis of class: his focus on the process "in which unpaid surplus labor is pumped out of direct producers" (Marx 1967, 3:791). Surplus labor represents the difference between the labor time required to reproduce productive laborers—what Marx termed necessary labor—and the total labor time expended by these producers.

Resnick and Wolff show how Marx's theory of class centered on the conceptual distinction between those individuals in society who perform necessary and surplus labor and those who extract it from direct producers, denoting this relation as the "fundamental" class process. Among the fundamental class processes they distinguish in Marx's work are the primitive communist, ancient, slave, feudal, and capitalist. Possibly the most important contribution Resnick and Wolff make in building a consistent theory of class is their distinction between the fundamental class process and what they describe as "subsumed" class processes. A subsumed class process consists of the distribution of surplus labor, whereas the fundamental class process refers to its performance and extraction. Subsumed classes neither perform nor extract surplus labor but rather "carry out certain specific social functions and sustain themselves by means of shares of extracted surplus labor distributed to them by one or another fundamental extracting class" (1982, 3).

In this formulation, subsumed classes can claim a share of the appropriated surplus, because they provide certain conditions of existence for the fundamental class process. The conditions of existence are economic, cultural, and political processes that condition and secure the reproduction of class processes (Resnick and Wolff 1979, 9). A condition of existence of a fundamental class process generates a subsumed class process—a distribution of the appropriated surplus labor—if it constitutes a process "without whose particular characteristics and interaction the class process could not and would not exist."

In their analysis of the capitalist fundamental class process, Resnick and Wolff examine three subsumed classes identified by Marx in *Capital*: merchants, moneylenders, and landlords. They argue that Marx treated these subsumed classes as directors of social processes that are conditions of existence of the capitalist class process: the circulation of commodities, the provision of capital, and access to land. The circulation of commodities is essential, for surplus value must be realized in money form. Merchants—pure buyers and sellers of commodities—earn a commercial profit that represents a transfer from capitalists of a portion of the surplus value they have extracted from productive laborers. Moneylenders control the money capital required by capitalists to set the labor process in motion. For providing this service, they earn interest that represents a transfer of a portion of the surplus value extracted by capitalists. Landlords earn a subsumed class payment from capitalists by virtue of their ownership of a limited resource. Because they control access to a condition of existence of capitalist agriculture, they must be paid a portion of the extracted surplus value in the form of capitalist rent payments.

Resnick and Wolff argue that in Marx's analysis societies can exhibit more than one fundamental class process at any time. He thus allowed for the possibility that multiple fundamental and subsumed classes could coexist. Most important, Marx also allowed for the possibility that individuals might occupy multiple class positions, based on their participation in distinct fundamental and subsumed class processes (Marx 1967, 2:129–152, cited in Resnick and Wolff 1982, 3). Within this framework, then, a social formation is defined as consisting of all the fundamental and subsumed class processes within a society. The task of analysis is understanding the overdetermined relationship and the potential struggle between fundamental classes and between fundamental and subsumed classes. Class struggle may occur over the form, manner, or size of surplus appropriation or its distribution, as well as over the economic, cultural, and political conditions of existence supporting different class processes.

In their attempt to rid Marxist class analysis of its essentialism, Resnick and Wolff distinguish class processes only on the basis of the different form and manner in which surplus labor is extracted or redistributed. In my view, in order to distinguish class processes further it is also necessary to specify how the means of production are distributed among producers and nonproducers and how this distribution is related to control of the labor process and to the mode of appropriation of surplus labor. I thus depart from the Resnick and Wolff formulation by employing the concept of "class relation" to refer to a fundamental class process and the conditions of existence necessary to distinguish different class processes from one another.[12]

I characterize feudal class relations by the existence of a class of landlords who own the principal means of production—land—and a class of direct producers who must pay rent in the form of labor services in order to obtain access to the means of production. Surplus labor is appropriated directly from the direct producers in a labor process controlled by landlords. Direct producers perform necessary labor in a labor process that they themselves control, for direct producers do possess certain means of production. This, in turn, may require other conditions of existence, such as economic or noneconomic coercion, to ensure that surplus labor is performed. These other specific

---

12. My definition of class relations is similar to what are commonly termed the "relations of production" in Marxist literature; it differs, however, in that 1) the entry point is taken to be the class process; and 2) property relations as well as control of the labor process are specified as conditions of existence of distinct forms of surplus labor appropriation. My definition is similar to Resnick and Wolff's (1979) early definition of class relations. They have subsequently dropped the specification of these conditions of existence and focused only on the class process, believing such specification to be essentialist.

conditions of existence are historically contingent, as is the form of ownership (feudal property, private property), and vary across social formations.[13]

Capitalist class relations are characterized by the existence of a class of workers dispossessed of the means of production and another class that owns the means of production. The workers, owning nothing but their labor power, sell their capacity to labor for a wage in order to acquire their means of subsistence. The capitalist class sets this labor power in motion in a labor process that it controls. Workers perform both necessary and surplus labor for the capitalists; necessary labor is equivalent to the value of labor power, defined as the value of the means of subsistence required to reproduce the commodity labor power. Surplus labor takes the form of surplus value and is equivalent to the difference between the total value of the commodities produced and the value of labor power. The capitalist class appropriates this surplus value as a result of its right of ownership over the product of labor.

Communal class relations are characterized by the collective possession of the means of production by direct producers, all of whom perform both necessary and surplus labor. Collective possession of the means of production and a collective labor process are what support the communal appropriation of surplus labor.[14] The class relations embodied in petty production are also characterized by the presence of only one fundamental class position: the petty producer. The petty producer's ownership of the means of production and control over the labor process in which both necessary and surplus labor are performed allows for the individual appropriation of surplus labor. As in the case of communal relations, no other class stands in opposition to the producing class in regard to control of the means of production and, hence, the ability to appropriate surplus labor. As in other fundamental class relations, however, subsumed classes may control certain conditions of existence of the petty class process and thus may be entitled to a share of the appropriated surplus. For example, to realize the value of their appropriated surplus product as exchange value (i.e., to engage in simple commodity production), petty producers may have to redistribute part of their appropriated surplus to merchants, if

13. The advantage of focusing on the class process as the form of production, appropriation, and distribution of surplus labor is that it draws attention to how similar forms of appropriation of surplus labor can exist in markedly different societies with historically specific conditions of existence. The "capitalism versus feudalism" debate in Latin America was rather sterile precisely because the debate was defined in terms of whether the same conditions governing feudal class relations in Europe could be found in Latin America (see Kay 1974). To get around the problem of historical specificity, many Latin American researchers (Harnecker 1985; Montoya 1978, 1980) refer to "servile relations"—what I define as feudal class relations.

14. I use the terms *communal* and *petty* class relations rather than *primitive communist* and *ancient* (as employed by Resnick and Wolff) in order to remove any notion of historical specificity from the concept. The words *primitive* and *ancient* imply a specification of the level of development of the productive forces. One of the aims of this reformulation of class analysis is to free class categories from their strict identification with historical epochs. For further development of the concept of the communal class process, see Amariglio (1984); on the petty class process, see Zalkin (1986).

merchants control a condition of existence of simple commodity production.[15]

The concepts of fundamental and subsumed class relations can be employed to produce an understanding of households—specifically, peasant households—that is quite different from standard analysis. First, it should be kept in mind that individuals, not households, are the bearers of class position. Moreover, individuals may occupy multiple class positions, participating in various fundamental class relations (as both petty producer and wage worker, for example) or in both a fundamental and a subsumed class relation (as petty producer and merchant). Because households are usually made up of more than one individual, and because individuals may occupy multiple class positions, the household must be reconceptualized as the potential site of multiple class relations.[16]

Second, what distinguishes the peasant household from the proletarian household is the former's access to means of production, making it both a unit of production and a unit of reproduction of labor power. This conceptualization of the peasant household, however, is compatible with a number of fundamental class relations—feudal, petty, communal, and capitalist—depending on the form of access to means of production and how surplus is appropriated. Within a rigorous framework of class analysis, there is no direct correspondence between the peasant household as a unit of production and reproduction, its relation to the means of production, and a specific form of surplus labor appropriation. Moreover, within this framework, household members may engage in feudal, petty, communal, and capitalist class relations at the same time.

Whether the primary fundamental class relation in which peasant households engage is in fact petty production depends on the conditions of existence of this class relation. These conditions in turn depend on the broader socioeconomic and political milieu, as well as on the economic, political, and ideological processes that support the peasant household as the site of reproduction of labor power.

THE HOUSEHOLD AS THE SITE OF REPRODUCTION OF LABOR POWER

The daily and generational reproduction of labor power is a general condition of existence for all class processes. For necessary and surplus labor to be

15. This approach both provides an explanation of how merchants may enrich themselves through transactions with the peasantry and preserves the consistency of Marx's analysis that required exploitation to take place in the sphere of production, not exchange. See Molano (1978, 52–53) and Zamósc (1979, 301–302) for similar views of the process of transfer or distribution of the peasant surplus product.

16. Most class designations of the peasant household invariably focus on the principal occupation of the male head of household, ignoring the gender and age division of labor within the household itself. Schmink (1984) also notes that it is problematic to assume that "supplementary" workers who have their own independent relation to the productive system necessarily belong to the class category of the head of household.

performed, the capacity to labor must be reproduced on a daily basis through such activities as cooking, cleaning, and washing clothes. And for a class process to be reproduced over time, biological reproduction (procreation), as well as the socialization of the next generation of productive workers, must also be ensured through child rearing, education, and so on.

But the specific form and manner of the reproduction of labor power, as well as the sites in which it takes place, are historically contingent. Aspects of daily and generational reproduction may be purchased as commodities, performed by direct producers for themselves, or carried out individually or collectively by other persons. The sites of labor power reproduction may include the marketplace, the state, the community, and households. The different sites, as well as the manner in which reproduction is carried out, will also influence whether these nonclass processes are subsumed class processes, that is, whether they are supported by a distribution of appropriated surplus labor from a fundamental class process.

A number of economic, political, and cultural practices influence whether or not and to what extent the household is the principal site of labor power reproduction. Such cultural practices include the rules and strategies governing kinship, marriage, and the constitution and dissolution of households. Also important are how individual and collective rights and obligations are structured and how these are ordered by gender and age.

Among the economic practices that determine whether the household is the principal site of reproduction of labor power are income pooling and shared consumption. These practices may depend in turn on whether the household is also the main unit of labor allocation, on whether it is a unit of production, and on the division of labor by gender and age. Other relevant economic practices include the distribution of resources and wealth between men and women, as well as how these resources are transmitted between generations.

Political practices that influence whether the household is the site of reproduction include the manner in which the state intervenes in defining and enforcing both the rules of household constitution and dissolution and the rights and responsibilities of individuals within the household to one another or among kin. The ability of states to legislate contractual relations between individuals is particularly important. Marriage and divorce, the ownership of property and inheritance, the mutual responsibilities of parents and children— all may be subject to state regulation. The state, for example, may intervene directly in determining whether the household is a unit of income pooling, legislating that a husband should control a wife's earnings or forcing fathers to contribute to child support.

These economic, cultural, and political practices are highly interrelated. In the analysis that follows, the economic, cultural, and political practices that support the constitution of households as the site of reproduction of labor power are referred to as *household relations*.

Conceptualizing the household as the principal site of the reproduction of labor power does *not* mean that at any given moment it is the only site where labor power is reproduced. The degree of development of commodity markets and of the state will influence the extent to which labor power is reproduced socially rather than in household units.[17] But the content of household relations cannot be derived simply from the degree of development of commodity markets, the state, or class relations.[18] Rather, these variables are all highly interactive.

For example, the cultural rules governing land inheritance are often important in determining whether households are constituted as units of production as well as of reproduction. Cultural rules regarding the timing of inheritance may also influence variables such as age at marriage and whether marriage is coterminous with the constitution of new households. Hence, the reproduction of the fundamental and subsumed class processes of petty production may be governed not only by the rules of the marketplace in a capitalist social formation but also by the practices encompassed in household relations.

Household and class relations also intersect with gender relations. How resources and wealth are distributed among men and women may influence each individual's relative bargaining position within the household and thus may influence practices such as income pooling, shared consumption, and the gender division of labor. Similarly, the gender division of labor within the household may influence the class relations in which given household members participate, in turn influencing the relative position of men and women in society and in the home.

Whether households are universally the site of income pooling and shared consumption has been the subject of considerable debate in the literature.[19] Kathie Friedman (1984, 45–46), for example, contends that sharing is the central characteristic of households; Hans-Dieter Evers, Wolfgang Clauss, and Diana Wong (1984, 33) argue that this assumption does not hold cross-culturally. There is mounting evidence that not all income sources are necessarily pooled within households. Ben White's admonition is helpful here:

---

17. In advanced capitalism, many activities required for the reproduction of labor power that had previously taken place in the household were either commoditized or taken over by the state (e.g., education). See Hartmann (1981) for an analysis of the changing composition of domestic labor.

18. Smith, Wallerstein, and Evers (1984, 7, 12), who define the household as a system of reproduction of labor power, also argue that it should not be considered as primordial but rather as a historically contingent site of labor power reproduction. Nevertheless, their analysis is quite essentialist, for they analyze the household totally in terms of its ability to provide cheap wage labor to capital. Also see Wallerstein (1984).

19. See Netting, Wilk, and Arnould (1984, xx–xxiv) for an excellent discussion of the problems of pursuing a definition of the household that holds universally.

"There is no clear-cut distinction between 'sharing' and 'not-sharing,' but rather a range of possible domestic arrangements in any society in which there are different areas of sharing, each with its own degree of sharing" (1980, 14). He notes, moreover, that "sharing" all or part of household income does not necessarily result in an egalitarian allocation of consumption, resources, or work among household members.

While White's work has centered on the analysis of intergenerational inequality, feminist researchers have highlighted the existence of gender inequality within households (Hartmann 1981; Bourque and Warren 1981). Reviewing a broad range of cross-cultural material, Folbre (1986) argues that women work more and consume less than men do within households and share less in household decision making. For Folbre, inequality within the household is linked to differences between men and women in bargaining power. She considers these differences not just culturally determined but directly related to the institutions of patriarchy; they include systematic differences in access to means of production, wealth, and wages.

Rather than positing female subordination as a result of patriarchy—a structured system of male dominance—I find it preferable to focus on gender relations as an arena of potential conflict and struggle. All of the conditions of household constitution and reproduction may involve struggle between men and women and adults and children. Procreation, child rearing, inheritance, consumption, and the division of work are but a few of the areas in which the interests of men and women may differ and come into conflict. To assume male dominance denies women a role as agents of social change.

Although the ordering of relationships among individuals on the basis of gender and age is certainly affected by material conditions internal and external to the household, it is also important to consider that cultural processes may be relatively autonomous. As Rayna Rapp has argued: "It is through commitment to the concept of family that people are recruited to the material relations of households. Because people accept the meaningfulness of family, they enter into relations of production, reproduction, and consumption with one another" (1978, 177).

The intersection of gender, household, and class relations is particularly important in thinking about whether the activities encompassed in the reproduction of labor power within households are supported by a subsumed class process. As discussed above, a condition of existence of all class relations is the daily and generational reproduction of labor power. But it is not a foregone conclusion that a subsumed class process (a distribution of surplus labor appropriated in a fundamental class relation) takes place to support this activity. Subsumed class processes are relations of struggle and may interact in contradictory ways with other arenas of potential conflict, such as those embodied in household and gender relations.

Under what conditions might domestic labor command a subsumed class payment? The most likely case would probably involve a peasant household constituted as a unit of production and reproduction through the practice of bilateral land inheritance.[20] Bilateral inheritance might provide women with the bargaining power both to support a gender division of labor whereby the man was the petty producer and the woman the domestic laborer and to guarantee income pooling and shared consumption of the fruits of petty production. In this case, income pooling represents a redistribution of the surplus labor appropriated by the petty producer to a nonproducer (the domestic laborer) for providing key conditions of the fundamental class process (daily and generational reproduction). The more typical case in peasant societies, however, is that the woman, in addition to being a domestic laborer, is also a petty producer, with the unit of production being a family farm. The characterization of the labor process might range from equality of participation in production, decision making, and control over income to the monopolization of control over decisions and income by the man. All of these factors might influence the degree of income pooling, from the "perfect exchange of equivalents" assumed in the literature to, literally, "unpaid family labor." The task of analysis is to bring together the potential tensions in household and gender relations to understand their interaction with class relations and the potential for social change.

The setting for the analysis of household and class relations presented here is the province of Cajamarca in the Peruvian department of the same name (see Map 1). The dominance of the hacienda system in Cajamarca and the relationship between the peasantry and the landlord class are the subjects of Part I. Part II analyzes the process through which capitalist class relations became predominant in the Cajamarcan countryside. In Part III, the peasant economy of the 1970s is examined quantitatively, drawing on a schematic model of peasant household reproduction and differentiation.

20. A historical example of domestic labor commanding a subsumed class payment in the case of the advanced capitalist economies is provided by the struggle for the family wage in the late nineteenth century. See Humphries's (1977) analysis.

PART ONE

The Cajamarcan Haciendas and the
Peasantry, 1900–1940

ONE

The Political Economy of the First Four Decades: The Dominance of the Hacienda System

The long period of sustained export growth that began after the War of the Pacific established the basis for the consolidation of Peru's modern economy. The expansion of the sugar industry contributed significantly to Peru's export boom. Sugar was the leading export product from 1895 to 1925, accounting for as much as 42 percent of the total value of exports in 1920 (Thorp and Bertram 1978, table 4.1). Moreover, during this period the sugar industry became increasingly concentrated on the north coast.[1]

Given its proximity to the coastal sugar-producing zones and its high population density, the department of Cajamarca had become a leading supplier of labor to the north coast by the 1920s. There is considerable disagreement, however, over the extent to which the expanding sugar industry spurred the growth of a dynamic regional internal market, the degree to which Cajamarca became an important supplier of foodstuffs, beef, and dairy products to coastal markets, and the effect of these developments on the class relations on the Cajamarcan haciendas.

During the 1940s, contemporaries considered the Cajamarcan highlands economically stagnant. The agronomist Jesús Silva Santisteban, evaluating agricultural and animal production in the province in the early 1940s, concluded that "rather than experiencing progress over the previous forty years, Cajamarca has fallen into a state of retrocession" (Silva Santisteban 1945, 65). Most researchers today share this view (Eslava 1973; Gitlitz 1975; Franco 1976). Lewis Taylor (1979, 6; 1984, 101), however, has argued that

1. In 1893–1895 the two northern departments of La Libertad and Lambayeque accounted for 45 percent of Peruvian sugar production, whereas by 1911–1913 they accounted for 61 percent (Albert 1976, tables 11a and 12a). The northern departments always contributed an even higher share of sugar exports (71 percent in 1911–1913) because the central and southern sugar-producing zones served the Lima market.

export-led growth at the turn of the century generated a vigorous internal market on the coast, creating the conditions to integrate Cajamarca firmly into the capitalist commodity market. According to Taylor, "capitalist social relations began to percolate" into the region between 1880 and 1930, and the haciendas of the department became "formally subsumed" to capital.

I am more skeptical than Taylor about the dynamizing effect of coastal export-led growth for the Cajamarcan haciendas. Undoubtedly, the volume of trade between highlands and coast was considerably greater in the early decades of the twentieth century than it was in the mid-nineteenth century, when the department was characterized by extreme economic stagnation.[2] But I believe that the increased integration of Cajamarca into the northern regional economy did not promote the development of capitalist class relations but rather spurred the expansion of feudal class relations on the Cajamarcan haciendas.

The growth of the regional internal market was insufficient to have allowed the haciendas to compete with the coastal plantations for highland labor on the basis of wages. Because hacienda land was abundant and underutilized, the cheapest labor force was maintained by ceding usufruct plots to peasant households and by landlord accumulation of wealth through unpaid labor services on the demesne and the collection of rents. In 1940 the hacienda system in Cajamarca was probably as strong as it had ever been.

HACIENDA CONTROL OVER LAND AND LABOR

The 1940 Peruvian census reveals that, of all highland departments, Cajamarca had the highest concentration of rural population living on haciendas—26 percent, compared to an average of 19 percent for the seven other sierra departments (Caballero 1981a, table 38).[3] In the province of Cajamarca, the focus of this study, the percentage of hacienda residents was slightly higher, 28 percent. The 1940 census listed 235 haciendas and *fundos* (smaller estates) in the province, with a total resident population of 30,468.

2. In the seventeenth and eighteenth centuries, Cajamarca had been an important textile production center, but textile production suffered considerably at the hands of British competition (Franco 1976, 23). In 1855 the value of textile imports to the province was six times greater than the value of its exports of wool cloth. Indicative of Cajamarca's nineteenth-century depression, textiles at this time constituted 15.6 percent of the total value of exports from the province, exceeded only by wheat flour (18.7 percent) and followed by cattle (9.3 percent) (Sarachaga, Degola, and Arana [1855] 1981, 32).

3. Caballero defined the rural population as those people residing in centers with fewer than two thousand inhabitants and the hacienda population as those residing on either haciendas or fundos, definitions I maintain in my analysis. The concentrations of population living on haciendas or fundos in the other highland departments were as follows: Apurímac, 13 percent; Ayacucho, 15 percent; Cuzco, 22 percent; Huancavelica, 21 percent; Junín, 10 percent; and Puno, 20 percent (Caballero 1981a, table 38).

TABLE 1. Districts of the Province of Cajamarca, Ranked by the Concentration of Rural Population on Haciendas, 1940

District	Number of Haciendas[a]	Average Number of Households Residing on Haciendas	Population Residing on Haciendas	Rural Population[b]	Percentage of Rural Population on Haciendas
Cospán	8	80.1	3,532	5,237	67.4
La Encañada	15	71.7	5,538	9,750	56.8
Magdalena	6	16.2	480	1.029	46.7
Cajamarca	89	18.0	8,413	23,578	35.7
Namora	14	20.7	1,402	3,992	35.1
Chetilla	10	19.0	925	3,322	27.8
San Marcos	20	47.4	5,099	19,481	26.2
Jesús	17	24.0	2,235	8,918	25.1
San Pablo	46	10.4	2,230	11,370	19.6
San Juan	2	27.5	231	2,101	11.0
Llacanora	6	7.3	269	3,033	8.9
Ichocán	1	37.0	107	8,184	1.3
Matara	1	1.0	7	2,807	0.2
Asunción	0	—	—	5,978	—
Total	235	24.9	30,468	108,780	28.0

SOURCE: Compiled from census data (Peru 1940, vol. 2, table 34).
[a]This column also includes census figures for fundos.
[b]The rural population includes all population centers of fewer than two thousand inhabitants.

The concentration of rural population on haciendas varied considerably across the province. Table 1 indicates that one-half to two-thirds of the rural population of the districts of Cospán, La Encañada, and Magdalena lived on haciendas. (Map 2 depicts the location of districts.)[4] In contrast, virtually none of the rural population in the districts of Asunción, Matara, and Ichocán—and few people in Llacanora and San Juan—lived on haciendas; these districts were composed principally of independent peasant communities. In the most populous districts of the province—Cajamarca, San Marcos, and San Pablo— the haciendas encompassed roughly 20 percent to 36 percent of the rural population. These districts also included the greatest number of haciendas.

Unfortunately, comparable data on the concentration of land within the haciendas were not available until the 1961 census. At that time, there were 189

4. Administratively, the department of Cajamarca contained eight provinces in 1940; the province of Cajamarca was divided into fourteen districts. By 1976 the number of provinces had increased to eleven and the number of districts in the province of Cajamarca to fifteen. During 1982–1983, two more provinces were created, San Pablo and San Marcos, raising the number of provinces in the department to thirteen and reducing the number of districts in the province of Cajamarca to twelve.

PIURA

AMAZONAS

Cutervo

To
Chiclayo

Santa Cruz

Chota

Bambamarca

Hualgayoc

Celendín

LAMBAYEQUE

San Miguel

San Pablo

La Encañada

Chetilla

Cajamarca

Baños del Inca

Llacanora

Magdalena

Namora

Chilete

San Juan

Matara

To Jequetepeque
Valley

Jesús

San Marcos

Asunción

Ichocán

Contumazá

Cospán

To Trujillo

Cajabamba

LA LIBERTAD

To Huamachuco

Legend

★ Department Capital

★ Province Capital

☆ District Capital

• Other towns

PIURA Surrounding Departments

---- Major roads

0   25
kilometers

Map 2. Southern Provinces of Department of Cajamarca, Provincial Capitals,
Province of Cajamarca and District Capitals Highlighted, 1970s

haciendas of more than 500 hectares in the department (Peru 1961a, vol. 6, table 2). Although these haciendas constituted only 0.2 percent of the total number of farm units, they held 59.1 percent of the land. In the province of Cajamarca, land was even more concentrated: 46 haciendas (0.2 percent of farm units) held 65.2 percent of the land.

The 1961 census data provide a minimum estimate of the degree of hacienda land concentration, for by then many Cajamarcan haciendas had been subdivided and sold. The data nonetheless indicate the high concentration of land held by the Cajamarcan landlord class. Whereas about one-quarter of the peasantry resided on haciendas, the landlord class controlled at least two-thirds of the province's land.

Most of the land encompassed by large haciendas consisted of either pastures (60 percent) or forest and wasteland (31 percent); only 9 percent of the land on farms larger than 500 hectares was cultivated (Peru 1961a, vol. 6, table 4.1). All told, these large haciendas held 23 percent of the province's cultivated land and 85 percent of the grazing land, thus conforming to the pattern typical of haciendas in all seven highland departments. Their near-monopoly of land was composed primarily of natural pastures (Caballero 1981a, 95–100).

Many haciendas in the department of Cajamarca were indeed mammoth. The largest, the Hacienda Araqueda in the province of Cajabamba, was reported in 1850 to have covered 100,000 hectares (Gorget 1975a, 8). The largest hacienda in the province of Cajamarca at that time, the Hacienda La Pauca, encompassed 54,000 hectares (Arce del Campo and Lora 1974, 2); it was followed in size by the haciendas Combayo (Santolalla [1918] 1977, 211) and Sunchubamba (Taylor 1984, 115), each measuring about 43,000 hectares.[5]

Fermín Málaga Santolalla, who wrote the first comprehensive monograph about the department, found the actual size of the haciendas impossible to estimate.[6] Many were so large that even their owners could not estimate their magnitude accurately. To emphasize their size, and to dramatize their importance in terms of accumulated wealth, Málaga Santolalla estimated the prevailing value of certain haciendas. The most valuable piece of property in

5. The Hacienda Combayo was inscribed in the public land registry in 1889 as consisting of 232,995 hectares, but Nicolás Santolalla ([1918] 1977, 211), the son of the owner, considered this figure exaggerated and reported the hacienda's size as 43,000 hectares. According to him, the hacienda had remained intact over the previous century.

The public land registry is located in the public registry of the city of Cajamarca (Registros Públicos de Cajamarca, Registro de la Propiedad, subsequently cited as RPC). Citations refer to the volume number (*tomo*) and the number of the specific entry (*folio*) for a specific hacienda. In cases where the information is appropriate and available, the entry number is followed by a paragraph number (*partida*), separated with a slash. The data cited for the Hacienda Combayo are reported in RPC (2:235).

6. Málaga Santolalla, a source I rely on heavily for early twentieth-century data, was a deputy from the province of Cajabamba to the national congress from 1903 to 1930 and served as its secretary. A mining engineer by training, he was also employed at the Algomarca mines on the Hacienda Araqueda for a number of years (Gorget 1975a, 9).

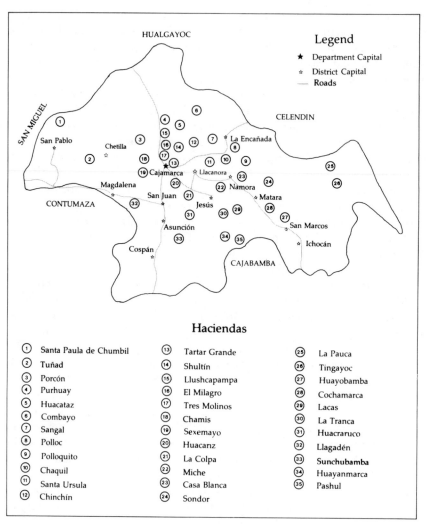

Legend

★ Department Capital
☆ District Capital
— Roads

HUALGAYOC

SAN MIGUEL

CELENDIN

San Pablo

Chetilla

La Encañada

Cajamarca

Llacanora

Magdalena

Namora

San Juan

Matara

CONTUMAZA

Jesús

Asunción

San Marcos

Cospán

Ichocán

CAJABAMBA

Haciendas

① Santa Paula de Chumbil
② Tuñad
③ Porcón
④ Purhuay
⑤ Huacataz
⑥ Combayo
⑦ Sangal
⑧ Polloc
⑨ Polloquito
⑩ Chaquil
⑪ Santa Ursula
⑫ Chinchín

⑬ Tartar Grande
⑭ Shultín
⑮ Llushcapampa
⑯ El Milagro
⑰ Tres Molinos
⑱ Chamis
⑲ Sexemayo
⑳ Huacanz
㉑ La Colpa
㉒ Miche
㉓ Casa Blanca
㉔ Sondor

㉕ La Pauca
㉖ Tingayoc
㉗ Huayobamba
㉘ Cochamarca
㉙ Lacas
㉚ La Tranca
㉛ Huacraruco
㉜ Llagadén
㉝ Sunchubamba
㉞ Huayanmarca
㉟ Pashul

Map 3. Province of Cajamarca, District Capitals and Selected Haciendas, 1940s

the department was the Hacienda Udima, then in the province of Hualgayoc, which he estimated as being worth about 50,000 Lp (Peruvian pounds)—a sum approximately equal to the total value of all imports to the department in 1904 (Málaga Santolalla 1906, 236, 197). In the province of Cajamarca, the haciendas Huacraruco and La Colpa combined were worth 15,000 Peruvian pounds; the Hacienda Combayo, 10,000; the haciendas Porcón, Sondor, and Llagadén 8,000 each; and the Hacienda Polloc, 6,000 pounds. (See Map 3 for location of the haciendas.)

Although archival work concerning the formation and expansion of the Cajamarcan haciendas has only recently begun, the available data suggest that the growth of the haciendas and the accompanying decimation of indigenous communities were phenomena that began in the colonial period. In this regard, the province of Cajamarca appears to differ from other highland areas, where the expansion of the haciendas is generally regarded a nineteenth-century phenomenon (Piel 1970; Spalding 1975).

The earlier consolidation of the Cajamarcan haciendas may be explained by the region's importance in the colonial social formation as a major wool and textile center and later as a mining center (Franco 1976, 20–21). At the end of the seventeenth century, there were thirty-five *obrajes* (textile production factories) in operation in the department, many of them located on what would become the major twentieth-century haciendas of Cajamarca province: Porcón, Sondor, Polloc, Huagal, La Pauca, Combayo, Huacraruco, Chaquil, and Huacataz (Gaitán 1975, 9–11; Silva Santisteban 1986). The discovery of silver at Hualgayoc in 1772 ushered in an unprecedented prosperity to the department for the next forty years. During this period, the haciendas' control over land and labor appears to have expanded considerably as they became suppliers of foodstuffs and livestock to the booming mining town.

The case of the Hacienda Porcón perhaps exemplifies the process of hacienda expansion in Cajamarca. In 1670 the Hacienda Porcón consisted of only 87 hectares. Available documents concerning border disputes with neighboring indigenous communities indicate that Porcón's holdings increased in 1689, 1780, and 1822 as a result of disputes settled in its favor. At the beginning of the twentieth century, this hacienda encompassed 28,000 hectares (Gaitán 1972, 27).

If the growth of the Cajamarcan haciendas, with the consequent demise of the land base of indigenous communities, occurred mainly during the colonial period rather than in the nineteenth century, this chronology may explain why Cajamarca has far fewer legally recognized Peasant Communities than do other highland departments.[7] Between 1926 and 1950, when some seven

7. Throughout the text, I use the term *independent peasant communities* to refer to the peasantry residing in *caseríos*, dispersed rural settlements or villages, outside the confines of hacienda property. Whenever reference is made to peasants belonging to officially recognized Comunidades Campesinas, Peasant Communities (or Comunidades Indígenas, as they were known until 1968), the term *Community* is capitalized.

hundred Comunidades Indígenas were legislatively constituted throughout the nation, only thirty-six Peasant Communities were registered in the department, and only nine in the province of Cajamarca (Chávez Aliaga 1957, 1:238–240).[8] The relatively early growth of haciendas in the province might also explain why in the twentieth century there are far fewer vestiges of communal class relations in Cajamarca than in other highland regions.[9]

Although the most important haciendas of the province were established by the end of the colonial period, they continued to expand their control over rural labor well into the 1900s. According to the 1876 census (Peru 1876b), some 24 percent of the rural population in the province of Cajamarca resided on 75 haciendas. By 1940 this figure had risen to 28 percent, and the number of haciendas and fundos in the province, had increased to 235 (Peru 1940).

TABLE 2. Average Annual Population Growth Rates, Province of Cajamarca, 1876–1940

District	Hacienda Residents	Non-Hacienda Rural Population	Total[a]
Cajamarca	9.3%	2.0%	2.3%
La Encañada	4.1	3.2	3.7
Llacanora	3.8	2.3	2.4
San Marcos	2.4	2.8	2.7
Chetilla	2.2	1.6	1.7
Jesús	1.3	1.0	1.1
Magdalena	1.3	− 0.1	0.3
Cospán	0.8	1.1	0.9
San Pablo	0.4	0.9	0.8
Matara	− 1.1	1.3	1.2
Ichocán	− 1.3	1.6	1.1
Asunción	− 1.6	0.7	0.6
Total Province	2.5	1.8	1.9

SOURCES: Compiled from census data (Peru 1876b, 299–311; Peru 1940, vol. 2, table 34).
[a]Total includes the urban population, defined as those residing in centers with more than two thousand inhabitants.

8. The minimal number of communities registering as Comunidades Indígenas may also have been affected by the fact that few of Cajamarca's peasants considered themselves to be indigenous. In the 1876 census, only 41 percent of the department's population was registered as Indian. Thirty-one percent registered as mestizo and 28 percent as white. Cajamarca held the largest proportion of population registered as white of any Peruvian department and ranked second with respect to the mestizo population, following Ancash (Díaz 1974, 29). At the beginning of the twentieth century, Quechua was spoken only on a few of the outlying haciendas (Porcón, Negritos, Combayo) and in the Cajamarca Valley (Málaga Santolalla 1906, 310).

9. In the 1961 census, only seventeen communities in the province reported owning land collectively (Peru 1961a, vol. 6, table 2.1).

During the interim, the population of the province grew at an average annual rate of 1.9 percent, the independent communities and pueblos grew by 1.8 percent, and the resident hacienda population grew by 2.5 percent (see Table 2).

Measurement problems may account for some of this impressive increase.[10] Interviews suggest, however, that the extent of effective hacienda control over rural labor was appreciably greater than that identified by the census.[11] Forty-one percent of the rural households surveyed in the province of Cajamarca reported that either members of the household or their parents had entered into rental arrangements with the haciendas between 1920 and 1950 (1976 Peasant Family Survey). These interviews reveal that, over the first half-century, increasing numbers of peasant households sought residence on the haciendas because of growing land pressure within the independent peasant communities. In addition, it became common for peasants in the independent communities to rent hacienda land.

In 1876 the department of Cajamarca held only 6.6 persons per square kilometer; this ratio increased to 10.3 by 1906 and reached 15.2 in 1940.[12] The person-land ratios for the province were substantially higher—14.1 in 1876 and 31.3 in 1940—but they tell only part of the story, for land was not equally distributed. Table 3 presents estimates of how person-land ratios for the haciendas may have differed from those of the independent peasant communities. These figures suggest that the number of persons per square kilometer in the independent communities of the province increased from 28.3 in 1876 to 60.3 in 1940. Relative land shortage was clearly a problem for the free peasantry, not for the landlord class.

During this period, if the children of independent peasant households wanted to farm, they increasingly had only one alternative: to rent hacienda lands. Whether they migrated to a hacienda or remained within their own community depended on both the location of the community and the demands of the landlord class. For the landlords, control over peasant labor was the basic source of wealth. The more households that could be enticed onto the hacienda or engaged in rental arrangements, the greater the total volume of rents and, thus, hacienda income. The greater the hacienda's control over peasant labor,

10. The problems surrounding the 1876 census are discussed in Appendix I. My estimates of the concentrations of rural population residing on haciendas are based on the most conservative assumptions regarding this population.

11. Macera (1974, clii; 1977, vol. 4) makes the same point, considering Peruvian haciendas to have had a much broader influence over the rural population than that captured by hacienda residency.

12. These figures are calculated on the basis of the Sociedad Geográfica del Perú's 1897 estimate that the department consisted of 32,482 square kilometers, as reported in Málaga Santolalla (1906, 6) and accepted as the official figure in the 1940 census (Peru 1940, vol. 2, table 1). Population data are from Peru (1876a, 3:448–533), Garland (1908, 114), and Peru (1940, vol. 2, table 34). See Table 3, p. 32, for the provincial estimates.

TABLE 3.   Estimated Person–Land Ratios, Province of Cajamarca, 1876 and 1940

	1876		1940	
	Population	Persons per Square Kilometer	Population	Persons per Square Kilometer
Population living on haciendas	11,605	4.4	30,468	11.6
Rural non-hacienda population	36,718	28.3	78,312	60.3
Total rural population	48,323 (87%)		108,780 (88%)	
City of Cajamarca	7,215 (13%)		14,290 (12%)	
Province of Cajamarca	55,538 (100%)	14.1	123,070 (100%)	31.3

SOURCES: Based on an estimated land surface of 3,935 square kilometers, calculated by the Sociedad Geográfica del Perú in 1896 and reported in Málaga Santolalla (1906, 143), Alvarez Saén (1908), and Peru (1940, vol. 2, table 1). I have allocated two-thirds of this area to haciendas (2,636.5 square kilometers) and one-third to independent communities (1,298.5 square kilometers).
Population figures are compiled from census data (Peru 1876b, 299–311; Peru 1940, vol. 2, table 34).

the more feasible it was to expand production on the demesne when market conditions warranted doing so.

The substantial growth of the resident population on haciendas is explained not only by voluntary immigration but also by hacienda usurpation of community lands. The dominant process varied by district, as seen in the two districts reporting the greatest growth in the number of hacienda residents, La Encañada and Cajamarca. Whereas the resident population of the haciendas of La Encañada grew primarily through immigration, the increase in the number of peasants on haciendas in the district of Cajamarca appears to be the result of the creation of a number of new haciendas and fundos at the expense of peasant communities.

The total population of La Encañada grew by an average annual rate of 3.7 percent, the highest rate of all districts in the province, suggesting considerable immigration into this district (see Table 2). The growth rate of the non-hacienda rural population was well above the provincial average, implying that the independent communities both attracted new immigrants and held their own against encroachments on their land by the haciendas.[13] Contemporary reports also indicate that the 4.1 percent annual growth rate of the resident

13. The only evidence of hacienda encroachment on peasant community lands in La Encañada involves Manuel Cacho Gálvez, deputy from Gajamarca to the national congress and owner of the Hacienda Polloc. In 1907 he usurped two sections belonging to the Community of Michiquillay

hacienda population was a result of voluntary immigration to the haciendas. Between 1912 and 1917, the number of peasant households on the Hacienda Combayo, the largest hacienda in La Encañada, increased by 50 percent (Santolalla 1977, 274). The hacienda management had embarked on a project of attracting additional resident labor by offering peasants advantageous conditions to settle on the hacienda. During the subsequent twenty-three years, population growth on this hacienda averaged 5 percent per year. Other haciendas in the district, such as Polloc, also encouraged peasants to settle on hacienda lands.[14]

Immigration was also significant for the district of Cajamarca during this period. Increased rural-urban migration does not account for the increase, for the city of Cajamarca grew by only 1.5 percent, compared with a growth rate of 3.1 percent for the rural population of the district. And whereas the non-hacienda rural population grew at an average annual rate of 2.0 percent, the hacienda population grew by a striking 9.3 percent. Moreover, the number of fundos and haciendas increased notably, from nine in 1876 to eighty-nine in 1940, suggesting that a number of new haciendas and fundos had been established at the expense of independent peasant communities. Seventeen of the new fundos and haciendas had been counted as *caseríos* in the 1876 census, accounting for more than one-third of the increase in hacienda residents between the two censuses. The better-known new fundos and haciendas included Miraflores, Otuzco, Santa Bárbara, Urubamba, Huacariz Grande, Huayrapongo, and Porconcillo.[15] The remaining new entries in the census listing may reflect the formation of new landholdings, the subdivision of larger haciendas, or simply their renaming.[16]

(Samaniego 1975b, 11–12; Burgos and Gaitán 1980, 19). That same year Mariano Cacho, renter of the Hacienda Santa Ursula, tried to take over a portion of the lands of the community of Shaullo, but the peasants brought suit and subsequently won their claim (Burgos and Gaitán 1980, 18; Taylor 1984, 105).

14. Taylor (1984, 107) also reports that a number of the major haciendas in the department were attempting to attract labor onto the haciendas including, in the province of Cajamarca, the haciendas Polloc, La Pauca, La Colpa, Huacraruco, and Sunchubamba. I differ with Taylor, however, in the interpretation of the haciendas' motivation.

15. Based on my interviews in the Cajamarca Valley during 1975–1976, I would venture that the majority of these land grabs took place in the late nineteenth century; in the life histories I collected, peasants were quite vague about when their communities lost land, although most alleged that the loss had taken place. My findings are similar to those reported by Chambeu (1975d, 10): "The Santabarbarinos do not have a precise idea about the history of their caserío. They affirm that Santa Bárbara had once been a very large community whose land encompassed all of the actually existing haciendas. Over the years its land was usurped by the hacendados of the region."

16. One of the few documented cases of hacienda formation in the twentieth century concerns the Hacienda La Colpa in the Cajamarca Valley. Taylor (1979, 98) reports that it was formed in 1901 through the amalgamation of three smaller fundos and the usurpation of lands belonging to the community of Yanamango in Jesús.

In sum, by the time the colonial period drew to a close, the haciendas in Cajamarca had consolidated their control over the land, particularly grazing pastures. But they also continued to increase their control over peasant labor well into the twentieth century. During the colonial period, the steady decline of the indigenous communities was probably a response to the desire of the landlord class to ensure a cheap labor force. During the Republican period, such a labor force was ensured partly through the landlords' near-monopoly of land, although this did not stop further land grabs altogether. As population pressure continued to mount within the independent communities of the province, the option of farming, especially animal raising, became increasingly dependent on the ability of peasant households to enter into rental arrangements with the landlord class.

THE LANDLORD CLASS

As late as the mid-twentieth century, the hacienda system remained the centerpiece of Cajamarcan economics and politics. The economic and political power of the landlord class rested on its control over land and labor as well as control over the state administrative, judicial, and repressive apparatus at the departmental, provincial, and district levels. The continuity of this class and its power was also reinforced by the practice of intermarriage, not only among the elite but also among potential hacienda heirs.

Many of the major provincial hacienda owners of the 1940s could trace family ownership of their hacienda at least as far back as the early Republican period, if not the colonial period (Departamento de Estudio e Investigación Social 1972). There was substantial continuity in the ownership of the major haciendas, involving such family names as Puga, Iglesias, Cacho, Bueno, and Castro, from the 1830s into the next century. New names appear occasionally, however, for some upward social mobility was provided by strategic marriages as well as by the rental of haciendas owned by the church and public charities.

From at least the nineteenth century, Peruvian laws have provided for partible inheritance. Among the Cajamarcan elite, inheritance was also bilateral, with male and female heirs generally receiving equal shares. Often, one heir would buy out the shares of the others, consolidating the landholding in his or her name after a certain period; but in some cases an extended family retained ownership, with one heir managing the hacienda for the family. In either case, it was not uncommon for a landlord to rent the hacienda or sections of it to his or her children at less than market price. According to Málaga Santolalla (1906, 188), this practice allowed parents to retire to the cities and live off the rental income while their children gained management experience. It may have also reduced disputes among siblings about who was to control a hacienda; it allowed those most disposed to living on the estate to consolidate their management while the parents were still alive. In addition, it may have reduced the likelihood that haciendas would be subdivided among heirs or sold to outsiders. These practices help to explain the continuity of family ownership in the Republican period.

The history of the Puga family landholdings provides a good example of these practices. In the 1820s, Juan Garcia Puga, a colonial *corregidor* of Cajamarca, acquired the Hacienda La Pauca and merged it with the Hacienda Huagal, which had been in the family for at least one generation. In the 1840s, his daughter, Carolina Puga Chavarry, married her first cousin, José Mercedes Puga Valera, and they managed both haciendas for the family until José Mercedes was killed after the War of the Pacific. Doña Carolina then managed the haciendas until one of her eight children, Victor Napoleón Puga y Puga, took over at the turn of the century. This hacienda was managed as an extended family enterprise until Victor Napoleón's son, Rafael Puga Estrada, took over and, in the 1940s and 1950s, began to purchase the shares of the other thirty-six heirs (Chambeu and Gorget 1975, 7, annex 1).

The Hacienda Combayo provides a somewhat different example of the role of marriage and kinship in maintaining the continuity of the landholding class. This hacienda, purchased by Juan Manuel Bernal de Gavaleta in the period after 1802, was left to his widow and ten heirs when he died in 1837.[17] For the next fifty years, the hacienda remained in the name of Doña María Arana vda. de Bernal; she then willed the hacienda to eleven grandchildren and several other heirs in 1888. Between 1890 and 1897, two brothers, Francisco and Eloy Santolalla Iglesias, began to buy the shares of Doña María Arana's grand-children. Francisco and Eloy were both married to Bernál-Arana cousins. They were also the land-poor nephews of Miguel Iglesias, the negotiator of the 1882 Treaty of Ancón and owner of the Hacienda Udima. In 1897 Eloy Santolalla inscribed the Hacienda Combayo in his name in the public registry, declaring that he had paid S/. 16,581 (Peruvian soles) for an undetermined portion of the hacienda.[18] Eloy, a trained mining engineer, managed the hacienda and mines of Combayo until his death in 1932. The hacienda then passed to his wife, María Bernal Arana vda. de Santolalla, who managed it through an administrator until 1947.

Although the women who owned the Hacienda Combayo during this period tended to be absentee landowners, residing in Cajamarca or Lima, it was not uncommon for women of the landlord class to manage haciendas themselves, particularly upon the death of their husbands. Thus, Carolina Puga de Puga is credited with developing the haciendas Huagal and La Pauca after her

17. All of the information on the Hacienda Combayo in this section is drawn from RPC (2:235).

18. In the early 1900s, 1 Peruvian pound was equivalent to 10.20 Peruvian soles (Málaga Santolalla 1906, 235).

Francisco Santolalla must have continued to own a share of the Hacienda Combayo, for in 1903 he put up his share as a guarantee so that his cousin Gustavo Iglesias could rent the Hacienda Llushcapampa (RPC, 2:235).

husband died. Paula Iturbe de Iglesias ran her own inheritance, the Hacienda Chumbil, even while her husband was still alive and she was bedridden. Nazario Chávez Aliaga reports that "the resident peasants would carry her from the city so that their dear *patrona* could satisfy her desires to personally visit her properties and dictate the most adequate measures to guarantee the organization and progress of the hacienda" (1957, 1:15). After her husband's death, Paula Iturbe even took on the management of another hacienda, renting the Hacienda Porcón for ten years.[19]

The hacienda rental market was composed primarily of those haciendas owned by religious groups or the provincial semipublic charity institutions, the Beneficiencia Pública. The church was a major landholder in the department of Cajamarca through the 1940s. For example, the Monasterio de las Consabidas Descalzas, also known as the Madres Concepcionistas, owned the vast estate Pallán in the province of Celendín as well as the haciendas Santa Ursula and Chotén in the province of Cajamarca. John Gitlitz (1975, 114) reports that the Hacienda Pallán was willed to the Madres Concepcionistas in 1710 by the great-grandson of the first Spanish owner in exchange for two weekly masses, one in his memory and another in honor of his parents. The convent also secured additional lands by purchase, through defaulted mortgages, and in the form of dowries when young elite women joined the convent.

The Beneficiencias were founded by members of the landlord class in the mid-nineteenth century to run the public hospitals, cemeteries, and some of the schools. They gradually accumulated landholdings, usually through bequests but also by purchases. In 1847, the year after its founding, the Beneficiencia Pública of Cajamarca acquired the Hacienda Porcón from the Hospitál Belemita in exchange for taking charge of the hospital's funding (Gorget 1975b, chap. 1). By the late 1940s, the Beneficiencia of Cajamarca also owned the Hacienda Chamis, the fundos Tartar de Otuzco, Tartar de los Baños, and Belempampa in the valley of Cajamarca, as well as a number of smaller properties scattered throughout the province (Chávez Aliaga 1957, 4:128).

The haciendas belonging to the church and the Beneficiencias were usually rented out through public auctions for a ten-year period. To guarantee their rental payment, the *arrendires* were often required to deposit the equivalent of two to three years' rent or to place their own haciendas or those of a relative as collateral. This requirement, as well as the control of the Beneficiencias by members of the landholding class, served to restrict entry to the Cajamarcan elite. Table 4 indicates that among the arrendires of the haciendas Santa Ursula and Porcón were often familiar Cajamarcan names: Puga, Iglesias,

---

19. Mallon (1987) also reports that women were substantial property owners in the central highlands in the late eighteenth and nineteenth centuries and often managed their own haciendas. She notes, however, that in order to sell their property or carry out other financial transactions women needed the permission of their husbands.

TABLE 4.   Arrendires of the Haciendas Santa Ursula and Porcón

Arrendire	Annual Rent (current soles)
Hacienda Santa Ursula (4,241 hectares)	
1903–1914 Mariano Cacho	1,100
1914–1922 Fidel Zevallos Palmer	1,250
1923–1939 Fidel Zevallos Palmer and Gregorio Fidel Zevallos	1,500
1939–1943 Antonio Otoya Puga	3,000
1943–1947 Serapio Montoya Cabanillas	3,000
1947–1952 Carlos Waslli	7,000
1952–1957 Cia. Agrícola Wipinar, S. A.	7,000
1957–1961 Gonzalo Pajares Goicochea	40,000
Hacienda Porcón (28,000 hectares)	
1875–1884 José Sousa	3,010
1884–1893 Paula Iturbe de Iglesias	3,010
1893 Juan Bautista Cacho	3,400
1894–1904 Diego López Uceda	3,601
1904–1914 Santiago y Federico Rojas Rodríguez	5,740
1914–1918 Federico Rojas and wife	10,292
1919 Edilberto Castro Pol and Santiago Rojas Rodríguez	10,300
1921–1931 Edilberto Castro Pol	11,000
1932–1935 Beneficiencia Pública of Cajamarca	not rented
1935–1936 Mariano Miranda	9,000
1937–1950 Beneficiencia Pública of Cajamarca	not rented

SOURCES: Information for the Hacienda Santa Ursula taken from the Registros Públicos de Cajamarca, Registro de la Propiedad, city of Cajamarca (8:104/1–14); information for the Hacienda Porcón taken from Gorget (1975b, chap. 1).

Cacho, and Castro. Through the 1940s, unfamiliar names usually belonged to persons related by marriage to members of the landlord class.

The rental of haciendas provided the religious groups and charities with a steady income, while for the land-poor relatives of the Cajamarcan elite it provided some opportunity for upward mobility. But these rental relationships, as well as the actual management of the haciendas, were strung by tension and conflict. The contents of the 1903 contract between the Madres Concepcionistas and Mariano Cacho for the rental of the Hacienda Santa Ursula illustrate such problems:

1. If the rent due the Madres was more than one month late, the contract was automatically rescinded.
2. The arrendire could not ask for a reduction of rent under any circumstances except the most unusual, such as destruction of the hacienda by an earthquake.

3. The arrendire was not allowed to sublet the hacienda without permission of the convent.

4. The arrendire was required to make all repairs to the *casa hacienda* (the main house) and the *tambo* (store) at his own expense.

5. At the end of the rental period, the arrendire could not claim more than S/. 200 for debts owed to him by the resident labor force for advances they had received. If debts exceeded this amount, they would be divided equally between the arrendire and the convent.

6. Under no circumstance could the arrendire expel any resident tenant from the hacienda, whatever that resident's sex or age. The arrendire was required to treat the resident population well.

7. If the arrendire died during the course of the agreement, management of the hacienda reverted to the convent. His heirs or representatives had no right to the hacienda. However, if the crops had already been planted, the heirs could continue to manage the hacienda until the harvest, if they paid the stipulated monthly rent to the convent.

8. The arrendire guaranteed the payment of rent, as well as the capital of the hacienda, by means of a mortgage on his house in Cajamarca.

9. Any improvements on the hacienda became the property of the convent, without any compensation to the arrendire.[20]

Until the late 1940s, rental contracts for the Hacienda Santa Ursula were similar for other arrendires. The only important variation concerned the required collateral. Thus Zevallos Palmer was required to put up Lp 4,000 in 1914, as well as a mortgage on a house he owned jointly with his father in the city. Otoyo Puga guaranteed his rent with the fundo Fustán, which belonged to his wife, Dorela Puga. Montoya Cabanillas guaranteed his with a mortgage on the Hacienda Cochambul. These required guarantees, even though the arrendires were generally family members of the landlord class, suggest that many rental properties were poorly managed and that their rental was sometimes a simple excuse for plunder.[21]

The Beneficiencias and religious groups not only had difficulty keeping their stock of capital on the haciendas intact; throughout the early twentieth century they were also engaged in some serious border disputes with members of the landowning class. In the 1914 contract between the Madres Concepcionistas and Fidel Zevallos Palmer for the rental of the Hacienda Santa Ursula, the

20. This rental contract is recorded in RPC (8:108). Information on other rental contracts for the Hacienda Santa Ursula is drawn from the same source.

21. In 1875 Vicente Sousa was charged S/. 16,693.50 for the animal inventories that disappeared from the Hacienda Porcón during his fifty years of management. In 1893, at the end of the contract held by Paula Iturbe de Iglesias, 403 female sheep, 168 male sheep, 106 lambs, and 687 head of cattle were missing from the hacienda. Charges of stealing animals were also made against the arrendires Diego Uceda, the Rojas Rodríguez brothers, and Edilberto Castro Pol (Gorget 1975b, chap. 1).

arrendire was warned about a dispute with the owners of the haciendas Chaquil and Chinchín over the lands of the community of Adacucho. The arrendire was to inform the convent of any usurpation of land or capital stock or any attempt by the neighboring haciendas to impose labor services on peasants of that community. The Hacienda Porcón experienced several conflicts: invasions of border lands by the landowners of the haciendas Porconcillo, Llushcapampa, and Negritos in 1885; a boundary conflict with the haciendas Chamis and Negritos between 1915 and 1920; and land invasions by the Hacienda Negritos and several peasant communities in 1923 (Gorget 1975b, chap. 1).

The land conflicts among the landowning class were not limited to aggressions against what was the weakest link in the hacienda system, property that was not managed directly. There were also serious conflicts among some of the major landlord families, such as the Puga and Bueno Cacho families, who struggled for more than twenty years over the boundaries of the haciendas La Pauca and Sondor (Chambeu and Gorget 1975, 8). Knowing how to take advantage of these struggles, peasants entered into labor service agreements with the landlord who was less exacting and thus often exacerbated the conflict.

Peasant struggle also affected the degree to which the rental of a hacienda could serve as an avenue of accumulation for the arrendires as well as for the owners. For example, after 1914 the Beneficiencia found it impossible to raise rents for the Hacienda Porcón because of peasant opposition. Peasants were well aware that increases in the lease for the hacienda negotiated at the auction would be passed down to them in the form of higher rents in cash, kind, and labor services for their parcels. The rental rates for these haciendas shown in Table 4 thus do not accurately indicate the land values or the relative profitability of the haciendas, for the level of rents depended on the manageability of the haciendas—that is, the arrendires' ability to collect rents from the resident peasantry—and hence on the nature of landlord-peasant struggle within the hacienda.

Chávez Aliaga (1957, 1:185) estimated that approximately 15 percent of the land surface of the province of Cajamarca consisted of these rental properties. Although the hacienda rental market was thus well developed in the first half of the twentieth century, providing access to land and labor, this opportunity for accumulating wealth and upward mobility was not without conflicts. The extent of landowners' struggles among themselves over land and labor, as well as landlord-peasant struggles over the conditions of extraction of the surplus, suggests that the power of the Cajamarcan landed elite was not monolithic.

Nevertheless, not until the 1940s, when APRA (Alianza Popular Revolucionaria Americana) gained a foothold in the department and provided some political expression for the urban middle sectors, was the economic and political power of the landowning class substantially challenged. Before then, members of this class not only occupied prestigious provincial and departmental government positions but also found ways to ensure that the judiciary, the army, and the police generally served their interests.[22]

The Puga family is the classic example of familial representation within the state over the course of four generations. In the 1820s, at the same time that Juan García Puga, who consolidated the haciendas La Pauca and Huagal, was the *corregidor* of Cajamarca, a relative, Manuel Márquez Puga, was the *síndico procurador general* of the city. Don Juan's son-in-law, José Mercedes Puga Valera, the next manager of the family holdings, was the deputy from Cajamarca to the national congress from 1868 to 1875, a member and later president of the Superior Court of Justice in Cajamarca, and then prefect of the department. His son, José Mercedes Puga y Puga, was a deputy from the province from 1905 to 1915, while another son, Pelayo, served in the Court of Justice.[23] Both José Mercedes and Pelayo were elected mayor of the city of Cajamarca at various times, and both served as officers of the College of Lawyers. Another son, Victor Napoleón Puga y Puga, was a senator in the national congress from 1931 to 1936 and from 1939 to 1945. His son, Rafael Puga Estrada, was a deputy from the province between 1956 and 1962 and mayor of the city in 1958. The Iglesias, Castro, Sousa, and Cacho families also contributed numerous public figures and continued to be directly represented in local and national politics through the mid-1950s.[24]

According to Frederick Pike (1964, 183) the sierra landowners could easily arrange to be elected as deputies or senators and "once installed, the *gamonales* were the bureaucratic puppets of the executive. . . . As a result, Presidents were not inclined to restrain their powers as absolute *caciques*."[25] Not surprisingly,

---

22. The principal governmental administrative positions were appointed. The prefect of the department was appointed by the president of the Republic, as was the subprefect of each province and the members of the Superior Court of Justice. Representation in the national congress was by direct vote, although until the middle of the twentieth century the vote was restricted to the literate male population. In the early 1900s, Cajamarca had three senators and nine deputies; the province of Cajamarca was entitled to two deputies, the other provinces to one (Málaga Santolalla 1906, 247–251).

23. Chambeu and Gorget (1975, annex 2) report José María Puga y Puga as deputy from the province from 1905 to 1915, but I believe this was actually José Mercedes, based on the parliaméntary report prepared by José Mercedes Puga y Puga for his term in the national congress, 1908–1914 (see Puga 1916). Data on the Puga family have also been drawn from Paz-Soldán (1917, 328).

24. For example, Mariano Castro was appointed *intendente* of Cajamarca by Simón Bolivar in 1823 and later served as a deputy from Cajamarca to the national congress, as well as prefect of the department of La Libertad (*Documentál del Perú: Cajamarca* 1967). His grandson, Victor Castro Iglesias, who was the nephew of the infamous Miguel Iglesias (briefly president of Peru during 1884–1885), was deputy from Cajamarca in 1899, mayor of the city from 1899 to 1901, and senator from 1901 to 1914 (Taylor 1979, 122). By the 1950s, the son of Castro Iglesias, Alejandro Castro Mendívil, had been prefect, mayor, and regional deputy from Cajamarca.

25. The terms *gamonales* and *caciques* are often used interchangeably to refer to the powerful highland landlords.

even though Indigenismo was a growing intellectual movement and the "Indian question" an increasingly significant political problem throughout the first four decades of the twentieth century, the power of the highland landlords in the national congress was usually sufficient to block any reformist agrarian measures.[26]

THE INTEGRATION OF COAST AND SIERRA

Peru's export boom at the turn of the twentieth century was fueled by the development of the sugar industry, increasingly centered on the north coast. Two important facts indicate that the expansion of the sugar industry contributed to the growth of the regional internal market: the growing concentration of the industry in this region and, hence, of sugar-sector employment; and the high rates of coastal population growth during this period. By 1912 the northern departments of La Libertad and Lambayeque accounted for 55 percent of national employment in the sugar industry, with this figure rising to 62 percent by 1922. The Chicama Valley in the department of La Libertad alone accounted for approximately one-third of the sugar industry's labor force during this period (Albert 1976, table 43).

The expansion of the sugar industry stimulated migration from the highlands to the coast, resulting in population growth on the north coast. Between 1876 and 1940, Pacasmayo and Trujillo, the two coastal provinces of the department of La Libertad, grew by an average annual rate of 2.6 percent and 4.0 percent, respectively.[27] Population more than doubled between 1876 and 1916 in the districts where the sugar plantations were located, with most of this expansion occurring in the years 1890 to 1916. The city of Trujillo, capital

---

Three presidents who were current or former sugar plantation owners governed Peru for most of the period from 1900 to 1920: López de Romaña, Pardo, and Leguía (Thorp and Bertram 1978, 50). Leguía was from the northern coastal department of Lambayeque. Although these presidents represented the interests of the emerging agrarian bourgeoisie, their legislative power often depended on their alliance with the highland landlords.

26. Indigenismo (literally, pro-Indianism) had its intellectual roots in the reassessment of Peruvian national identity that followed Peru's defeat in the War of the Pacific. As a result of Indigenista pressures, the Constitution of 1920, promulgated by Leguía, contained Article 58, which obligated the state to "rehabilitate" the Indians through assimilation and the provision of education. More important, Indian ownership of communal lands was protected. The Roca Commission was subsequently established to investigate the growing problem of land disputes in the southern sierra, and it prepared what was considered to be a comprehensive legal code to implement Article 58. The sierra gamonales raised an outcry, and the commission was dissolved (Pike 1964, 220–222). Not until 1933, under the government of Oscar Benavides, was legislation passed providing for the legal recognition of the Indigenous Communities.

27. These figures were calculated from Peru (1940, 3: xx, vii). The simple average annual growth rates, however, are significantly higher than the cumulative annual growth rates estimated by Maletta (1980).

of the department of La Libertad, was the main urban center of the north coast, with a population of twenty-three thousand in 1923; its annual growth during the period 1876 to 1923 averaged 2.1 percent, far outpacing that of Chiclayo, capital of Lambayeque, which grew by only 0.75 percent (Klarén 1976, 142–143; Hunt 1977, table 2).

Population growth rates suggest that the internal market on the north coast, particularly in La Libertad, grew steadily as a result of the expansion of the sugar industry. But the characteristics of this industry's development—its vulnerability to international price fluctuations, its high degree of concentration, and the effect of low real wages—raise some doubt about the extent to which it played a dynamizing role within the broader regional economy of the north of Peru.

According to Peter Klarén (1976, 140–141), the coastal provinces of La Libertad did prosper steadily from 1890 until the beginning of World War I. Not only Trujillo but also the smaller district capitals enjoyed a vigorous commercial expansion, largely based on European imports. But Klarén considers this period of prosperity to have been rather short-lived, for in the 1920s towns such as Ascope, Chicama, and Santiago de Cao almost ceased to be commercial centers, and the city of Trujillo stagnated. By 1929, before the Great Depression, thirty large commercial houses, as well as scores of small businesses, went bankrupt (Klarén 1976, 262).

Klarén attributes the decline in the regional economy to the increasing concentration of the sugar industry—and particularly to the near-monopoly of trade that resulted from the vertical integration of the Empresa Agrícola Chicama Ltda., the major sugar enterprise and owner of the plantation Casa Grande. In the mid-nineteenth century, sixty-four plantations had existed in the Chicama Valley. By 1918 there were only four: Casa Grande, held by the Gildermeister family (after 1910 controlled by German capital); Roma, owned by Victor Larco; Cartavio, owned by W. R. Grace and Co.; and Chiclín, the property of Rafael Larco. Casa Grande and Roma together held approximately three-quarters of the land in the valley. In 1927 Casa Grande eliminated its major rival by purchasing the plantation Roma (Klarén 1976, table 1).

The concentration of land in the hands of the major plantations came at the expense of both smaller sugar cane plantations and peasant producers who previously had been integrated into local trade circuits. Moreover, the plantation work force became increasingly concentrated in company towns, with wage goods directly provided by company-run bazaars. Klarén finds it especially significant that Casa Grande obtained permission from the Benavides government in 1915 to reopen the abandoned port at Malabrigo and build a railroad through the Chicama Valley from the port directly to the plantation. The company apparently also received the privilege of importing European goods through this port duty-free (Klarén 1976, 145). Casa Grande was then able to bypass both the import houses in Trujillo and the local merchants and sell wage goods at its company store at a much lower price. The commercial influence of the Casa Grande bazaar reportedly extended far beyond the plantation's gates, allowing it to compete in other provincial markets as well. As regional trade declined in the postwar years, both the commercial import houses of Trujillo and smaller provincial merchants blamed this development on Casa Grande and the Gildermeisters.[28]

Bill Albert (1976) is more skeptical about the specific role of Casa Grande in the demise of regional trade. He explains the region's commercial crisis between the wars by analyzing the difficulties faced by the sugar industry in the international market. The 1920s brought a downward trend in world sugar prices as a result of global overproduction. The average annual growth of Peruvian sugar output declined from 8.3 percent in the 1910s to 2.7 percent in the 1920s (Thorp and Bertram 1978, table A.2.3). The Depression accentuated this trend when growth in output fell to 1.8 percent in the 1930s. According to Albert (1976, 87a), the urban areas were dependent on the export sector, and when the sugar industry went into decline in the 1920s, both the towns and regional commerce declined as well.

Rosemary Thorp and Geoffrey Bertram (1978; 47–50) argue that the sugar industry was a relatively inefficient generator of demand-led growth for the local economy, primarily because this sector is so capital-intensive. Overall employment hardly changed between 1894 and 1930, whereas output quadrupled.[29] Although the north coast benefited from the increased employment, as central and southern Peruvian sugar production became displaced, wages in the north lagged behind those in other sugar-producing areas (Albert 1976, table 47). Moreover, during the boom years of World War I, real wages fell, a trend that continued through the 1920s (Albert 1976, table 52; Thorp and Bertram 1978, table 6.2).

Even with real wages falling, population growth could still provide for a modest increase in the demand for basic foodstuffs, with possible spin-off effects for highland food-producing areas such as Cajamarca. Contemporaries considered the rising cost of living during these decades to be led by food prices, an increase they blamed on the displacement of food production on the coast.

28. Klarén (1976) attributes the rise of APRA and its fervent support among the middle class partly to the stagnancy of this region in the 1920s and the discontent generated in Trujillo and in the coastal provinces by Casa Grande's operations.

29. Employment in the sugar industry did fluctuate quite a bit during this period, as can be seen in Table 5 (p. 48). Over the long run, however, employment appears relatively static when one considers that in 1894 total employment in the industry was twenty-four thousand (Thorp and Bertram 1978, 48–49). Thorp and Bertram argue that the switch from Chinese coolie labor to local wage labor did result in a one-time increase in the contribution of sugar workers' wages to aggregate demand. But the system of labor recruitment probably modified even this effect, for most of the wage income earned by the highland migrant labor in the early decades of the century consisted of cash advances spent in the sierra.

Thorp and Bertram (1978, 132–140) argue, however, that food production was not displaced by the expansion of export agriculture. They report that the acreage in nonexport food crops remained virtually constant from the early 1900s to the late 1920s. Only in the later 1920s do they find evidence of export production (in this case, cotton) displacing foodstuff production on the coast. In addition, in the late 1930s, a considerable amount of coastal land was diverted from cattle raising to crops (Thorp and Bertram 1978, 394).

Perhaps most significant for the agricultural development prospects of the Cajamarcan highlands was the fact that the increased demand for foodstuffs on the coast was met by increased food imports. In 1900 food imports constituted 13 percent of total imports; they reached 21 precent in 1915, dropping slightly in the last half of the decade; throughout the 1920s, this figure hovered at approximately 22 percent (Thorp and Bertram 1978, table 6.18). The major food items imported throughout the period were wheat and wheat flour, Cajamarca's potential regional export crop.

The importing of hard red winter wheat and wheat flour from Chile had another damaging effect on Cajamarca's export possibilities: it permanently changed consumer preferences on the coast. The type of bread that could be produced from the traditional highland soft wheat varieties became an inferior good. Thus Cajamarca's regional export possibilities shifted principally to cattle and seasonal migrant labor, rather than grains. Whereas the cattle trade was sensitive to the health and vigor of the coastal internal market, fluctuating cyclically, the migrant labor flow permanently integrated coast and highlands.

The Development of the Regional Labor Market

Demographics partly explain why Cajamarca became integrated into the broader regional economy as a supplier of labor power with the growth of the coastal sugar industry. The population of the sugar-producing region of the north coast in 1876 totaled 135,065, compared with Cajamarca's population of 212,246.[30] Moreover, in the late nineteenth century, the northern coastal region suffered a wave of epidemics: typhus was endemic from 1881 to 1888; a smallpox epidemic occurred in 1886; and in 1888 there was a regional outbreak of malaria. In 1903 bubonic plague appeared in the Jequetepeque Valley, Cajamarca's main outlet to the coast (Burga 1976, 228–231).

Not surprisingly, contemporaries lamented the small population on the northern coast and the resulting relative scarcity of labor for the expanding sugar industry (Garland 1908, 204; Hunt 1977, 3; Thorp and Bertram 1978, 44). In contrast, Málaga Santolalla (1906, 184) observed that "in a region such as Cajamarca that is so populated, it is natural for labor to be abundant and

---

30. This estimate includes the provinces of Trujillo and Pacasmayo in the department of La Libertad and the department of Lambayeque; it is based on Peru (1940, 3:vii, xx). The highland provinces of La Libertad had a population of only 99,009 in 1876. The population data for Cajamarca are drawn from Peru (1940, 2:viii).

cheap," a view shared by other observers (Solano 1906, 2; Córdova Muñoz 1913, 3). Labor was relatively abundant in Cajamarca, as well as cheap, because of the unequal distribution of land between haciendas and independent peasant communities and the resultant growing land pressure in the communities as the twentieth century progressed (see Table 3).

In the first period of expansion of the sugar industry (1854–1870), the labor requirements of the plantations were met by importing Chinese coolie labor (Klarén 1976, 73–74). In the 1870s, following an international scandal over the treatment of the Chinese en route to Peru, this labor source was closed off. After the War of the Pacific and the recovery and subsequent expansion of the sugar industry, the coastal landowners had little choice but to turn to the sierra as a source for unskilled labor.[31] Thus began the system of labor recruitment known as *enganche*—literally, "the hook."

The enganche system functioned on the basis of cash advances. To induce peasants to migrate temporarily to the coast, labor contractors, usually financed by the plantations, combed the highlands of the Cajamarca and La Libertad departments to offer peasant men advances, called *socorros*. Upon receiving a socorro, usually a sum of gold, a peasant would sign a contract (despite his illiteracy) agreeing to work off the debt on a certain plantation, usually during the slack agricultural period in the sierra. The contract sometimes stipulated the wage to be paid or, if not, the minimum amount of time that the peasant was required to remain on the plantation in order to cancel his debt, usually two to three months. In the early decades of the century, the advance was often in the range of S/. 10 to S/. 50 (Klarén 1976, 77; Gonzales 1980, 305). Peasants were usually required to guarantee the repayment of the cash advance not only with their potential labor power but also with their personal possessions. They were often required to have a co-signer (*fiador*) whose property also served as collateral for the agreement (Gonzales 1978, 239).

The degree of coercion employed in this recruitment system has been the subject of considerable debate. Writers of the period generally denounced the system as abusive and extremely exploitive of indigenous labor, implying that peasants were recruited against their will (Málaga Santolalla 1906, 184; Means 1920, 527; Gonzales 1980, 291–292). Current analysts tend to place more emphasis on the monetary incentives that induced impoverished highland peasants to migrate seasonally (Albert 1976, 94a; Blanchard 1979, 74–76; Bauer 1979, 38). My own research supports Klarén's (1977, 293) reinterpretation that noneconomic coercion was initially necessary to establish the

31. Gonzales (1978, 222) reports that the plantations turned to the sierra as a source of labor reluctantly, for their previous experience with workers from the highlands had not been promising. Those workers who had migrated to the coast on their own volition during the first sugar boom tended to stay only for very short periods, and they were more prone to illness than were the Chinese.

practice of seasonal migration. Cajamarcan peasants considered the coast an unhealthy place, and with good reason.[32]

Nevertheless, poorer peasant households clearly took recruiters' cash advances very willingly, whether to meet family emergencies, sponsor religious celebrations, or pay off debts. Interviews indicate that over the course of the first four decades of the twentieth century, as land shortage became more acute in the province, more and more peasants were migrating voluntarily as a strategy for generating part of the household's income. Enganche increasingly became the peasantry's credit system, facilitating consumption in advance of labor performed. By the 1920s, growing numbers of peasants were migrating on their own volition, without an advance, attracted by the wage difference— seven to one—between coast and sierra.

Michael Gonzales (1978, 1980) has amply demonstrated the ingenious mechanisms by which the plantations and their recruiters imposed the practice of highland-coastal migration on a skeptical peasantry. Local fiestas and market days, when peasants tended to drink too much, were popular times to recruit. Not infrequently, the contractors provided the liquor. Sometimes, merchants also served as recruiters, enlisting peasants by providing them with goods on credit; the peasants would then be required to pay off their debts by laboring on the sugar plantations. Some contractors even rented highland haciendas and then forced their tenants to pay off their rental obligations by working for a sugar cane plantation on the coast (Gonzales 1978, 228, 231, 225).[33]

In the initial period of enganche, extraeconomic coercion also prolonged the stay of highland peasants on the sugar cane plantations (Klarén 1976, 80–81). Once on the coast, peasants became further indebted to the labor contractor through the latter's control over wages and through forced purchases at high interest rates, which sometimes reached 50 percent (Blanchard 1979, 72–79). In some cases, contractors were paid a percentage (usually 20 percent) of the total advances given; in other cases, they earned a commission based on the total wage income of the peasants they had recruited—providing another incentive to prolong the stay of their recruits on the coast.

32. Workers from the Cajamarcan highlands seemed to be particularly vulnerable to malaria. On the rice plantation Lurifico in the Jequetepeque Valley, as much as 5 percent of the work force would be in the hospital during the summer months of December to March, when malaria hit hardest (Burga 1976, 186–188).

33. Gonzales (1978, 225) reports that contractors for the plantation Cayalti in the department of Lambayeque rented the Hacienda Llaucán from the Colegio San Juan de Chota in 1890 because of the large number of peasants residing on this hacienda. The majority of the labor contractors servicing Cayalti at the turn of the century were merchants or hacienda owners from the highland provinces of Bambamarca, Chota, and Santa Cruz. According to Gonzales, the plantation preferred hacienda owners or lessees as contractors because they could deliver more peasants and could use property as collateral to guarantee the plantation's advance to them. See Scott (1976, 327) for a discussion of the labor recruiters employed by the plantation Casa Grande in the 1950s; he notes that many of these were cattle traders.

But as Gonzales (1980, 293) argues, indebted bondage was not only based on the greed of the labor contractors. It also responded to the labor requirements of the sugar cane plantations. Because the cultivation of sugar cane in Peru relies on irrigation, planting and harvesting activities can be carried out almost year round. Until the 1950s, the sugar planters complained continually that the work force was unstable and that the expansion of the industry was limited by the available labor supply (Roquez 1979, 41). Indebted bondage served their interests as long as the degree of peasant exploitation did not lead to labor unrest or encourage too many runaways.[34]

Solomon Miller (1967, 199) suggests that the widespread practice of paying plantation workers a mixed wage, partly in cash (credited against the advance) and partly in foodstuffs (typically, one pound of meat and one pound of rice per day worked), also served to prolong the stay of the highland migrants. The food ration kept the monetary portion of the wage low, so that the workers could repay the advance or accumulate cash only slowly, if at all. Meanwhile, the food ration also ensured a moderately healthy work force, despite the abuses of the labor contractors.

The first labor struggles on the plantations were indeed tied to these abuses, forcing most of the plantations to become directly involved in labor recruitment rather than relying on independent contractors (Klarén 1976, 78–81; de Osma 1912).[35] In 1912 the major plantation of the Chicama Valley, Casa Grande, established its own recruitment agency in the city of Cajamarca. The agency was also charged with purchasing cattle to supply the rations furnished to plantation workers. By 1940 Casa Grande had such agencies in thirteen of the province's pueblos (Franco 1976, 30).

In the early decades of enganche, the coastal plantations appeared to divide up the migrant labor cache among themselves. The provinces of Cajamarca and Cajabamba were the domain of Casa Grande, partly shared with the other plantations of La Libertad. Other major areas of independent communities further north—the provinces of Hualgayoc, Chota, and Santa Cruz—were the primary recruiting areas for Lambayeque plantations such as Cayalti (Gonzales 1978, 225). The rice plantations of the Jequetepeque Valley recruited in the adjacent Cajamarcan province of San Miguel and in the district of San Pablo (Burga 1976, 241–244). Competition for labor among the plantations, however, often made these tacitly agreed-upon boundaries meaningless. In 1919, for example, near the peak of the sugar export boom, Casa Grande was planning to recruit more workers from Bambamarca than all the Lambayeque plantations combined had planned to do (Albert 1976, table 56).

During the 1890s, most workers on the sugar plantations were still Chinese. By 1900 there were already some one thousand permanent workers on the five

34. See Scott (1976, 328) and Gonzales (1980, 312–313) on the problem of runaways. It generally fell to the recruiters and labor contractors to ensure that peasants fulfilled their contracts.

35. On the subsequent development of the coastal trade union movement, see Klarén (1976) and Albert (1976, 185a–212a).

major plantations of the Chicama Valley, the majority of them highland migrants (Klarén 1976, 74–79). The flow of seasonal highland labor increased steadily, and by 1912 the great majority of the 6,197 field workers in the Chicama Valley were from the highlands. By 1920 the total work force in this valley had expanded to 10,131 (Albert 1976, table 43). Seasonal workers greatly outnumbered the permanent labor force on the estates.

The unprecedented high sugar prices during World War I led not only to increased acreage and employment but also to inflation. Food prices, as well as the general cost of living, doubled between 1913 and 1920 (Hunt 1977, table 16). In this period, some of the major coastal plantations purchased highland haciendas both to secure peasant labor, by requiring that tenants pay off their labor services on the sugar plantations, and to produce foodstuffs directly for the expanding labor force, thus maintaining low wages. The Gildermeisters of Casa Grande purchased the Hacienda Huacraruco in Cajamarca province in 1917 and the nearby Hacienda Sunchubamba in 1919. The plantation Pomalca purchased the Hacienda Udima in 1920, and

TABLE 5. Employment in the Peruvian Sugar and Rice Industries, 1912–1940

Years	Sugar	Rice
	Average Annual Employment	
1912–1915	24,650	9,020[a]
1916–1920	25,346	12,059
1921–1925	29,231	14,325
1926–1929	30,780[b]	16,652
1931–1935	26,356	38,233
1936–1940	25,895[c]	27,803
	Average Annual Rate of Growth	
1912–1920	2.7%	6.0%[d]
1920–1929	2.5%	9.1%
1931–1940	1.4%	1.5%

SOURCE: Compiled from Hunt (1977, table 8).
NOTE: Data for 1930 are not available for either the sugar or rice industries. Employment estimates for the rice industry until 1926 include males only. In 1931, 8,000 women were employed in the industry, but by 1934 this figure had dropped to 2,000.
[a] Employment figure for 1915 only
[b] Based on data for 1926 and 1929 only.
[c] The 1940 figure has been taken from Hunt's own series, rather than from his reported census figure, to maintain consistency.
[d] Based on data for 1915–1920 only.

Cartavio purchased a hacienda in the department of La Libertad (Klarén 1976, 139; Horton 1976, 160; Miller 1967, 169). Other plantations leased haciendas in the Cajamarcan sierra for the same purposes.[36]

The collapse of the sugar market in the 1920s led sugar planters on the central and southern coast to change crops, but those in the north were unable to do so because of their large capital investments. Thus, by the 1920s, the northern plantations were producing 75 percent of Peru's sugar output (Thorp and Bertram 1978, 47, 42). They apparently held production at full capacity to offset low prices, for, as Table 5 shows, industry employment continued to grow during this period.

In the 1920s, more and more Cajamarcan peasants migrated independently to the coast, a migration no doubt facilitated by the experience of other Cajamarquinos with the enganche system.[37] At the same time, a permanent nucleus of highland migrant workers began to form on many of the plantations.[38] The contribution of Cajamarcan migrants to population growth on the north coast is captured in the fact that, in 1940, Cajamarquinos constituted 62 percent of the total migrants to the department of La Libertad and 59 percent of those to Lambayeque (Peru 1940, vol 3, table 19).

The sugar sector was especially hard hit by the Great Depression of the 1930s. Growth in output was reduced to 1.8 percent, while employment grew by only 1.4 percent. But as growth in sugar production declined, rice production expanded dramatically in response to tariffs on rice imports. One of the major rice-producing areas was the Jequetepeque Valley.[39] The Empresa Agrícola Chicama, Ltda., of Casa Grande formed the Negociación Agrícola

36. The plantation Roma leased the Hacienda Llaucán, and Laredo leased the Hacienda Chusyán (Gonzales 1978, 242). Some plantations were more successful than others in securing a labor supply in this fashion, as well as in developing their highland haciendas as foodstuff producers. See Horton (1976) on the problems of turning the Hacienda Udima into a profitable enterprise; see Taylor (1984) on the success of Casa Grande with the haciendas Huacraruco and Sunchubamba.

37. Data for the plantation Cayalti illustrate this trend. In 1905, 88 percent of the temporary labor force had been recruited through enganche; by 1924 this proportion had fallen to 44 percent (Gonzales 1978, 245). Nonetheless, the absolute number of peasants recruited by the agency of Casa Grande in Cajamarca continued to increase at least through the 1920s. Taylor (1979, 159) reports that in 1913 the agency recruited a monthly average of 960 peasants from the province; this figure rose steadily, to 1,672 in 1917, dropping for the next two years, and then increasing to 2,738 workers in 1923.

38. By 1923 half of the plantation work force on Cayalti consisted of permanent workers, considered settled in plantation households. This proportion increased to 65 percent in 1932 (Gonzales 1978, 267–269). The population of Casa Grande increased from 5,000 in 1912 (de Osma 1912, 15) to 9,251 in 1940 (Peru 1940, vol. 3, table 34).

39. The Jequetepeque Valley was the second leading rice-producing zone in the country until 1945, when it became the leading producer (Burga 1976, 206). The rice promotion policy was so successful, with land switched from export crops into rice, that rice was in oversupply in the 1930s, leading to the downturn in employment reported in Table 5.

Jequetepeque, purchasing five rice plantations there in 1931 (Burga 1976, 214). Casa Grande's diversification undoubtedly ensured peasants from Cajamarca continued access to seasonal employment. Many peasants from the district of Jesús, where land pressure had become especially acute and seasonal migration a way of life, remember the Great Depression only as the period when they worked on the rice estates rather than the sugar plantations.

The continuing competition for labor on the coast was one major reason why the enganche system functioned well through the 1950s. The sugar plantations of the Chicama Valley and Lambayeque had to compete not only with the rice industry but also, subsequently, with the expanding cotton plantations in the far north. The end of enganche, as well as the generation of a relative surplus population on the coast, would have to await more profound changes in the class relations in the Cajamarcan highlands.

Developments in the Product Market

At the turn of the century, Málaga Santolalla lamented the weakness of Cajamarca's commercial agriculture: "In the fifty years since the department of Cajamarca was constituted, agriculture has advanced little, for the methods of planting, cultivation, and harvesting have not changed at all; all that one notes is an expansion of the cultivable area and an increase in sugar production and alfalfa, but this is the consequence of natural population growth and the associated growth in consumption" (1906, 200). Most of the agricultural surface of the province of Cajamarca was dedicated to producing barley, the primary foodstuff of the peasantry.

Commenting on the trade statistics compiled in 1855, the year the department was officially constituted, Málaga Santolalla thought that the volume of trade had "undoubtedly increased considerably" since then.[40] The value of mineral exports was substantially higher, and Cajamarca was providing increased quantities of livestock, as well as lard and butter, to the coast. But Cajamarca's only agricultural export product was processed coca leaves, destined for German markets. In 1855 wheat flour had been the leading regional export product; by the early 1900s the sale of this product was limited to highland interprovincial trade (Málaga Santolalla 1906, 196–200).

Málaga Santolalla thought Cajamarca had the potential to meet total coastal consumption of both wheat and potatoes. He argued that if only transportation costs were lower, highland wheat production could compete with Chilean imports. Other observers of the period concurred; with transpor-

40. Málaga Santolalla (1906, 243) was commenting on the regional trade data presented in Sarachaga, Degola, and Arana ([1855] 1981). He himself found it impossible to estimate the volume of regional trade at the turn of the century, noting that the only reliable figures available were those for the mining industry. According to Málaga Santolalla's rough calculations, imports to the department were on the order of Lp 50,000, not that much greater than the total volume of mineral exports alone, estimated at Lp 39,278 (1906, 236).

tation costly, it made sense for the haciendas to export only high-value products such as wool, hides, and dairy products, or beef, which could be transported on the hoof (Solano 1906, 4; Córdova Muñoz 1913, 16; de León 1911, 36).

The coastal markets were a five-day mule trek from the capital city of Cajamarca. In 1864 the national congress had authorized the construction of a railroad from the Pacasmayo to the city of Cajamarca. Enrique Meiggs, who built the railroads in most of Peru during this period, won the bid. Meiggs completed the 65-kilometer Pacasmayo–La Viña trajectory in 1873; however, all but one bridge was destroyed in the 1878 floods. With the War of the Pacific and the subsequent disorder, reconstruction was not contemplated until 1889, when, under the Grace Contract, the Peruvian Corporation assumed the management of this and all other Peruvian railroads as partial compensation for canceling Peru's external debt.[41]

The Peruvian Corporation restored rail traffic only as far as Yonán in the Jequetepeque Valley; thus, at the turn of the century, a three-day mule trek from Cajamarca was still required to reach the railhead. Moreover, as a student delegation from the National University of San Marcos observed in 1917, "One could say that [Cajamarca] does not even have the trails to stimulate a minimum degree of commercial exchange, for those existing trails barely allow travelers and small amounts of merchandise to pass" (UMSM 1917, 33).

The city of Cajamarca became accessible by road only in the late 1920s, when a 90-kilometer road was built to Chilete under the Leguía administration's Road Conscription Law.[42] This was not an all-weather road; during six months of the year, it was barely passable by motor traffic. Pike observed that until the late 1930s traveling to Cajamarca meant enduring "rigours of travel nearly as severe as those faced by the conquistadores" (1964, 2). Exports from the region continued to depend on mule transport. Not until 1945 was the province of Cajamarca connected to coastal markets by an all-weather road.

The export of cattle was not so dependent on good transportation, and the available data suggest that cattle production expanded significantly until the 1920s. In 1855 the department stocked an estimated 32,615 head of cattle and 164,950 head of sheep (Sarachaga, Degola, and Arana [1855] 1981, 29). Edmundo de León (1911, 17), who conducted a study of the livestock potential of the four northern Peruvian departments, estimated that Cajamarca held between 185,000 and 200,000 head of cattle and sheep, in roughly equal

41. The dates cited here are those reported by Málaga Santolalla (1906, 157–161); they differ slightly from those reported by Chávez Aliaga (1957, 1:99–101). On the Grace Contract, see Yepes del Castillo (1972, 138–139) and Cotler (1978, 124–126).

42. The Road Conscription Law (Ley de Conscripción Vial), passed in 1920, required Peruvian males between the ages of twenty-one and fifty to provide twelve days of labor on road construction; those aged eighteen to twenty-one or fifty to sixty had to provide only six days of labor. The unpopular law was abrogated in 1930 with the fall of Leguía.

numbers. These figures imply that over the last half of the nineteenth century and the first decade of the twentieth, the sheep herd was reduced approximately by half, whereas the stock of cattle tripled.[43] This increase in the cattle stock was even more impressive in the province of Cajamarca. Data for sixteen haciendas show that the stock increased from 3,700 head in 1855 to approximately 35,000 in 1911.

Important changes also occurred in the location of animal stock. In 1855 indigenous communities held 30 percent of sheep and cattle stock; the haciendas held 70 percent (Sarachaga, Degola, and Arana 1981, 29). In 1911 de León estimated this distribution at 5 percent and 95 percent. Most of the cattle grazing on hacienda lands, however, belonged to the peasantry, who paid rents to the landlord class for grazing rights. These data are thus consistent with the earlier description of the haciendas' expanded control over peasant labor in this period.

Although the cattle stock had grown rapidly, the available data indicate that exports of cattle to the coast during the years of the sugar boom were only approximately equivalent to local highland consumption. Nicolás Santolalla (1977, 234) estimated that approximately 4,000 head of cattle were traded each year in the provinces of Cajamarca, Celendín, and Hualgayoc. The city of Cajamarca was the major highland market, consuming 1,460 head per year; 360 head were slaughtered in the provincial capital of Celendín, and 180 head in the mining center of Hualgayoc. Some 2,000 head were exported to the north coast, only 500 more than had been reported from these same provinces in 1855 (Sarachaga, Degola, and Arana 1981, 32). Sufficient profit incentive did exist, however, to increase the volume of regional exports. Santolalla (1977, 233) estimated the price of beef by live weight to be 30 percent higher on the coast, net of transportation costs, than in the highlands.

Barriers other than transportation also hampered intraregional trade. The lack of a developed financial system and the chaotic state of the medium of exchange also hindered rapid commercial development. Until the 1920s, the Spanish colonial peso circulated along with the British pound sterling, in addition to the Peruvian pound, silver soles, and gold soles (Montoya 1980, 168). All except the largest transactions were carried out in cash, and trade was thus encumbered by the weight of gold and silver coins. Moreover, trade and travel were risky because of banditry. The Leguía administration finally established some order by replacing the pound sterling and silver sole with

43. Data for twenty haciendas are available for both 1855 and 1911. The size of the cattle stock and sheep herd had increased significantly on twelve of these haciendas. Among those showing important increases were La Pauca (from 800 to 10,000), Polloc (4,100 to 8,000), Tuñad (1,100 to 5,000), and Huacraruco (6,600 to 8,000). The most striking decreases were shown by Porcón, traditionally the largest sheep-raising hacienda in the province (12,500 to 7,000), Llushcapampa (5,300 to 1,000), and Combayo (8,400 to 6,000). The figures are drawn from Sarachaga, Degola, and Arana (1981) and de León (1911).

paper currency backed in gold soles and creating the Banco de Reserva del Perú to centralize monetary emission and credit (Cotler 1978, 187).

Taylor's (1984, 101–102) archival research suggests that in the 1920s the cattle trade was quite dynamic. Taylor also argues that the Empresa Agrícola Chicama, Ltda., played a pivotal role in integrating Cajamarca with the northern regional economy. He reports that during the 1920s Casa Grande's Cajamarca agency was buying some 200 to 400 head of cattle a month in the provinces of Cajamarca, Hualgayoc, and Celendín, in addition to significant amounts of barley and other cereals. Annual exports in the range of 2,400 to 4,800 head by one firm represent a significant increase over the total estimated volume of the cattle export trade (2,000) in the previous decade. After purchasing Huacraruco and Sunchubamba, Casa Grande developed these haciendas as cattle production centers for its coastal plantations. In the first six months of 1929 alone, these haciendas sent 1,721 head to the coast, with its buyers in the highlands sending an additional 1,230 head directly to Casa Grande. Taylor then argues that during the 1920s "there was not an hacienda of importance in these provinces that was not integrated into the commercial orbit of this enterprise" (1984, 102).

There is overwhelming evidence that the Cajamarcan haciendas were not bastions of self-sufficiency.[44] Luxury consumption by the landlord class depended on the integration of the haciendas into the market economy. At the turn of the century, there were at least five foreign import houses in the city of Cajamarca, as well as one in each of the provincial capitals and even in some of the districts (Málaga Santolalla 1906, 235). In the early 1920s, these import houses stocked such goods as liquors, photographic equipment, and imported cotton, wool, and silk cloth (Aviles et al. 1921, 40–58).

The *casas comerciales* controlled not only the importation of luxury goods to the province but also interprovincial trade and the export of Cajamarcan commodities to the coast (Aviles et al. 1921, 40–58; Alvarez Saén 1908, 1).[45] The foreign commercial houses also had a network of stores on the coast and were linked to the main international banks operating in Peru. For example, in addition to four stores in the department, the commercial house of León y Ruppert operated stores in the coastal cities of Pacasmayo and Chiclayo. The Casa Grace had its main subsidiaries in Trujillo and Lima. Hilbck, Kuntz and

44. The market and profit orientation of haciendas and its compatibility with feudal class relations internally are well established in the literature. See Macera (1971, 15–16) and Spalding (1975, 113–114), for example, on the colonial period in Peru.

45. The locally owned commercial houses tended to be owned by members of the landlord class. For example, Domingo Querzola, who owned the oldest commercial house, the Casa Comercial Querzola, also owned the Hacienda Succhubamba. Nicanór Chavarri, the owner of the commercial house Neira y Chavarri, founded in 1908, owned the fundo Otuzco in the Cajamarca Valley (Aviles et al. 1921, 40–58). A superb analysis of the role of the landlord/merchant/cattle trader in southern Peru is provided by Montoya (1980). The role of these individuals in Cajamarca, and how they related to the foreign commercial houses, requires further study.

Cia. was linked to the Banco Alemán Transatlantico as well as the Banco del Perú y Londres. Sattui and Cia., which specialized in high-value products from the *selva* (Amazonian, or jungle) region, such as coffee, cacao, and rubber, was the agent of the Banco Italiano.

In 1930 these firms, along with the Casa Grande agency and five of the more progressive landowners (Alejandro Castro Mendívil, Manuel Cacho Sousa, Leopoldo Rodríguez, Luis Querzola, and Oscar Barrantes), formed the Cajamarcan Chamber of Commerce, Agriculture, and Industry to lobby the state for improved transportation to the coast to facilitate commerce (Chávez Aliaga 1957, 3:133–134). The Chamber of Commerce looked to the coast rather than internally for the expansion of the internal market; peasants were regarded as no more than subsistence producers. As the subprefect of Cajamarca noted, because of the lack of transportation, agricultural production was small-scale and "people plant what they will eat" (quoted in Alvarez Saén 1908, 1).

But these contemporaries could not have been altogether correct, for a good segment of the peasantry was paying for access to grazing or cultivable land on the haciendas through rents in cash (see Chapter 2). Those peasants, at least, were compelled to engage in commodity exchange. But because the peasantry owned the majority of the cattle stock of the province, it is likely that the sale of cattle, rather than the production and sale of foodstuffs, constituted the primary nexus of the peasantry to the provincial product market.

There was also a substantial degree of specialization in artisan craft production among different villages, as well as differing ecological conditions for agricultural production, which spurred trade in the weekly pueblo markets.[46] Although barter was not insignificant, Cajamarca could hardly have been characterized as a "natural economy," devoid of the market nexus. Peasant trade, however, was generally small-scale. Until the 1940s, women controlled the rural trading circuits in peasant agricultural and artisan production, crisscrossing the province on mules.

The development of the enganche system also spurred the monetization of the local economy and had at least some effect in broadening the internal market. In the early years of the system, most of the wage income earned by seasonal migrants consisted of the cash advances received and spent in the sierra. Not until the 1920s and 1930s does the proportion of cash advance to total wage income appear to decline, favoring the consumption of wage goods on the coast. Nonetheless, it is also from this later period that peasant migrants report accumulating some savings from coastal wage labor that were subsequently invested in the sierra.

46. For example, artisans in the district of Jesús specialized in pottery, baskets, and other reed products, while those in the district of San Miguel and the northern portion of the district of Cajamarca (the Porcón area) specialized in woolen textiles.

The first anthropological account of the province, written by Eulogio Elespuru Bernizón (1939, 153–155) in the 1930s, included in the list of commodities purchased by the peasantry salt, *aguardiente* (sugar cane alcohol), *chancaca* (brown sugar cakes), dyes and thread, and leather and rubber for making sandals. Also, *bayeta* (rough wool cloth) was generally purchased for clothing. Every peasant man and woman sported a straw hat, imported from the province of Celendín. Occasionally, peasants would purchase agricultural implements such as steel plowheads or hoes.

Elespuru Bernizón considered candles, matches, sugar, gunpowder, and cotton cloth for shirts or blouses to be luxuries for the peasantry. Significantly, although thousands of Cajamarcan peasants had migrated seasonally to the coast by the 1930s, processed foodstuffs had not yet penetrated the rural Cajamarcan diet. Only when the all-weather road opened did rice, noodles, and bread made of imported wheat flour, which migrant workers were learning to eat on the coast, begin to become standard fare in highland diets.

Determining the precise effect of the Depression in Cajamarca is difficult. The picture that emerges from available data shows the decade of the 1920s as perhaps the most dynamic for the province's economy. But because the coast was characterized by relative stagnation during this decade, a stagnation that lasted into the 1930s, Cajamarca's economic growth, although perhaps exceeding that of earlier periods, could have been only relatively modest.

One effect of Cajamarca's integration with the coast as a supplier of cattle may have been a significant decline in the province's cattle stock. After growing rapidly in the late nineteenth century, the size of the provincial cattle stock stabilized in the first two decades of the twentieth century.[47] In 1944 Silva Santisteban (1945, 50–51) noted that the stock had decreased considerably since the 1929 census. He may have been observing the result of an overly rapid supply response to the possible expansion of market opportunities on the coast in the late 1930s, when grazing lands there were put into crop production. In the early 1940s, meat was scarce in the city of Cajamarca, reflected in unusually high prices. In 1944 only 637 cattle had been processed at the city's slaughterhouse, compared with 3,500 in the early 1910s (de León 1911, 17; Córdova Muñoz 1913, 18) and 1,460 in 1917 (Santolalla 1977, 234).

The available data are only suggestive of the main trends characterizing Cajamarca's integration into the circuit of capitalist exchange. Obviously, a great deal more primary research must be done before we can conclude that the integration of the province with the coast as a supplier of cattle and labor power ushered in a period of relative prosperity in the 1920s, followed by stagnation in

47. According to de León's (1911, 17) data, sixteen provincial haciendas held 35,000 head of cattle at the beginning of the 1910s. This estimate is roughly comparable to Córdova Muñoz's (1913, 3) estimate that the province contained 42,000 head of cattle. The 1929 census reports 42,265 head of cattle in the province (Pinto 1972).

the 1930s and early 1940s. But the observations of contemporaries about the development of the productive forces do support this proposition.

According to Málaga Santolalla (1906, 150, 191), agricultural technology in the early 1900s was more primitive than it had been in the period of the Incan hegemony in the region, when complex irrigation systems had been utilized. He blamed the lack of irrigation development on the fact that agriculture was small-scale and oriented only to the local, internal market.

The results of the first national agricultural census, taken in 1929, indicate the state of agricultural development in the department. Of all Peruvian departments, Cajamarca had the largest area dedicated to the production of corn and was second in wheat and barley acreage; but the department ranked fifth in corn yields and reported the lowest yields of all departments for wheat and barley (Pinto 1972, 32, 36–37, 38–39, 77). Nonetheless, the very best lands, including those of the Cajamarca Valley, were still dedicated to the cultivation of wheat and barley during this period (UMSM 1917, 32).

Studies of the cattle industry suggest that its level of technological development was also quite low. One student of the industry wrote: "The method of raising cattle is so perverse and rustic that it brings the degeneration of the cattle" (Córdova Muñoz, 1913, 29). There was little attention to breed selection. Reportedly, one landowner imported a Holstein bull from the United States, hoping to improve the stock, but then simply put the bull out to wander the range, without any attention to crossbreeding control. Moreover, most landowners gave no importance at all to the quality of animal feed. Consequently, the dairy cows of the province produced at most 2 liters of milk a day (Córdova Muñoz 1913, 18–29).

Nonetheless, in the 1911 study of the four northern Peruvian departments, Cajamarca was described as the department with the greatest potential for cattle production because of its favorable climatic conditions that yielded abundant natural pastures. But de León (1911, 31), the author of this study, was also dismayed by the poor management and utilization of the cattle herd.

The technological innovations that were introduced on the Cajamarcan haciendas between 1900 and 1940 were largely in cattle and dairy production. Various landowners, such as Villanueva on the Hacienda Purhuay and Rodríguez on Quilcate, experimented in the 1910s with improved alfalfa and clover pastures (Córdova Muñoz 1913, 14). Although alfalfa was grown primarily to fatten cattle for export to the coast and to feed beasts of burden, there were also indications of an incipient modern dairy industry. De León was surprised to find that Castro Iglesias had purchased the most modern equipment for a butter factory on La Colpa. At least two other butter and cheese factories were in operation in the province, on the haciendas Yanacancha and Quilcate (de León 1911, 30). Obviously impressed, de León predicted that the dairy industry would become the primary industry of Cajamarca: "I am convinced that once dairy production takes hold on several of the haciendas, this will become the 'mother' industry, one that could supply all of the country with milk with even a surplus to export.... Of the many valleys which I have visited, I have found in this department regions which do not have anything to envy the conditions of the pastures of Holland" (1911, 29). He would not have been disappointed by events in the province in the 1940s and 1950s.

Two landowners, Alejandro Castro Mendívil and Manuel Cacho Sousa, took the lead in the initial development of the Cajamarcan dairy industry. Cacho Sousa's father, Manuel Cacho Galvez of the Hacienda Polloc, was the first to carry out serious work on cattle breeding. In 1916–1917 he imported Brown Swiss cattle from Argentina and began the difficult process of crossing them with the best criollo cattle (Chávez Aliaga 1957, 1:247). Cacho Sousa later managed the major portion of this hacienda, renamed Santa Teresita de la Quispa, and with Castro Mendívil brought the first planeload of Holsteins to Cajamarca in the early 1920s. Castro Mendívil and Cacho Sousa are also credited with a number of technological innovations, such as adapting Holsteins for the first time to altitudes above 2,800 meters. During this decade, Castro Mendívil developed the first capitalist dairy enterprise in Cajamarca (Taylor 1979).

Nevertheless, some twenty years later, the agronomist Silva Santisteban (1945, 47) described these innovating landowners as the exception rather than the rule in the region's cattle industry. Few landlords actually practiced breed selection. The majority of the Cajamarcan cattle stock was of poor quality and very low productivity. Even in the Cajamarca Valley, cows maintained on alfalfa feed produced only 3 to 4 liters of milk daily. Sheep production was even more pitiful. Silva Santisteban thus concluded that Cajamarca's agriculture had fallen into a state of retrocession over the previous forty years, an observation with which other contemporaries agreed (Alayza Escardo 1943).

CONCLUSION

The dominance of the hacienda system in Cajamarca was based on the control by the landlord class over land and labor—the basis for the accumulation of wealth—and the political hegemony of this class. Moreover, its control over rural labor continued to increase during the first part of the century, while its political power went relatively unchallenged.

The first challenge to the hacienda system was economic. Highland peasant labor now had a positive opportunity cost through seasonal migration to the coast. The existence of this alternative precluded the development of capitalist class relations on the haciendas during this period. If the haciendas had depended on wage labor, they would have had to compete with the coastal plantations, which would have required that the use of wage labor be as profitable in the sierra as it was on the coast.

The internal market at the haciendas' command was no doubt growing, but it was limited by high transportation costs and national trade policy. There was little incentive to expand and improve production significantly, although some agricultural experimentation was underway. Because the haciendas held a virtual monopoly of grazing land, which was underutilized, land had a low opportunity cost. The cheapest labor force could be maintained by ceding land in usufruct. Peasants could generate their own subsistence requirements at little or no cost to the landlord while providing both a permanent and temporary labor reserve for the landlord's demesne. The luxury consumption patterns of the landlord class could be maintained without much effort through the accumulation of rents and minimal direct production.

Growing land pressure in the independent communities was the main factor compelling peasant households into multiple class relations—either through wage work based on temporary migration or a rental arrangement on a hacienda. The sufficient condition for peasants to be willing to enter into feudal class relations was the near-monopoly control over uncultivated land and pastures by the haciendas. But most important in determining the particular content of feudal class relations in the province, as I discuss in the next chapter, was the fact that peasants from the independent communities *did* have a potential alternative: seasonal wage work on the coast. The conditions of existence of feudal class relations were indeed changing.

TWO

Class Relations on the Cajamarcan Haciendas

According to Málaga Santolalla, "the surface of most haciendas in the department is divided into three sections. The first section consists of the lands worked directly by the owner with the labor of the *colonos*. The second section is given to *arrendadores* or *arrendatarios* who cultivate the lands on their own account for an annual payment. Finally, the third section is given over to individuals; the owner provides the land, seed, and sometimes the oxen, and the *partidario* plows and cultivates. The crop is divided in the fields into generally equal shares" (1906, 196).

The organization of production on the Cajamarcan haciendas and the rental arrangements between peasants and landlords were hardly this straightforward, although most of the large haciendas of the province were characterized by peasants paying rent in some combination of labor services, products, or cash. The salient feature of class relations on the haciendas was the peasants' obligation to provide unpaid labor services, regardless of whether the primary rental payment was in kind or in cash. Another feature was the large variation in the quantity of labor services demanded; this variation existed not only between haciendas but also among peasants with the same rental contract within a hacienda.

Peasants were distinguished according to the primary form of rental payment required of them. The colonos (also called *peones, la gente de hacienda,* or *quinceneros*) were members of those peasant households who, in return for a parcel of land and grazing rights, paid rent only in the form of labor services. They constituted the permanent work force for the landlord's direct production on the demesne. The colonos were always hacienda residents. Sharecroppers (partidarios or *aparceros*) included households residing on the hacienda, as well as peasants from neighboring communities. Their rent was paid in kind, and their labor services were termed *faena*. The arrendatarios or arrendires paid rent

TABLE 6.   Rental   Arrangements   on   Haciendas   in   the   Province   of
Cajamarca, 1920–1950

Type of Rental Arrangement	Respondents' Self-Categorization	Haciendas
Colonos	14%	Chaquil, Huacariz, La Tranca, La Colpa
Sharecroppers	44%	Polloc, Chaquil, Sangal, La Tranca, Huacraruco, Miche, Porfía, La Colpa, Porcón, Chamis, Yumagual, Huacariz de San Antonio, Shultín, Ajoscancha, Las Vegas, San Luis, El Molino, San Cristóbal
Arrendires	42%	Polloc, Chaquil, Combayo, Polloquito, Sondor, Huacraruco, Porcón, Llushcapampa, Llagadén, Urubamba, Ronquillo
Total	100% (N = 43)	

SOURCE: 1976 Peasant Family Survey.
NOTE: Only those haciendas reported by survey respondents are included.

in cash; their labor services were also termed *faena* or, if in exchange for grazing rights only, *hierbaje*. The primary rental relationship between the landlord class and households in independent peasant communities involved arrendire arrangements, although these agreements were also made with hacienda residents.

Sharecropper and arrendire arrangements were by far the most common (see Table 6). Analysis of the tems of these rental agreements reveals their heterogeneity, however. The obligations of an arrendire on one hacienda might be considered those of a colono on another.[1] The variation in the amount of labor service required of different households is only partially explained by the different amounts and quality of land given in usufruct and by different demands for peasant labor. Three other factors are equally important in explaining variations in the appropriation of surplus labor; 1) the personalized and paternalistic nature of landlord-peasant relations; 2) the locale of residence, that is, whether the household resided on the hacienda itself or in a nearby community; and 3) the role of the enganche system and wage labor

1. The diversity of rental arrangements on the haciendas was first pointed out by Gitlitz (1975, 136, 143). In my interviews, I was nevertheless surprised by the wide variation in the content of these agreements; I had expected to find more consistency, at least among those in the same rental category on one hacienda. I initially thought that faulty memories might be to blame, but after cross-checking a number of informants' reports with their sworn declarations to the Agrarian Reform Office of the Ministry of Agriculture in Cajamarca, I found that my interview data (collected in 1975–1976) were usually consistent with what informants had reported in 1972 for agrarian reform purposes.

opportunities on the coast, which increased the bargaining power of the peasantry as the century progressed.

VARIATIONS IN RENTAL ARRANGEMENTS

Of all the rental arrangements, those of colonos show the most consistency over time. Colonos are considered to have made up the permanent labor force on the haciendas since the colonial period (Silva Santisteban 1945, 93). Most commonly, members of colono households had been born on the hacienda, as had their parents. The colonos were always required to perform more days of labor service than any other group on the hacienda.

The earliest contemporary description reported that four days a week was the standard labor requirement for the head of a colono household (Málaga Santolalla 1906, 185). Nicolás Santolalla ([1918] 1977, 221, 225), writing in 1917, thought that colonos on most haciendas worked a minimum of twenty days a month for the landlord, as was the case on the Hacienda Combayo. Several decades later, the most common arrangement was still for the colono to work three or four days a week for the landlord and to farm a subsistence parcel the remainder of the week. Other variations included providing labor services every other week or for fifteen days at a time; colonos under this latter arrangement were known as quinceneros (Hacienda Llushcapampa).[2] In the majority of cases, the basic arrangement was that half of the labor time of adult male colonos consisted of unpaid labor services; this constituted the surplus labor time appropriated by the landlord.[3]

But there were some important exceptions. On the Hacienda La Pauca, some colono heads of household worked full-time for the landlord (Chambeu and Gorget 1975, 10). In return, they were allowed to pasture their animals

2. This chapter, as well as chapters 3, 6, 7, and 9, draws heavily on my interviews during 1975 and 1976 with peasant men and women residing in caserios that had once been part of haciendas before the haciendas were broken up and sold in the 1950s and 1960s. The data reported in the text are taken from three types of interviews: 1) structured interviews I and my assistants carried out as part of the 1976 Peasant Family Survey (see Table 6 for a list of the haciendas included in the quantitative data on the hacienda system; see Appendix IV for details on this survey of 105 households; 2) unstructured interviews I carried out in the context of participant observation in the caserios that were once part of the haciendas Combayo, Polloc, Santa Ursula, Tres Molinos, Cristo Rey, Huacariz de San Antonio, Porcón, and Huayobamba, as well as in a number of the independent villages of the province; and 3) detailed life histories I compiled of former tenants of the haciendas Combayo, Polloc, Santa Ursula, and Huacariz de San Antonio. In the text, only the material collected as part of the 1976 Peasant Family Survey is explicitly referenced. The haciendas to which specific descriptions refer are noted in parentheses.

3. The rate of exploitation of colono labor may have been higher in Cajamarca than in other Peruvian highland regions. Montoya (1978, 43) reports that he considered the standard range of labor services on the haciendas in Andahuaylas to be approximately two to three days per week or one hundred to one hundred fifty days per year.

freely on hacienda land, and they received periodic gifts such as salt or *ají* (chili peppers). They also received generous land allotments that they, in turn, sharecropped with other peasants. Nevertheless, these colonos on the Puga family's hacienda were the most dominated group, considered by the others to be *"gente esclava"* (slaves).[4]

On most haciendas, only a few of the colonos worked full-time for the landlord, usually as *mitayos* or *punteros* caring for the landlord's sheep or cattle, respectively. In addition to a plot of land and permission to graze their own animals along with the landlord's, these full-time workers sometimes received a small cash payment (Hacienda Combayo) or a percentage of the newborn animals from the landlord's stock (Hacienda Polloc). On some haciendas, other colonos who worked full-time were the *huasicamas*, permanent servants in the casa hacienda (haciendas Llushcapampa, Huacariz de San Antonio). Although they too were sometimes given access to a small parcel of land and had grazing rights for their animals on the hacienda, members of these households actually lived in the casa hacienda and served at the landlord's will.

A more common pattern in the province was for such servant duties to be rotated among the women and children of households residing on the hacienda as *semaneras* (literally, weekly workers) (Málaga Santolalla 1906, 185). Along with housekeeping, semanera duty usually included caring for the hacienda's yard and work animals, as well as cleaning out corrals, milking cows, and collecting wood. It also involved cooking the noon meal for the colono work force. The number of weeks of required semanera duty varied with the total number of dependent households and whether the landlord family resided on the hacienda rather than in the city of Cajamarca. The reported time required ranged from two weeks to three months a year, with the higher figures given for haciendas where the landlord family was in residence (haciendas Chamis, Llushcapampa).

Besides performing semanera duty, which was an obligation of all women residing on the haciendas, colono women were also required to attend special work parties, sometimes called *mingas*, to process the hacienda's products (haciendas Polloc, Sangal, Combayo, La Tranca, Llagadén, Chamis, Llushcapampa). They were also required to carry out a number of other tasks, such as spinning wool, at home or on their own time (haciendas Porcón, Llushcapampa). Younger children usually accompanied their mother while she was involved in semanera duty. Young girls participated in the mingas, while young boys performed agricultural labor services along with their fathers.

---

4. Gitlitz (1975, 125–127) similarly describes the peons on the Hacienda Pallán in the province of Celendín. They worked full-time for the landlord, six or even seven days a week, in return for one meal a day, a 1-hectare plot, and grazing rights. Not until the late 1930s was the work week reduced to five days and the labor service requirements of some peons to fifteen days a month.

The obligations of colono status clearly fell upon the whole peasant family.[5]

Not only the labor of a colono household but also the household's means of production were subject to the landlord's disposition. Work animals (oxen and horses) and pack animals (burros and donkeys) had to be provided whenever the landlord required them. Colono households were also sometimes required to provide their sheep to fertilize the landlord's fields; movable corrals would be built for such a purpose and rotated over the fields before planting (Hacienda Santa Ursula).

Peasants born on the hacienda were the most dependent on the hacienda's resources and the landlord's good will, and, not surprisingly, these colonos were the most subservient element of the landlord's labor force. The importance of residence in determining the degree of exploitation and servility is underscored by the fact that in Cajamarcan parlance the term *colono* often denoted any hacienda resident, whatever the primary form of rental payment. On the Hacienda Combayo, for example, all residents were called colonos, although these were in turn distinguished as peons or arrendires (Santolalla 1977).

The resident peasants on the haciendas Santa Ursula and Porcón were also generally referred to as colonos, although the few existing written rental contracts between peasant tenants and landlord-arrendires show that these tenants were in fact sub-arrendires, with an important portion of their rent being paid in cash. In a 1918 contract between the arrendire of the Hacienda Santa Ursula and a tenant sub-arrendire, the peasant household agreed to an annual cash payment of S/. 40 in addition to the following services:[6]

1. Twelve days of faena were to be provided for agricultural work on the landlord's demesne—six days during the planting season, with a team of oxen, and six days during the harvest. The peasant would receive S/. 1.00 for the former services and S/. 3.00 for the latter.
2. A woman from the household was to be sent for the sorting of wheat or whatever job she could perform, "always and whenever asked."
3. A semanera was to clean the casa hacienda whenever it was that household's turn.
4. The head of the household was to transport wood and bamboo for the hacienda whenever asked.
5. The household was to provide all the burros required to take the hacienda's potato crop to Cajamarca. This service would be remunerated at the rate of S/. 0.10 per day plus pasture.

5. The requirement that women and children perform unpaid labor services on the hacienda has been widely reported but not analyzed in much depth. See, for example, Favre (1976, 129–130) on Huancavelica; Tullis (1970, 90–91, 99) on Junín; Montoya (1980, 70–71) on Andahuaylas; and Craig (1969, 279) on the La Convención Valley in Cuzco.

6. "Contrato entre Julián Condor and Fidel G. Zevallos Palmer, Octubre 1918," Hacienda Santa Ursula files, Agrarian Reform Office, Ministry of Agriculture, Agrarian Zone II, Cajamarca.

6. The household was allowed to pasture fifty sheep rent-free as long as all of the household's sheep were provided to fertilize the landlord's fields for forty days.

The number of days of agricultural faena was clearly specified, but several other unspecified labor services were also required of this resident household. These fell into two categories: women's labor services and the use of the household's animals. (The differential treatment of male and female labor services is analyzed in Chapter 3). The unspecified services were required because these sub-arrendires resided on the hacienda. Their obligations in this regard hardly differed from those reported by resident colono households on other haciendas where rent was paid exclusively by labor services.

The sub-arrendires residing on haciendas owned by the church or the Beneficiencias, such as Santa Ursula, were not the only resident tenants subject to labor service requirements as severe as those placed on colonos. For example, on the haciendas Chaquil and Polloquito, several resident households paid 150 days a year in labor services in addition to cash rents. Nevertheless, there is little question that the peasants on the estates owned by the church or the Beneficiencias were among the most exploited. Because landlord-arrendires had to pay a fixed money rent to the hacienda owners, their management of the hacienda had to generate a predetermined level of cash income. They passed this burden on to the tenants, who were forced to pay a given amount of cash rent regardless of their own production levels. Moreover, labor services were also imposed to provide the work force for the landlord-arrendire's own profit-generating activities. Not surprisingly, it was on these rental properties that the most acute landlord-peasant conflicts occurred.

On most haciendas, fewer labor services were required of sharecroppers and arrendires than of colonos, because the principal form of rent for these first two groups was in kind or in cash. The faena required of sharecroppers ranged from twelve or fifteen days (haciendas Huayobamba and Shultín) to three months per year (haciendas Chaquil, La Tranca). The other variation in sharecropping arrangements was that the landlord might provide work animals in addition to seed. Many households were forced into sharecropping simply because they did not own an ox for plowing or a horse for threshing grain. If the landlord provided work animals as well as seed, the cost of the seed was deducted before the crop was divided into equal shares (Huacariz de San Antonio). Otherwise, sharecropping was based on the division of gross output into equal shares.

Rental arrangements with arrendires varied even more than those for sharecroppers, for the former could cover grazing rights or the rental of crop land. Santolalla (1977, 221–224) described a typical agreement as covering both of those items and consisting of a cash payment on the order of S/. 5.00 to S/. 7.50 per hectare, plus the provision of fifteen days faena per year. During the 1930s and 1940s, a typical arrangement of this kind included payment of a specified sum in cash and twelve days of faena per year (haciendas Llagadén, Sondor, Ronquillo).[7]

On other haciendas, arrendires paid a fixed sum per hectare sown and per animal grazed, in addition to labor services. On the Hacienda La Pauca in the 1920s, a typical arrendire might have paid S/. 25 annually for a good-sized parcel of land, as well as S/. 1.00 per head of cattle and S/. 0.50 per head of sheep grazed on hacienda lands. The faena requirement was usually twelve days per year, six during the planting season, with oxen, and six during the harvest (Chambeu and Gorget 1975, 10–11).

By the 1920s, increasing numbers of peasant households from the independent communities were entering into rental arrangements for grazing rights only, sometimes called *piseros*, on the hacienda. A common arrendire arrangement of this sort was the annual payment of S/. 0.20 per head of sheep, plus the provision of twelve days of faena per fifty head of sheep (Hacienda San Antonio). The arrangement could be more exacting, however, requiring in addition to the cash payment as much as one day of faena annually per head of sheep (Hacienda Lacas). The grazing fee for cattle, usually S/. 1.00 per head, was four to five times greater than the fee for sheep. On the Hacienda Polloc, arrendires were required to provide anywhere from one to twelve days of faena per head of cattle, depending on the personal relationship between landlord and arrendire. Silva Santisteban (1945, 92) considered the payment of S/. 2.00 and two to three days of faena per head of cattle to be most typical in the 1940s.

Sometimes the arrendire household could choose to pay its rent in a combination of labor services and cash. On the Hacienda Llushcapampa, for example, a peasant could either work one day every two weeks per head of cattle (i.e., twenty-six days per year) or pay a fine of S/. 0.20 per day of faena missed. The equivalent cash rental for grazing was thus S/. 5.20 per head per year. On the Hacienda La Pauca, arrendires could choose to pay S/. 15 per year rather than provide the twelve days of faena required (Chambeu and Gorget 1975, 11). Chambeu and Gorget suggest that this flexibility was a sign of the abundance of the labor force relative to the demesne's labor requirements in the 1920s.

On other haciendas, such as Huacraruco, arrendires could pay for grazing rights only with faena. In the 1930s and 1940s, arrendires reported paying from two to sixteen days a year per head of cattle. José Manuel Mejía (1974, 1), estimating that arrendires on Huacraruco provided an average of ninety days of labor services per year, argues that the faena requirement was prompted by this hacienda's low population density and relative labor scarcity.[8]

---

7. Gitlitz (1975, 131–132), analyzing the arrendire contracts on the Hacienda Pallán, found no correlation between the size and quality of arrendire plots and the level of cash rent. The number of days of faena also varied, but about thirty days per year was most common.

8. See Taylor (1984) for an analysis of labor relations on the Hacienda Huacraruco, based on archival research, that differs from that provided by Mejía (1974), which is based on interviews.

TABLE 7.   Rental Rates for Grazing Rights on Haciendas, 1900–1944 (Annual Rate per Head in Current Peruvian Soles)

Area of Reference		Cattle	Pigs	Sheep and Goats	Horses	Mules
1900s	Department	1.00	—	0.20	1.00	—
1905	Porcón	0.80	0.40	0.20	0.80	0.80
1910s	La Colpa	0.80	0.50	0.50	0.80	0.80
1911	Department	1.00	—	0.50	0.80	0.80
1915	La Colpa	1.00	0.80	—	1.00	1.00
1917	Department	1.00–1.50	—	0.25–0.50	1.00–1.50	1.00–1.50
1917	Combayo	1.00	0.80	0.25	0.25	1.00
1920s	La Pauca	1.00	—	0.20	—	—
1930s	Province	1.00	—	0.20	1.00	—
1940	Santa Ursula	0.50	—	0.20	—	free[a]
1940s	La Pauca	2.00	—	0.40	—	—
1942	Santa Ursula	2.00	0.80	0.40	—	—
1944	Province	2.00	0.50	0.50	2.00	—

SOURCES: Information for 1900s (Department) from Málaga Santolalla (1906, 185); for 1905, from Gorget (1975b, appendix 1); for 1910s and 1915 (La Colpa) from Taylor (1979, 123, 129); for 1911, from de León (1911, 12); for 1917, from Santolalla ([1918] 1977, 223–224); for 1920s and 1940s (La Pauca), from Chambeu and Gorget (1975, 11); for 1930s, from Elespuru Bernizón (1939, 157); for 1940 and 1942, from "Contrato entre Resurección Culqui y el Sr. Antonio Otoya Puga, Abril 18, 1940," and "Proyecto de reglamentación de relaciones contractuales y de trabajo entre el conductor don Antonio Otoya Puga y los colonos sub-arrendatarios de la Hacienda Santa Ursula, 5 Junio 1942," respectively, Hacienda Santa Ursula files, Agrarian Reform Office, Ministry of Agriculture, Agrarian Zone II, Cajamarca; and for 1944, from Silva Santisteban (1945, 94).
[a]Grazing rights were free if provided to the hacienda when demanded.

Table 7 summarizes the available data on cash rental rates for grazing rights. The table does not adequately reflect the great variation in arrendire arrangements, because these rental rates do not include the faena associated with the arrendire arrangement and are not market prices. Nonetheless, the data indicate that nominal rental rates rose only gradually over the four decades; in real terms, rental rates fell drastically until the 1940s.[9] These trends suggest that the haciendas' resources were underutilized and that the haciendas were trying to attract peasant households from the independent communities into rental agreements.

My 1976 Peasant Family Survey interviews in La Laimina and other communities surrounding Huacraruco support Mejía's report that arrendire arrangements continued to be common on this hacienda at least until the 1940s and, in some cases, the 1960s.

9. Using data on price changes reported in Wilkie (1984, vol. 23, table 2618) to construct a consumer price index based on 1915 prices, we can estimate that the rental rates per head of cattle (in constant Peruvian soles) fell from S/. 1.00 in 1915 to S/. 0.53 in 1920 and S/. 0.58 in 1930, increasing to S/. 1.12 in the 1940s.

One labor requirement not considered a faena but required of hacienda residents and nonresidents alike was participation in the *rodeos*, animal roundups. Several times a year, all the animals grazing on hacienda lands were rounded up for identification, so that the landlord could determine the rent owed by each peasant household. Fines were imposed for animals that had not been reported to the landlord initially. It was also common for the landlord to exact an additional "tax" of a share of the newborn calves or lambs discovered at this time (haciendas Polloc, Chaquil). The rodeos were termed an activity "for the common good" (*de beneficio común*), but in most cases not even a meal was provided.

Another task "for the common good"—but which fell only to hacienda residents to carry out—was cleaning and repairing the canals and irrigation ditches. Because all households on the hacienda were supposed to benefit from the available water supplies (even though they rarely had irrigation rights), these labor services were not counted as a faena. In addition, resident households were required to spend several days a year maintaining the trails on the haciendas. These services were known as *repúblicas* and were enforced by the local district government rather than by the landlord.[10] Although a bill passed by the national congress in 1909 prohibited all government authorities from requiring the free services of Indians or peons on haciendas for either public or private projects, labor services for trail maintenance continued in Cajamarca throughout the first four decades of the century, as they did in much of highland Peru (Davies 1974, 52; Cotler 1978, 169).

In terms of required obligations, colono status was clearly the most demanding. Household reproduction was always somewhat precarious, because the time available for subsistence production largely depended on the landlord's good will. In sharecropping and arrendire arrangements, households were much freer to concentrate on their own productive activities. Because landlords had a stake in the sharecroppers' harvest, they were less motivated to impose requirements for labor services that might have curtailed peasant production. Under arrendire arrangements, peasant households had the least to do with the landlords, for the productive process was totally under the households' control. But because landlords did not share the risks of production, they had fewer incentives to limit the appropriation of labor services. Other factors, such as the landlords' desire to accumulate money capital with little effort or to attract peasant labor to the estate, also influenced the number of labor services demanded in this arrangement.

Whereas the rental arrangement determined the primary form for extracting surplus labor—either directly as labor services or indirectly through the

10. I did not quantify these additional days of labor requirements in my structured interviews. Gitlitz (1975, 127) reports that on the Hacienda Pallán tenants served as much as twenty-five days a year in repúblicas and that the rodeos took another five days annually.

redistribution of surplus labor in the form of products or cash—residence on or off the hacienda was crucial in determining the actual rate of exploitation. Resident households were totally dependent on the hacienda for their livelihood. Nonresidents, in contrast, generally entered into rental arrangements on the hacienda in order to complement their access to resources.

As noted in Chapter 1, by the turn of the century common pasture land had all but disappeared within many of the independent peasant communities. The landlord class held a virtual monopoly of the grazing lands of the province, and peasants who wished to raise sheep or cattle had little alternative but to pay rent for the privilege of grazing on hacienda lands. Also, population growth continually exerted pressure on forests and water supplies, providing additional incentives for independent peasants to seek rental arrangements on the haciendas. During the first forty years of the century, peasants could find good farm land only on the haciendas (Santolalla 1977).

Thus, by the 1930s and 1940s, many peasant households in the communities of La Shita, La Tranca, Cebadín, and La Laimina in the district of Jesús were arrendires of the haciendas La Tranca or Huacraruco.[11] Households in the communities of Hualqui, La Succha, and Yanamango rented land and grazing rights on other haciendas of the district. Such arrangements were also common in the district of San Marcos. Peasants in the communities of Manzanilla and Asunción were arrendires on the haciendas Sondor or La Pauca; those in La Laguna became arrendires of the haciendas Noriega or Huayobamba. Other arrendires of this latter hacienda lived in the communities of Saparcón and Milco (Rivera 1974).

In contrast to the exactions imposed on peasant households resident on the haciendas, the labor service obligations of nonresident arrendires and share-croppers were less severe and were clearly delineated. Peasants from the community of Tambo who rented pastures from the Hacienda Santa Ursula reported that they never had to provide semanera duty, and the various landlords there did not demand that the peasants provide their animals for transportation on the hacienda. Women of nonresident arrendire households were also not required to perform unremunerated labor services for the landlord. As one woman in the community of Sarín explained, "Those female mingas were only the obligation of the Indian women on the hacienda."

Similar reports were made by arrendires and sharecroppers of the independent communities in the district of Jesús. Arrendires of the Hacienda Huacraruco from the neighboring communities of La Laimina and La Shita, for example, noted that the faena was always clearly stipulated and paid off by men, usually on road construction or in sheep-shearing activities. Arrendires on

11. The information in the next several paragraphs is drawn both from the 1976 Peasant Family Survey and from my unstructured interviews in these communities during 1975 and 1976. Garay (1975c) found that one-third of the households residing in the community of La Laimina had been arrendires of the Hacienda La Tranca through 1972.

the Hacienda Miche from the community of La Succha were not even required to pay faena, for colono households satisfied the landlord's demand for labor services there.

Peasants from independent communities who entered into rental agreements, however, did not have all of the same privileges as those who lived on the haciendas. Resident households were generally entitled to collect wood and other raw materials on hacienda land for artisan production or constructing houses, whereas nonresidents commonly had to pay cash for access to these resources (haciendas Huayobamba, Noriega).

Nevertheless, nonresident households were not totally dependent on the hacienda for their survival. They usually had access to at least some land within the villages, held as private property or in sharecropping arrangements made possible through the network of kinship and *compadrazco* (fictive kinship) relations. Moreover, seasonal migration to the sugar plantations provided these independent households with another possibility for generating income. Should a landlord prove too demanding, peasants from these households could simply withdraw from the rental arrangement.

It also became increasingly common for whole families to migrate onto the haciendas (haciendas Combayo, La Pauca, Polloc).[12] Although these immigrants also became resident tenants, they continued to have more independence than the traditional colonos, the gente de hacienda. Chambeu and Gorget (1975, 11) suggest that this was because they usually continued to own some land in their communities of origin and thus had the option of leaving the hacienda if conditions became too bad. My interviews indicate that young, landless households were the most likely to have sought residence on the haciendas. The greater independence of these new residents was more likely explained by the existence of the wage labor alternative. Even if they became indebted to the landlord, they could acquire a cash advance from the *enganchador*, pay off their debt, and leave the hacienda for the coast. The result of this possibility was an intricately stratified labor force within the hacienda, with differing labor services and degrees of economic and noneconomic coercion imposed on arrendires from independent communities, new immigrants, and peasants born on the hacienda.

ECONOMIC AND NONECONOMIC COERCION

Outright restrictions on peasant mobility were probably not necessary on most haciendas, although residents on the Hacienda La Pauca considered themselves completely bound to the estate (Arce del Campo and Lora 1974, 51). Potential landlessness, indebtedness, and the power of the landlord class to

---

12. There was also heavy immigration onto the Hacienda Pallán in Celendín from 1920 to 1940, with the number of residents increasing by around 50 percent (Gitlitz 1975, 136).

enforce debt payments were sufficient conditions to tie resident labor to the hacienda. As a peasant on Rafael Puga's hacienda said of his landlord, "He had the authorities in his hand" (Chambeu and Gorget 1975, 13).

The principal form of economic coercion was indebtedness.[13] Peasants became indebted in many ways: through fines for noncompliance with hacienda regulations, through purchases at hacienda stores, and through the credit landlords provided to help meet household emergencies. In addition, some landlords gave cash advances to peasants to secure their labor services.

A 1940 rental contract between Antonio Otoya Puga and a sub-arrendire, Resurección Culqui, on the Hacienda Santa Ursula illustrates some of the ways peasants could fall into debt.[14] This tenant was to pay an annual rent of S/. 130 for his household's usufruct parcel. Half of the rent was to be paid in cash and the other half in labor services that included the following:

1. Twelve days a year of agricultural faena—six with oxen during the wheat planting and six during the harvest, without remuneration.
2. The tenant was required to work an additional six days a week for as long as the landlord required for plowing and planting the hacienda's crops. This additional labor would be remunerated at the rate of S/. 0.20 per day (for purposes of the rent payment) plus food. The peasant was to provide his own oxen for four of the six days each week.
3. The working day was from 8 A.M. to 5 P.M. If a peasant missed work, he was fined S/. 2.00 per day.
4. The household was required to toast barley and to make *chochoca* (toasted corn kernels) whenever required by the landlord.
5. The household was required to send one woman to cook food for the peons, to sort wheat, and to do whatever other job she could whenever the landlord required it, without any remuneration in cash.
6. The household was to provide the landlord with sixty days' worth of sheep manure (by corralling the sheep over the landlord's fields). If the landlord did not need the manure, then the household was obligated to pay S/. 0.20 per head of sheep and S/. 0.50 per head of cattle for grazing rights. Bulls could be pastured free on the hacienda, and a grazing fee need not be paid for burros if they were provided to the landlord whenever required.
7. The household was required to sell two sheepskins to the landlord at the price of S/. 0.10 each and one pig at the price of S/. 0.80.

13. Neither Gitlitz (1975) nor Taylor (1979, 1984) considered indebtedness a major factor in limiting peasant mobility on the estates they studied. On the broader debate over the extent of debt peonage on the Andean haciendas, see Martínez Alier (1973), Bauer (1979), Loveman (1979), and Montoya (1980, 37, 74).

14. "Contrato entre Resurección Culqui y el Sr. Antonio Otoya Puga, Abril 18, 1940," Hacienda Santa Ursula files, Agrarian Reform Office.

8. The members of the peasant household were not allowed to leave the hacienda. If they did so, they were subject to a fine.
9. The household guaranteed the payment of rent and the provision of the specified services with their personal belongings.

Note that the rental payment of this sub-arrendire was to be provided half in cash and half in labor services. In order to generate the cash payment of S/. 65 through work on the hacienda at S/. 0.20 per day, the tenant had to work 325 days for the landlord, in addition to the stipulated faena requirements. Because women's labor services were explicitly excluded as a means of paying off the rent, this implies that the head of the household or a male replacement was required to work full-time for the landlord—considerably reducing the family labor force available for subsistence production on the usufruct plot.

The only way such heavy obligations could be met was by having a large family (see Chapter 3) or by sharecropping the usufruct parcel with peasants from outside the hacienda—a mechanism that left it to the self-interest of peasant sub-arrendires to extract surplus labor from other peasants. But although the sub-arrendires might have required their own sharecroppers to meet part of the labor service obligations, these requirements were never as severe as those imposed by the landlords themselves; if they had been, the sharecropper might as well have entered into a rental arrangement directly with a landlord. This sharecropping practice helps to explain the comments of peasants in independent communities who described the labor services associated with their access to hacienda land as much less onerous than those of the resident peasantry. It is also important to note that the sub-arrendire was the person responsible for meeting the contractual terms of the tenancy agreement, guaranteeing payment with the household's accumulated stock of animals or wealth. The alternative was indebted servitude; debts were accumulated over one's lifetime and passed on to the next generation.

The system of fines imposed on tenants for noncompliance was another effective means of economic coercion. The fine for failing to perform labor services on Santa Ursula was ten times the level of remuneration: if a peasant missed one day of required work, he was then indebted to work an additional ten days for free. On the Hacienda Combayo in 1928, five arrendires were fined amounts ranging from S/. 1 to S/. 2.50 for not completing a full week of the required faena.[15] Given the prevailing level of daily remuneration, S/. 0.20, these arrendires became indebted to the landlord for an additional five to twelve days of labor service. This escalating fine–labor indebtedness system was a fairly consistent feature of hacienda rental arrangements throughout the province (haciendas Polloc, Llushcapampa, Huayobamba).

15. Hacienda Combayo, Planillas de Trabajo, 1928, week 42, files of Gonzalo Pajares, Cajamarca.

Peasants were also fined for grazing more animals on the hacienda than they reported to the landlord and for grazing animals on the hacienda's reserved pastures. Some landlords simply confiscated the "illegal" animals (Hacienda Polloc), whereas others doubled the payment of rent and faena required per head (Hacienda Chaquil). Called the *mostrencaje*, the fine could reach four to ten times the normal level of rent (Málaga Santolalla 1906, 222). On the Hacienda Combayo, arrendires could be fined as much as one month of labor services for pasturing animals on the reserved pastures.[16] Moreover, peasant households were held responsible for any damage their animals caused to the landlord's crops. These fines served both to increase the pool of labor services on which landlords could draw and to tie labor effectively to the hacienda.

Peasant households also fell into debt through commercial transactions with the landlord class. The 1940 Santa Ursula contract illustrates how peasants were sometimes required to sell certain items to the landlord at a predetermined (and usually much below market) price. The pricing arrangement represented another source of surplus extraction from the peasantry. Noncompliance with the obligation could result in an additional debt to the landlord. One former tenant explained to me that if the households failed to sell the two sheepskins or the pig to this landlord, they would be charged with the market value of the pig or the hide. In the 1940s, a good-sized pig was worth about S/. 10 in the Cajamarca market. At the prevailing rate of remuneration for labor services, not complying with this forced sale would result in the addition of some fifty days of labor service. On at least one other hacienda, peasants were also required to sell to the landlord any surplus grain produced by the household, as well as an occasional sheep or cow (Hacienda Porcón, described in Gorget 1975b).

A few landlords operated tambos, or general stores, where residents could purchase such items as salt, coca, kerosene, and matches on credit (haciendas Santa Ursula, Polloc). Although peasants were not forced to buy these goods, the effective isolation of the haciendas, the restrictions on peasants' excursions outside the hacienda, and the attractiveness of credit in a liquidity-tight economy would have encouraged such purchases.

A more common practice than the operation of hacienda stores was the liberal extension of credit to the peasantry by landlords. In lean years, landlords advanced seed to the peasants; if the harvest failed, the resident peasants could depend on the landlord to advance them foodstuffs and cash to see them through a bad year. These advances were then credited against future crop surpluses or labor services. Peasants were also given loans to help pay for funerals and weddings, to celebrate religious festivals, and sometimes to help buy animals or implements. The extension of credit certainly provided

16. See the case of the arrendire Mercedes Llanos; Hacienda Combayo, Planillas de Trabajo, 1928, week 13, Pajares files.

households on the hacienda with a form of social security and might be considered part of an instrumental exchange between landlord and peasant; but credit naturally led to indebtedness and to restricted mobility.

The magnitude of potential peasant indebtedness is illustrated in the 1903 contract between the Madres Concepcionistas and Mariano Cacho for the rental of the Hacienda Santa Ursula (described in Chapter 1). This rental contract explicitly stated that the arrendire could claim no more than S/. 200 from the owners at the end of his contract for debts incurred to him by peasants. At that time, this sum represented two thousand days of labor services.[17] When haciendas were sold, the new owners usually had to compensate the sellers for the outstanding debts owed by the resident peasantry (Hacienda Combayo).

The next section of this chapter will examine in detail peasant indebtedness and the use of credit in the context of the development of wage payments on the haciendas. Here, I want to emphasize that indebtedness functioned as an effective mechanism for preventing peasant mobility. A peasant on the Hacienda Combayo explained the situation this way to me: "Yes, one could leave the hacienda—every year we would go to Cajamarca to market—but one just wouldn't leave without asking don Eloy [Santolalla]. He might think that one wasn't planning to come back, and what would happen to one's animals and things?"

As the 1940 Santa Ursula contract showed, a peasant who left the hacienda without permission was subject to a fine; and if a peasant did not comply with the stated obligations, the landlord was contractually, if not legally, entitled to the peasant household's animals, tools, and other meager possessions. Debt peonage in Peru was formally illegal by 1916 (Davies 1974, 62–63); the inclusion of these provisions in a contract written as late as 1940 indicates that landlords generally had the backing of social practice, if not the legal system, to enforce peasant indebtedness.[18]

Interviews suggest that economic and noneconomic forms of coercion on the haciendas were interrelated and complementary. Strong discipline was imposed internally on all the larger haciendas. Peasants were subject not only to fines but also to whippings and incarceration. Various contemporaries noted the extensive use of physical punishment (Málaga Santolalla 1906; Silva Santisteban 1945). The typical hacienda had a jail (*calabozo*), usually a cell

17. This figure is calculated on the basis of Málaga Santolalla's (1906, 185) estimate of wage payments to colonos at S/. 0.10 per day.

18. Taylor (1984, 111) found two cases in the archives of the department from the period 1900 to 1935 in which peasants brought litigation against landlords who attempted to limit their mobility. In both cases, the peasants won. Taylor argues that this provides evidence that peasants freely entered and left the haciendas and that landlords had limited ability to restrict their mobility. He does not mention, however, whether these cases involved peasants attempting to run out on their debts.

under the landlord's house, where recalcitrant peasants were locked up without food for several days at a time.

Landlords ruled supreme within their haciendas.[19] Local government officials hardly ever interfered within the hacienda boundaries; if they did, it was at the landlord's behest. District governors and the local lieutenant governors were usually appointed with the landlords' consent. The power of the landlord class also extended far beyond the haciendas' boundaries.

A complementary ideological condition of existence of feudal class relations on the haciendas was the "natural inequality" between peasant and landlord. Their different places in the world were part of a hierarchy supported by traditional Catholic teaching. It was "God's will" that a peasant had been born a colono. Such fatalism, which explained every natural calamity befalling the peasant household, was easily transposed to "the landlord's will" to explain every transgression against the peasantry. The *patron* appeared to replace God within the confines of the hacienda and typically was referred to as "*amito*," a title with religious connotations.

The "natural inequality" between landlord and peasant was also maintained by racism. The colono of the hacienda was always referred to as "Indio," even though in some cases he or she might be mestizo or white. Calling tenants "Indio" put them in their place; it forced tenants to show respect for a "superior" race, as well as for the economic and political power of the landlord class. Hacienda residents demonstrated their respect in many ways—pulling aside off a hacienda trail if the landlord wanted to pass, not speaking unless first addressed and then holding one's hands folded in prayer. On the Hacienda La Pauca, resident peasants reportedly had to kneel before the landlord at a distance of some fifteen meters, taking off their hats (Chambeu and Gorget 1975, 12).

Inequality was also maintained through illiteracy. Although primary schooling was supposedly compulsory, few public schools were built on hacienda lands until mid-century. On some haciendas, peasant families organized private schools in the 1930s and 1940s, paying for the teachers themselves; at least one landlord (Rafael Puga of the Hacienda La Pauca) stopped these private efforts as late as the 1950s (Chambeu and Gorget 1975, 27–28).

The hacienda system was repressive, but it was also highly paternalistic. As long as the peasant household met its obligations, it was guaranteed access to cultivable land and pasture, water, and wood. The landlord was always there

19. The power of the landlord class was not limited to the major provincial landowning families. One might expect that landlords ruled supreme in the vast and relatively isolated haciendas such as La Pauca, Sondor, Combayo, and Polloc; but they also did so in the smaller fundos of the Cajamarca Valley. Several peasant informants reported that family members had been beaten or shot to death with total impunity by these less powerful landlords.

to help the household meet emergencies. Moreover, the continuity of the system, whereby children were guaranteed their place on the hacienda, ensured security for the parents in old age. The hacienda system also offered peasants political protection, whether from the encroachment of other landlords, military conscription, or rural banditry.[20]

The hacienda system had a highly personal dimension. As previously noted, the size of the household's usufruct plot, as well as its total labor obligations and other forms of rent, depended on the individual relationship between the head of the peasant household and the landlord.[21] Colonos in good favor could have access to large tracts of land and could raise sizable animal herds. Even more benefits were possible if one became a *mayordomo* or foreman.

Peasants won the landlord's favor by complying with the rental agreement, demonstrating good behavior and loyalty, offering periodic gifts, and fostering ties of compadrazco. The significance of gifts should not be underestimated. Almost all the peasants I interviewed who at one time had resided on haciendas recounted taking chickens to the landlord for the harvest feast or eggs to the estate house when serving the semanera duty. Any major event in the landlord's family, such as a birth or a wedding, would be an occasion for the peasant household to deliver a sheep or a goat. These gifts were not required by any formal agreement but rather by social custom.

Although the hacienda system was all-encompassing, it was not rigid. During the first forty years of this century, it managed to accommodate new entrants and to extend significant control over the rural labor force by modifying some of its rules. An increasing number of rural households gained access to hacienda land on much more favorable terms than had previously been the case. This was possible partly because of the personalized nature of landlord-peasant realtions. Better rental terms became necessary when seasonal migration to the coast offered peasants an alternative opportunity to generate income, while the landlord class remained dependent on the accumulation of peasants' rent for income and wealth.

THE DEVELOPMENT OF WAGE PAYMENTS ON THE HACIENDAS

The concept of remuneration has quite different meanings in feudal and capitalist class relations. In feudal class relations, labor services are provided by peasants to landlords as full or partial payment for the usufruct of land. The

20. Rural banditry, particularly cattle rustling, was endemic in many provinces of Cajamarca at this time, although the problem was not as severe in the province of Cajamarca itself. See Gitlitz (1975) and Taylor (1979, 106–115).

21. See Gitlitz (1975) for a detailed analysis of how the personalistic nature of landlord-peasant relations fits into the model of the "triangle without a base." This is also discussed, for other regions of Peru, by McClintock (1981) and Tullis (1970).

direct appropriation of surplus labor is justified ideologically as a remuneration to the landlord for granting means of production to a landless class. Any additional compensation to peasants for services rendered is attributed to the landlord's role as patron or benefactor.

In capitalist class relations, in contrast, the appropriation of surplus labor in the form of surplus value requires that workers be compensated for labor performed. This form of appropriation of surplus—where the value of what labor produces is greater than the value of labor power—in order to be justified ideologically, requires that labor be remunerated per day worked. The transition, then, from feudal to capitalist class relations within the haciendas can be characterized as the transition from labor services as a payment to the landlord for ceding land to peasants to the payment of a wage as remuneration to peasant laborers for work performed.

Theoretically, capitalist class relations require that labor be dispossessed of access to the means of production and totally dependent on a wage for its reproduction, because the value of labor power must be socially determined in the marketplace. In the process of developing a free wage-labor force, however, a land parcel is often a complementary portion of the wage payment for labor performed. Giving land in usufruct for subsistence production serves to lower the value of labor power indirectly, by reducing the number of wage goods, and thus maintains money wages at a lower level than would otherwise be the case.

From the conceptual viewpoint of capitalist class relations, feudal class relations could be described as the payment for labor services in the form of the usufruct of land. But this transformation takes place only in the context of the transition in the relations of production themselves, not in a vacuum. It requires certain economic, political, and ideological conditions of existence, explained in this and subsequent chapters.

In the early 1900s, important political and ideological changes were taking place at the national level that would eventually have an impact on class relations in Cajamarca. In 1916, under the Pardo administration, the national congress passed the Right to Remuneration Bill, which for the first time institutionalized the notion of remuneration for work performed. The bill was a substantial piece of pro-Indian legislation (Davies 1974, 62–63). Indigenous laborers in the sierra were guaranteed the right to payment for services rendered of at least S/. 0.20 per day, in addition to meals. This payment was to be forthcoming regardless of whether the peasant was also granted a usufruct parcel or grazing lands.

The bill also intended to abolish debt peonage and other restrictions on peasant mobility from the haciendas. For example, if food or other items were distributed by the landowner, the total value could not exceed the total weekly earnings of the peasant workers. In cases where a peasant was in debt to the landowner, the animals or personal belongings of the peasant household could not be seized in partial payment of the debt, nor could the peasant be forced to work off the debt in labor services. Moreover, the bill specified that if daily wages were not paid, peasants were free to leave a hacienda at any time with their animals and personal belongings.

Thomas Davies (1974, 44–65) traces the political origins of this bill to the rise of "Indigenismo" within Peru and to the changing balance of political and economic power that characterized the first two decades of the twentieth century. Nonetheless, one can only speculate on the specific forces behind its passage, for it preceded the organization of peasants not only in the sierra but also on the coast. Not until the period of World War I did the coastal union movement become organized (Klarén 1976, chap. 2). The organization of *yanaconas* (tenants on the coastal estates)—demanding payment for work performed, written contracts, and security of tenure—did not become an important political force until the 1930s (Harding 1975, 226–227).[22] The Right to Remuneration Bill was, however, perfectly consistent with the ideological requirements of capitalist class relations. It established the legal principle of remuneration according to work performed and labor's right to dispose of its own labor power.

At the national level, political control of the state was the focus of struggle between the emerging bourgeoisie and the sierra landowning class (with the bourgeoisie clearly in the ascendancy). At the regional and local level in the highlands, the landowning class still reigned supreme. Davies (1974, 64) notes that landowners and local government officials throughout the highlands paid scant attention to the Right to Remuneration Bill, and the national executive was powerless to enforce it.

This deficiency is clearly seen in the case of Cajamarca. The 1940 rental contract for the Hacienda Santa Ursula, which explicitly limited labor mobility by requiring peasant households to guarantee the payment of labor services with their possessions and to provide some labor services without remuneration, was written twenty-four years after the Right to Remuneration Bill. Perhaps the inclusion of a specified payment for some labor services in contracts, from at least 1918, can be explained by the changing political and ideological currents at the national level; nevertheless, the contractual stipulation of a wage payment was not enforced as long as the regional power of the landowning class went unchallenged.[23]

Whether labor services were ever remunerated on the haciendas is a point of contention among peasants and landlords. Contemporaries reported that

22. Kapsoli (1977, 39–40), however, sees the bill as a product of the conflicts between colonos and landlords in southern Peru and notes that even if the bill was subsequently not enforced, it had great symbolic value. Blanchard (1979, 81) sees it instead as a product of the reported abuses of the enganche system.

23. The changing national current did have some effect on Cajamarca's local press. Taylor 1979, 40), who carefully worked through the archives of local newspapers, reports several articles in the late 1920s and 1930s denouncing unremunerated peasant labor services on the haciendas.

wages were paid both to free labor and to colonos. For example, Málaga Santolalla (1906, 319) noted that colonos were paid for their labor services at the rate of S/. 0.10 per day in addition to meals and that free workers in the province were paid S/. 0.20 per day. Most peasants, however, swear that they were never paid "*un real*" (one cent) for their labor services through the 1950s. The various rental contracts for the Hacienda Santa Ursula always stipulated some remuneration for services performed, but peasants I interviewed on this former hacienda in 1976 denied that they were ever paid for their efforts. Silva Santisteban (1945, 93) supports the peasants' claims with his observation that the colonos on the haciendas were provided a meal whenever they performed labor services but that they did not "have any security of being remunerated (such is the general case)." Moreover, he specifically notes that peasant women were never remunerated for their services as semaneras or for processing the haciendas' products.

Only for the Hacienda La Colpa (Taylor 1979, 123) and the Hacienda Combayo is there strong evidence that wages were actually paid before 1940. In my interviews, peasants reported that wage payments were first introduced on the Hacienda Huacariz de San Antonio and Huacraruco in the early 1940s, on Porcón in the 1950s (when the Ministry of Agriculture established an experiment station there), and during that decade on Polloc (1954) and La Pauca (1958). Not until the 1950s and 1960s would wage payments for services performed become common on the haciendas, as a result of changing political winds, peasant demands, and the reorganization of the productive process on many of the haciendas.

The fact that peasants were not usually paid cash wages, based on a strict accounting of remuneration for labor performed, does not mean that their labor services were always unremunerated. Several forms of remuneration for services rendered were perfectly compatible with feudal class relations. The origin of the rural labor market in the province, as well as the payment of faena, probably evolved around the hacienda harvests. In the early part of the century, landlords often used the same system of labor recruitment that was common among the peasantry both on and off the hacienda: the mingas, or collective work parties, that have their roots in the precolonial period. The principal remuneration for those who participated was a large feast, with plenty of food, *chicha* (a corn-based brew), and coca served throughout the day. By tradition, the feast included plenty of meat, and several cows, pigs, and sheep might be butchered on the hacienda for the occasion.

Under the prevailing social relations, it was incumbent on the landlords to differentiate themselves by showing their generosity toward both "their gente" and peasants from neighboring communities whom landlords wanted to attract as seasonal labor. This required not only that the feasts of the patron be more sumptuous than those of the rich peasantry but also that landlords show their good will by giving *propinas*, or tips, to those who participated, including both faena labor and "free" labor (Málaga Santolalla 1906, 193). These tips were clearly payment in kind for labor performed. Moreover, they became fairly standardized. In the 1930s and 1940s, it was common to receive 1 *arroba* of potatoes for each day worked at the potato harvest and 1 *almud* of barley or half an almud of wheat during the harvest of these grains.[24] Women and children traditionally received half the amount that men were paid.

The other form of wage payment consistent with feudal class relations was the remuneration implicit in the credit-indebtedness relationship. The distribution of seed and foodstuffs during bad years and the provision of nonproduced goods on credit at hacienda tambos allowed peasants to receive exchange values in advance of labor services. These mechanisms also reinforced the positions of the landlord as benefactor and the peasants as dependents. Cash advances granted by landlords and credited against the future provision of labor services were a somewhat different matter. Such advances were an embryonic form of remuneration for labor performed, explained by the Peruvian saying "Sin deudas no hay trabajador" (Without debt there are no workers).[25]

Wage Payments and Indebtedness on the Hacienda Combayo

The Hacienda Combayo is one of the few haciendas in the province of Cajamarca where archival materials report the payment of wages in the early decades of the century and where peasants confirm that cash wages were in fact paid. The development of wage payments on this hacienda was clearly tied to the credit–labor indebtedness system and to the particular needs of the hacienda for a steady labor supply.

The Hacienda Combayo was different from others in the province because from 1898 to 1932 the principal economic activity of its owner, Eloy Santolalla Iglesias, was mining. But although mining was the primary focus of Santolalla's entrepreneurial talents, agricultural activities on the hacienda were not neglected. In a monograph written at "La Molina," the National Agrarian University, don Eloy's son, Nicolás Santolalla, describes the hacienda as having 143 hectares of cultivable land in direct production and a sizable herd of cattle in 1917 (1977, 224). Moreover, some investments had been made in improved pastures and cattle breads.

The hacienda labor force had three categories of tenants: peons, arrendires, and *agregados*. The agregados did not have a direct rental arrangement with the hacienda but rather were affiliated with the arrendires, either as part of the

---

24. An arroba equals 25 pounds. An almud is a measure of volume rather than weight; an almud of wheat equals about 22 pounds and an almud of potatoes 20 pounds. Another weight measure frequently used in Cajamarca is the *quintal*, equal to 4 arrobas, or 46 kilograms. A *carga*, what a pack animal could carry, equals approximately 12 arrobas (Santolalla 1977, 219–220).

25. Horton's data (1976, table 3:34) also suggest that advances were necessary to establish the practice of wage labor on the Hacienda Udima. See Montoya (1980, 37, 74) for another example (in Andahuaylas) of the use of indebtedness to secure a labor force.

extended family labor force or as sharecroppers. According to Santolalla (1977, 223, 225), the resident labor force consisted of 225 men (72 arrendires, 133 agregados, and 20 peons) and 450 women and children. On any given day, the hacienda could count on approximately 70 men and boys and 25 women workers; one-third of the daily labor force was deployed in agricultural activities.

From archival data, a detailed labor utilization schematic for this hacienda during the late 1920s can be reconstructed. In Table 8, the Oficina Combayo data refer to the foundry operations at the casa hacienda. The mines in operation included La Estrella, La Boya, La Merced, Quinuacucho, Chirimayo, and El Lago, all on hacienda lands. The agricultural and animal-raising operations of the hacienda are listed under the category "Hacienda."

The data indicate that fewer workers were employed on a daily basis in the late 1920s than indicated by Santolalla for the late 1910s. This difference appears to result from the omission of women workers from the payroll lists in the late 1920s rather than from a contraction in hacienda activity. The 1920s data are, however, consistent with Santolalla's estimate of the division between

TABLE 8.   Labor Use on the Hacienda Combayo,
Late 1920s

| | Average Number of Workers per Week | | |
Category	Men	Women	Total
Oficina Combayo			
Peons	13.9	—	13.9
Muleteers	2.3	—	2.3
Semaneras	1.3	—	1.3
Servants	1.7	—	1.7
Shepherds	1.2	—	1.2
Faeneras	—	1.8	1.8
Administrators	1.3	—	1.3
Subtotal	21.7	1.8	23.5
Mines			
Peons	17.2	—	17.2
Hacienda			
Agricultural peons	12.4	—	12.4
Livestock peons	4.0	2.0	6.0
Faeneras	—	0.1	0.1
Church maintenance	1.0	—	1.0
Subtotal	17.4	2.1	19.5
Total labor	56.3	3.9	60.2

SOURCES: Oficina Combayo, Planillas de Trabajo, 1926; Hacienda Combayo, Planillas de Trabajo, 1928; both in the files of Gonzalo Pajares, Cajamarca.

mining and agricultural activities: approximately two-thirds of the daily labor force engaged in activities related to mining.

The payroll lists from the 1920s also allow a partial reconstruction of the different rental arrangements used to secure this labor force. The majority of workers in the foundry were peons who worked an average of thirty-five weeks a year. From the ranks of the peons also came the servants and the shepherds, the other workers employed approximately full-time by the Oficina Combayo. The semaneras and faeneras were also from peon households; the semanera duty on this hacienda was rotated monthly, whereas the faenera duty was rotated weekly.

The arrendires who worked for the Oficina Combayo most often served as muleteers, transporting the hacienda's mineral and agricultural products to Cajamarca. They rarely were required to provide their own beasts of burden, for the hacienda had a large stock of mules and burros. From the ranks of the arrendires also came the *capataz* (supervisor) of the foundry. In addition, the Oficina had two employees, the bookkeepers of the hacienda, who were not drawn from the ranks of the resident laborers, most of whom were illiterate.

Most of the mine workers were secured through the arrendire rental arrangement. According to Santolalla (1977, 222), the faena requirements of the arrendires had been recently eliminated in order to attract labor to the hacienda. My interviews on this hacienda, however, revealed that arrendires were required to work one month each year in the mines for remuneration. The payroll lists for the six mines in operation in the late 1920s confirm this. The arrendires usually sent a substitute, one of their agregados, to fulfill the labor requirement.

Few of the hacienda's peons worked inside the mines. They were distributed almost equally between the foundry and the agricultural sector of the hacienda. Of the fifteen peons in the agricultural sector, six worked full-time in livestock activities, and nine constituted the core of the hacienda's agricultural work force. The other agricultural workers, approximately six per week, were drawn from the ranks of the agregados. Santolalla (1977, 224) reported that the peons worked an average of 250 days, or forty-two weeks, a year, a period consistent with the data reported on the payroll lists. The agricultural work force was also supervised by peasants drawn from the ranks of the arrendires.

The detailed payroll lists provide good evidence that the labor performed on this hacienda was remunerated. They also show that wage levels varied according to the rental agreement of the tenant, according to the type of work performed, and according to age and sex. As Table 9 shows, arrendires usually earned more than peons for similar work. As Santolalla (1977, 225) explained it, this was because peons earned an implicit wage through their rent-free access to a plot of cultivable land and grazing rights. These usufruct rights were termed the *salario* (salary), a term (and concept) that came to be used in Cajamarca with increasing frequency in the 1940s and 1950s (haciendas Santa

TABLE 9. Daily Wage Rates on the Hacienda Combayo, 1917–1928 (in Current Peruvian Soles)

	1917	1926		1928	
		Mode	Range	Mode	Range
Arrendire	0.30	0.40	0.10–0.60	—	—
Peon	0.20	0.20	0.10–0.60	—	—
Child	0.15	—	—	—	—
Woman	0.05	—	—	0.10	—
Foundry worker	—	0.20	0.10–0.60	—	—
Agricultural worker	—	—	—	0.25	0.10–0.60
Miner	—	0.40	0.15–0.60	—	—
Muleteer	0.40–0.50	0.50	0.10–1.00	—	—
Semanera	—	0.20	0.10–0.50	—	—
Servant	—	0.10	0.10–0.50	0.25	—
Faenera	—	0.10	0.10–0.50	0.10	—
Shepherd	0.10–0.15	0.10	0.10–0.30	0.10	—
Puntero	0.13–0.25	—	—	0.45	—
Overseer	0.25	0.50	0.50–0.60	0.50	0.40–0.60

SOURCES: Santolalla ([1918] 1977, 225); Oficina Combayo, Planillas de Trabajo, 1926; Hacienda Combayo, Planillas de Trabajo, 1928 (the last two in the files of Gonzalo Pajares, Cajamarca).
NOTE: These rates exclude the value of the noon meal, estimated at S/.0.10 in 1917.

Ursula, Sangal). Santolalla calculated the value of these usufruct rights as approximately S/.0.13 per day, making the real wages of arrendires and peons in 1917 approximately equal. In addition, when they worked for the hacienda, workers received a noon meal that Santolalla valued at S/.0.10 per day.

Wages also varied according to the particular job performed. Muleteers and mining workers received the highest remuneration. Both jobs required that peasants spend time away from their home and fields. Work in the mines was especially arduous, for working conditions were very poor. Clearly, a material incentive was required to entice workers to agree to this form of paying off their debts. Work in the mines was remunerated at a higher level than work in the foundry or in agriculture, and all three were more highly paid than personal services, that is, the work of semaneras, servants, and faeneras.

There was a fairly large variation in wage rates within certain job categories because of the personalistic nature of wage determination. There also was discrimination by sex. Although both men and women formed part of the agricultural labor force and often carried out the same tasks, men earned an average of S/.0.25 per day whereas women were paid only S/.0.10, if they were reported on the payroll books at all. Wage rates on the hacienda also fluctuated according to season. The highest wages for all categories of work were paid

TABLE 10. Peasant Indebtedness on the Hacienda Combayo, 1928 and 1929 (in Current Peruvian Soles)

	1928	*1929*
Number of peasants with debts at year end	85	67
Mean value of debt	32.18	33.24
Median value of debt	15.45	15.29
Total indebtedness of peasants on hacienda	2,734.89	2,226.95

SOURCE: Debt book, Hacienda Combayo, 1928–1930, files of Gonzalo Pajares, Cajamarca.

during the months in which peasants needed to plow their fields in preparation for planting (February–March and October–November). But other mechanisms besides incentive wages were also necessary to ensure that the resident peasantry would provide its labor power to the hacienda.

A debt book for 1928–1930 supports the agrument that indebtedness was a powerful incentive for resident peasants to offer labor power "for sale." During this three-year period, 103 peasants contracted debts on this hacienda. As Table 10 shows, the average debt was S/. 32 to S/. 33, almost three times the average annual wage income (S/. 12). The amount of debt ranged from S/. 1 to S/. 333.25, with the median approximately S/. 15.

The majority of peasants incurred debt by taking advances, which they agreed to pay off with labor services. For example, during one week in November 1928, seven peasants received advances ranging from S/. 3 to S/. 5 to work in the mines at Pilancones.[26] The advances functioned much like the enganche system that was utilized by the coastal plantations to recruit highland labor. The systems differed in that peasants could pay off the advances over the span of the year, making work for the hacienda much more compatible with their own agricultural production than coastal migration would have been. Moreover, if need be, they could also pay off their debts over the course of their lifetime or pass on the debt to their children.

Advances were also given to commission specific kinds of tasks. For example, several peasants were given advances to weave sacks of *linza*, which were used to pack minerals. Advances were also paid to peasants to fix roads on the hacienda.[27] Peasants also incurred debts in the form of fines for breaking the rules of the hacienda—failing to work a full six-day week, for example, or allowing their animals to graze on the hacienda's reserved pastures.[28]

26. Hacienda Combayo, Planillas de Trabajo, 1928, week 44, Pajares files.
27. Hacienda Combayo, Planillas de Trabajo, 1929, weeks 11 and 20; Oficina Combayo, Planillas de Trabajo, May 30, 1926; both in Pajares files.
28. Hacienda Combayo, Planillas de Trabajo, 1928, weeks 13 and 42, Pajares files.

Of the 103 peasants with entries in the debt book, 6 percent managed to cancel their debt and 34 percent to reduce it. Four percent maintained the same level of debt and 29 percent increased their level of indebtedness. (There was incomplete information for 28 percent of the entries.) Two-thirds of those listed in the debt book provided labor services during this period, working an average of 5.2 weeks and earning an average credit of S/. 11.74 against their contracted debt. Others reduced their debt by selling agricultural or animal products to the hacienda, but these were a minority; this hacienda's primary interest was in securing labor for its diversified economic activities.

From 1928 to 1929, peasant indebtedness to the hacienda was reduced slightly (see Table 10), but the broader trend was for the total level of peasant debt to increase over time. In 1910 peasant indebtedness had stood at only S/. 883.45; it had increased threefold in fewer than twenty years.[29] Peasant indebtedness had a long history on this hacienda. In 1898, when don Eloy Santolalla consolidated his ownership of the hacienda, he assumed the outstanding debts owed by peasants on the hacienda to the previous managers.[30]

Don Eloy rationalized the use of labor services on the hacienda, abolishing unpaid faena and instituting accountability between labor performed and its remuneration. Moreover, to entice peasants to provide the labor power necessary to develop the resources of this vast hacienda, the level of remuneration gradually increased over the next few decades. Nonetheless, as long as peasants had sufficient access to the means of production, economic coercion was necessary to ensure an adequate labor force. The development of wage payments on the Hacienda Combayo was thus closely linked to the system of credit, advances, and peasant indebtedness.

THE ORGANIZATION OF PRODUCTION ON THE HACIENDAS

The combination of rental arrangements on most haciendas provided landlords with diverse income sources—cash and agricultural and livestock products as rent—and with both permanent and temporary workers who could be mobilized for the landlord's direct production. Nevertheless, a landlord's production decisions and the precise combination of rental agreements did not

29. Personal communication from Françoise Chambeu (handwritten draft report of case study of the Hacienda Combayo). Chambeu carried out fieldwork on the Hacienda Combayo during 1974 and began the process of quantifying the hacienda's debt books, but she completed tabulating the data only for 1910. She reports that at the time of her visit the Santolalla library at the casa hacienda was in total disarray, although it contained a good number of debt and payroll books. Most of these had disappeared by the time of my visit to the casa hacienda in 1981.

30. Personal communication from Françoise Chambeu, based on documents examined in the Santolalla library at the casa hacienda during 1974.

simply respond to the dictates of profit maximization; they were constrained by the class relations of which they were a part. Whether a landlord reserved a portion of hacienda lands for direct cultivation or animal raising, and how large this demesne might be, depended on the prevailing market conditions, on whether surplus labor could be appropriated effectively, and—not least—on the landowner's disposition toward farming. No direct intervention in the productive process was required for the landowner to realize at least a modicum of wealth based on the accumulation of the fruits of productive labor by sharecroppers or arrendires. As long as land was relatively plentiful, renting or sharecropping it simply increased the total surplus that could be accumulated. In fact, Santolalla (1977, 273) observed that the most profitable haciendas in the province were those that left productive activity to the peasantry and simply collected cash rents.

The available data suggest that on most Cajamarcan haciendas the demesne covered only a small portion of the estate and colonos constituted a minority of the work force. Moreover, there is little evidence that landlords attempted to expand the demesne at the expense of the peasantry or tried to convert sharecroppers and arrendires into colonos (or any of the three groups into wage workers) before the 1940s and 1950s. On the Hacienda Combayo, which measured 47,000 hectares, only 765 hectares had been plowed in 1917, approximately 16 percent of the estimated cultivable land. Peasant holdings accounted for 81 percent of the land in production, the landlord's demesne for 19 percent. The number of arrendire households (seventy-two) considerably exceeded that of peon households (thirty) (Santolalla 1977, 211–212, 223). Similarly, the demesne of the Hacienda La Pauca covered only a small portion of the potential cultivable land, and through the 1940s the number of arrendires on the hacienda significantly exceeded the number of peons (Arce del Campo and Lora 1974; Chambeu and Gorget 1975).[31]

The landlord intervened in the production process of those crops that had an urban market, such as wheat and potatoes (haciendas Combayo, Polloc, La Pauca). At the lowest elevations, high-value crops such as coca, sugar cane, and coffee were grown (Hacienda La Pauca). On most haciendas, however, animal production constituted the principal income-generating activity, with cattle dominating on Combayo, Polloc, Chaquil, and La Pauca and sheep on the

---

31. Gitlitz (1975, 122–125) estimated that the Caballeros, arrendires of the Hacienda Pallán in the late 1930s, reserved no more than one-tenth of this vast estate for direct production. In the early 1940s, the estate counted 60 peon households, 15 to 20 sharecroppers, and 300 to 340 arrendires. According to Gorget (1975a, 14–15), when Luis José Orbegoso bought the Hacienda Araqueda in the province of Cajabamba in 1930, he was displeased to find that the 300 resident households had such large extensions of quality land. Horton (1976, 159) reported that in the early decades of this century there was no agricultural demesne on the Hacienda Udima, the main activity of the Iglesias family being cattle production. Moreover, tenants were allowed to cultivate whatever amount of land they desired.

haciendas Porcón and Huacraruco.[32] The advantage of animal production was that, under prevailing techniques, it required little labor or supervision. Crop production was another matter. Peasants had to be coerced to work, and the landlord had to assume all the losses resulting from the vagaries of either the weather or the market.

What is particularly interesting in the Cajamarcan case is that the most dynamic economic activity, cattle production, was in the hands of the peasantry (de León 1911, 17). On the Hacienda Combayo, three-quarters of the cattle herd belonged to peasants (Santolalla 1977, 223–224). On the Hacienda La Pauca, through the 1940s, peasants had three times as many cattle as the landlord did (Chambeu and Gorget 1975, 11).[33]

Landlords did attempt to enlarge their stocks through various means. Peasants were sometimes required to give a share of their newborn calves to the landlord as "gifts," or these animals were simply confiscated at the rodeos or when found grazing on reserved pastures. A few landowners built up their herds by imposing rent in kind. In order to become a sharecropper on the Hacienda La Colpa in the 1910s, peasants were required to pay one ox as an entry fee (Taylor 1979, 125). The landowner first built up his stock of *chusco* cattle in this manner and then gradually replaced it with improved breeds. In the 1940s, Rafael Puga built up his herd on the Hacienda La Pauca by similar means. He expanded the number of arrendires on this hacienda and required that the annual rent be paid in cattle. When he had accumulated a herd of 150 to 200 head in the late 1940s, he sold them to purchase Holsteins and develop a dairy enterprise (Chambeu and Gorget 1975).

Not until the 1940s and 1950s, however, was there sufficient market incentive to capitalize the productive process by investing in improved pastures and breeds. Until then, the accumulation of wealth was largely from the collection of rents; the accumulation of money rent rested on cattle production by peasants, for it was primarily through the sale of cattle that peasants generated cash.

· The location of the hacienda was another factor influencing the exact crop mix and the combination of rental arrangements. The greater the distance to

32. In 1917, for example, the gross income of the agricultural sector of the Hacienda Combayo came from cattle sales (27 percent), wheat sales (23 percent), fattened pigs (19.5 percent), and cheese (13.3 percent), with other less significant products contributing 17.2 percent (Santolalla 1977, 239).

33. Similar data have been reported for other haciendas in the department. On the Hacienda Araqueda in 1930, peasants owned 84 percent of the sheep and 85 percent of the cattle. Between 1930 and 1945, the hacienda management increased its holdings of both significantly, importing improved breeds from the coast; by 1945 peasant herds had been considerably reduced in size (Gorget 1975a, 15, 33). On the Hacienda Udima early in the century, peasants owned three-quarters of the cattle stock. Under the management of the owners of the plantation Pomalca, hacienda stocks were gradually increased and those of the peasantry reduced; by 1940 peasants owned only 45 percent of the stock (Horton 1976, 158, table III–33).

market, the more important arrendire arrangements appear to have been, as compared to sharecropping or demesne production. Many of the smaller haciendas in the valley of Cajamarca were sharecropped in their entirety until the 1940s (Huacariz de San Antonio, Shultín, Tres Molinos). According to Silva Santisteban (1945, 93), few landowners were interested in working their fundos directly. The ease of marketing valley foodstuffs in the city of Cajamarca probably explains why these haciendas were sharecropped rather than given over to arrendires. That they were not worked directly by landlords could have reflected fear of risk; although it contains extremely fertile land, the valley is also prone to unexpected frosts, giving Cajamarca its name, "place of the frosts." By giving land to the peasantry in sharecropping arrangements, landlords kept costs at a minimum, a practice that was perfectly rational as long as the opportunity cost of land was low.

The preference for sharecropping could also have reflected landlord-peasant struggle over the conditions of appropriation and distribution of surplus labor. Common themes in writings of the period spoke of the difficulty of coercing labor out of colonos and ensuring that the faenas of arrendires and sharecroppers were met. The elaborate list of fines for not meeting labor obligations attests to this resistance. The peasants always preferred to work their own plots. Although the predominance of arrendire and sharecropping arrangements in Cajamarca can be explained from the point of view of the economic interests of the landlord class, peasant resistance and the existence of an economic alternative—migration—may have been just as important.

Attempts to Increase the Rate of Exploitation

Peasant resistance, as well as a lack of market incentives, could explain why there are few known cases of landlords successfully turning their arrendires or sharecroppers into peons or colonos and why wage labor on the haciendas did not proliferate until the 1950s. By then, the worst fate for a peasant household was to be thrown off a hacienda.

Research thus far suggests that Cajamarca in the first half-century was not as conflict-ridden a region as other highland departments were.[34] But the majority of landlord-peasant struggles that did take place involved the conditions of appropriation of surplus labor, especially on the properties of the church and Beneficiencias, when landlord-arrendires attempted to increase the level of unpaid labor services.

An important example of such a struggle affecting the conditions of

34. Gitlitz (1975, 41–42) compiled a list of thirty major peasant conflicts in the department of Cajamarca between 1580 and 1971. Seventeen involved peasant challenges to the level of expropriation of surplus on the haciendas; only seven were community-hacienda struggles over land. The best-known conflict in the department, in 1916 on the church-owned Hacienda Llaucán in Hualgayoc, resulted in the death of three hundred peasants. See Gitlitz (1975, appendix to chap. 1) and Taylor (1979).

exploitation in the peasants' favor is provided by a conflict on the Hacienda Porcón. In 1905 peasants there achieved what peasants on no other hacienda had been able to: standardization of rental requirements for all peasant sub-arrendires. As mentioned previously, an important way landlords maintained their power over the peasantry was through a "divide and rule" strategy whereby the welfare of each household depended on its individual relationship to the landlord, with the result that rental contracts within a single general rental category differed markedly.

The history of peasant struggle on the Hacienda Porcón dates from the colonial period, when the resident peasantry burned down the obraje several times.[35] In 1878 the peasants of this Quechua-speaking indigenous community first proposed taking over the payment of rent, to make payments to the Beneficiencia directly. That suggestion was rejected by the Beneficiencia "as a subversive idea," but the resident peasantry continued to attempt to rent the hacienda themselves in subsequent rental auctions.

The tenants of Porcón first demanded that the Beneficiencia regulate their rental rates directly in 1904. The Beneficiencia had just leased the hacienda, increasing the rent by 50 precent. It was clear to the peasants who would pay for this increase. They refused to allow the new arrendires on the hacienda and again offered to rent it directly themselves. Nonetheless, the arrendire managed to take possession and immediately began to increase the exactions imposed on the peasantry. The Beneficiencia was finally forced to act when a growing number of peasants refused to pay their cash rents and threatened to leave the hacienda.

The "Reglamento de la Hacienda Porcón" of 1905 not only standardized the rental rates and faena obligations for all peasant sub-arrendires on Porcón; it actually lowered the total level of both. The success of the Porcón peasantry had much to do with this community's long tradition of struggle and its internal organization. But its success also reflected the fact that the community's ultimate threat, to abandon the hacienda, was a real one in 1905. Peasant households did have an alternative, migrating either to other haciendas (many of which had border conflicts with Porcón) or to the coast.[36] The Beneficiencia apparently understood that the level of income for its charitable activities depended on the size of the resident labor force. Landlord-arrendires could not

35. This account of the struggle on Porcón is based on the unpublished monograph and documents in Gorget (1975b). François Gorget worked through the files of the Beneficiencia Pública of Cajamarca in 1974.

36. There were restrictions on peasant mobility from this hacienda, such as the prohibition against peasants marrying off the hacienda, but the landlord-arrendires often did not have the stature to enforce these restrictions (Escalante 1972). The complaints of these arrendires show that the peasants often did not abide by the rules of the game, "showing respect" ("Pedido de apoyo represivo de los arrendadores R. Rodriguez y Federico Rojas a la BPC," Cajamarca, July 8, 1904; "Queja de los arrendadores Rojas y Rodriguez en relación con el Reglamento de 1905"; both in Gorget 1975b, annexes 2 and 4).

be allowed to be so exploitive that the appropriation and redistribution of peasant surplus labor would be jeopardized.

Not until 1942 would peasants on another hacienda obtain a standardized set of rent schedules and labor services. This struggle took place on a church property, the Hacienda Santa Ursula. It was provoked by an increase in the rental level secured at the hacienda auction in 1939, when the hacienda was ceded to Antonio Otoya Puga. This increase was subsequently passed on by the landlord-arrendire to the resident peasantry in the form of higher rents and increased labor services. But, in contrast to the struggle on Porcón at the turn of the century, the major demand on the Hacienda Santa Ursula in the early 1940s was that wages be paid for labor performed. The peasants were advised by lawyers sympathetic to APRA, and they successfully carried out a rent strike. The settlement of the conflict standardized the contract for all sub-arrendires and increased the stipulated wage payment for labor services from S/. 0.20 to S/. 0.30 per day. The principal form of tenancy was now to be sharecropping, with the landlord required to provide seed in order to claim 50 percent of the crop.[37]

Only one case of a landowner successfully increasing the labor services required of resident peasants has been well documented and this took place in an entirely different context—the incipient process of capitalist development on the Hacienda La Colpa. Taylor (1979, 128–134) reports that as soon as Castro Mendívil took over this hacienda from his father in the late 1910s, he proceeded to increase from fifteen to twenty the number of days colonos had to work for the hacienda; he also raised the rents of arrendires. At the same time, however, he increased the wage payments for labor performed and thus maintained social peace.

In the 1920s, Castro Mendívil then increased the size of the demesne at the expense of the peasantry. Some arrendires were expelled and the peons relocated to less productive plots, a process that was repeated throughout the province with increasing frequency some three decades later. In Taylor's analysis, Castro Mendívil was able to move the peasants without incurring protest by continually increasing the level of wages. And he was able to increase wages by capitalizing the hacienda, turning it into the region's first modern dairy establishment by the late 1920s. Taylor considers La Colpa to have become a fully mature capitalist enterprise by the 1930s.

Another experience with wage payments and attempted proletarianization of the peasantry in the province, on the Hacienda Combayo, was to turn out quite differently. The difficulty of getting the resident peasantry to work for the Hacienda Combayo, even at wages much higher than the provincial average,

37. "Proyecto de reglamentación de relaciones contractuales y de trabajo entre el conductor don Antonio Otoya Puga y los colonos sub-arrendatarios de la Hacienda Santa Ursula, 5 Junio 1942," Hacienda Santa Ursula files, Agrarian Reform Office.

was a source of concern to the young heir of this hacienda (Santolalla 1977, 273–277). In order to attract sufficient labor for the hacienda's agricultural and mining activities, wages had to be even higher than those paid in 1917. But Santolalla doubted that the hacienda could afford to pay a wage that would satisfy the basic needs of the peons. It would still be necessary to cede land in usufruct to the peons and arrendires to cover part of their costs of reproduction. The landlords' dilemma was that the resident peasants always preferred to work their own land rather than work for the hacienda.

Analyzing these factors, Santolalla came to the novel conclusion (novel for an agricultural entrepreneur) that the most profitable solution for the hacienda was simply to forfeit demesne production and to increase both the total number of resident households on the hacienda and the size of their respective holdings. He reasoned that in 1917 the net profit of the hacienda's agricultural sector had been S/. 7,800; approximately S/. 3,000 had been earned from productive activities on the demesne, and S/. 4,000 had been collected in rents. The amount collected in rents should have been much greater, approximately S/. 6,700, but because the hacienda was trying to attract labor to the hacienda, rents had been reduced recently.

In order to net a profit of S/. 3,000 on agricultural and animal-raising activities, the management had invested S/. 21,606, yielding a 14 percent return on investment. Although this rate was certainly not low, Santolalla reasoned that if the hacienda's capital were switched to other, less labor-intensive activities and the resident laborers were left free to exploit the hacienda's resources on their own volition, the net return would be even greater. Santolalla's recommendation was to "divide the pastures and lands which are currently in direct exploitation as well as the cattle and tools; charge the established rent schedule to all colonos; forget about employing wage labor or faenas and leave peasants in complete liberty, which would be easy to do since it would be to their total satisfaction. The earnings of the hacienda would increase without the bother of exploiting the fundo" (1977, 273). According to his calculations, a net profit of S/. 10,000 could be made.[38]

The profitability of the hacienda could be increased still further, he believed, if more peasants were attracted onto the hacienda. Santolalla thus devised a colonization scheme involving the settlement of 250 new arrendires, each to be given 10 hectares of cultivable land. To implement the plan, he proposed that the hacienda provide these new residents with the working capital to get established, with improved seeds and tools, and with technical assistance. The hacienda would also gain through judicious investments in the most profitable activities: Santolalla recommended that the management invest in a grain mill

---

38. Horton (1976) argues that the reason the transition to capitalist class relations on the Hacienda Udima was not achieved was that the collection of rents was the most dependable source of estate profits. He also cites peasant resistance to proletarianization.

and butter and cheese factory. He also thought that it might be profitable to market peasant products. All these activities would yield a return on the hacienda's capital much higher than the current 14 percent.

Nicolás Santolalla's modernization project was never attempted, however. The same system of advances and wage payments for work in the mines and in demesne production continued in effect. After the death of don Eloy in 1932, the mining activity of the hacienda fell into decay, and under successive administrators the systematic accounting of wage payments and labor performed was abandoned. In the 1940s, the principal activity of the hacienda was sheep raising. The only wage employees left were the mitayos and punteros who tended the hacienda's flock and herd.[39] Not until after 1947, when Nicolás and his sister, Rosalía Santolalla Bernal, purchased the hacienda from the other heirs, was an attempt made to transform the hacienda into a capitalist enterprise.

The case of Combayo shows how the development of wage payments based on cash advances was by itself insufficient to induce peasants to offer their labor power for sale.[40] As long as the peasantry had access to sufficient land, the payment of wages could not ensure an adequate supply of labor. Demesne production was caught in a double bind. On the one hand, there was a tension between the wage level that could be paid and the maintenance of the hacienda's profitability. As long as the opportunity cost of land was low, ceding land in usufruct was an attractive mechanism to keep wages low. On the other hand, ceding land in usufruct to the peasantry reduced the available supply of labor for demesne production. As long as market incentives were insufficient to bring about the dispossession of the peasantry, economic coercion was necessary to induce peasant labor to work on the estate. The credit-indebtedness system was only a partially effective mechanism.

CONCLUSION: THE CLASS ANALYTICS OF THE HACIENDA SYSTEM

Until the 1940s, the primary source of landlord wealth was the accumulation of rents. Rental arrangements on the hacienda led to a varied combination of income sources based on distinct class processes. Landlord income included the product of demesne production, the fruit of unpaid labor services. These labor services constituted part of a feudal class process, for they were based on the

39. This information is based on my interviews on the Hacienda Combayo in July 1976 and December 1981; Registros Públicos de Cajamarca, Registro de la Propiedad, city of Cajamarca (2:235); and Hacienda Combayo, Planillas de Trabajo, 1944–1946, Pajares files.

40. The example of Combayo supports Martínez Alier's (1973, 160) thesis that the slow development of wage labor on the Peruvian haciendas was largely a result of peasant unwillingness to give up hacienda resources and the landlords' inability to overcome this resistance. Also see Gorget (1975a, 21–24) on the Hacienda Araqueda.

direct appropriation of surplus labor in a labor process controlled by the landlord in return for granting peasants access to a usufruct plot of land.

The other components of landlord income, rents in cash and kind, represented a redistribution of surplus labor to landlords from peasant producers. I consider sharecropping and arrendire production to be part of the fundamental class process of petty production, because sharecroppers and arrendires controlled their own labor process, performing necessary and surplus labor, and they were the first appropriators of surplus labor. Landlords, however, provided a key condition of existence of petty production—namely, access to land—that entitled them to a subsumed class payment in the form of rent. These rental arrangements thus constituted a subsumed class process of petty production.

In order to acquire land in sharecropping and arrendire arrangements, however, households were often required not only to pay rent in kind and cash but also to surrender surplus labor directly, providing labor services (faena). The reproduction of petty production on the haciendas was therefore tied to the feudal class process as well. The majority of hacienda households participated in multiple class relations: the fundamental class processes of feudal and petty production and the subsumed class process of land rental.

Near-monopoly control by landlords over access to uncultivated lands and grazing pastures served as the necessary condition for peasant households to be willing to surrender rent in the form of labor services, products, and cash for access to means of production. Other economic conditions of existence of feudal surplus accumulation included credit and indebtedness and indeed the development (but also the limited size) of the internal market. The political power and ideological dominance of the landlord class were other conditions of existence that served to tie colono labor to the haciendas, ensuring that peasants honored their agreements and debts, while allowing a heterogeneous system of rental arrangements on the estate, with differing degrees of servility.

The growing integration of the province into the national political economy during the first four decades of the twentieth century began to change some of these conditions of feudal class relations but reinforced others. The accumulation of wealth depended on the total peasant labor under the landlord's control. Growing land pressure within the independent peasant communities allowed the haciendas to extend their control over rural labor as the century progessed. But the expansion of the sugar industry on the coastal plantations and the enganche system also provided "free" peasants with an alternative opportunity to generate income. In order to maintain resident labor, attract migrants to the haciendas, and encourage peasant households from independent communities to enter into new rental arrangements, the terms of surplus appropriation and redistribution had to change. This change was facilitated by one of the ideological conditions of existence of feudal class relations, the personalized nature of landlord-peasant relationships, which allowed individual rental arrangements to vary widely.

One important change was the way the hacienda system came to support the reproduction of the petty class process within the independent peasant communities. These "free" peasants obtained access to land on quite different terms. Most notable was the reduction or absence of the requirement to perform labor services. In other words, the reproduction of the fundamental class process of petty production began to occur without participation in the feudal class process as its precondition.

The possibility of seasonal wage employment on the coast also constrained the development of wage labor on the haciendas. The principal way the haciendas could compete for labor was by ceding land in usufruct. The development of the internal market was not vigorous enough to motivate either substantial expansion of the landlord's demesne or its capitalization. Giving peasants access to land continued to be the most effective means of maximizing landlord rental income.

The development of the conditions for capitalist class relations at the national level—for example, through legislation establishing the right to remuneration for labor performed and abolishing the legal basis for debt servitude—also began to challenge the hegemony of the highland landlord class. The incipient development of wage payments on the estates must be located in this context of changing political and ideological conditions for capitalist and feudal class relations. To increase the amount of peasant labor at their disposal for work on the demesne, modernizing landlords had to remunerate peasants per labor day worked. Landlords had little choice but to turn to the system of cash advances for future labor services and peasant indebtedness, given the peasantry's access to land and its preference for petty production. But this system was only partially successful in developing a wage labor force as long as the opportunity cost of land was low and peasants had sufficient access to resources to guarantee their primary reproduction requirements.

A number of subsumed class processes governed the redistribution of the appropriated surplus within the hacienda system. The development of the market was a condition of existence for the realization of money rents. Merchants were thus a subsumed class in relation to both arrendires and landlords. Surely the size of the subsumed class payment surrendered by arrendires to merchants was also an important disincentive to demesne production. Sometimes, landlords occupied the class position of merchant directly, selling demesne or peasant production, as well as products to the resident peasantry. This position served to increase their cut of the appropriated surplus. More commonly, however, landlords relied on the commercial houses of Cajamarca for interdepartmental and provincial trade; these commercial houses also supplied the luxury and productive consumption of the landlord class.

The redistribution of feudal rents maintained not only the merchant class but also the church and the public charities. By providing a key condition of existence for land-poor members of the elite—access to a hacienda—they were entitled to a predetermined share of the accumulated surplus. These landlord-arrendire rental agreements served to increase the rate of exploitation on these properties, in some cases undermining the conditions of feudal appropriation and surplus redistribution. The church and the public charities also provided other important conditions for feudal class relations, often legitimizing the power of the gamonales both politically and ideologically.

Various other subsumed class processes operated within the haciendas. The hacienda administrators, employees, and foreman, whose role was to ensure that surplus labor was in fact performed, constituted another subsumed class on the hacienda. They were a crucial link in the internal hierarchy of the hacienda, maintaining discipline, order, and "respect." Their incomes, drawn from the accumulated surplus of landlords, represent a subsumed class payment for another condition of existence of feudal class relations.

Another subsumed class process governed rental arrangements among the peasantry. Notably, an important mechanism for increasing the total volume of feudal rent was the practice of giving peasants land allotments sufficient in size for them in turn to sharecrop with other peasants. In this case, while the colonos themselves participated in a feudal class process, they engaged in a subsumed class process with other peasants, being entitled to a subsumed class payment (as rent) for providing access to land to other peasant households. The redistribution of the appropriated surplus to colono households represented the latter's subsistence consumption, so that they could in turn provide surplus labor to the landlord class.

In sum, within this framework, the hacienda system was class-differentiated in a complex manner. Two fundamental class relations—feudal and petty—governed the production, appropriation, and redistribution of surplus labor. Each class relation was a relation of struggle, with the outcome and the particular balance of forces between the fundamental and subsumed class processes in a continual process of evolution and change as the century progressed.

THREE

The Peasant Household on
the Hacienda

To prosper on the hacienda, a peasant household needed access to sufficient land and family labor power. Both were contingent on feudal class relations. Peasant households on haciendas constituted units of production precisely because they were granted access to land by the landlord class. But a good-sized holding could be farmed and a large herd maintained only by having a large family and by retaining grown children within the household. Feudal class relations impinged upon the household as a unit of reproduction through such factors as the landlords' influence over marriage and their ability to constitute new rent-paying households.

Feudal class relations impinged upon peasant household reproduction in other ways, too, for a household's ability to allocate labor was constrained by the obligation to provide labor services to the landlord. The degree of appropriation of surplus labor and the extent of its extraction through rents were important determinants of the level of household income, the quality of reproduction of household labor power, and the possibility for accumulation of means of production.

An important characteristic of feudal class relations in Cajamarca was that rental agreements were made only with male heads of households. Because only men acquired access to land, households on the hacienda were most patriarchal. With their mobility and income-generating possibilities restricted, women had no choice but to marry, bear large numbers of children, and perform domestic labor. This subordination of women enhanced the appropriation of surplus labor time by the landlord class while it lowered the standard of living of the feudal peasant class.

CONSTITUTION AND COMPOSITION OF HOUSEHOLDS

The average peasant woman on a Cajamarcan hacienda gave birth to nine children during her lifetime. Of these, an average of five would reach adulthood.[1] But not all children were welcomed equally. There was a strong preference for males, because only male heirs could assure parents of security on the hacienda in their old age. Midwives, in fact, charged twice as much for the delivery of a male baby as for a female.[2]

On the hacienda, large families were prized by both the peasantry and the landlord class. Having many children, both sons and daughters, was important to the economic success of the household. Schools were virtually nonexistent on the haciendas through the 1950s, and the primary activity of children was to perform productive labor for their parents until the children formed their own households. Large families conferred status on the parents, mainly because of the material benefits associated with them. A family with many children brought esteem to a woman, for it spoke well of her capabilities in raising and caring for her babies; for a man, having many children was a sign of prosperity and, to a lesser extent, virility. The landlord class also valued large peasant families, because the market value of a hacienda was often determined by the size of its resident peasantry. Moreover, children performed labor services, either assisting their parents or being directly charged with certain tasks. Although large family size increased the potential labor force of the hacienda, there is little evidence that the common condition of most peasant women— either being pregnant or lactating for twenty to thirty years of their lives— ameliorated the conditions of their exploitation.

Social sanctions against women who could not bear children were common. Barren women were often abandoned by their husbands, with the full approval of the community. Their only recourse was to return to their parents' homestead, because they themselves could not enter into a rental agreement with the landlord. These women, though sometimes pitied, were generally held in contempt by other women, as were those who never married. Single women were often the victims of gossip and ridicule: "There must be something wrong with her" (*algo le pasa*). They were criticized as vain, sassy, or lacking in domestic skills.[3]

1. I isolated the demographic characteristics of women on the hacienda by dividing the sample from the 1976 Peasant Family Survey into cohort groups by age. Of fifty-one women in the sample who were more than forty-five years old in 1976, eighteen had been hacienda residents. These women were born between 1901 and 1931 and married during the period from 1926 to 1956. Twenty-eight women in the age group from thirty-five to forty-four were married during the period of dissolution of the hacienda system, the 1950s and 1960s; eighteen of these women had been born and raised on haciendas. Twenty women under thirty-four years of age in 1976 were married after the system dissolved; nine of these had been born on haciendas.

2. Although male children were preferred by parents, I did not uncover any evidence of female infanticide. Females were valued for their productive contribution.

3. Whether single women were considered to be a burden on their parents largely depended on the household's access to resources. Poor households, those with few sheep, might not have been able to employ another grown woman productively. Rich peasant households, however, with large herds of sheep, probably welcomed an additional female hand for sheep raising, spinning, and weaving. Nonetheless, the overwhelming majority of women married.

Children tended to form their own unions relatively late and, on balance, sons and daughters married at similar ages. Survey data indicate that most women gave birth to their first child by the age of twenty-four, suggesting that women were involved in unions by at least the age of twenty-three; the same data indicate that men had spouses by their mid-twenties (1976 Peasant Family Survey). The relatively late marriage age was probably encouraged by the important economic contribution that grown children made to parental households and enforced by the patriarchal authority over children embodied in feudal class relations.

According to Elespuru Bernizón (1939, 157), marital unions on the hacienda were "nothing more than agreements between parents." The life histories I collected, however, reveal that personal choice did play a role, although it was subject to the constraint of parental approval. Amorous relationships often developed while young people tended the household's stock of sheep and cattle. Premarital sex was condoned, but it was expected to lead to a formal union.

Marriages were formed through two mechanisms. If her parents approved of the union, the young man would go to the woman's home with his relatives, bearing gifts. The young woman's parents would signal their approval by accepting the gifts—usually items appropriate for a celebration—and the celebration could begin immediately. If the couple thought one set of parents would disapprove of their union, they would often simply "run away" for a couple of days or so, a common practice in the independent peasant communities. Upon their return, the young woman's father, if he approved of the man, would accompany the couple to the young man's home to enforce the union. In order to increase the likelihood of agreement, the young woman would be provisioned with blankets (which she herself had been weaving for several years in preparation for marriage), as well as some smaller farm animals. If the young man's parents agreed to the union, then the toasting and celebration would begin. If they did not, the woman's father could request that the landlord enforce the union, for the woman would have been *engañada* (deceived) and the family disgraced.

If the young woman's father disapproved of her choice of a man, the running away would be quickly forgotten, even if she became pregnant. There was relatively little stigma attached to out of wedlock pregnancies; not infrequently, a child born outside of marriage would be raised by the woman's mother, particularly if the woman subsequently married another man.[4] Parental disapproval was sometimes related to the character traits of the young man or to differences in status. One elderly woman on the Hacienda Combayo tearfully

4. One can only speculate on whether the tolerance for out of wedlock pregnancies on the hacienda was related to the sexual abuse sometimes faced by peasant daughters from landlords and their sons. Rarely would "illegitimate" children from such unions be recognized by a hacendado, although sometimes later in life these offspring might receive special favors. See Gitlitz (1975) and Chambeu (1975a) for similar observations.

related to me how her father, an arrendire of the hacienda, had forbidden her union with the son of a peon: "It was for my own good, he said, for his family would simply eat my sheep."

Rarely were marriages consummated religiously or legally. In the first half of the twentieth century, the rural parishes of the northern highlands were in advanced disarray. All haciendas had a chapel, but only the patron saint day would be an occasion for celebrating mass; sometimes the couples who had formed unions during the previous year would then take religious vows (haciendas Combayo, Polloc). Some landlords were more concerned than others with the morality of their hacienda's inhabitants: at the turn of the century, Paula Iturbe de Iglesias reportedly consecrated unions on the Hacienda Chumbil until a priest could make the trek to San Pablo (Chávez Aliaga 1957, 5:15).

Landlords intervened in marriage choice primarily by prohibiting the children of tenants from marrying outside the hacienda (Escalante 1972). Probably more significant, given the generally restricted mobility of tenants and their need to remain on the hacienda to secure farmland, was the landlord's ability to influence the constitution of households through the allotment of new tenancies. On some haciendas, an agreement to form a new tenancy was in fact a permission to marry.

Considerable pressure was usually exerted by the son's family for a young couple to reside patrilocally, at least in the initial years of marriage. The son would continue working alongside the father, and the bride would be incorporated into the household's female labor force under the direction of the mother-in-law. Mother-in-law and daughter-in-law relationships were notoriously bad, the daughter-in-law often complaining that she was treated like a slave.

Daughters usually received their inheritance of sheep when they formed a stable union, and, in the initial years of marriage, sheep raising may have been the only independent economic activity of the young couple. Sons did not receive their inheritance (usually in the form of work animals or cattle) until they left the parental homestead. A young couple customarily did not build their own house and form a separate household economy until after their first child was born. A child confirmed the stability of the union, proving that the bride was not barren. Given the tension between mothers-in-law and daughters-in-law, this practice must have also served as an incentive for childbearing.

The location of the couple's dwelling depended on the labor arrangement and distribution of land between fathers and sons, as well as on the specific rental contract with the landlord. Life histories reveal three patterns of household formation on the hacienda, based on differing arrangements for access to land and the payment of rent. Sometimes, the patriarch's landholding would continue to be worked in common by all of his sons, under his direction.

In this case, each son would usually build a house in the same compound as the parents. In other cases, the patriarch would cede each son a subtenancy. Father and son would agree on the amount of rent the son was to contribute to the father's overall rent obligation. This subtenancy arrangement commonly involved a sharecropping agreement between father and son, whereby the father provided the usufruct parcel, seed, and sometimes the oxen; the son and his family provided the labor, and the crop was divided into equal shares. The new household usually constructed its dwelling on the land ceded to it. A third arrangement was for each son to enter into his own rental contract with the landlord. In this case, the new household might settle on a different section of the hacienda.

On the Hacienda Combayo, arrendires and peons had quite different options. Arrendires had large extensions of cultivable land, averaging 7.7 hectares but ranging up to several hundred. A number of households could be accommodated on the holding as agregados. In 1917 each arrendire (called *cabezonario*, or head of holding) had an average of 1.85 agregados attached to him (derived from Santolalla [1918] 1977, 223). Interviews on this hacienda reveal that most agregados were sons or other members of the arrendire's family, that it was common for married sons to build their dwellings in the patriarch's compound, and that the patriarch was usually successful in exploiting the landholding as a collective unit. After the patriarch retired from active work in the fields, he would continue to direct the work, as well as the distribution of the crop among the households in the compound, and to coordinate the payment of rent and the provision of labor services to the landlord. But when the patriarch died, considerable struggle could develop among brothers over whether the eldest son would continue to exert patriarchal authority or whether the land would be divided, with each son negotiating his own contract with the landlord.[5]

The situation of the peons on the Hacienda Combayo was not the same, for their usufruct parcels were usually small, averaging around 2 hectares, and married sons could not be accommodated on the holding. Sons usually entered into their own rental agreements with the landlord, most commonly as new peons. During the 1920s, most peon sons reportedly asked the landlord, don Eloy Santolalla, for permission to marry, because in their case marriage constituted a new tenancy relation.

The most common arrangement on the Hacienda Santa Ursula, where peasants were sub-arrendires, was for sons to sharecrop a subtenancy with the father and to share in the labor obligations. When all the land had been thus

5. See Miller (1967) for similar data on sibling conflict on a hacienda in the neighboring highland valley of La Libertad. The system of compounds on the Hacienda Combayo is also evident in the land titles registered for the subdivision and sale of this hacienda in the Cajamarcan public registry (Registros Públicos de Cajamarca, Registro de la Propiedad, city of Cajamarca [RPC], 2:235).

subdivided among the sons, the sharecropping arrangement was expected to be sufficient to maintain the parents in old age. And as the parents grew older, the sons and daughters-in-law were also expected to assume an increasing share of the labor services. By custom, the youngest son remained with his wife in the parents' home until their deaths. It was understood that he would inherit the parents' house and immediate possessions in return for the care provided. If the land parcel had already been divided into subtenancies, the sons would renegotiate their tenancy with the landlord when the father died.

Rarely would widows assume the contractual obligation with the landlord if their sons were already of working age. Most pitied were the women who might be left without any sons, for it was not uncommon for an exacting landlord simply to throw a widowed or abandoned woman off the hacienda. Thus, in the 1903 rental contract signed with Mariano Cacho for the Hacienda Santa Ursula, the Madres Concepcionistas had to prohibit the landlord from expelling any tenants from the hacienda, "whatever that resident's sex or age."[6]

My interviews with women who had once lived on the haciendas illustrate the precarious situation in which widows found themselves. The landlord of the Hacienda Huacariz de San Antonio threw the mother of Rosa Aquino off this hacienda when she was widowed in the 1930s. The couple had been sharecroppers, but the rental contract was rescinded when the husband died, and the wife was forced to move to the neighboring community of Agopampa. The landlord, perhaps finding his role as "benefactor" in contradiction with such treatment of a widow, finally allowed Rosa's mother to continue pasturing her sheep and pigs on hacienda land as long as she provided faena whenever he asked. That widows were treated this way reflects the undervaluation of female labor, a topic to be discussed later.

In order to remain on the hacienda, the main recourse for a widow with young children was either to remarry quickly or to become a full-time domestic servant. According to Pola Huamán, the landlord of the Hacienda Llushcapampa tried to throw her out, with her five children, in the late 1930s when her husband abandoned her for another woman. She refused to leave, pleading that her family had always been "gente de la hacienda," and she finally convinced the landlord to let her become a huasicama. Without access to land or wages, she supported her family through the landlord's gifts of food and clothing.

In all my interviews, I found only one case, on the Hacienda Huayobamba, of a young widow who did not remarry, apparently by choice. In the 1940s, this hacienda was developing a dairy specialization, and this young widow was allowed to remain on the hacienda, renting pastures, by providing labor services as a milkmaid. Men who were widowed, at whatever age, always

6. This contract was recorded in RPC (8: 108).

remarried quickly, reflecting their dependence on women for domestic labor and child rearing.

Class Relations and Household Size

A patriarch's ability to control sufficient land and to maintain authority over his sons largely depended on the landlord's good will. If, for example, a son demanded his own subtenancy and the father was reluctant to accede, the son could turn to the landlord to negotiate his own access to land. The maintenance of patriarchal control over family labor was thus conditioned by the personalized nature of landlord-tenant relationships. These relationships also influenced the degree of feudal social differentiation, household size, and the prevalence of nuclear versus extended households.

A noted feature of the hacienda system in Cajamarca was the high degree of differentiation among peasant households according to the amount of land to which they had access. The differentiation of the peasantry on the hacienda was expressed in terms of the possibility for accumulation, on the one hand, and by household size and structure, on the other. As peasants recount it, poor peasants formed nuclear households with access to land sufficient only to reproduce their own labor power and the means of production. Rich peasants were those patriarchs who not only had abundant land to farm but also were surrounded by their married sons. The landlord-peasant relationship was what made patriarchal control over labor and an extended household possible, allowing some sectors of the peasantry to accumulate a modicum of wealth.

Given this potential degree of social differentiation on the haciendas, it would not be surprising if there had been little difference in the average household size between hacienda households and households in the independent peasant communities. Households on the hacienda in 1940, however, were somewhat larger, averaging 5.2 residents, compared to 4.6 residents in households in the independent communities (Peru 1940, vol. 2, table 34). The larger hacienda households may reflect the effect of feudal class relations in fostering extended families, a greater patriarchal control over children (suggested by later age at marriage), higher fertility, and lower mortality— these last two related to the more favorable material conditions for the peasantry on the estates.[7]

A comparison of vital statistics for hacienda and non-hacienda residents reveals no statistically significant difference in the sample means. Women in independent communities had their first live birth at the mean age of 22.6; hacienda residents were slightly older, bearing children at the age of 24.2. This

7. In the literature on Peruvian haciendas, it is generally assumed that hacienda residents fared better than independent peasant producers, because hacienda households had greater access to cultivable land and other hacienda resources such as pasture, water, and forests (McClintock 1981, 74; Martínez Alier 1977, 146). This proposition is investigated in the next section of this chapter.

suggests that non-hacienda women probably did marry earlier; they also had a slightly higher fertility rate (an average of 9.4 live births versus 9.0). But child mortality was slightly higher in the independent communities, too, with women losing 48 percent of their children, compared to 41 percent for hacienda women. Overall, the differences in fertility and mortality do not account for the differences in household size.[8]

Feudal class relations probably reinforced larger household size on the haciendas through restrictions on mobility and support for patriarchal control over children, as well as extended household structures. But the incipient effect of capitalist class relations on household size within the independent peasant communities cannot be discounted. Within these communities, temporary migration to the coast through the enganche system provided young men with the possibility of an independent income source, which could have encouraged marriage at an earlier age and the formation of nuclear households. Also, as land shortages became more acute toward the 1930s and 1940s, the pattern of temporary migration gradually gave way to permanent migration, perhaps reflected in the smaller size of the remaining sierra households. The differences in household size between the haciendas and the independent communities may thus involve aspects of both capitalist and feudal class relations exerting different pressures on patriarchal control of children and family structure and composition.

NECESSARY AND SURPLUS LABOR TIME AND THE GENDER DIVISION OF LABOR

The household labor process on the haciendas was based on a well-defined yet flexible division of labor by gender. Agricultural production and animal raising were the two principal activities of most peasant households, complemented by artisan production. Whereas men were regarded as the primary agricultural-ists, women were generally charged with animal care. Nonetheless, both men and women participated in some of the myriad tasks associated with these two concerns. In these overall patterns, the gender division of labor on haciendas differed little from that in the independent peasant communities.

Men generally coordinated the agricultural production process, deciding when, where, and what to plant, directing the work process, and taking part in all work activities in the fields. Women usually participated in the agricultural field tasks that were most labor-intensive, such as weeding, harvesting, and threshing. They also assisted during the planting, shaking soil free from the weeds that were overturned during the plowing and placing seed in the furrows. In the Quechua region of Porcón, sowing the seeds was associated with women's

8. Child mortality has been defined broadly as the loss of a child to whom a woman has given birth, regardless of the child's age. The data are drawn from the 1976 Peasant Family Survey for the cohort of fifty-one women more than forty-five years of age in 1976.

power of fertility and was done only by women. Young children of both sexes helped in the agricultural tasks carried out by women. When boys became eight or nine years old, they joined in the male agricultural tasks, alongside their fathers.

Although household members constituted the primary labor force for agricultural activities, reciprocal labor exchanges among households were common. Called *ayni* labor, or *un tal por otro tal*, these labor exchanges occurred most frequently among men for tasks such as field preparation and planting. Whenever a number of men from outside the household helped with work in the fields, a large noonday meal was prepared by the women. Sometimes women also exchanged labor for such cooking. These labor exchanges were usually conducted among extended family members or compadres but were not limited to these individuals.

Through the 1950s, hacienda households sponsored mingas for the harvests. The mingas differed from the typical labor exchange in that a strict accounting of work was not usually kept; it was expected, however, that if one household participated in the minga of another, the second household would also attend the minga of the first. Rich peasants did not need to reciprocate in this fashion, because such a large group of peasant households participated in their mingas, given their greater demand for harvest workers. Their mingas were usually more festive occasions than those of other peasant groups on the hacienda, requiring abundant food and generous quantities of chicha and coca. When I asked a peasant woman on the Hacienda Combayo how one could distinguish poor, middle, and rich peasants, she said, "You just had to go to their mingas to see."

The hacienda harvests (those of landlords and the rich peasantry) in the district of La Encañada attracted peasants from communities throughout the province. Bringing valley products to barter (*trueque*), these migrants were also remunerated for their participation. For example, in the potato harvest, they were often designated a row or two to harvest as their "salary."[9]

Animal raising, including both sheep herding and the tending of cattle, was generally the responsibility of women, aided by children. Only in the area of the Hacienda Porcón was sheep herding a male occupation. Because most of this hacienda was located in the *jalca* (at the highest elevations of the province), sheep herding was the principal economic activity of most households. Women were also charged with raising the smaller farm animals (pigs, chickens, guinea pigs, and rabbits), whereas men usually cared for the work animals (oxen,

9. The case studies by Garay (1975a, 1975b, 1975c, 1975d) of the communities of Chilacát, La Laguna, La Laimina, and Pariamarca all provide good detail on intraprovincial migration aimed at securing products produced at different elevations. By the 1970s, the scale of these seasonal migrations had been significantly reduced. On this general phenomenon in Peru, as well as the many variations in the minga, or *minka*, practice, see the essays in Alberti and Mayer (1974) and Orlove (1977).

donkeys, mules, and horses). If the work animals had to be taken out to graze on hacienda pastures, the women or older children might take them. During an especially dry winter season, if pastures were poor, the men of the household might take all the larger farm animals to graze at higher elevations, sometimes leaving for several weeks at a time (haciendas Polloc, Combayo). These examples illustrate the flexibility that was required in the household's gender division of labor.

All household members, as well as close relatives, participated in activities such as the slaughter of a cow or a pig, which could occupy several days. The men butchered the animal and cured the hide, while the women prepared sausages and beef jerky and cooked the large midday feast. Sheep shearing often involved reciprocal labor exchanges among households. Men sheared the sheep, and women washed the wool and later carded it.

Women were responsible for food-processing tasks and other food production such as making cheese. Corn husking and shelling and the preparation of grains for milling were done immediately after the harvest only if some surplus production was going to be sold. More commonly, the crop was stored and processed over the course of the year, in accordance with the household's consumption requirements. Milling was usually done by hand, although in the 1920s some haciendas such as Combayo and Polloc had their own grain mills.

Artisan production was based on a fairly flexible although specialized gender division of labor. Women were generally responsible for spinning and dyeing wool for textile production. Only in the environs of the Hacienda Porcón did men spin wool; presumably this was because they were the shepherds on this hacienda and spinning is an activity especially complementary to watching over the herds. Both men and women might weave, but only men wove textiles on the standing Spanish loom, introduced during the colonial obraje period. Women wove on the less productive backstrap looms. Bayeta (the wool cloth used for trousers and skirts) was usually produced on the Spanish loom, whereas the backstrap loom was used for producing blankets and ponchos. Both men and women usually knew how to sew and produced their own clothes, although by the early decades of the century tailoring was developing as a specialized occupation (among men and only for men's clothes) on the haciendas, as it was within the independent peasant communities. There was also a tendency for carpentry to develop as a specialized male skill. Although textile production was the most important artisan activity of hacienda households in this period, rope (made out of *penca*), straw baskets, gourd bowls, and wooden spoons were also produced domestically by men, women, and children. Ceramic production, in contrast, was quite specialized, carried out only in certain villages of the province with the appropriate raw materials.

Both men and women participated in household production activities, but women were responsible for those associated with daily reproduction: food preparation, wood gathering, hauling water, and washing clothes. They were aided by children, although by the time boys were nine or ten, their participation in domestic chores was minimal unless the household had no daughters. The only reproductive task in which men commonly participated was wood gathering, particularly if a tree needed to be felled and chopped. Child care was a complementary activity to both domestic labor and household production, for very young children accompanied the mother in every task, usually tied on her back.

The allocation of labor between household and hacienda production was especially interactive. The provision of labor services to the landlord by men or by women often required a particular gender division of labor within the household; but the prevailing gender division of labor within peasant households could also be the basis for the overall determination of male and female tasks on the hacienda. For example, if the male head of the household had to provide full-time labor services to the landlord, subsistence agricultural production fell to the women and children, as it did among peon households on the Hacienda Combayo.[10] On haciendas such as Porcón, where sheep herding was a male occupation, women also had to work more in subsistence agriculture. In contrast, on those haciendas where women herded the hacienda's sheep or cattle, women worked relatively less in agriculture. The prevailing gender division of labor on the hacienda thus had singularly important repercussions for the availability of family labor power and the gender division of labor within the household.

The prevailing gender division of labor among the peasantry also influenced how work was divided in the provision of labor services to the landlord. Because peasant men were generally considered the principal agriculturalists, and women considered the "helpers," on most haciendas men provided the negotiated number of days of labor services for agricultural work on the demesne, and women were expected to "help" in the most labor-intensive tasks. This additional labor was rarely formally recognized.

Some landlords did not exploit this subtle means of increasing the surplus labor time appropriated from the peasantry and instead imposed their own conceptions of the proper gender division of labor. On the Hacienda Polloc, for example, Manuel Cacho Galvez did not consider it proper for women to work in the fields, believing that only men should be agriculturalists. Likewise, the landlord of the Hacienda Adacucho did not allow women to perform agricultural work on the demesne, reportedly because he feared that women would steal agricultural products under their skirts. According to Chambeu

---

10. Gitlitz (1975, 127) notes that on the Hacienda Pallán in the neighboring province of Celendín the full-time hacienda workers (the peons) complained that they did not have sufficient time to work their own fields, which consequently had to be farmed with the labor of wives and children.

(1975a, 11), these policies in turn influenced the gender division of labor in peasant production, with women rarely working in the fields.

Women were charged with the activities required for household reproduction, and their labor services for the landlord class were often similar. For example, the semanera duty extended women's domestic work from their own household to the landlord's. As a servant in the casa hacienda, a peasant woman was responsible, for one week, for housekeeping tasks, animal care, and food preparation. Cooking the field hands' noonday meal was no simple task. Cooking for a group of twenty peons, as one peasant woman recounted it, meant getting up by three in the morning to start sorting, toasting, and grinding the arroba of wheat or barley for the meal. The corn had to be shelled and toasted, the soup made, and enough wood gathered for a three- or four-hour fire. The children helped, of course, carrying water and gathering wood. But they also had their own tasks, such as feeding the smaller farm animals and sweeping out the casa hacienda. After the noon meal was served, the semanera might be responsible for milking the hacienda's cows, making butter or cheese, or perhaps grazing the landlord's pigs and goats.

If the hacienda was large, or if the landlord's family lived on the hacienda, several semaneras were required each week. Daily maintenance of the landlord's family—cooking, washing clothes, cleaning, child care, running errands—required the services of at least one or two peasant women, with an additional woman required to cook for the peons.

If the landlord's family lived in the city of Cajamarca, the hacienda women were also sometimes required to take a turn at semanera duty in the town house, where they served as maids. Occasionally, they also processed the hacienda's agricultural products in the city, because absentee landlords may have considered it unsafe to store their crops on the hacienda where they could be pilfered. In one case, that of a dairy farm in the valley, the semaneras were charged with selling the farm's milk production door to door in the city (fundo El Molino).

Married women considered the semanera duty in town to be particularly onerous, for it required them to be away from their families for weeks at a time, interfering with household reproduction. Because of the distances between the haciendas and the city, these turns tended to be prolonged; but serving in the city did relieve them from having to take their weekly turn later on during the year. For some unmarried women, the semanera duty in town served as an escape from the confines of the hacienda. For example, among my interviewees was Lucila, unmarried at the age of thirty, who begged her mistress, doña Olga Bueno, to take her to the city of Cajamarca as a permanent semanera. There, she met her husband.

Málaga Santolalla (1906, 184–185) reported that at the turn of the century the majority of maids in the city of Cajamarca were semaneras. By the 1940s, as increasing numbers of young peasant girls migrated to the city from the independent communities, full-time domestic servants largely replaced the hacienda semaneras in the homes of Cajamarca.

Underlying the servile relationship between landlords and the resident peasantry was the understanding that the labor power of the whole peasant family was at the landlord's disposal. In practice, the undefined appropriation of surplus labor was differentiated by gender, for the rental arrangements between landlord and peasant were agreements between men. Peasant men's tasks were well delineated, involving the obligation to carry out a negotiated number of days of labor services in specified tasks. In contrast, women's obligations, with the exception of the semanera duty, were rarely negotiated in advance and involved a broad range of services both in the casa hacienda and in the peasant woman's own home.

This gender difference in the form of surplus labor appropriation—with a specified commitment for peasant men and an unspecified commitment for women's labor time—is readily apparent in the written rental contracts we have examined for the Hacienda Santa Ursula. In a 1918 contract, the peasant man agreed to provide twelve days of labor services for agricultural work; the peasant woman, in addition to the semanera duty, was to be available "for the sorting of wheat or whatever other job she could perform."[11] Some of these "other jobs" were more clearly delineated in a 1940 contract for this hacienda, although the amount of labor time required was not so clear.[12] Women were required to toast the hacienda's barley, to make corn meal for the landlord, and to "send one woman to cook food for the peons, to sort wheat, and to do whatever other job she could whenever the landlord required it, without any remuneration in cash."

On the Hacienda Santa Ursula, female mingas were organized for the husking and shucking of corn, the sorting of wheat and barley, toasting, and milling. During the barley-toasting minga, for example, each woman would be given one sack of 125 pounds to toast each day. Usually the minga went on for four or five days, until all the grain was ready for milling. There was no grain mill on Santa Ursula, so another female minga would be organized to process the toasted grains into flour for the landlord's consumption. Because the milling technology was so rudimentary (the grains were milled by hand between two large stones), preparing 1 arroba, or 25 pounds, could take three to four hours.

The duration of the mingas depended on the extension and composition of the landlord's demesne, as well as the total number of resident households on the hacienda. Peasant women reported spending as much as three months a year in these labor-intensive processing tasks (Hacienda Chaquil). Mingas were also organized to prepare wool for spinning. On the haciendas Porcón and

11. "Contrato entre Julián Condor y Fidel G. Zevallos Palmer, Octubre 1918," in Hacienda Santa Ursula files, Agrarian Reform Office, Ministry of Agriculture, Agrarian Zone II, Cajamarca.

12. "Contrato entre Resurrección Culqui y el Sr. Antonio Otoya Puga, Abril 18, 1940," Hacienda Santa Ursula files, Agrarian Reform Office.

Chaquil, where sheep raising was an important concern for the landlord, women spent from three to four weeks a year in this task.

In addition to attending these special work parties, women were required to produce use and exchange values for the landlord in their own homes. This performance of surplus labor differed from the socialized labor services in that the distinction between necessary and surplus labor was blurred, often serving to reduce the necessary labor time for the reproduction of household labor power. In these "home" tasks, the household also usually had to provide some of the raw materials for the production process, increasing the exploitation of labor still further. On several haciendas, the women had to make barrels of the corn-based liquor called chicha, which the landlord used for special occasions on the hacienda, such as the harvest minga or the celebration of the patron saint's day. A barrel of chicha requires 2 arrobas of corn and 10 pounds of chancaca (brown sugar cakes). The landlord supplied the corn, but the household sometimes had to supply the sugar cakes, which generally had to be purchased (Hacienda Polloc). The production of chicha first entailed one day of shelling corn; then, after the corn had been soaked for several days, it took another day of cooking and continually stirring the brew. Wood collection for a day's worth of flame certainly occupied the children for at least one day.

Women were also commonly required to make butter and cheese in their homes for the landlord. Sometimes these products were for the landlord's consumption, but on the Hacienda Llushcapampa, they were produced for the Cajamarca market. One woman on this hacienda, the wife of a quincenero, claimed that she was required to make cheese daily without remuneration. Again, these were time-consuming, labor-intensive tasks, but they could be combined with women's other domestic responsibilities.

Especially detrimental to the household economy was the requirement that women spin the hacienda's wool. On some haciendas, women would incur obligations to spin as a faena for pasturing sheep on hacienda lands—for example, on the Hacienda Lacas, 1 pound of spun wool was charged per ten sheep grazed per annum. On the largest sheep-raising hacienda in the province, the Hacienda Porcón, however, the women had to spin the landlord's wool not as a faena but because they were hacienda residents (Gorget 1975b). Women in the Andes often spin as they pasture their sheep, as they sit to chat, or even as they walk down the village paths. But spinning full-time with the primitive hand spindle (*rueca*) results in at most a pound of wool spun per week. When combined with other tasks, spinning a pound could take three to four weeks. Given that 6 to 8 pounds of wool yarn are required for a blanket or a poncho and that a family of six needed at least 10 to 18 pounds of spun wool a year, the appropriation of a woman's spinning time by the landlord interfered with the peasant's ability to clothe her own family.

Also detrimental to the household economy was the demand on some haciendas that a child be sent to work full-time to tend the landlord's sheep.

One woman I interviewed on the Hacienda Chaquil had become a mitaya at the age of four; another, on the Hacienda Polloc, at the age of six. The landlord's appropriation of children's labor deprived the parents of a key resource and augmented the mother's workload.

The well-defined gender division of labor between productive and reproductive tasks served to increase the mass of surplus labor subject to appropriation by the landlord class at the same fixed cost, that is, the household usufruct parcel. Under colono arrangements, peasant men spent approximately half of their labor time performing labor services for the landlord and the other half in subsistence production. The rate of exploitation of male labor was thus approximately 100 percent. The exploitation of colono women may initially appear less severe. Semanera duty required on average two to four weeks a year, and the maximum number of days reported spent in female mingas equaled about three months a year. In addition to these obligations, however, the gender division of labor and the undervaluation of women's labor in reproductive tasks allowed the appropriation of female labor time by the landlord class to continue inside the peasant home. The rate of exploitation of female labor may have been equivalent to that of male labor.

The undervaluation of women's labor is also evident in the relative remuneration of male and female labor. When wage payments were introduced on the haciendas, they were strictly for men's work obligations (Silva Santisteban 1945, 94). Women and children were never paid for their work as semaneras or for attending the female work parties. Furthermore, women were never remunerated for the additional demands placed on them by exacting landlords, such as processing food at home. The 1940 Santa Ursula contract referred to earlier provides clear evidence of this practice. Whereas it stipulated that men were to be remunerated at the rate of S/. 0.20 per day for their labor services, the contract specifically noted that women's performance of surplus labor was to be "without any remuneration in cash." The 1942 regulation of contracts on this hacienda stipulated that no labor service was to be unremunerated.[13] Nonetheless, the women I interviewed who had once resided on the Hacienda Santa Ursula alleged that they were never paid for their labor services, even though men did begin to receive cash wages. This pattern was also reported to me concerning the fundo Shultín and the haciendas Huacariz de San Antonio, Adacucho, and Noriega.

In those cases where women were remunerated in kind for their participation in a given activity, such as the grain harvest, their remuneration was unequal to men's. Men were typically paid twice as much as women. Even when men and women worked side by side, as in the potato harvest, men

13. "Proyecto de reglamentación de relaciones contractuales y de trabajo entre el conductor don Antonio Otoya Puga y los colonos sub-arrendatarios de la Hacienda Santa Ursula, 5 Junio 1942," Hacienda Santa Ursula files, Agrarian Reform Office.

received 1 arroba of potatoes per day worked, whereas women received only half an arroba (haciendas Combayo, Huacariz de San Antonio). Although in the 1970s men and women tended to be paid equal harvest shares for equal work, wage payments were more gender-differentiated in communities that once had been part of the haciendas.

The economic rationale of the landlord class for devaluing female labor is self-evident: this devaluation enhanced the mass of appropriated surplus labor. The more interesting question is why peasant men allowed their household's standard of living to be less than it might have been had they struggled against the conditions of exploitation of female labor. There was clearly a close relationship between the number and duration of labor services that women performed for the landlord and the level and quality of reproduction of household labor power.

The exploitation of female labor persisted partly because it was largely unseen. Domestic labor, including processing and transformation activities, was not categorized as "work" but rather was considered part of being female. Because it was perfectly justified at the ideological level that women should serve men, it was "natural" that women would serve the landlord as well. The social construction of gender also devalued women's participation in certain productive activities. Men were regarded as the primary agriculturalists, and thus women only "helped men" in productive tasks; such a notion justified unequal wage payments by sex, if women's labor was remunerated at all.

Another mechanism that reproduced women's subordination and facilitated their exploitation involved the way the patriarchal peasant family was constituted. Recall that feudal class relations were rental arrangements between men and that the reproduction of feudal class relations placed disproportionate importance on the personal relationship between landlord and peasant. These personalized relations enhanced the landlord's authority within the hacienda and, in a parallel fashion, served to reproduce the authority of peasant men over women. Only men had access to land, and this exclusion of women from access to the means of production meant that women were totally dependent on men for subsistence. Even carrying out their own traditionally defined female activity of animal raising generally depended on men securing access to grazing land. The consequence was that women had to marry if they were to have access to the means of production.

Of course, men were also dependent on women. Only women could bear children, who could guarantee a household's future prosperity. The constitution of patriarchal peasant households, mediated by the landlord class, was thus the mechanism for allocating women to men and for ensuring that only one gender would perform domestic labor. Peasant men appeared to be compensated for their own exploitation through the subordination of women.

Although household relations on the hacienda were firmly bound in class relations, other factors tended to support a relatively egalitarian distribution of consumption, if not of work. One of the ways hacienda households differed significantly from those in the independent communities was the degree of income pooling. The great majority of households on the hacienda had sufficient access to land so that their primary economic activities were agricultural production and animal raising, based on the family labor force. Households were relatively self-sufficient—or at least able to guarantee their subsistence consumption requirements of grains and to generate surpluses that could be traded for crops produced at other elevations. The relative lack of commoditization of agricultural production before 1940 meant that the net agricultural product was indeed a family labor product, consumed by those who had produced it. Income pooling and shared consumption were thus facilitated by the ability to generate subsistence consumption, the small share of total production that was commercialized, and the relatively few independent income-generating activities that were not family-based.

As the century progressed, the growing monetization of the peasant economy within the hacienda introduced a wedge into the practice of household income pooling by giving more control of household income to men. For example, the payment of rent in cash, as compared to sharecropping and colono arrangements, tied hacienda households quite firmly into commodity markets, particularly the cattle trade. Although women continued to be responsible for cattle raising, men represented the household in its commercial dealings with the outside world, negotiating the sale of cattle. In addition, men were responsible for the payment of rent. Similarly, the system of cash advances and indebtedness, mediated as it was by the landlord–male peasant relationship, reinforced male control of cash income.

Activities that would allow women to generate cash income on the hacienda were few—basically, the making of chicha and, among rich peasant women, running small stores in their homes. As we will see in the next chapter, women's income-generating activities in the independent peasant communities were much broader in scope, partly because of the greater monetization of the rural economy as compared with that of the hacienda. But the inability to maintain household subsistence from agricultural and animal production (which forced peasants to engage in multiple income-generating activities) also weakened the basis for household income pooling. Before pursuing these comparisons in more detail, however, we should consider the level of household income that was possible on the haciendas.

PEASANT HOUSEHOLD INCOME LEVELS IN 1917

As noted previously, the Hacienda Combayo was not typical of haciendas in the province, because it relied on the use of cash advances to secure a labor force for its diversified agricultural and mining activities. Nevertheless, the monographic and archival material available for this hacienda allows us to construct income profiles to illustrate the level of farm income that could be generated by hacienda households. In addition, the income profiles allow us to explore the significance of feudal differentiation on the haciendas and the effects of the subordination of women in lowering the living standards of peasant households. Moreover, the data shed some light on why peasants might have been willing to enter into feudal class relations voluntarily rather than seeking wage labor on the coast.

In 1917, 81 percent of the cultivable lands of the Hacienda Combayo were in the hands of the resident peasantry (Santolalla 1977, 224). Given the relatively high elevation of this hacienda, more than half of the 420 hectares cultivated by the peasantry were planted in barley. Barley was also the principal grain in peasant diets, consumed principally as barley flour (*mashca*) mixed with water to form a porridge. Nineteen percent of the peasants' cultivated area was planted in wheat, consumed locally as bread. A similar area was dedicated to potato cultivation, the principal crop bartered by Combayo peasants with peasants from the Cajamarca Valley. Corn was another important staple, consumed as toasted kernels (*cancha*), but it could be grown only at the lowest elevations of this hacienda, near the narrow river bottom. Its cultivation thus accounted for only 2 percent of the cultivated land. Sufficient broad beans and lentils were planted to meet household consumption needs.

The reported yields on this hacienda for wheat, barley, and tubers were considerably higher than those reported for the department in the 1929 agricultural census. Bean yields were slightly lower, and those for corn significantly lower, than the departmental average (Pinto 1972, 12). Table 11 presents the gross and net returns per hectare for the five major crops on the Hacienda Combayo. Potatoes and beans yielded the highest net return per hectare; in comparison, the return for grains and corn was quite low. When the labor input for each crop is taken into account, however, the data show that production of barley, the major crop of this hacienda, yielded the highest return per labor day worked.[14]

The peasants of the Hacienda Combayo not only worked the largest share of the cultivable lands but also held the majority of the livestock grazed on the 13,000 hectares of natural pastures. In 1917 the peons and arrendires owned 73 percent of the 3,503 cattle and beasts of burden, 79 percent of the 388 pigs, and 60 percent of the 6,504 sheep.[15] Cattle production was an important

14. Only the cost of seed has been included in the costs of production, because the available data do not allow estimates of the value of animal fertilizer or the depreciation of tools and animal power. The net return to labor is thus a net return to labor and capital before the payment of rent. Also, the net return per labor day may be overstated, because the labor utilization data were drawn from those calculated by Santolalla (1977) for demesne production. Santolalla considered these data to be applicable to the rich peasantry also.

15. These statistics are derived from the figures provided in Santolalla (1977, 223–224, 270). The Planillas de Trabajo for the Oficina Combayo and the Hacienda Combayo for the late 1920s

TABLE 11. Return per Hectare and per Labor Day Worked in Peasant Production on the Hacienda Combayo, 1917 (in Current Peruvian Soles)

Crops	Gross Return per Hectare	Costs per Hectare	Net Return per Hectare	Number of Days Worked	Return to Labor
Wheat	44	7.0	37	43	0.80
Barley	50	5.0	45	43	0.99
Corn	37	2.0	35	97	0.34
Potatoes	160	24.7	135	199	0.67
Broad beans/Lentils	80	6.0	74	93	0.77
Weighted average	70.9	9.2	61.7	76.4	0.77

SOURCE: Compiled from Santolalla ([1918] 1977, 228–229, 265).

TABLE 12. Average Amount of Landholdings, Animal Holdings, and Rental Payments by Resident Peasantry on the Hacienda Combayo, 1917

	Arrendires	Peons
Average amount of land	7.72 hectares	2.20 hectares
Average number of large animals	28	18
Average number of small animals	46	30
Average amount of rental payment:		
For landholding	S/. 19.3	S/. 5.5
For large animals	28.0	17.7
For small animals	13.3	8.7
Total rent	S/. 60.6	S/. 31.9
Average amount of land in cultivation	5.21 hectares	1.49 hectares
Gross value of agricultural production	S/. 369	S/. 106
Gross value of animal stocks	S/. 958	S/. 598

SOURCE: Compiled from Santolalla ([1918] 1977); see Appendix II for the estimating procedure.
NOTE: Large animals include cattle, horses, donkeys, and mules; small animals include sheep, goats, and pigs.

income-generating activity among arrendire households, providing the cash to pay the rent. Merchants from Cajamarca came to the weekly plaza at the casa hacienda to buy cattle that subsequently would be fattened in the valley and then exported to the coast. Peasant households also marketed sheep, but on a smaller scale, selling them to generate cash for a family emergency or

---

suggest that the sheep-raising and cattle-raising operations of the hacienda were managed separately, with sheep under the management of the foundry operation (the Oficina Combayo) and cattle part of the mixed agricultural activities of the Hacienda Combayo (see Table 8). This is probably the reason Santolalla gives little attention to sheep raising in his monograph.

other extraordinary expense. The primary objective of sheep production, besides being a store of wealth, was to provide wool for household textile production. The smaller farm animals—pigs, chickens, goats, and guinea pigs—were raised primarily to meet the household's consumption requirements. Milk processing was rare; only a few households made *cuajada* (a soft white cheese) from their temporary excess of milk.

In order to estimate peasant farm income on the hacienda, it is necessary to estimate the average size of peasant landholdings, animal holdings, and rental payments (see Table 12). To explore the variation in income levels and possible composition of household income under the varying rental arrangements, I have estimated three income profiles, presented in Table 13. They include income profiles of typical arrendire and peon households, with the average amount of land and animal holdings (estimated in Table 12), and a peon

TABLE 13.   Levels and Composition of Annual Household Income on the Hacienda Combayo, 1917 (in Current Peruvian Soles)

	Arrendire	*Peon*	*Puntero*
Net agricultural income			
Net value of agricultural production	321.5	91.9	46.0
Rental payment	−19.3	—	—
	302.2	91.9	46.0
	(79.8%)	(33.9%)	(13.8%)
Net income from animal production			
10% of value of animal stocks	96.0	60.0	96.0
Rental payment	−41.3	—	—
	54.7	60.0	96.0
	(14.4%)	(22.2%)	(28.8%)
Wage income			
Male labor	21.7	75.0	72.0
Female labor	—	6.8	36.0
Child labor	—	5.2	36.0
Subtotal	21.7	87.0	144.0
Imputed wage income	—	+31.9	+47.0
	21.7	118.9	191.0
	(5.8%)	(43.9%)	(57.4%)
Total net income	378.6	270.8	333.0
Per capita net income[a]	69.6	49.8	61.2

SOURCE: Compiled from Santolalla ([1918] 1977); see Appendix II.
[a]This figure assumes a mean household size of 5.44 (Peru 1940, vol. 2, table 34).

household whose members, denoted as punteros, worked full-time for the landlord raising animals.

Some of the assumptions embodied in these calculations need to be explained. If both adults in a puntero household worked full-time, they probably sharecropped their usufruct parcel with other peasants. I assumed that they received 50 percent of the net value of production as agricultural income. Because data were not available to calculate income from animal production on the basis of the net change in animal stocks, I assumed 10 percent of the value of animal stocks as a proxy for the value of animals consumed and sold. I also assumed that the herds of the puntero household were at least the size of those of an arrendire household, since punteros could tend to their own herds while they cared for those of the landlord.

With respect to wage income, I assumed that the man from the peon household spent 250 days a year in agricultural work for the landlord; the woman, 45 days in agricultural work and as a semanera; and a child, 21 days in agricultural work for the hacienda (see Appendix II). Also, because peons paid no rent as such, the value of the resources under their command is shown as an imputed wage. For the puntero household, I assumed that the man worked full-time as a puntero, the woman worked full-time as a mitaya, and their male child worked full-time as an assistant puntero. In addition, their imputed wage includes tips given by the landlord for newborn animals. For the arrendire household, wage income includes the provision of 30 days of labor in the mines and 16.7 days of demesne agricultural work. The wages applicable to each of these activities are drawn from Table 9.

Based on these intentionally conservative assumptions, the income of an arrendire household was approximately 40 percent higher than that of the average peon household, and 14 percent higher than that of the best-paid peon household, one where all family members were remunerated for full-time work. The composition of household income differs substantially among the three groups, particularly in relation to the relative importance of agricultural and wage income. Whereas nearly 80 percent of the income of the arrendire household was from agricultural production, only 34 percent of the income of the peon household was from this source. For a puntero household whose members worked full-time, wage income constituted nearly 58 percent of net annual income, compared to 44 percent for a peon household where only the man worked full-time and 6 percent for arrendire households who were obligated to work only one month out of the year.

These estimates understate the value of farm production, for they do not include estimates of the value of agricultural processing and product transformation. They also exclude the value of artisan production and possible income generated from commercial activities such as the sale of chicha. The estimates of per capita income also do not take into account a possibly significant variation in household size. Arrendire households were presumably larger than peon households, because arrendire households had an average of 1.85 male agregados affiliated with them, mostly sons or relatives. As discussed earlier, peons did not have the option of holding on to the labor of their children. If it is assumed that all of the agregados were indeed family members of the arrendires and in most cases lived on the family compound, the extended households of arrendires may have averaged 7.5 members, compared with 4.5 members in peon households.[16]

Taking these assumptions into account, the per capita income of arrendires turns out to be lower (S/. 50.5) than that of peon households (S/. 60.1). For per capita income to have been equal, arrendire households would have had to work another 146 days in the mines. This they could have easily done, for they counted on 2.85 adult male workers. Alternatively, arrendires would have needed to work an additional 1.2 hectares of land for per capita income to have been equal. The level and composition of household income on the hacienda probably varied significantly among different households, even within the same rental arrangement. Not the least variation was the household's disposition to work in the mines and the need to seek cash advances repaid in labor services.

Household income also varied according to the available employment for different household members and the relative remuneration for male and female labor services. The highest *wage* income profile on the hacienda required that the man, the woman, and one child work full-time. But because women and children were paid only half of what men earned for similar work, the wage income such a household could earn was lowered accordingly. Moreover, if the woman worked full-time, and if the usufruct parcel was sharecropped rather than worked directly, the foregone income from agricultural production was greater than a woman's annual wage income. Only if a child had full-time employment on the hacienda would full-time wage work for all family members be an income-maximizing proposition. But this was a rare case on the Hacienda Combayo. In 1917 only eight to ten men and women worked full-time in the hacienda's cattle and sheep operations.

The women of the peon households rotated the available wage work among themselves—semanera duty, milking cows, and occasional agricultural work—but this yielded no more than six or eight weeks of employment a year. In 1917 only 161 female labor days were employed in total by the hacienda for agricultural production, principally for the corn and potato harvests. All women's jobs on the hacienda were remunerated at the same wage, S/. 0.05 per day plus meals. The lowest male nominal wage was four times greater, S/. 0.20;

16. To arrive at this distribution, I assumed that each arrendire household had, in addition to 2.85 adult male workers, 1.43 adult female workers, or 4.3 adults, whereas peon households had only 2 adult workers. The total number of children on the hacienda was then distributed proportionately between the two groups, giving arrendire households an average 3.2 children and peon households 2.5. The estimate was constrained by the total hacienda population of 675 and the 1940 census average of 5.44 members per household.

if the value of meals was equal for the two sexes, S/.0.10 per day, then the difference in the remuneration to labor was twofold. Clearly, the subordination of women lowered the peasant household's level of income and thus the family's well-being.

The data also illustrate the landlord's dilemma. At the going hacienda wage rate and current prices, farming was a much more attractive proposition for the peasantry than wage work. A hectare of land yielded an average annual net income of S/.61.7 (excluding rent); to earn this much through wage work, a peasant would have had to work 118 days in the mines, the highest paid but most onerous job on the hacienda, or perform 154 days of agricultural labor on the demesne. At current prices, the average net return per day worked on the usufruct plot was S/.0.77, significantly higher than the wage for any job on the hacienda.

Paying resident labor the equivalent of their opportunity cost would have affected the profitability of the hacienda considerably. In 1917 the Hacienda Combayo realized a net income of S/.3,040, which amounted to a rate of profit of 14 percent on capital invested. If agricultural wages had been raised to the level of peasant opportunity cost in agricultural production, and if all men and women had been remunerated at this rate, the hacienda's net income would have been reduced to S/.1,401, and the rate of profit to 6.5 percent.[17] If wages had been raised to the level of those on the sugar plantations (see Table 14) net income and the rate of profit would have been negative.

This is one important explanation of why both economic and noneconomic coercion were necessary even on "modernizing" haciendas. The peasants wanted to farm; without either a wage at least equivalent to opportunity costs or their substantial dispossession from the means of production, the credit-indebtedness system and the ideological reinforcement of servitude were necessary to compel peasants into wage labor. Nonetheless, according to Santolalla (1977), neither mechanism guaranteed the hacienda a sufficient labor supply for mining and agricultural activities.

The data for the Hacienda Combayo also illustrate why, for the peasantry, acquiring land in usufruct under feudal class relations may have been a more attractive proposition than migrating to the coast to earn wage income. Acquiring a single hectare of land at a rental rate of S/.2.5, with an average net return of S/.61.7, yielded an income equivalent to 43 days of wage labor on the Chicama sugar plantations in 1917 (see Table 14). Earning the minimum estimated net annual income of an arrendire on the Hacienda Combayo would have required 272 days of coastal wage labor; earning the net annual income of the peon would have required 195 days.

---

17. These statistics are derived from the data in Santolalla (1977, 238–240, 229–230). If the salaries of all employees had been increased proportionately, the net income would have been negative.

Because temporary migration to the coast also involved monetary costs, the equivalencies noted above actually understate the required stay. Moreover, as described in Chapter 1, there was always the possibility of incurring more debt on the coastal plantations. Thus, for example, peasants from the village of Adacucho received advances from the *socorrista* of the plantation Casa Grande in 1925 ranging from S/. 20 to S/. 50 (Chambeu 1975a, 1–11). On average, it took them four months of work on the coast to pay back their debt, although the average wage of field hands in that year might have been as high as S/. 1.81 (see Table 14).

The composition of peasant household income on the Hacienda Combayo differed from that on other haciendas because wages were paid in the form of advances for labor performed. This, of course, means that peasant income levels on this hacienda were higher than on most provincial haciendas, given equal amounts and quality of land and available family labor.

The data for the Hacienda Combayo also indicate that the income levels of hacienda residents considerably exceeded those of smallholders in the independent peasant communities. The average holding in the communities was

TABLE 14. Average Daily Wages Paid to Agricultural Field Hands in the Sugar Industry, 1912–1928 (in Current Peruvian Soles)

	National Average	National Average, Males	Average for Chicama Valley Sugar Plantations, Males
1912	1.25	1.27	1.33
1913	1.27	1.29	1.40[a]
1914	1.23	1.26	1.30
1915	1.27	1.30	1.30
1916	1.19	1.13	1.09
1917	1.44	1.37	1.39
1918	1.59	1.60	1.52
1919	1.91	1.83	1.64
1920	1.83	1.62	1.27
1921	1.82	1.85	1.79[a]
1922	1.78	1.58	1.30
1923	1.84		
1924	1.84		
1925	1.81		
1926	1.67		
1927	1.72		
1928	1.75		

SOURCES: National averages (first column) from Hunt (1977, table 12); based on *Extracto Estadístico del Perú*. Averages for males (second and third columns) from Albert (1976, table 47); based on *Estadística de la Industria Azucarera*.

[a]These figures include the value of a food ration; all other figures exclude this value.

probably not much greater than that estimated for a peon household on the hacienda, 2.20 hectares, with 1.49 hectares in production. Animal stocks were likely to have been considerably smaller, given the lack of access to grazing pastures in most communities. If we assume that smallholders earned the same net agricultural income as peons did, S/. 92 per year, and one-quarter of the net animal income, S/. 15 per year, net farm income may have been on the order of S/. 107 for a typical household. If net wage income was equal only to the advance of S/. 30 typical in the 1910s, total annual household income would have been in the range of S/. 137—about half of that earned by a peon household on the Hacienda Combayo.

To begin to approximate earning the income of a hacienda peon or arrendire would have required either a migration much longer than the typical four months or less abusive conditions on the coastal plantations that would have allowed the accumulation of savings as well as significantly greater consumption levels. The wage gap between coast and sierra—on the order of seven to one in 1917—was certainly sufficient to attract increasing numbers of highland migrants to the expanding employment opportunities on the sugar plantations over the decade of the 1920s. The wage gap may even have increased in the early 1920s—to nine to one—because of the stagnancy of monetary wages in Cajamarca.[18] But there is little evidence that provincial landlords attempted to compete for seasonal labor either through the payment of wages or by offering steadily higher wages. They did not have to compete in that fashion, as long as they had vast tracts of unutilized land on the estates.

CONCLUSION

Even though the Cajamarcan peasantry had an alternative opportunity to generate income through migration, hacienda control over rural labor expanded during the first four decades of the century precisely because it was in the interest of both peasants and landlords. But because the hacienda peasantry had gained access to sufficient means of production, landlords continually had to coerce the peasants through economic and noneconomic means to put aside their own productive activities and perform surplus labor. Although peasant struggle, if only in subdued forms, affected the profitability of feudal class relations for landlords, the cheapest labor force was nevertheless maintained by ceding land in usufruct as long as land was relatively plentiful.

18. My interviews suggest that the wage rate for "free" agricultural labor stayed at around S/.0.20 from the late 1910s until the late 1920s. Also, Santolalla (1977) considered that the Hacienda Combayo paid peons the going market rate, S/.0.20, in 1917. Peons on this hacienda were paid this same rate until 1928, when it was raised to S/.0.25 (see Table 9). Chambeu (1975a, 11) reports that in 1925 the going wage for free male labor was S/.0.20 in the district of Namora. Taylor (1979, 167) estimates wages in the Cajamarca Valley as S/.0.15 in 1915, S/.0.20 in 1920, and S/.0.25 in 1925 and 1930.

As this chapter has shown, the particular content of feudal class relations also had singularly important implications for the level of peasant household reproduction. Class relations affected how hacienda peasant households were constituted and the size and structure of households. Moreover, the level of household income and the quality of reproduction of labor power, as well as the possibility for peasant accumulation, were closely governed by the personalized landlord-peasant relationship.

One important element in this relationship was the subordination of women, which while seemingly compensating peasant men for their exploitation, served to increase the surplus labor time appropriated by landlords. Undoubtedly, the particular forms of exploitation of female labor lowered the standard of living of hacienda peasant households. Nevertheless, the hacienda system also offered women and men a greater level of security than was possible within the independent communities, both economic security—access to resources to generate higher levels of household income and the possibility of credit to meet family emergencies—and social security, through the reproduction of household relations that generated family stability and the support and care of elderly parents. As the next chapter shows, household life in both respects differed markedly in the independent peasant communities.

FOUR

The Peasant Household in the Independent Community

In contrast to peasant households on most haciendas, households in the independent peasant communities of the province increasingly participated in capitalist class relations during this period. Although farming was still the principal activity of most households, land shortage and monetization of the rural economy forced a growing number of peasants to seek wage labor. By the end of the 1920s, probably a majority of poor peasant households in the districts of Jesús, Namora, Matara, and Cajamarca had sent a temporary migrant to the sugar plantations of the north coast.

But temporary participation in wage labor did not necessarily signal proletarianization. As Florencia Mallon (1983, 248) notes for the central highlands, temporary migration was often the best insurance policy against complete dispossession. In Cajamarca, migration to the coast was indeed seasonal, tied to the highland agricultural cycle, with the two main periods of migration coming after the fall planting of grains (roughly December to March, depending on the rains and elevation) and after the harvests (June to August).[1] Household reproduction strategies in the highlands continued until the 1950s to frustrate the attempts of the plantations to develop a larger and more stable work force. Not until the end of that decade would permanent migrants to the coast begin to outnumber their temporary and seasonal counterparts (see Chapter 7).

The possibility of wage employment had its initial impact on household

---

1. The seasonal pattern of migration and how it was constrained by the labor requirements of highland peasant agriculture are well documented in the twenty-six community case studies carried out by the Socio-Economic Study Program of the Cajamarca–La Libertad Project. See Chambeu, Garay, and Samaniego (1975, table 1) for a summary of these studies. My own research reveals that the timing of seasonal migration was also related to household composition by age and sex.

reproduction strategies by providing a new source of credit (the enganche system) and a more lucrative alternative to artisan activities. The dead season in highland agriculture had always been the period for carpentry, weaving, sewing, making household utensils (gourd plates, wooden spoons, baskets) and work implements, and carrying out those tasks that had accumulated over the year (making tiles for a new roof or building a penca fence). With the alternative of sending one household member to the coast to earn cash, many of these activities were considerably curtailed as the century progressed—a change that was both a cause and a result of the growing monetization of the rural economy.

Although vigorous population growth on a relatively static land base led to growing fragmentation of peasant holdings during the first half of this century, peasant households also had other income-generating alternatives to forestall their proletarianization. Some households skirted temporary migration by acquiring additional lands in usufruct on the haciendas or by sharecropping the lands of relatives and neighbors. Other households maintained themselves as petty producers by having a household member become a trader or muleteer. In other words, by participating in multiple class relations (both fundamental and subsumed), households were able to remain units of production and reproduction.

The income-generating strategies pursued by the peasantry were closely associated with a household's access to land; this access was in turn related to inheritance practices, the degree of development of the local land market, and the particular locale of the community with respect to a hacienda. Differing household reproduction strategies also reflected particular processes of household formation, as well as the composition of households by gender and age.

Land inheritance within the independent communities was generally bilateral, with all children—male and female—receiving approximately equal shares.[2] This pattern of inheritance had important implications for women's economic position and, especially, for their bargaining position in marriage. In contrast to the hacienda, there was little material basis within the independent peasant communities for patriarchal households. Households in these communities were also much less stable. Although family stability has long been considered a characteristic of peasant societies, common features of village life in the early part of the century in Cajamarca included marital infidelity,

2. The community case studies of the Socio-Economic Study Program also substantiated the fact that the inheritance of land was generally bilateral in the independent communities; see Chambeu, Garay, and Samaniego (1975, 16) and Chambeu (1975c, 12). The only kinds of property that were gender-differentiated in inheritance were kitchen implements, which daughters would inherit, and agricultural tools, which would be divided among sons. The parental homestead was inherited by the child still living at home, who was responsible for caring for the parents in their old age. If no heir resided with the parents, the house might be dismantled upon their death, and the beams, tiles, and other useful materials distributed among the remaining kin.

separation and divorce, childred born out of wedlock, and even the abandonment of children by their parents. These characteristics are illustrated in this
chapter through the life histories of peasant women in two of the independent
communities of the province.

PEASANT COMMUNITIES AND THE STATE

According to the 1940 Peruvian census (Peru 1940, vol. 2, table 34), the
province of Cajamarca contained 382 independent peasant communities. But
to call the villages and the dispersed rural settlements (caseríos) "independent"
because they were situated outside the confines of hacienda property does not
mean that they were independent of the influence of either the haciendas or the
state authority. Before turning to the study of household relations, it is
important first to situate these communities in terms of provincial political
structures and peasant-state relations.

Centralized administrative control by the state extended down to the level of
the districts, where the *gobernador* was appointed by the prefect of the
department from a list drawn up by the subprefect of the province (Málaga
Santolalla 1906, 247). In the early decades of the century, only the most
important villages were deemed worthy of having a *teniente gobernador*,
appointed by the subprefect. During the Leguía presidency, the number of
villages with these direct representatives of the national state increased
considerably, in concert with the modernization of the state apparatus.

Village administration was in the hands of an *agente municipal* who was, in
theory, elected. If the population was less than three hundred, these functionaries were appointed by the elected provincial council. But few peasants recall
participating in elections until recent decades; they considered these positions
to be the appointments of landlords, important pueblo merchants, or "of
Cajamarca" (referring to the capital city and administrative center of the
department). The municipal agents and lieutenant governors were usually
local residents. They tended to be drawn from the middle and rich peasantry,
because few others could afford to pay a replacement while they were away
from their fields, dealing with problem after problem (*"un lío después de otro"*).
According to a 1908 report of the subprefect of the province, it was often hard to
staff these positions. But he also noted that "in some pueblos the position [of
lieutenant governor] constitutes permission to carry out every kind of abuse and
crime" (quoted in Alvarez Saén 1908).[3]

The list of abuses compiled by peasants was probably even longer than the
list described by this concerned subprefect. Topping the list for many was the

3. I did not investigate local political relations in any detail. See Edwards (1912) and Gitlitz
(1975). The most detailed historical study of politics at the local level during this period is Mallon's
(1983) pioneering work.

Municipal Law (Ley Municipál). This statute obligated all citizens to participate in public works projects, both in the local community and in the district capital. The tasks carried out under what at times seemed like forced conscription were trail (and, later, road) maintenance, plaza and school construction, and church repair. This labor obligation did not fall equally on all citizens, nor did these projects always benefit the communities. A great deal of coercion had to be applied to make peasants from the caseríos perform unpaid labor for the pueblos, the district capitals (Burgos and Gaitán 1980, 14). The tension generated between reluctant caseríos and demanding pueblos over these services is one of the major reasons for the proliferation of new district capitals in Peru in the twentieth century.

Projects organized by local municipal agents for their own villages were another matter. Beginning in the 1920s, but particularly in the 1940s, village after village began to build its own school and to demand that the prefect provide teachers. Similarly, the construction of feeder roads between caseríos and the pueblos in the 1940s was often undertaken at local initiative.

Another major source of tension between peasants and the state was the Military Conscription Law of 1898 (Ley de Conscripción Vial), which subjected all males between the ages of nineteen and fifty to military draft. Those between nineteen and twenty-three years of age were chosen by lottery for a three-year service; those who were not chosen were placed on a waiting list. Those older than twenty-three served in a rather complicated reserve system (Málaga Santolalla 1906). The lists of those eligible would be drawn up at the district level by a committee consisting of the governor, the mayor, and the justice of the peace. Military service was not equitably distributed, falling disproportionately on the poor peasantry. Manuel Burgos and Evelio Gaitán (1980, 14) note that the system was riddled with abuse and that peasants were forced to pay substantial sums to avoid being "chosen" by the lottery. Not until the 1940s, however, did significant numbers of peasants actually serve as military recruits.

Much more onerous in the 1920s was Leguía's Road Conscription Law, which required all males between the ages of eighteen and sixty to provide specified amounts of unpaid labor services for road construction. Even in this case, though, not all Peruvians had to perform this service; one could hire a substitute or pay a S/. 10 fine.

Although peasants in Cajamarca were not subject to a property or land tax, they did have to pay a number of indirect taxes that served to transfer a portion of the appropriated surplus labor of petty producers to the state. Particularly regressive was the tax on aguardiente, which in Cajamarca was as heavily consumed as chicha. In 1905 this tax constituted 53 percent of the taxes collected in Cajamarca by the Cia. Nacional de Recaudación, the national tax collection company. The tax on sugar, the second major income source for this company, was somewhat less regressive, because most peasants relied on the locally produced chancaca as a sweetener. The third major source of tax revenue was the sale of official paper and stamps, required for every official transaction (Málaga Santolalla 1906, 271–280). Peasants were to become increasingly adept at using the legal system to solve disputes—not only with landlords, merchants, and other creditors, but also among themselves—over these decades, and thus the sale of these stamps and paper provided another lucrative source of state surplus accumulation.[4] The main source of departmental revenue was a property tax on haciendas, whereas the main source of municipal income was a tax on local trade, charged to those who participated in the weekly pueblo markets (Málaga Santolalla 1906, 262).

The two communities in which the following case studies of household and class relations are located—Pariamarca, in the district of Cajamarca, and La Succha, in the district of Jesús—illustrate some of the province's diversity. Pariamarca is only 12 kilometers from the departmental capital, slightly less than a two-hour walk. Its location largely explains its early integration into the city's product and labor market. In 1940 the village center held sixty households, with a population of 245; its administrative area of influence spanned thirteen annexes with a total population of 3,532 (Hafer 1971, table 1.1). Because of its proximity to the capital city, however, Pariamarca never developed as a marketing center or as a focal point of political or social activity.

Pariamarca is on the western slope of the Cajamarca Valley, at an elevation ranging from 2,700 to 3,100 meters (Hafer 1971, 3). Near the valley bottom, the lands are quite fertile, and corn and wheat are grown. At higher altitudes, cultivable land is dedicated to potatoes and other tubers, barley, or garlic; at still higher elevations, the land is sandy and poor, suitable only for grazing. Few haciendas were located on this side of the valley, and only one, the Hacienda San Antonio, exerted some influence over the villagers of Pariamarca. The extension of this hacienda was small, however, and in the 1920s and 1930s only sixteen families sharecropped lands here. In this period, few Pariamarcan households owned more than 5 hectares of land. Most households participated in wage labor, either in the city of Cajamarca or through seasonal migration to the north coast.

The caserío of La Succha is at the southern end of the Cajamarca Valley, about forty minutes by trail from the district capital of Jesús, which serves as

---

4. Almost every life history I collected included at least one official litigation, whether over provisions of an inheritance or the delineation of property lines. The notary records of Cajamarca have only recently been opened for historical examination and will certainly yield a wealth of data on the extent to which peasants relied on the judicial system. A photo in Málaga Santolalla's (1906, 197) monograph—depicting a long line of peasants waiting outside the building that housed the court and other government offices in Cajamarca—hints at what awaits future researchers. The best-documented study of peasant use of the legal system in Peru during this period is, again, Mallon (1983, 156, 212).

marketing and administrative center for villagers within the district. The district capital was connected to the city of Cajamarca in 1920 by a 20-kilometer road. In 1940 the pueblo of Jesús had 1,401 inhabitants (Peru 1940, vol. 2, table 34), fewer than the 1,885 counted in 1876 (Peru 1876b), reflecting the heavy emigration from the district during this period.[5] The village of La Succha registered ninety-four households in 1940, with a total population of 462.

The district of Jesús is at a lower elevation than the district of Cajamarca, with La Succha situated at approximately 2,500 meters. The soils are generally considered fertile, but since the turn of the century land pressure has been acute. Moreover, the communities on the eastern slope of the river valley had minimal access to grazing pastures, as compared to those on the western slope. The eastern highlands (jalca) of this valley belonged to various small haciendas of the districts of Namora and Matara. Throughout the first half of the twentieth century, peasants from La Succha and neighboring communities rented pastures on these haciendas; they also migrated in significant numbers on both a seasonal and a permanent basis to the northern coast.

The following analysis of household and class relations at the village level is based on life histories of two peasant women, María Rumay of Pariamarca, born in 1912, and Rosa Fernández of La Succha, born in 1911.[6]

GROWING UP IN PARIAMARCA, 1910–1930

María Rumay, like her older sister, was born out of wedlock. Her young mother was the *enamorada* of a relatively prosperous Cajamarcan middle peasant. María was only nine months old when her mother died from a bad fall, which apparently caused her to hemorrhage. María's three-year-old sister died shortly thereafter from fright (*espanto*).

María was raised by her aunt and her grandparents. María's aunt had a daughter a year older than María, also born out of wedlock, and María considers this cousin her sister. Her aunt went to live with another man when María was about five years old, and she and her cousin stayed with their

5. See Llanos Aguero (1972, 101–102) for the argument that the permanent migration of peasants from Jesús to the coast contributed to the decline of the district capital. Bazán (1978, 41, 74) found that 80 percent of the households in the Community of Hualqui had sent a migrant to the coast at some point. He believes that the massive emigration from Jesús did not occur until 1940, the year the Casa Grande recruitment office in this pueblo was set up. He notes, however, that Casa Grande recruiters worked the villages in the northern section of the district, such as Yanamango and Huacariz, earlier than 1940.

6. I began to collect the life histories in 1976; they are based on multiple interviews with María over a twelve-month period and with Rosa over a six-month period. I also lived in Rosa's home for two weeks in the fall of 1976. The data presented here were rechecked with members of both households during a return visit in December 1981. The names of the women and their families have been changed to protect their privacy.

grandparents. This was not an uncommon pattern, for, as María explained years later, "What man would like it if a woman brought her children by another man into marriage?"

When María was nine years old, she learned that her mother had allegedly been killed by the wife of her biological father. At the annual Pariamarca fiesta, María was standing next to her aunt and the aunt's *compañero* when they overheard a conversation between the local *brujo* (witch doctor) and her father's wife. They were laughing about how they had succeeded in putting a spell on her mother and causing her death. María vividly remembers how her uncle (her aunt's compañero), the teniente of Pariamarca, beat up the brujo. Although her uncle was the highest political and legal authority in the village, there was no thought of prosecuting the brujo. Instead, after beating him up, her uncle simply urinated in his mouth. Her mother's death had been avenged in the eyes of the community.

From the time María was little, her grandmother, Celestina, counseled her never to become involved with a married man. Celestina greatly lamented that two of her three daughters had become involved with married men; in her opinion, such involvement had caused one daughter's death. Her grandmother warned María that a young woman shouldn't trust men, because they would take advantage of her, she also blamed women for not being able to keep their men faithful: "You should never leave your home. Always stay with the man so that he won't abandon you, leaving you pregnant."

But it was not unusual that María and her cousin had been born from such informal unions. For men, it was a source of prestige to have an enamorada, although only the wealthiest villagers could actually maintain more than one household (Althaus 1975, 28). Both María and her cousin had been recognized by their respective fathers, who turned out to be brothers.

María's great-grandfather had owned a considerable amount of land in Pariamarca. The major portion of the hill on which María's family resides today had once belonged to the family. But by the time María was born, her grandfather owned only 2 hectares or so, just enough to satisfy the household's basic grain requirements.

Celestina earned the family's cash income through her trading activities. From her neighbors she bought garlic, and from artisans near the city of Cajamarca she bought earthen pots, which she sold in the market of Jesús, then a two-day mule ride from Pariamarca. On Sundays, peasants from all over the district brought their produce to Jesús, where Celestina purchased corn, beans, lentils, and peppers to later resell in the market of the city of Cajamarca.

Celestina also dyed wool as a source of income. She was considered the expert dyer of the village, and peasants from miles around brought their wool to her. María and her cousin were charged with collecting wood for the fire that would be used to boil the dye mixture. Celestina waited until she had thirty or forty pounds of wool before she began to dye it, and María and her cousin would have to spend three or four days gathering sufficient wood. They also helped their grandmother prepare the spun yarn for dyeing, wrapping it around poles to form "rabbit ears." After it was dyed, they wound the wool into balls.

The two cousins also helped with the agricultural field work. Upon her husband's death, Celestina had taken charge of agricultural production. She did all the agricultural tasks except plowing, and for that she paid a neighbor. The family had never owned its own oxen; when María's grandfather was alive, he had exchanged his labor for the use of a team. The usual exchange was one day of male labor for each day's use of an ox. Without a man in the household, Celestina had to pay cash both for the team of oxen and for a worker to plow.

Perhaps because of the difficulty of trying to manage agricultural production and maintain her trading activities at the same time, Celestina quickly found a new partner. Her new compañero was much younger than she was, a landless worker from outside the village who had migrated to the city of Cajamarca. According to María, Celestina simply brought him home from the market one day. He subsequently assumed the heavy agricultural work, although the girls continued to help in weeding and harvesting. In her forties, Celestina had her fourth daughter with this man.

While their grandmother traded, María and her cousin usually stayed at home, looking after the baby and the animals. When they were eight or nine, their grandmother began to accumulate a small herd of sheep so the girls could be productively employed. They then spent their days wandering up and down the village paths and on the steep hillsides of the mountain seeking pasture for the herd. Grazing lands were scarce, and their household did not have sufficient land to let a field lie fallow so that the sheep could at least graze on weeds during the rainy season. María and her cousin attended school only for one year, the year they were twelve. María wanted to continue, but her grandmother could not afford to pay for the pencils and notebooks.[7]

María first participated in agricultural work for wages when she was about ten. In the 1920s, Pariamarca was an important center of garlic production. Peasants who planted garlic usually held a special minga for the labor-intensive harvest, inviting everyone from the village to participate. Work began around six in the morning; everything that was harvested before the midday meal was served, around one o'clock, constituted the owner's crop. After lunch, the people harvested for themselves, earning their wage (*el jornalito*). María recalls that when she was only twelve she was able to harvest a full arroba of garlic (25 pounds), worth close to S/. 0.20, the equivalent of the male agricultural wage in the village. Celestina then sold the garlic in the Jesús market.

---

7. The cousins probably attended a private school, because the first public school in Pariamarca was not built until 1944; thus the cost of schooling must have also included tuition. The school must have been in existence for some time, however, because María's aunts also completed the first grade. In 1912 there were only 161 primary schools in the entire department (Edwards 1912, 23).

Celestina's young partner also worked as a wage laborer. In the early 1920s, he worked on the road that was being built from Cajamarca to the coast under President Leguía's Road Conscription Law. María remembers this as paid work; payment was the only way workers would stay on the job, given the more lucrative alternative of migrating to the coast. But her grandmother's partner did not care for the coast and preferred to earn S/. 0.15 per day working near home. María thought that her grandmother earned at least this much from her trading activities, for Celestina sometimes returned with as much as 1 sol when she made the full trading round from Pariamarca to Cajamarca and Jesús and back.

Celestina controlled the household's finances and managed to save enough from her trading activities and her partner's wages to buy almost 1 hectare of land. According to María, her partner took advantage of Celestina's lack of education and registered the land title in his name only. Not long after, he abandoned Celestina, running away with her niece. This was considered to be quite a betrayal, for female family members usually showed more solidarity toward one another with respect to amorous relationships. He subsequently sold the parcel of land and, because it was registered in his name, kept all the profits. Celestina never forgave him on either count. Several years later, when the niece died during childbirth, he tried to return to Celestina, but she would not have anything to do with him.

Celestina paid a high price for this involvement. She not only lost her savings but also was disinherited by her own mother, who had disapproved of her relationship with a man who was much younger and who was a landless worker from outside the village. Celestina's mother died the year before the couple split up. Her attitudes suggest that she might have been from the rural petty bourgeoisie. It was actually quite common for older women to form unions with younger men, particularly if the woman owned land (Chambeu 1975c, 20).

After Celestina was abandoned by her partner, she sharecropped out her remaining land, for she considered herself too old to take charge of the agricultural work. At this time, she also designated how the property would be divided after her death. Because the 2 hectares had belonged to her first husband, the land was to be divided between their three daughters. María was to receive what would have been her mother's share. When María's mother died, however, her grandmother had taken out what is termed an *hipoteca* from one of the richer peasants of the village to pay the costs of the funeral. The hipoteca is a form of loan whereby the lender gets the usufruct rights of a land parcel until the loan is repaid. María's aunts had tried to pay back the loan in order to work the additional land, but the rich villager refused to return the land, treating the hipoteca as if it had been a land sale. The lost parcels were considered part of María's inheritance, because they had been put in hipoteca to pay the costs of her mother's funeral. Thus María was to inherit only four-tenths of a hectare of land.

Although María's father had recognized her as his child, she inherited nothing from him. He would give her presents, a few *reales* (cents) whenever she ran into him. She had hoped that he would remember her when he died. He did call her to his deathbed, but by the time she arrived he was unable to speak, and no one ever determined what he had wanted to tell her.

At the age of fifteen, María found herself on her own when her grandmother died. She tried living with each of her aunts, but things did not work out. She sold the sheep she had inherited from her grandmother, sharecropped out her inheritance of land, and went to the city of Cajamarca to find work as a maid. Her first job was with the Noriega family, at that time the landlord-arrendires of a small fundo called Las Torrecitas in the valley of Cajamarca. María stayed with them only six months before one of her aunts made her quit, believing that the Noriegas were working her too hard. Not only did she have to cook for the patron's family, but she was also made to wash and peel the wheat and barley brought in from the fundo for sale in Cajamarca. They were forcing her to do semanera work, which, according to María's kin, was not appropriate for a maid.

Maids, by the very fact that they were "free" workers, were generally considered a social step above the "hacienda Indias." Moreover, María was from one of the independent peasant communities that had not been subject to servile relations with a hacienda. And María, like many peasants from Pariamarca, was white. Her family considered it demeaning that she was being treated like "just another India."

In this first job (in 1927), María had earned S/. 2.50 per month plus room and board.[8] In her second job, with a Chinese merchant family in Cajamarca, she earned almost double that amount. Her salary was now sufficient for her to clothe herself (one could buy cloth for a blouse for approximately S/. 0.50), as well as save a sol or two. In three years, she saved enough to quit her job as a maid and, with her capital, to begin trading. At first, she limited her activities to buying products in Pariamarca and taking them to sell in small piles on the sidewalks of the marketplace in the city of Cajamarca. But before long she was buying products in Cajamarca and taking them by burro to different parts of the valley, as her grandmother had done. Her favorite trip was between

8. Elespuru Bernizón (1939, 57) reported that at the time he was writing "free" maids in the city of Cajamarca earned between S/. 1.00 and S/. 1.50 per month plus room and board. The higher earnings reported by María for the previous decade could be the product of faulty memory or could reflect the immigration of large numbers of young women into the city of Cajamarca in the 1930s, causing wages to fall. The latter interpretation is supported by the widely reported observation that free maids had replaced semaneras by the 1940s. For a comparison of female and male earning opportunities, note that the daily wage reported by Elespuru Bernizón for free agricultural workers in the province in the late 1930s was S/. 0.80 plus food; thus, a full-time male wage worker (working twenty-four days) could have earned approximately S/. 19 per month, as compared to a maid's S/. 1.00 to S/. 1.50.

Asunción, in the western highlands, and Cajamarca. She purchased clay pots in the city to sell in Asunción and bought hot peppers there to resell in the city market. Over the course of the next fifteen years, she worked the markets of Namora, San Marcos, La Encañada, and Chetilla, as well as Asunción, "always buying and selling."

At the age of nineteen, she formed her first union, with a man from Pariamarca. Her aunts wanted them to marry formally, but María did not consider that important. They went to live with his family, which turned out to be a mistake, for María did not get along at all with her mother-in-law. Her mother-in-law continually complained about María's trading activities, claiming that she would not stay home long enough "to be useful." But María was also helping her partner. He worked the black market in aguardiente, purchasing the sugar cane alcohol on the coast and distributing it in Cajamarca and Namora. To avoid paying taxes, he had to transport and distribute the alcohol at night, and María usually accompanied him, carrying out her own trading activities.

María blames her mother-in-law for this man abandoning her after only two years. Needing cash, his parents asked him to take an advance from the Casa Grande agency in Cajamarca. He promised to stay on the coast only long enough to pay back the advance, but he never returned to Pariamarca. Such behavior was repeated with increasing frequency throughout the province.

After several months, María's mother-in-law threw her out of the house, leaving María alone with a six-month-old baby. She went to live in a house that she and her cousin had inherited from Celestina on the plaza of Pariamarca. It was then that she realized the importance of having one's own property: she had somewhere to go when she was abandoned. María blames herself for the death of her daughter shortly thereafter, saying that she hated her mother-in-law so much that it tainted her breast milk and gave her daughter *colera*.

GROWING UP IN JESÚS, 1910–1930

Rosa Fernández grew up in the town of Jesús. Her mother's family was from La Shita, a village to the west of Jesús, but her grandmother had always maintained a good house in the pueblo. The family had quite a bit of land in La Shita, and the dual residence suggests that they were from the rich peasant stratum. In contrast, her father was from a poor peasant household in Cebadín, an hour's walk south of Jesús. He had left home at an early age to learn the basket-weaving trade in the pueblo. Jesús was noted for its fine wicker and reed baskets, some of which were exported to the coast.

Her parents had met in the pueblo, and, when Rosa was born, her father earned the household's cash income through his artisan activities. He was a womanizer ("*muy mujeriego*"); soon after Rosa was born, he was caught in the bed of a lover by the woman's husband. He was beaten until he was left crippled. He died a few years later, when Rosa was only three and her mother pregnant with a third child.

Less than a year after his death, Rosa's mother ran off with a man from the jalcas near Huayobamba. She left each of her three children with different neighbors. Although Rosa's grandmother was quite old by then, she considered it a disgrace that Rosa's mother had abandoned her children, so she brought them to live with her.[9] Rosa remembers these as wonderful years. She and her sister raised her younger brother and tended her grandmother's small animals. They never suffered from want, for the grandmother sharecropped out the family lands in La Shita, and the household had a steady source of foodstuffs and income.

But her grandmother died when Rosa was eight. Her mother had moved back to Jesús the previous year with her new husband and his four children. Rosa did not want to live with them, but she had no other choice. Her older sister went to live with their paternal grandmother in Cebadín, but that side of the family was too poor to take in Rosa and her brother as well.

Rosa's stepfather was a trader and muleteer. Although he did quite well by Jesús standards, he refused to send his sons or Rosa to school. And Rosa lived in terror of him. Reportedly, he was a drunk and often violent. One night, he almost killed one of his sons with a hatchet, because the son had forgotten to tie up the sheep. Soon after, when she was nine, Rosa obtained a job as a maid and moved out.

In her first job, where she was charged with looking after some small children, Rosa was paid only room and board and was sometimes given used clothing. After several years with this family, she found another job, where she was paid small tips. Her employers also clothed her and her brother, whom she continued to look after.

About this time, Rosa's stepfather convinced her mother to sell the family inheritance in La Shita. Rosa went to the local judge and begged him not to let her mother sell the land: "What will happen to us if we don't have any land? Where will we go?" The judge explained that he could have blocked the sale if it had been her father's land, because Rosa would have been an underage heir, but that her mother had the right to do anything she pleased with her own inheritance. The family land was sold.

Rosa then started planning how to leave Jesús for Lima. She thought she could easily obtain a job as a maid in Lima, for she had heard of other pueblo girls finding work without difficulty in the nation's capital. But her worry was her younger brother. Rosa had managed to pay for books and a uniform for him

9. There was a definite stigma to being raised by others, particularly by those who were not members of the family. Such orphans were called *huacchas*, stray sheep. My fieldwork suggests that this was fairly common, however; also see Chambeu's (1975c, 23) study of Jocos in the district of Matara.

to start school. If she left, she was certain her stepfather would take him out of school and make him work on his mule train, as his own sons did.

Before she could act on her plan, her mother forced her to marry Julio Sangay of La Succha. Julio had seen her in the plaza of Jesús and wrote Rosa a letter asking for her hand. Rosa, who was only fifteen, was shocked. She did not answer the letter, and she avoided Julio as much as possible on market days when he came to town. The next year, however, Julio visited Rosa's mother and arranged the marriage. Rosa was terrified. She really did not know Julio and did not want to marry him. Nonetheless, in 1927 they were married in the church on the plaza of Jesús.

After their marriage, they settled in La Succha, a village that was a forty-minute walk from Jesús, with Julio's widowed mother. Julio was one of eight brothers, although by that time only two other brothers lived at home. The other five had all migrated permanently to the coast. The three remaining sons jointly worked the family lands, approximately 3 hectares.

Rosa was miserable during the first years of her marriage. It was not because she had been raised in Jesús and now had to live in the countryside, for the lines between town and country were somewhat blurred. Rather, she suffered the more common affliction of young brides who resided with their mothers-in-law: in Rosa's words, "I was expected to be the maid." In addition, she did not like her husband much. She resented the fact that her mother had forced her to marry him, supposedly "for her own good." Finally, when she arrived in La Succha, she learned that Julio had already had a wife, a woman older than he was, who had abandoned him for another man. He had three children by her, but only one son was still alive.

One day, Julio's first wife returned from the coast with their seven-year-old son, wanting Julio to take responsibility for the child. Rosa was upset and refused. She hated the woman, hated Julio, and hated her mother and mother-in-law. She felt sorry for the son, however, because she too had been abandoned by her mother. Julio's mother finally agreed to raise the child, and Rosa was relieved. But her mother-in-law really did not want the child around, and the boy was miserable. He finally returned to his mother's home, contracted pneumonia, and died. Rosa thought it was his own mother's doing, because the woman had bathed him at night.

After Rosa had been married for two years, her mother died during childbirth. Although Rosa had had a stormy relationship with her mother, she felt compelled to give her a good funeral, which she knew her stepfather was incapable of doing. Proper funerals were expensive: one had to buy a casket and pay a priest to give a mass; one also had to provide plentiful food and aguardiente for the wake. Rosa convinced Julio to take out an advance from the Casa Grande labor contractor in Jesús to pay the costs.

Julio was experienced in the ways of coastal migration. His first migration had been made at the age of twelve. He had gone *socorrido* with his uncle, who had acted as his guarantor. Several of his older brothers already lived at Casa Grande, and he and his uncle usually stayed with them during the four months they spent on the coast. Julio's first job on the plantation was to plant cane, a job reserved for young boys, who were paid half the adult wage.[10] Before his marriage to Rosa, he had migrated nearly every year. In the early years, he always took an advance, but more recently, since he was known at Casa Grande, he simply migrated on his own and always found work.

Women from Jesús seldom accompanied their men when they migrated seasonally.[11] Rosa, however, refused to stay alone with her mother-in-law and convinced Julio to let her go with him. They left La Succha for the Casa Grande plantation in late 1929. Accompanying them was Rosa's fourteen-year-old brother, whom she refused to leave behind.

STRATEGIES OF THE NEAR-LANDLESS:
THE AGUILAR-RUMAY HOUSEHOLD, 1930–1950

In 1933 María married Manuel Aguilar in a formal church ceremony. This time, she was determined not to be fooled by a man; marriage in the church appeared to promise more security.[12] Manuel was the son of Pariamarcan middle peasants; his father owned 4.5 hectares of fairly good land. His four brothers and sisters had all migrated from Pariamarca. When his father died, Manuel sharecropped the family lands with his mother. When María married him, his prospects as an agriculturalist looked quite good. Soon after their marriage, however, Manuel's mother died without having formally divided the land among her five children. Because she had left no will, it was up to the five to actually divide the land inheritance.

The siblings fought bitterly over the division. Everyone wanted the best parcels, those which had access to irrigation. The five split into two camps. Manuel and a brother wanted to draw straws for each of the major land parcels,

10. Young boys made up the plantation work force for planting through at least the 1940s. Another life history, that of Abelardo Rojas (collected in December 1981), revealed that he too had migrated to Casa Grande at the age of twelve. In 1934, as many as 120 boys might have been working each day in these planting activities, earning S/. 0.50 per day plus half a food ration. Rojas believed that the great majority of these young migrants were from the districts of Jesús and Cajamarca.

11. Although few women from Jesús migrated to the coast during this period, there are reports of women from other regions of the department accompanying their men. According to Gonzales (1980, 309), it was not unusual for migrants from Bambamarca to the plantation Cayalti to migrate with their families.

12. Although both couples described here were married in the church, they were the exception rather than the rule in Cajamarca; both Jesús and Pariamarca, unlike many other communities in Cajamarca, had functioning parishes at that time. Elespuru Bernizón (1939, 157) reported that there were few formal weddings in the independent peasant communities he observed in the 1930s.

thus ensuring that each parcel was large enough to make plowing worthwhile. The other three wanted to divide each parcel into five segments, thus ensuring that each sibling received land of comparable quality. At one point, physical violence between the brothers broke out, and even María and her sister-in-law started pulling each other's hair. Finally, the group of three sought redress in the courts of Cajamarca. As a result, the lands were embargoed and could not be worked. The court embargo (*juicio*) lasted fifteen years.

María and Manuel suffered most from the suit, for they were the only ones trying to succeed as petty producers. Manuel's brothers and sisters all lived in the city of Cajamarca and had jobs. For most of their married life, María and Manuel would have access to minimal amounts of land. The only piece of property was María's inheritance, four-tenths of a hectare of land. The burden of generating the household's income was also to fall primarily on María.

María had not stopped her trading activities when she married. She had settled into a pattern of working the Namora and Asunción markets primarily on alternate Saturdays; she was usually gone from home for three days at a time. During the week, she sold on the sidewalks of the Cajamarca market the products she had purchased in the outlying districts. According to her, in the 1930s, one could do quite well as a trader, for there was little competition. Sometimes Manuel accompanied María to market, to help her load the sacks of grain, but small-scale trading was a woman's activity. Only women could sit on the sidewalks and sell their produce in small mounds. This was a more lucrative activity than having a stand in the marketplace, especially if one had minimal capital.

Manuel did accompany her regularly to the annual potato harvest in La Encañada. They would bring gifts of salt and other products from the city to friends in that area, and, in return for the gifts, they would be assigned a row of potatoes to harvest for their own benefit. The size of the row depended on the quality and quantity of the gifts. Because their labor in the potato harvest was part of a commercial venture—they later resold the potatoes in Cajamarca— they usually arrived in La Encañada with two or three burros loaded down. This practice was a variant of the typical exchange of products that took place between peasants living at different ecological levels. In María's case, the practice reflected the fact that she was a trader and an experienced buyer in the city markets.

Continual pregnancy and lactation seemed not to hamper María's trading activities. She would take the baby that she was currently nursing with her, while the other children stayed at home, first under her husband's supervision and, later, her eldest daughter's. María had a child almost every two years until she was thirty-nine years old. Only four of her seven children, all daughters, survived past early childhood.

María gave birth to all her children at home with the help of the local midwife, her *comadre*. Her comadre was considered one of the best midwives in

Pariamarca, for very few women or babies died when she was attending. María lost all three of her sons, at the age of two or three, in the same way, of a diarrhea that dehydrated them. She accepted this as God's will, but at the same time she was somewhat bitter that none of her sons lived. A son could have protected her. She blames her husband's abandonment of her in old age on the fact that she never gave him a surviving son.

Manuel tried migrating to the coast several times to earn wage income, but he did not like the work. In 1935 he went to Chepén to work in the rice harvest; although he easily found work, he returned after only fifteen days. He tried again several years later, when María's trading income fell as a result of the drought in the highlands; but the drought had affected the rice plantings on the coast, and this time he had difficulty finding work.

Throughout the period that María and Manuel were raising their family, they had to sharecrop the lands of other villagers in order to grow their corn and beans. It was María, offering gifts of eggs or a chicken, who usually had to convince her relatives and other neighbors to sharecrop with them. Manuel was much too proud. In a good year, they secured access to four or five parcels, so that in total they might have almost a hectare in production.

Manuel was in charge of the agricultural work. While their daughters were young, he exchanged labor with male relatives or neighbors whenever he needed help in the fields. Sometimes, when they had cash, they paid a peon to help with some of the heaviest tasks. Whenever nonhousehold labor was utilized for agricultural work, María stayed home from her trading activities to cook the large midday meal for the workers. María's daughters began helping in the fields when they were six or seven. They accompanied their father just "as if they were boys." They weeded corn, garlic, and barley and worked in the harvests, doing a good job by the time they were twelve or so. María considered that they carried their own weight as adult workers by the time they were fifteen. The daughters also helped cook for the peons; at the age of twelve, her eldest daughter could handle the cooking by herself, freeing María to pursue her trading activities.

The daughters also accompanied Manuel whenever he worked as an agricultural laborer in the village. Each daughter was earning the equivalent of an adult's wage by the time she was fifteen. In the 1940s, harvest labor was still remunerated in kind during the harvests, usually an almud of barley or peas (approximately 18 pounds). Even though María had worked as an agricultural laborer herself as a child, she lamented the fact that her daughters had to go to work on their neighbors' land, considering it a public sign of their economic difficulties.

María's daughters also shared in the domestic work, helped care for the household's sheep and smaller animals, and aided in spinning the wool that was produced each year. Her eldest, Francisca, gradually assumed primary responsibility for domestic chores and cared for the younger children of the family, freeing María to trade. Because of her household responsibilities, Francisca finished only first grade. María did value schooling, however, and her other three daughters finished second grade.

The second major tragedy of the Aguilár-Rumay household occurred in 1945, when their house burned down. They never determined exactly how the fire started, although María thought that it might have been set by one of Manuel's brothers. They lost everything in the fire—all their blankets, clothes, pots, and what money María had stowed away.

After the fire, María tried to move back to her house on the plaza, but one of her nephews was living in it, and he refused to give it up. As the son of María's cousin, he did have a claim on the house. María did not try to fight; one family juicio was simply enough. Instead, she, Manuel, and their four daughters lived in a *chosita* (a straw hut), "just like pigs," according to María, until they could save enough to build a proper adobe home. María encouraged Manuel to migrate to the coast to earn some income, but he refused. It took five years to save enough money from her trading activities to build a home as good as their last one, with clay tiles on the roof.

The Aguilar family dispute over land was finally settled with the intervention of Dr. Pastor, the owner of the only hacienda in the vicinity of Pariamarca. Manuel's father had rented lands from the Hacienda San Antonio in the 1920s and had bought two of the disputed parcels from him. Pastor sided with Manuel in the family dispute, because Manuel was the only sibling who had worked the lands. Pastor used his influence, and the courts finally ruled in Manuel's favor, but not until 1949.

In the final settlement, Manuel received slightly more land than the other brothers, a total of about 1 hectare. Most of the parcels were left intact, with the exception of the irrigated lands, which were divided equally into five very small strips. Of Manuel's four siblings, only his sister ever worked her share of the land directly. The others sharecropped out their land to relatives in the area.

Once Manuel had his land back, María started to reduce her trading activities. The all-weather road linking Cajamarca to the coast had been completed in 1945, opening up the district markets to large-scale truck trade. Small traders like María found it difficult to compete. With only a pair of burros, one could not buy as much and consequently had to pay more for the goods. According to María, "the large merchants with their trucks ruined it all."

PROLETARIANIZATION AND RETURN TO FARMING: THE SANGAY-FERNANDEZ HOUSEHOLD, 1930–1950

Rosa and Julio were among the forerunners of a trend—permanent migration to the coast—that gained momentum over the next decades. Like many

Cajamarquinos, they planned to migrate for only a short time, long enough to pay back the advance and accumulate some savings, but they ended up staying five years. Perhaps they were most unusual in that they did eventually return to the Cajamarcan highlands to farm.

When they arrived at Casa Grande, Julio, Rosa, and her brother first went to live with Julio's cousin, a permanent worker on the plantation. Living conditions were crowded, with eight of them sleeping in one room. But conditions with Julio's brothers, the only alternative, would have been even worse. Rosa became accustomed to the situation, as well as to the ways of the coastal woman who was the current companion of Julio's cousin.[13]

Rosa and Julio planned to stay at the plantation only one year. They had borrowed approximately S/. 200 from the enganchador, and they thought they could pay off the debt at the rate of S/. 1.00 per day and still have enough to live on, for the hacienda also gave each worker a ration of a pound of rice and meat per day worked, which Rosa cooked for the three of them. The average wage on Casa Grande, including the value of food rations, was then about S/. 1.75 per day (Hunt 1977, table 12).

At the end of the first year, they had not paid back even half their debt. Life on the coast was much more expensive than Julio had recalled, and their first child, Teodoro, had been born. Julio decided to apply for permanent status in the plantation work force. This status entitled them to their own room in the plantation housing complex and guaranteed that Julio would not be laid off during the dead season, when the mill was closed for cleaning and repairs.

Julio was happy with work on the plantation. Rosa, however, longed for the sierra. She found it hard to get used to the bustle of the company town, and it was difficult to find work.[14] The main income-generating activities for women in the plantation town were to wash or cook for groups of single men or to make chicha for sale. Julio was jealous and did not want her to mingle with other men,

13. Rosa was quite disdainful of the "loose" morality and character of coastal women. Her view of family life on the plantation was similar to that reported by de Osma (1912) and Miller (1967). Miller found that all the men and women in his study who were over the age of forty and had been on the coast for more than ten years had been married at least twice and that it was common to find people who had been in three or four relationships. Moreover, he reported that men almost never claimed the children from such unions; when a union broke up, the man usually moved to another plantation, and the woman hurriedly tried to find another man so that she would not be evicted from plantation housing. That was usually relatively easy to do, because women were still somewhat scarce on the coast, even in the 1960s.

14. According to Rosa, Casa Grande did not employ women for any task. Data provided by Albert (1976, tables 44–46) show that some women were employed as field hands in the Chicama Valley plantations earlier, between 1912 and 1922, becoming at most 2.3 percent of the work force in 1917. The employment of women was more prevalent in the central and southern sugar-producing valleys, where greater numbers of Japanese immigrants were employed. These immigrants usually came from Japan in family groups.

and Rosa was not eager to turn her home into a *chicheria*. Yet she hated not having something "useful" to do and being totally dependent on Julio for her needs. At least in the highlands one could always raise animals.

Rosa also did not like Julio's behavior on the coast. He always lingered in the chicherias or canteens after work and was turning into a drunk, often physically abusing her (*"con el aguardiente vienen los golpes"*).[15] Moreover, as the years passed, she felt that they were making little material progress. They were continually in debt, and although they had finally paid back their original advance, they had not managed to save much. Rosa did feel good about the fact that her brother was able to go to secondary school. He still lived with them, and he contributed to the household economy by doing odd jobs around Casa Grande and working in the fields during school vacations. The final blow for Rosa came when her brother contracted tuberculosis, still a common disease on the coast in this period, and died at the age of nineteen.

After five years on the coast, Rosa finally convinced Julio to ask for a month's leave to visit Cajamarca. Once in La Succha, she convinced him to stay. His mother agreed to divide up the family property, and Julio inherited approximately half a hectare of land, which he sharecropped with his mother until her death. He also sharecropped several of the parcels that made up the inheritance of the brothers who were living on the coast. With the savings they had accumulated on the coast, Rosa and Julio were able to buy a few animals and build an adobe house on Julio's land.

Rosa was pregnant when they returned from the coast, but she lost this daughter at birth. She soon was pregnant again, and in 1937 Lucho was born. The couple needed more land to work, so about this time they became arrendires of the Hacienda Miche, in the jalca near San Nicolás Lake, to the east of La Succha. They were to rent lands on this hacienda for the next twenty-six years.

By Cajamarcan standards, the Hacienda Miche was rather small, covering perhaps 300 hectares of land. In 1940 only ten households lived on the hacienda itself, all sharecropping with the landlord (Peru 1940, vol. 2, table 34). Only these households provided labor services, consisting of repair work on the irrigation canal or hacienda trails several times a year. Because the landlord did not even have a house on the property and never became interested in farming the hacienda himself, he usually left the peasants to their own self-interests, coming out only during the potato harvest to collect his half of the crop.

The bulk of hacienda land was rented out as grazing pastures to peasants from neighboring communities such as La Succha. According to Rosa, perhaps thirty or forty families grazed their animals on the hacienda; only a few families

15. The problem of alcoholism among the sugar cane plantation work force was a recurrent theme of contemporaries. See de Osma (1912, 19).

actually rented cultivable land, as Rosa and Julio did. When they first began renting, they paid S/. 10 per hectare per growing season for their 2.5 hectares. In addition, they paid S/. 0.50 per head of sheep grazed on the common pasture of the hacienda.

Rosa dedicated herself to sheep raising. In most years, she had a herd of between fifteen and twenty-five head. Every morning, after making breakfast and feeding her pigs, chickens, and guinea pigs, she walked the 5 kilometers to the hacienda's common pasture, taking all her children with her. By the mid-1940s, she had five children, four sons and a daughter. She carried the baby on her back, and the older children helped her look after the sheep. As she grazed her sheep, she spun her wool and the children played. On their way home, they all collected wood for the fire. Besides housework, child care, and animal raising, Rosa became a weaver. She usually wove two blankets each year for the household and made a poncho or two for the children.

Julio was in charge of the agricultural work. He planted barley and potatoes on the lands rented from the hacienda and corn, beans, potatoes, and alfalfa on his lands in La Succha. He usually met his additional labor needs through labor exchanges with the two brothers who resided in the village. Sometimes Rosa helped in the fields, but usually she cooked for the workers and watched the children and sheep. She did not care for field work, so she was quite happy when her eldest son, Teodoro, could replace her in the fields. He started helping his father when he was only five or six, and Rosa claimed that at this age he did much more field work than she ever did. By the time Teodoro was twelve, he could handle the oxen with ease.

Rosa was in charge of marketing the farm produce. They never sold large quantities of agricultural or animal products. Rather, every Sunday, Rosa took 25 pounds of potatoes or barley or a stack of alfalfa to sell in small piles or bundles at the Jesús market. With what she earned that day, she then bought the household's weekly necessities: salt, cooking oil, soap, candles, and matches. Two or three times a year, when they had to make a larger purchase such as agricultural tools or clothing, they would sell one of Rosa's animals. Following the common pattern among smallholders in the independent peasant communities (Elespuru Bernizón 1939, 157), Rosa managed the family finances.

By the late 1940s, Rosa and Julio were doing quite well by La Succha standards. They worked 3 hectares of land, which, in most years, was sufficient to meet their basic consumption needs. They had also managed to save enough from their sales of sheep, pigs, and good crops to buy the major farm animals that would help them to be self-sufficient. Counting the ox Julio had inherited from his mother, they now had three oxen, two burros, and a horse, along with a good-sized herd of sheep, several pigs, and numerous chickens and guinea pigs. Their two older sons finished the second grade, the highest level of schooling available in La Succha, and in their teens worked full-time with Julio in the fields. The third son was in school in Jesús, and they hoped he would finish primary school. At home with Rosa was her young daughter and the baby, Rodolfo. For the first time in her life, Rosa was quite content.

CONCLUSION

The life histories of María and Rosa illustrate how the commonly cited characteristics of family instability—informal and extramarital unions, the abandonment of women and children—were features of peasant life in Cajamarca even before this region was substantially proletarianized. The integration of the Cajamarcan peasantry into capitalist class relations during this period only accentuated these practices.

Even before the development of wage labor and male migration, two factors distinguished household relations on haciendas from those within the independent communities: the form in which households were constituted as units of production and the way community mores and social sanctions were determined and applied. On the haciendas, households were constituted as units of production and reproduction by virtue of their participation in feudal class relations. Within the independent communities, the most important factor in shaping the contour of household relations and a household's access to at least some land was a cultural practice, inheritance. In the independent communities, inheritance was bilateral, usually guaranteeing the equal division of resources among all heirs. This practice had contradictory effects on household relations, sometimes supporting and at other times undermining the stability of households as units of production and reproduction. Most important, access to land through inheritance provided women with a measure of economic security and bargaining power not available to women on the haciendas.

Miller (1967, 186) has argued that in the neighboring highlands of La Libertad, households formed matrilocally were much less stable than those formed patrilocally, because men suffered a loss of status by having to work for their fathers-in-law, who often treated them poorly. He attributes the high rate of abandonment of women to this loss of status and accompanying problems. Moreover, he notes that without access to land men could enforce their authority within the family only through the force of personality. But it must also be remembered that bilateral inheritance and matrilocality provided women with an economic base for divorce. They, too, could withdraw from relationships that became too oppressive, and they could attract new partners because of their access to means of production. One can even argue that female land ownership could have contributed to household stability at times by ensuring that men would have sufficient land to farm only if they remained in a union.

Another difference between household relations on haciendas and those within the communities was the much weaker role of community ideology in defining social mores and sanctioning social deviance, as compared to the landlords' role in this realm on haciendas. Although this topic requires further research, the lack of social sanctions against behavior that did not support patriarchal household units may perhaps be tied to the disintegration of communal structures and community identity in Cajamarca in earlier centuries.[16]

In the early decades of this century, income pooling and shared consumption were important practices contributing to household stability both on the haciendas and within the independent communities. As noted previously, income pooling was facilitated by the use value character of most agricultural, animal, and artisan production and by cultural practices in which household production was an indivisible product and a return accrued by family, rather than purely individualized labor. This practice in turn was supported by the rather flexible, though gender-based, household division of labor in productive activities. Men and women had different but complementary spheres of productive activities.

Rising land shortage within the independent communities no doubt contributed to the instability of petty production as the dominant class relation and the primary occupation of men and women. Lack of access to sufficient resources weakened the complementary gender-based division of labor between agriculture and animal production. It also reduced the economic contribution of children. The need to engage in multiple income-generating activities created the basis for independent income streams among men and women, perhaps weakening the basis for shared consumption and commitment to the unit of reproduction. This situation was aggravated by the fact that, in the early decades, only men had the opportunity to participate in wage labor, resulting in their greater control over this increasingly important household income source.

Seasonal male migration also contributed to the instability of sierra households, because permanent wage employment on the coast provided men with the opportunity to disentangle themselves from household commitments. Sierra men often formed a second union on the coast, even during temporary migration (Miller 1967). Although male migration certainty increased the rate of female and child abandonment, it did not, however, lead to the dissolution of all familial ties or of reciprocal obligations between the migrants and their

16. This hypothesis is suggested by Bourque and Warren's (1981) analysis of how the structure of the Comunidades Campesinas reproduced patriarchal relations and women's subordination to men. In contrast, Cajamarcan communities are often not so much communities as groupings of households with little sense of community (Silva Santisteban 1945, 94; Chambeu, Garay, and Samaniego 1975). Although lack of community cohesion in Cajamarca has been attributed to seasonal migration, the temporary absence of males, and the permanent loss of potential community leaders (Chambeu 1975c), I believe that the low level of social cohesion in many of these communities should be traced much further back, to the disintegration of the indigenous communities in the colonial period.

parents and siblings.[17] Migrant remittances continued to be an important source of sierra household income through the 1970s, and as long as kinship obligations were met, migrants continued to have a claim on their highland inheritances, exacerbating land fragmentation within the independent communities.

Although I have focused on the tensions in household relations that contributed to growing instability, it is important to remember that the majority of Cajamarcan peasants, such as María and Rosa, did live in households that managed to sustain themselves as units of production and reproduction for a considerable length of time. That they did so is partly explained by their participation in multiple class relations. Members of a household could acquire additional land to reproduce themselves as petty producers through a variety of subsumed class processes. Sharecropping the lands of relatives who had migrated and of richer peasants in the community was one such possibility. So was acquiring access to hacienda lands. Households could also engage in other income-generating activities such as dyeing wool or trading, with income from these sources serving—through the purchase of land—to reproduce the household as a unit of production. Women's income-generating activities, as in the case of María's household, sometimes reduced the need for male migration and participation in capitalist class relations. Participation in wage labor, as in the case of Rosa's household, also provided the material basis to constitute households as units of production. These trends were accentuated over subsequent decades.

17. The relationship between migrants and their parental households is analyzed in more quantitative detail in chapters 10 and 11. The Cajamarca data differ from Miller's (1967, 186) analysis of these relationships in the neighboring highland region of La Libertad. He reported that the majority of migrants broke all ties with their highland kin.

PART TWO

The Process of Capitalist
Transition, 1940–1980

FIVE

The Development of the Market in Milk, Land, and Labor

The decade of the 1940s might have been propitious for the development of the northern highlands as the granary of northern Peru. Manuel Prado's election to the presidency in 1939 brought to the fore expansionary economic policies, drawing the Peruvian economy out of the stagnation that had characterized the 1930s.[1] The demand for foodstuffs increased steadily, and, with the completion of the road network integrating Cajamarca and the coast, the department's haciendas should have been able to expand their production of wheat and other foodstuffs significantly. National economic policies, however, were to prove most unfavorable for highland producers.

In the early 1940s, the north coast was producing an important share of its own food requirements. Between 1929 and 1944, the land area dedicated to food production on the coast had increased by an average annual rate of 3.5 percent, comparable to coastal population growth. This increase was a result of both governmental restrictions on land use, which favored food production over export crops, and the difficulties in the international market for cotton during World War II (Thorp and Bertram 1978, 196, 179, 199).

Coastal food production increased, even though the agricultural sector received little protection during this period. Despite the lack of protection, food imports per capita remained below 1920 levels, not rising significantly until the late 1940s. Nonetheless, the major food import in this period was wheat, Cajamarca's potential regional export crop. Imports of wheat and wheat flour increased from 9 percent of total Peruvian imports in 1936 to 14 percent in

1. Thorp and Bertram (1978, 151–153, 185) argue that the stagnancy of the 1930s was largely self-induced, for Peru's exports recovered relatively quickly from the slump of the Great Depression. Moreover, Peru had been stagnant before the Depression, so the Peruvian economy was not as adversely affected as that of other countries. Throughout the 1930s, however, government spending declined more rapidly than export earnings and resulted in little stimulus for economic growth.

1948, while beef imports increased from 0.3 percent to 3.5 percent over the same period (Thorp and Bertram 1978, 394, 200).

Perhaps the most unfavorable development for highland producers was the changing national political configuration, which coalesced around cheap food policies that favored the urban sector. The eruption of World War II produced inflationary pressures on the Peruvian economy, partly because of the rising prices of imports. Although food prices were increasing only moderately, domestic price controls on foodstuffs were imposed in 1942 (Thorp and Bertram 1978, 179, 191, 197). As a result, the internal terms of trade moved steadily against agriculture; among the most severely affected products were wheat and beef. By the late 1940s, the crisis of profitability in highland agriculture contributed to growing food shortages and to increasing food prices spurring inflation. The lost credibility of expansionary macroeconomic policies contributed to General Odría's seizure of power in 1948 and the redirection of the economy toward economic liberalism.

In this overall negative macroeconomic picture, a new constellation of forces emerged, favoring the development of the province of Cajamarca as a dairy region. The interactive roles of the incipient Cajamarcan bourgeoisie, foreign capital, and the Peruvian state were crucial in setting the stage for the development of agrarian capitalism.

CREATING THE CONDITIONS FOR PROFITABLE PRODUCTION

In the early 1950s, Nicolás Santolalla remarked that "those who knew the Cajamarca Valley one quarter of a century ago cannot but observe the marvelous transformations that have taken place in just the last decade. Twenty-five years ago, not even on the same haciendas of the leaders of today's movement could you raise cattle. The valley of Cajamarca was a great marsh" (cited in Chávez Aliaga 1957, 1: 195).

Luis Amorín, editor of *El Rodeo*, the new publication of the Association of Agriculturalists and Cattlemen of Cajamarca, concurred: "In the last few years, considerable progress has been made in the field of dairy cattle. All of the medium and large landowners of the Cajamarca Valley are rapidly putting agricultural production aside and going totally into the production of dairy cattle....Only three or four years ago the pampas of Cajamarca had only degenerated criollo cattle. Today one sees Holsteins" (Amorín 1948, 1).

Some experimentation with improved cattle breeds and pastures had taken place in the province in previous decades, but technological innovation had been the exception rather than the rule (Silva Santisteban 1945). Moreover, such experimentation had little, if any, effect on the prevailing class relations on most of the Cajamarcan haciendas. The 1940s and 1950s were to prove different on both counts.

Much of the credit for the rapid transformation rests with the modernizing landowners themselves, who, from 1930 on, became increasingly effective at drawing state resources to Cajamarca. They were also instrumental in creating an internal market for milk in the province by lobbying the Swiss multinational corporation Nestlé, S.A., to locate a milk-processing shop in the valley. That Nestlé did so was in turn a result of the concessions that the Peruvian state was willing to offer foreign capital at the time.

The first organization of entrepreneurs in Cajamarca—the Chamber of Commerce, Agriculture, and Industry—was formed in 1930 to develop local commerce. It immediately began to lobby the national government to build roads, for poor transportation was considered the main obstacle to increased interregional trade. Throughout the next decades, the Chamber of Commerce was also to pressure the state into extending the services of the Ministry of Agriculture to the province (setting up an experiment station), extending air service to the city of Cajamarca, and, in the late 1950s, building a tourist hotel.

Two major roads had been completed by 1930, the Cajamarca-Chilete trajectory to the coastal railhead and the road from Cajabamba to Trujillo, linking the southern tip of the department with the coast directly. The absence of intradepartmental roads minimized the benefit of this second link for the province of Cajamarca, however. Extensions of the road network within the department, and particularly the construction of a road from the city of Cajamarca to the coast, were relatively expensive propositions, because they had to be based on free wage labor. The political climate of the 1930s and 1940s would not allow a repetition of Leguía's conscription of unpaid Indian labor. Moreover, given the steady demand of the coastal plantations, highland labor had a high opportunity cost. Road construction in this period thus required that the national state make a significant commitment of funds; but not until the 1940s, under the expansionist fiscal and monetary policies of the Prado and Benavides administrations, did the state do so, largely as a response to the pressures of the Cajamarcan Chamber of Commerce.

The Chilete-Pacasmayo road, linking Cajamarca directly to the coast, was begun in 1941 and completed in 1945. Also in that year the Cajamarca-Cajabamba link was finished, finally giving the departmental capital two outlets to coastal markets (Chávez Aliaga 1957, 1: 107).

With the completion of the central road network, conditions should have been favorable for the expansion of foodstuff production in Cajamarca, if transportation costs had been the only barrier to increased output on the haciendas. As noted earlier, however, the terms of trade had been moving steadily against food production since the 1930s, and few positive national agricultural policies had been generated.

In 1943 the Association of Agriculturalists and Cattlemen of Cajamarca (also known as the Cattlemen's Association) was formed to lobby for more favorable governmental pricing and tariff policies. Its first act was to demand that the government rescind a recent decree lowering the price of wheat (Eslava 1973, 67–68). Represented among the association's founding membership of forty-six were both the traditional members of the Cajamarcan landlord class and the more modern entrepreneurs of the Cajamarca Valley who were developing the incipient dairy industry. The leadership of the association fell to the latter group; Alejandro Castro Mendívil, owner of the Hacienda La Colpa, was elected its first president. The association was subsequently to focus its energy on developing the conditions for a profitable dairy industry.

Given the prevailing price structure, dairy production (or the production of alfalfa, either for direct sale or as feed for fattening cattle) was more profitable than grain production. According to the calculations of the Cattlemen's Association, the production of 1 hectare of wheat in 1949 yielded a loss of S/. 4.40 per hectare (*El Rodeo* 1949, no. 15, 1). This accounting was probably exaggerated—it was contained in a petition asking the Odría government to raise the price of wheat, with complaints of unfair competition from cheap Chilean wheat imports—but it illustrates the growing disparity between the profitability of dairy production and that of grain production during these years.

The net annual return on 1 hectare of irrigated alfalfa was on the order of S/. 929.[2] The more profitable activity, however, was dairy production: ten cows could be maintained on 2.5 hectares of alfalfa, yielding a net annual profit of S/. 2,640, or a return of S/. 1,056 per hectare.[3] Dairy production was even more profitable if the cows grazed on pastures that were less costly than alfalfa, such as rye grass. Also, producers could increase average daily milk production to 8 liters by investing in mixed dairy breeds, significantly raising profitability. Profits could be increased still further by processing the milk into butter.

In 1948 the editors of the Cattlemen's Association journal reported that no one had followed the examples of Castro Mendívil and Cacho Sousa in developing a dairy specialization twenty years earlier because the market had been limited. Improved transportation now served to broaden the market for Cajamarcan producers, and this perhaps explains why, in the valley of Cajamarca in the mid-1940s, "enclosed pastures were being built daily" (*El Rodeo* 1948, no. 12).

A number of other conditions were also required to allow the fledgling dairy industry to expand and prosper. The development of dairy herds required significant capital investment and therefore new sources of credit. Although private efforts in breed selection and pasture improvement had been successful

2. This figure is derived from Silva Santisteban (1945, 71), on the basis of the average dry and rainy season prices for alfalfa in the Cajamarca Valley.

3. According to Silva Santisteban (1945, 71), the daily cost of one dairy cow was S/. 0.49, based on a herd of ten. A good criollo cow produced 5 liters of milk per day; at the 1944 price of S/. 0.24 per liter, milk production yielded a net profit of S/. 0.15 per liter.

on a small scale, more systematic technical assistance was needed.[4] Moreover, given the distance between Cajamarca and the coast a local milk-processing plant was a prerequisite if milk production was to develop on a large scale. The Association of Agriculturalists and Cattlemen pressured the state to direct financial resources to Cajamarca and helped bring Nestlé to the province.

PERULAC (Compañía Peruana de Alimentos Lacteos, S.A.), a wholly owned subsidiary of Nestlé, S.A., began its operations in the province in the mid-1940s. This company had been active in Peru for a number of years, serving as the licensed importer and distributor of Nestlé milk products. It also operated a major milk-processing plant in Lima and, beginning in 1933, a factory in Chiclayo that produced various milk-based products.

PERULAC's interest in the dairy potential of Cajamarca dates from the construction of its Chiclayo plant (Chávez Aliaga 1957, 1: 254). Not until World War II, however, were conditions favorable for the company to expand its operations to the sierra. First, from the 1930s on, increasing amounts of coastal lands were being switched from pastures and cattle production to food crops, a move that threatened the company's potential supply of local milk. Second, in 1939 both Nestlé and its international competitor Carnation were granted tariff protection on final milk products as inducements to expand their Peruvian operations.[5] Carnation subsequently built a milk-processing plant in Arequipa, in southern Peru, in 1942. Third, during World War II, trade with Europe was severely curtailed. As a major importer of milk products for its processing industry, PERULAC had to look for domestic milk suppliers if its local production activities, and its profits, were to be maintained.

Following the completion of the road from Cajamarca to the coast, PERULAC began its activities in Cajamarca on an experimental basis, collecting milk in the Cajamarca Valley in refrigerated trucks. In the first year, 1947, some twenty suppliers provided an average of 3,349 liters per day to the company (derived from Eslava 1973, 92–94). But 265 kilometers of unpaved road separated the supply of milk from its processing destination, the Chiclayo plant.

Because of continual pressure from the Cattlemen's Association and PERULAC's own interest in securing reliable and increasing supplies of fresh milk, the company finally decided in 1949 to install a pre-processing, or condensation, plant in Cajamarca (*El Rodeo* 1948, no. 12). A prefabricated

4. A few landowners had already developed their breeding systems to the point of selling pure and mixed-breed bulls as reproducers. The ads in *El Rodeo* show Cacho Sousa, Bisiak, Dobbertin, and Rossell operating on this scale in 1948 (*El Rodeo* 1948, no. 9).

5. According to Lajo Lazo (n.d., 179, 288), tariff exemption was provided by a 1939 *Resolución Suprema* (government decree). Eslava (1973, 143) reports, however, that the government granted PERULAC tariff protection on Peruvian-produced products in 1940. That was the year in which the Industrial Promotion Law was passed, basically giving the government carte blanche to grant special incentives for industry and other productive activity (Thorp and Bertram 1978, 187).

TABLE 15.   PERULAC Suppliers, Daily Milk Collection, and Capacity Utilization, 1949–1978

	Number of Suppliers	Average Daily Milk Collection (liters)	Capacity Utilization (%)
1949	59	4,417	6
1950	120	7,205	9
1952	160	14,014	18
1955	205	19,519	24
1957	243	23,304	29
1960	355	29,034	36
1962	397	26,712	33
1965	470	33,151	41
1967	531	35,710	45
1970	681	48,360	60
1972	728	46,565	58
1975	1,126	54,219	68
1978	1,400	75,365	94

SOURCES: Data for 1949 to 1972 compiled from Eslava (1973, tables 8, 8b,
and 9); data for 1975 and 1978 compiled from Burga Bartra (1981, 29).

aluminum factory was imported from the United States for this purpose, and
forty workers became employed in Cajamarca's first industrial establishment.

Although the valley of Cajamarca had a nascent dairy industry at this time,
PERULAC had to undertake considerable promotional activity for its investment to pay off. As Table 15 shows, in 1950 the new plant was operating
at only 9 percent of capacity. PERULAC's most important short-run promotional strategy was incentive pricing. To attract suppliers, it began by
offering prices of S/. 0.60 per liter—well above the previous market rate of
S/. 0.24. The incentive price was necessary both to induce current dairy
producers who processed their own milk into butter and cheese to become
PERULAC suppliers and to induce other landowners to invest in improved
pastures and dairy cattle. But this was a highly inflationary period, and by 1949
the Cattlemen's Association was petitioning the government to raise the price of
milk (*El Rodeo* 1949, no. 15). In 1950 the government gave PERULAC
permission to pay S/.0.80 per liter (Eslava 1973, 145). Over the years, price
policy would be one of the major sources of tension among PERULAC, the
Cattlemen's Association, and the state.[6]

PERULAC also implemented a prototypical agricultural development
program. The company set up a credit program to allow landowners to import

6. See the minutes of the Cattlemen's Association meetings and its bulletins, summarized in
Eslava (1973, 138–143). These tensions are analyzed in Chapter 8, below.

improved dairy breeds. It also organized an artificial insemination program, paying 50 percent of the costs. To encourage the development of enclosed pastures, PERULAC brought in its own fleet of heavy machinery to Cajamarca, organizing a machine bank of tractors, bulldozers, and trucks for rental to the landowners. Its technical experts developed experimental pastures planted in improved varieties of seeds. In addition, it published a series of technical assistance pamphlets and promoted the construction of stables and silos (Eslava 1973, 107, 123).

In order to extend the basic milk collection routes and increase the number of suppliers, PERULAC also carried out an extensive road construction program, partly supported by financial contributions from the state. Over the next two decades, it opened approximately 179 kilometers of road in the province and maintained another 160 kilometers (Eslava 1973, 125).

In the first years of PERULAC's operation, its suppliers were limited to the fundos and haciendas of the Cajamarca Valley. In the 1950s, when the newly built roads penetrated surrounding districts, the number of milk providers increased steadily. By the late 1950s, the growing volume of milk processed reflects both a substantial increase in the number of suppliers (see Table 15) and the technical development of the industry. Productivity continually increased, especially on the valley farms, as a result of improved dairy breeds and the intensive cultivation of improved pastures. In the early 1960s, PERULAC's milk collection routes were extended to three other provinces of the department, first Cajabamba, then Celendín and San Miguel, doubling the number of suppliers during this decade.

In its efforts to develop the dairy potential of the region, PERULAC was assisted by new state agricultural development programs. Before the 1940s, state assistance to Cajamarca's landowners had been limited to such passive forms of support as granting permission to Castro Mendívil and Cacho Sousa to import planeloads of improved cattle breeds from the United States and Argentina.[7] Under the Prado administration, the Peruvian state began to assume a more developmental role, gradually directing increased state resources to the sierra for infrastructural development such as irrigation. In 1943, the first national agricultural development program, SCIPA (Servicio Cooperativo Interamericano de Producción de Alimentos), was organized under the Ministry of Agriculture. These programs were largely directed to the commercial farming sector, and Cajamarca was no exception, given the well-organized lobbying effort of the Cattlemen's Association and PERULAC.

In 1944 SCIPA began its technical assistance activities in Cajamarca with a

7. Some modest material support was also given. Chávez Aliaga (1957, 1:241) reports that at one point the national director of the Ministry of Agriculture was so convinced of the enthusiasm and efforts of the cattle producers of Cajamarca that, without a budget entry for such a purpose, he sent two Ayrshire bulls to Castro Mendívil. The Ministry of Agriculture was to be repaid with twelve crossed Holstein-Ayrshire bulls, to be distributed among other cattle producers in the area.

project for improved seed for pastures, potatoes, and wheat. SCIPA organized demonstration plots, usually on the haciendas of the members of the Cattlemen's Association (Puga's Laguna Seca or Miranda's Llushcapampa, for example), to test the new varieties and then disseminated the results among the landowners (Chávez Aliaga 1957, 1: 258).

SCIPA also completed numerous small irrigation projects designed to tap underground water reserves in the valley, such as on the fundos Huacariz, Pilancón, and Shultín. In support of the dairy development initiative, it also distributed free plans for the construction of stables and silos, organized a small tractor pool, and initiated an animal health project.

SCIPA's main project for small farmers promoted the use of guano fertilizer and improved agricultural implements. The efforts of SCIPA in sheep improvement, however, also benefited the peasantry. In 1951 SCIPA organized an experiment station to work with sheep on a tract of land purchased from the Hacienda Porcón. Over the next two decades, its breed-selection program gradually improved the stocks belonging to peasants in the area.

Some state irrigation projects also benefited the peasantry. The first major state-funded irrigation project in the department was begun in 1937 in the district of Jesús. According to Silva Santisteban (1945, 12), this project, covering 1,500 hectares, was intended primarily to stem the massive temporary migration of peasants from the area, suggesting that Cajamarca was experiencing seasonal labor shortages. The project was not completed until 1951, however, and did little to decrease either temporary or permanent migration from the district of Jesús to the coast, which was prompted by the extreme land pressure in the zone.

The second major irrigation project, in the Huacaríz area of the Cajamarca Valley, was more clearly directed to the development of the dairy industry.[8] When state approval for the project was pending in 1944, Silva Santisteban (1945, 70) voiced his concern that the project would only spur the dispossession of the peasantry in the valley, facilitating the conversion of former grain-producing lands to improved pastures. He worried about the subsequent effect on food prices in Cajamarca if foodstuff production were to be abandoned, and on the local labor supply if the sharecroppers and arrendires of the valley were forced to migrate to the coast or to the haciendas at the higher elevations. Although a number of peasant communities were helped by this 2,500-hectare irrigation project, Castro Mendívil was among the major beneficiaries.[9]

8. An account by a native of Jesús, José Rosario Llanos Aguero (1972, 101–106), suggests that the two irrigation projects described by Silva Santisteban were actually one.

9. According to Llanos Aguero (1972, 105–106), the communities of Jesús had serious conflicts with Alejandro Castro Mendívil over canal rights, for "he tried to make himself owner of the water." Llanos Aguero notes that only by organizing and struggling against Castro Mendívil in the national senate and chamber and within the Ministry of Public Works were the small farmers of Jesús assured of getting access to water.

In the 1940s, although coastal agro-export production continued to claim the lion's share of its resources, the state also began to channel increasing amounts of credit to highland agricultural development. During 1951 and 1952, for example, the state agricultural development bank, the Banco de Fomento Agropecuario, made loans totaling S/. 4.2 million in Cajamarca, representing 2.3 percent of all loans extended nationally (Chávez Aliaga 1957, 1:217).[10] The Cattlemen's Association kept up its pressure for increased agricultural credit, and by 1965 the local banking agency had been converted into a full-service branch bank, with Cajamarca receiving S/. 32 million in agricultural credit.[11] Throughout the following years, the total volume of credit continued to increase steadily.[12]

The state also directly financed some of the projects of the Association of Agriculturalists and Cattlemen. For example, in the 1966–1967 fiscal year, a total of S/. 2.36 million was allocated from the national budget to the association to finance the building of its headquarters, in addition to constructing eight tube wells for irrigation and supporting the now-annual regional cattle fair (Malpica 1967, 6).

LAND, LABOR, AND MILK: FEUDAL VERSUS CAPITALIST CLASS RELATIONS

Feudal class relations on the Cajamarcan haciendas in the twentieth century were economically rational as long as land had a low opportunity cost and labor a relatively high one. The cheapest labor force was maintained by ceding land

10. The private banking sector also responded to the increased demand for credit, with loans placed in Cajamarca increasing tenfold between 1941 and 1951. Private credit to Cajamarcan borrowers in 1951 slightly exceeded public loans, amounting to S/. 4.7 million. According to the data presented by Chávez Aliaga (1957, 1:215–216), Cajamarca's share of the total credit extended nationally by private banks had increased from 14 percent to 21 percent; those figures seem extremely high, however.

11. The lobbying efforts of the Cattlemen's Association are documented in the association's minutes, summarized in Eslava (1973, 138–140). There is a reference to the agricultural bank establishing a branch in Cajamarca in 1960, although Burga Bartra (1981, 14–16), the source of the 1965 data, reports that the *sucursal* was established in 1965.

12. The available data do not agree on the question of whether Cajamarca's share of the national total increased or decreased over time. According to the data presented by Burga Bartra (1981, 14–16), Cajamarca's share fell from 1.6 percent of the total agricultural credit extended nationally in 1965 to 1.0 percent in 1970, 0.4 percent in 1975, and 0.5 percent in 1980; in these last two years, however, the province of Jaén was listed separately, and it alone claimed 6.4 percent and 6.2 percent of the national total. The data reported in Matos Mar and Mejía (1980, table 45) show that the department received 1.5 percent of the total in 1965, 3.2 percent in 1968, 4.2 percent in 1976, and 4.4 percent in 1978. By either data set, Cajamarca's share of credit was less than its contribution to the total value of agricultural production; Cajamarca contributed 4 percent of national output in 1963, 5 percent in 1968, and 7 percent in 1976 (Matos Mar and Mejía 1980, table 39).

to peasants and appropriating unpaid labor services. The first important change in the conditions of production in the province was the rising value of land.

Valley bottom land in Cajamarca was reported to have increased sixfold in value between 1930 and 1950 (Eslava 1973, 68), and contemporaries complained of rises in the price of land and the rental rates of haciendas (Silva Santisteban 1945; Chávez Aliaga 1957, 1: 196). Although inflation was high in the 1940s, with the cost-of-living index increasing fourfold over the decade, the available data suggest that the value of land was rising significantly faster than consumer prices, a trend accentuated by the return to relative price stability in the next decade.[13]

In the early 1950s, the value of 1 hectare of well-irrigated land in the province was on the order of S/. 2,500 (Chávez Aliaga 1957, 1: 196). Hacienda land prices were rising not only in the valley but also at the higher elevations, even when the land was not particularly suitable for dairy farming. The sale price of the 8,196-hectare Hacienda Huacataz (located above 2,800 meters, at the edge of the Cajamarca Valley) increased sixteenfold between 1936 and 1958, doubling in real terms.[14]

The rental rates for the haciendas belonging to the church and public charities were also increasing in real terms in the 1950s. The rent on the Hacienda Huayobamba in the district of San Marcos tripled between 1942 and 1957, as the hacienda was developed as a dairy enterprise (Mejía and Correa 1979, 11). Between 1955 and 1961, the rental rate for the fundo Cristo Rey in the Cajamarca Valley doubled in real terms (derived from Burga Posito et al. 1980, 13–14). Even the rental rate on the Hacienda Santa Ursula, which was poorly irrigated, doubled between 1947 and 1957.[15]

This rise in land values is partially explained by the high inflation of the late 1940s, which made land an attractive investment. But the potential for profitable milk production in the Cajamarca Valley was even more important in explaining these impressive increases. One of the conditions supporting

13. Taking 1953 as the base year of 100, the Lima CPI (consumer price index) in 1940 was 19, the same as in 1929. By 1950 it had risen to 78 (Wilkie 1974, supplement 3, table 1). Throughout the following discussion in Part II, this index has been used to construct constant 1953 prices. Average annual inflation rates have been calculated from the International Monetary Fund series on price changes reported in the *Statistical Abstract of Latin America* (Wilkie 1984, vol. 23, table 2618).

14. "Minuta de Escritura de Compra-Venta, Hacienda Huacataz, Noviembre 1958," files of Gonzalo Pajares, Cajamarca. In 1953 constant soles, the price of the hacienda increased from S/. 176,471 to S/. 370,370.

15. Registros Públicos de Cajamarca, Registro de la Propiedad, city of Cajamarca (8:104). Caution must be used, however, in interpreting dramatic changes in hacienda rental rates. It was not unheard-of for a bidder to offer a rental rate totally out of proportion to the economic value of a hacienda. Gitlitz (1975, 288) reports that this is what happened on the Hacienda Pallán in 1954 when Alejandro Soto offered S/. 130,000, outbidding the longtime arrendires, the Caballeros, who had rented this hacienda previously for S/. 60,000.

feudal class relations on the haciendas had indeed changed: land no longer had a low opportunity cost.

Throughout the 1950s, labor continued to have a relatively high opportunity cost. But, combined with rising land values, the high opportunity cost of labor now encouraged the switch from agricultural production to less labor-intensive activities, rather than providing a stimulus to settle peasant labor on the haciendas.

The demand for highland peasant labor on the coast continued to grow in the 1940s and 1950s. By 1940 sugar production had recovered from the trauma of the 1930s' world market; subsequently, the Korean War caused an increase in international prices comparable to that of the 1910s. Moreover, domestic consumption of sugar increased substantially in this period. As a result, the acreage devoted to sugar cultivation expanded significantly in the 1950s, although output grew even more rapidly as productivity increased (Thorp and Bertram 1978, 232–235). The area under cultivation continued to depend on the availability of highland braceros. A 1950 editorial in the journal *Azucar* stated: "We find ourselves at the beginning of an era of intense mechanization and technological change that will allow us to face *the extreme shortage of labor* and compete in terms of costs with the sugar produced and refined in the other sugar-producing countries of the world" (quoted in Róquez 1979, 41; my emphasis).

The first labor-saving innovations in the sugar industry were introduced in the 1950s, and by 1964 all the major sugar plantations had mechanized soil preparation and weeding (Collin-Delavaud 1976, table 1). Only the plantation Cartavio had at this point mechanized the harvest, although the other plantations eventually followed suit, significantly reducing the demand for temporary labor. Collin-Delavaud (1976, 171) writes that the relative labor shortage came to an end in Lambayeque in 1959 but that it continued in La Libertad because of the heavy migration from this region to the booming fishing port of Chimbote.[16]

Throughout this period, the coastal sugar plantations competed with the expanding rice industry for Cajamarcan peasant labor. In the 1950s, the demand for unskilled labor on the Jequetepeque rice plantations increased

16. The precise changes in total employment in the sugar industry are difficult to pinpoint because of conflicting estimates of total employment in 1940. Hunt (1977, table 8) estimates 1940 employment at 27,758 but also reports the 1940 census figure of 46,197. Scott (1976) uses this latter figure to report a dramatic decrease in jobs in the sugar industry as a result of mechanization, with employment plummeting to 24,000 in 1969. Data collected by the "Informe de la Commissión de Abril" show 1962 employment as 26,181, decreasing to 23,070 in 1964 (cited in Róquez 1979, 51). The average employment for these two years, 24,625, is only slightly lower than the average of 25,895 between 1936 and 1940 (see Table 5). The data provided in Róquez's (1979) analysis of the sugar industry suggest that mechanization did not have a significant impact on employment levels until the early 1960s, and thus that the 1940 census estimate of employment was way off base.

substantially because of a switch to a more productive and labor-intensive rice-transplanting technique.

In the highlands, another source of competition for labor in the 1950s came from the expanding mining industry. The Algomarca mines and the Northern Peru Mining and Smelting Company, operating in Quirovilva and Paredones, recruited in the Cajamarca area. They too adopted the enganche system of labor contracting. Road construction provided yet another source of demand for unskilled labor, as did military conscription (Scott 1976, 330).

On the supply side, population growth in the province was relatively modest between 1940 and 1961, especially compared to the first part of the century. The cumulative annual growth rate was only 1.5 percent, compared with 2.0 percent in the previous period between censuses, reflecting heavy emigration from the province.[17] Permanent highland-to-coast migration during this period, of course, contributed to the relative labor surplus on the coast in the 1960s.

According to Chávez Aliaga (1957, 1: 187–189), the growing demand for labor put pressure on provincial wages. He noted that "even with a high population density, one finds a scarcity of labor in many districts," and he believed that rising wages were seriously affecting the profitability of the Cajamarcan haciendas. He observed that the haciendas were forced to limit the extension of their agricultural production to the number of resident peons, because landlords could not count on the availability of temporary workers. He also noted growing absenteeism on the haciendas, as "the workers were migrating in search of higher wages to the sugar haciendas on the coast, to the coca haciendas on the Marañon River, to the road and public works, and to the guano islands." Chávez Aliaga suggested that for all these reasons many landowners preferred to dedicate themselves to cattle raising, which required fewer workers, rather than continuing to produce agricultural foodstuffs.

The available data support the argument that nominal wages for agricultural workers were rising in the province. But in the late 1940s, inflation averaged around 22 percent; thus, as Table 16 shows, real wages declined dramatically. Furthermore, the data suggest that highland wages were stagnant in real terms throughout the 1950s and 1960s, as surplus labor, in relation to employment opportunities, grew both on the coast and in the highlands. Table 16 also shows the significant difference between the wages paid to free labor and those paid to the hacienda's resident labor force when cash payments for labor services were introduced. The gap narrowed considerably by the late 1950s, as the haciendas developed a permanent wage

17. Between 1961 and 1972, the cumulative population growth rate again increased, to an annual 1.83 percent (Maletta 1980, 37). In terms of average annual growth rates, the change in the period from 1940 to 1961 is not as drastic—1.8 percent, compared with the previous 1.9 percent; over the period from 1961 to 1972, it reached 2.0 percent.

labor force for their dairy activities. Nonetheless, these workers' wages continued to be considerably below the legal minimum wage that applied to permanent workers after 1962.

The development of the dairy industry in the province had its own contradictory impact on the demand for, and supply of, peasant labor. The conversion of part or all of an estate to dairy production first increased the demand for labor but then greatly reduced it. The development of the physical infrastructure for dairy production was quite labor-intensive. Irrigation canals had to be dug, drainage systems installed, new pastures planted, and field dividers constructed. Very little machinery was available for the task—in the early 1950s, there were still only ten tractors in all of the Cajamarcan highlands—and the new infrastructure had to be installed by manual labor (Chávez Aliaga 1957, 1: 191).

Once the initial investment in land improvements had been made, however, the labor requirements of the new dairy enterprise were significantly reduced, especially if the landlord totally abandoned agricultural production on the demesne. Dairy production demanded a small, skilled, permanent labor force that could take responsibility for the increased capital investment in improved cattle breeds, equipment, and installations. A proletarianized work force was thus a rational goal. The way in which some of the haciendas succeeded in creating a small, permanent labor force—through the dispossession of the resident peasantry—then increased the supply of free labor, contributing to a relative labor surplus in the highlands in the 1960s.

Several other factors supported the switch from agricultural to dairy production, as well as the development of capitalist class relations, in the 1940s and 1950s. Wages on the hacienda now actually had to be paid, not only because inflation was eroding the value of accumulated peasant debts but also—and more important—because the peasants were becoming increasingly aware of their rights as citizens of Peru. Landlords had often attempted to keep hacienda tenants uneducated and tied to the haciendas, but by the 1940s the resident peasants were learning both that they had the right to be remunerated for their labor and that there was a positive opportunity cost in coastal wage employment. These realizations were undoubtedly facilitated by the improved means of communication and transportation that characterized the period. The seasonal migrations of two generations of peasants from neighboring independent communities to the coast and their exposure to the growing strength of the coastal labor movement and new political ideas must also have had an impact on hacienda residents.[18]

The editors of *El Rodeo* (1949, no. 14) voiced their concern about the influence of these factors in generating perceived labor shortages and "labor

18. The coastal trade union movement emerged during the second decade of the twentieth century, in concert with the rise of APRA (Klarén 1976; Pareja 1980).

TABLE 16. Observations on Daily Agricultural Wages for Males, Province of Cajamarca, 1942–1976

	Free labor		Hacienda labor		Minimum Wage	
	Current Soles	1953 Constant	Current Soles	1953 Constant	Current Soles[a]	1953 Constant
1942			0.30[b]	1.3		
			.50–1.0[c]	2.1–4.2		
1944	3.0[d]	10.0				
1945			1.0[e]	3.0		
1946			1.0–1.2[f]	2.8–3.3		
1948			1.0[g]	1.7		
1949	4.0[h]	5.7				
1957			3.0[i]	2.4		
1958			8.0[j]	5.9		
1959	8.0[k]	5.2				
1960			10.0[l]	6.1		
1962					15	8.1
1965	15.0[m]	5.8			23	8.9
1966	15.0[n]	5.3			23	8.1
1968			15.0[o]	4.0	30	8.1
1970					36	8.7
1972					43	9.1
1973	31.3[p]	6.2			43	8.5
	48.0[q]	9.5				
1975					73	11.3
1976	34.4[r]	4.3			92[s]	11.5

SOURCES AND NOTES:

[a] Minimum wage series applies to the districts of Cajamarca, Magdalena, San Pablo, Los Baños, Ichocán, Jesús, and San Marcos; the minimum wage for the other districts of the province is slightly lower (Ministry of Labor 1981).

[b] Hacienda Santa Ursula ("Proyecto de reglamentación de relaciones contractuales y de trabajo entre el conductor don Antonio Otoya Puga y los colonos sub-arrendatarios de la Hacienda Santa Ursula, 5 Junio 1942," Hacienda Santa Ursula files, Agrarian Reform Office, Ministry of Agriculture, Agrarian Zone II, Cajamarca).

[c] Hacienda Huacariz de San Antonio (author's interviews with former hacienda tenants, CAP Huacariz de San Antonio, February, April, and September 1976).

[d] Wages for cowhands in the Cajamarca Valley (Silva Santisteban 1945, 72).

[e] Hacienda Tartar Grande (author's interview with Abelardo Rojas, former administrator of this hacienda, Cajamarca, December 1981).

[f] Hacienda Sunchubamba, for workers employed in road construction and in agricultural field work. As a result of a strike by the union of the Sección Andina of the Empresa Chicama, Ltda., wages were increased to S/. 1.20 in September 1946 (Taylor 1984, 121).

[g] Hacienda Huayobamba (author's interviews with former hacienda tenants, CAP Huayobamba, October 1976).

[h] Wages for field hands in wheat production (El Rodeo 1949, no. 15).

[i] Haciendas in the Condebamba Valley owned by Gonzalo Pajares (author's interview with Gonzalo Pajares, Cajamarca, December 1981).

[j] Hacienda La Pauca (Chambeu and Gorget 1975, 36).

[k] Wages for cowhands in the Cajamarca Valley (Boletín 1960, no. 1).

[l] For the Hacienda Huacariz de San Antonio (author's interviews with former hacienda tenants, CAP Huacariz de San Antonio, February, April, and September 1976).

problems": "The Indians won't work.... They are being stirred up by leftists and this has resulted in a lack of discipline and a lack of respect for private property... [and] a stirring up of the traditional order within the heart of the haciendas. The provision of labor by the peasantry is becoming expensive and difficult to acquire in sufficient supply."

Determining whether and to what extent APRA was actually organizing on the Cajamarcan haciendas in the 1940s will require further research. From 1933 to 1945, the party was illegal, although it remained politically active on the north coast. Gitlitz (1975, 249–250) found no evidence that Apristas actively went out to the haciendas to agitate. Rather, he notes that Bustamante's legalization of the party in 1945 allowed Aprista lawyers, many of whom were idealistic reformers, to come out of jail, hiding and exile. He concludes that the peasantry actively sought them out as allies in the late 1940s.

But there is some evidence, developed in the next chapter, that lawyers who were at least sympathetic to APRA were indeed actively involved in several of the most notable conflicts of the early 1940s, on the Hacienda Santa Ursula and the fundo Chamis, the rental properties owned by a religious order and a public charity. In these years, the *comuneros* of a few communities, such as Hualqui in Jesús, began to organize, with an Aprista orientation, to obtain legal recognition and recover lands that had been lost to the haciendas over previous centuries (Bazán 1978, 15).

Changing national political currents must also be considered in explaining why the conditions for feudal class relations on the haciendas were undermined during this period, with the effect of supporting the consolidation of capitalist dairy enterprises in the province. According to Harding (1975, 229–230), what had begun as a struggle of the coastal yanaconas against the sugar plantations in the 1930s had spread to the sierra in the 1940s through the activities of APRA, leading to increased rural unrest and land invasions in the southern highlands in the 1950s. The most noted agrarian conflict of this period was the struggle in La Convención, Cuzco (Blanco 1972). Subsequently, land takeovers increased in intensity all over southern Peru, and the peasantry's demand for land could no longer be ignored. The attack on feudalism was to develop as the rallying cry of all the liberal parties in the 1960s, finally resulting in the 1964 Agrarian Reform Law of President Belaunde.

---

[m] Hacienda Urubamba (1976 Peasant Family Survey).

[n] Hacienda La Colpa (1976 Peasant Family Survey).

[o] For the Hacienda Huayobamba (author's interviews with former hacienda tenants, CAP Huayobamba, October 1976).

[p] Mean wage earned by peasant agricultural wage workers (1973 Cajamarca Income Survey).

[q] Fundo Cristo Rey ("Informe de Empadronamiento y Verificación, Fundo Cristo Rey, Septiembre 1973," fundo Cristo Rey file, Agrarian Reform Office, Ministry of Agriculture, Agrarian Zone II, Cajamarca).

[r] Mean wage earned by peasant agricultural wage workers (1976 Peasant Family Survey).

[s] Minimum wage as of July 1, 1976.

CONCLUSION

The changing market conditions for milk, land, and labor, combined with local and national political trends, provided the impetus for the development of capitalist class relations on the Cajamarcan haciendas. During the 1940s and 1950s, feudal class relations gradually lost their economic rationale. This change resulted in large part from the development of relatively profitable dairy enterprises as alternatives to hacienda foodstuff production. This development itself was a product of the interactive role of the state, multinational capital, and the modernizing landowners of Cajamarca.

State economic policy was largely responsible for the deteriorating terms of trade for foodstuff production and, hence, the attractiveness of the dairy alternative. The deteriorating terms of trade for grain production meant that there was little stimulus to expand or even maintain agricultural production or a large, readily available supply of cheap labor on the haciendas. Moreover, with the rising value of land, this resident labor force was no longer so cheap. The need to pay the resident labor force cash wages and the difficulties of recruiting cheap labor from neighboring communities when additional labor was required encouraged the transition to a less labor-intensive productive activity.

The relatively high opportunity cost of highland labor, which now encouraged the development of dairy production rather than the extension of feudal class relations on the estates, was in turn related to the fate of Peru's export crops in the world market and the continuing high demand for sierra labor on the coast. The creation of a regional internal market for milk, together with the supporting conditions for dairy production—credit, technical assistance, availability of machinery, development of the road network—made dairy farming too attractive for most landlords to resist. That it was to be based on capitalist, rather than feudal, class relations was largely a consequence of the relatively small size and highly developed skills of the labor force that dairy farming required.

But this transition in class relations did not depend on economic factors alone. Equally important were the political changes taking place during these decades. The landlord class no longer ruled supreme in the highlands; landlords now had to contend with the political aspirations of the growing urban middle sectors and the increasing influence of the party, APRA, that inspired those hopes. The political configuration was changing both regionally and nationally. The highland landlords were no longer the national actors they had been in previous decades, nor could they take for granted the support of the undisputably dominant capitalist class in defending their interests unless they, too, became capitalists.

SIX

The Development of Agrarian
Capitalism: Junker and Farmer Paths

Landlord reactions to the changing conditions of production were many and varied. The most violent response to the prospect of profitable dairy enterprises was simply to throw peasants off hacienda land and then to recruit a permanent wage labor force from the most loyal former tenants. More commonly, however, the evolution from feudal to capitalist class relations was gradual and uneven, often characterized by an intensification of feudal exploitation of peasant labor while the infrastructure for dairy production and a wage labor force were being created.

A major feature of the internal transition in class relations on the Cajamarcan haciendas—or of the "Junker" path of capitalist development— was that it was accompanied by a relatively massive, privately initiated land reform.[1] This subdivision and sale of hacienda lands served to rid landlords of feudal obligations and allowed them to consolidate a small, permanent wage labor force on the estates. The land sales also diminished the threat of militant peasant opposition to the new conditions of production and constituted an important source of capitalization for the new dairy enterprises. Moreover, the land sales contributed both to the expansion of petty production among the

---

1. See Winson (1982) for a careful examination of the concept of the "Junker," or "Prussian," road of agricultural development, drawing on a historical analysis of capitalist transition in the German Democratic Republic (East Germany). I am not using the concept in a comparative historical sense but rather in the more limited manner Lenin (1971) employed in "The Agrarian Programme of Social Democracy in the First Russian Revolution, 1905–1907" to refer to the process of internal transition of class relations on estates, that is, the transformation of feudal peasants into wage workers.

peasantry and to engendering a "farmer" path of capitalist development in Cajamarca.[2]

CLEARING THE LAND OF FEUDAL OBLIGATIONS: TENANT EVICTIONS

Interviewing cattle producers in 1944, Silva Santisteban asked what would happen to the indigenous population if the peasants were no longer allowed to work the agricultural lands of the valley. The cattle producers made the following prediction: "The indigenous folks will go to the neighboring haciendas, as already is occurring; they are moving to the higher elevations looking for land to plant and upon which to graze their animals, since the landowners of the valley are already enclosing their land for pastures and taking away land formerly rented out to the Indians, such as on the fundos Shultín, Tres Molinos, and Tartar. These landowners are already enclosing their lands to make fenced-in pastures" (Silva Santisteban 1945, 69).

The dispossession of the peasantry in the 1940s was concentrated in the rich valley area surrounding the city of Cajamarca, where peasant usufruct plots often had access to irrigation. In 1946, most of the sharecroppers on the fundo Chamis were expelled; in the early 1950s, the remaining peasants on the fundo Shultín, as well as on Ajoscancha and the Hacienda Yumagual were also expelled; and in 1955, evictions hit the fundos San Luis, Las Vegas, El Molino, and Huacariz Chico.[3] By the end of the 1950s, the vast majority of peasant sharecroppers had been cleared off the valley floor. The only peasant producers who remained were property owners, concentrated around the communities of Tartar and Otuzco and, in the district of Jesús, in Yanamango and Yanamarca.

In some cases, these peasants were resettled from the valley floor to the hills surrounding the valley and the sharecropping arrangements continued, though on very marginal lands. More frequently, they were given the opportunity to purchase these marginal plots, whereby all obligations between landlord and

---

2. Marx and Lenin used the term *farmer* in different ways. In *Capital*, Marx employed the concept to refer to a capitalist who extracted surplus value from wage workers and rented land from landowners, illustrating that property was not the central feature of a fundamental class process. Lenin (1971, 155–163), in "The Agrarian Programme of Social Democracy," used the term *farmer way* to describe a situation in which there was no landlord economy or where the estates were broken up as a result of revolution. His focus was on the process of social differentiation among direct producers and the conditions that led to the emergence of an entrepreneurial group, capitalist farmers, who employed wage labor. In this chapter, my use of the term *farmer way* covers the processes described by both Marx and Lenin; the distinguishing feature of the capitalist farm is that it is based on the relation between capital and wage labor.

3. The data on peasant expulsions from the valley of Cajamarca were collected primarily through the 1976 Peasant Family Survey.

tenant ended. The landlords then selected their most loyal former tenants to make up the permanent wage labor force of the emerging dairy enterprise.

The labor requirements of dairy farming were indeed less than those of foodstuff production. The Hacienda Tres Molinos provides a good example. After Juan Miguel Rossell purchased the property in 1952, the majority of the sharecroppers on this hacienda were resettled on the steep and rocky hillside where the caserío Tres Molinos is located. Some fifty families had previously sharecropped this 150-hectare hacienda, but the dairy enterprise employed only thirty permanent wage workers. One-third of the new wage labor force was female, and these milkmaids were often wives, daughters, or sisters of the male workers; thus only some twenty families gained access to permanent wage employment on the dairy farm.[4] The magnitude of the change in employment was on the order of 2.5 to 1.

Most of the former tenants managed to purchase small plots from Rossell; the majority of these plots were less than half a hectare.[5] Given the small size and poor quality of these lands, few households could meet a significant portion of their subsistence requirements as petty producers. Some sought employment in the city of Cajamarca, which was only 10 kilometers away; most joined the ranks of the temporary coastal migrants.

Peasants on other fundos of the valley were less fortunate. Often, they were not relocated or given the opportunity to purchase even marginal land parcels. Their only recourse was to emigrate permanently. Some moved to districts at higher elevations or to other provinces in search of land, for example, to the Hacienda Pallán in Celendín (Gitlitz 1975). For many dispossessed peasants, however, migration meant full proletarianization as they sought work in the city of Cajamarca, in the mines, or on the coast.

MORE GRADUAL TRANSITIONS: THE USE OF FEUDAL LABOR TO CAPITALIZE THE HACIENDAS

On some of the valley haciendas, and on most of the larger haciendas in the province, the transition to a wage labor force was smoother and the dissolution of feudal class relations not so abrupt. Rather, landowners utilized unpaid labor services to develop the productive core of the hacienda and to capitalize the productive process.

4. I carried out the case study of the Hacienda Tres Molinos in January 1976. I interviewed Fernando, the son of Juan Rossell; Rossell's nephew, Ernesto (the manager of the dairy farm); and all the milkmaids employed on the dairy farm.

5. According to a community survey carried out by students from the National Technical University of Cajamarca in 1980, 87 percent of the parcels were smaller than one-quarter of a hectare (Becerra Bazán et al. 1981). They also found that 41 percent of the fifty-five households residing in the caserío had moved there when the caserío was constituted in the 1950s; the rest were new residents.

Until 1940, the Hacienda Huacariz de San Antonio in the Cajamarca Valley had been sharecropped almost in its entirety.[6] The owner, María Velgara, bought her first dairy cows in 1941. During the 1940s, she gradually put in rye pastures and built up a herd of improved dairy cattle. The development of the pastures and the construction of the other portions of the infrastructure for dairy production were based on the unpaid labor services of the twenty-seven sharecropper households. Velgara centered her dairy activities on the production of butter and *manjar blanco* (a milk sweet) for the Lima market. Ten men from the resident households worked almost full-time, at token wages, in this rudimentary industry.

In the 1950s, after the Huacariz irrigation project was completed, more land was put into pastures, and the peasants' usufruct parcels were reduced in size and confined to the more marginal hacienda lands. By 1960 no household had access to more than 3 hectares of land. The sharecroppers who were not employed as wage workers on Huacariz were given permission to migrate seasonally to the coast, once the hacienda's infrastructure was completed, and the labor service obligations of the men were rescinded. The wages of the permanent workers steadily increased, and the more privileged workers were allowed to graze their own improved cattle on the hacienda's pastures. As a result, the hacienda's tenant labor force was gradually proletarianized without much conflict. This pattern of internal proletarianization, based on a steady reduction in the size of the usufruct plots but accompanied by rising wages, is similar to that on the Hacienda La Colpa two decades earlier, reported by Taylor (1979). In the 1960s, the tenants on the Hacienda Huacariz de San Antonio peacefully accepted the reduction in the size of their land parcels also because they were well aware of the successful dispossession of sharecroppers elsewhere in the valley. Most had faith that "Señorita Marita," as she was affectionately known, would not do the same.

But she was getting on in years, and in 1964 her nephew, José Velgara, took over management of the farm. Upon his aunt's death, he attempted to end all sharecropping arrangements. At first, he was subtle; he simply refused to give the peasants seed to plant and refused to provide the oxen for plowing. By this time, however, Peru's first agrarian reform legislation had been passed, and when Velgara tried to claim the cattle of Concepción Durán, one of the sharecroppers, as his own, Durán turned to the agrarian reform to seek redress, filing a *declaración jurada* (a sworn declaration) that he had been a feudal tenant of the estate. The 1964 Agrarian Reform Law protected sharecropping arrangements, and consequently a judge came out from the city of Cajamarca

6. The case study of the Hacienda Huacariz de San Antonio was carried out during February and September 1976. Interviews included the management of the cooperative, all the milkmaids and their families, and members of various households who had been employed as wage workers by José Velgara but who had not joined the cooperative. I also collected detailed life histories of Concepción Durán and his wife, Rosa Aquino.

and ordered Velgara to provide seed to his tenants and return Durán's dairy cattle. Velgara did provide the seed, but later that year he sent in his cattle to eat the peasants' crops. The former sharecroppers initiated a juicio against Velgara that was to last eight years.

Cajamarca's judicial system in the 1960s still tended to favor the landlord class, and Velgara eventually was able to rid his estate of sharecroppers. Moreover, he fired most of his aunt's wage workers, because they too were sharecroppers and had joined the lawsuit. He then hired and trained a new labor force of peasants from neighboring communities. Some of the new workers were members of the families of the ex-sharecroppers, and this created bitter family disputes. Velgara successfully converted the full extension of the hacienda into a modern capitalist dairy enterprise by the late 1960s.

On the larger haciendas in the more remote reaches of the province, the process of conversion to new class relations was much more gradual and the transition even more exploitive of feudal peasant labor. The labor services demanded of the peasants often increased while the size of their subsistence parcels decreased, and they were not compensated by wage payments. On the Hacienda La Pauca, the largest in the province, feudal class relations continued to coexist with capitalist class relations well into the 1970s (Chambeu and Gorget 1975, 23–31).

Rafael Puga assumed the management of La Pauca in 1943 and quickly began to expand cattle production on the estate. He first focused on beef cattle for export to the coast and later introduced dairy cattle. Through the 1950s, the hacienda produced butter and cheese mainly for direct export to Lima. When the road to this hacienda was completed, around 1960, Puga became a PERULAC milk supplier. By then he had also developed a nationally famous herd of fighting bulls.

Puga's initial response to the growing market opportunities of the 1940s was to change the form of payment of rent for the vast expanses of land on the hacienda that were ceded to arrendires. Rather than accept payment in cash, he demanded that rent be paid with cattle, as he was attempting to increase the size of his own stock. This was probably also a strategy to deal with inflation, because the real value of cash rentals was falling rapidly. In the mid-1940s, a one-year-old criollo calf cost approximately S/. 130 in the Cajamarca market and a bull S/. 250. Most arrendires had been paying between S/. 30 to S/. 40 for their parcels, and the switch in the form of rental payment thus amounted to an increase in the absolute level of rent appropriated.[7] At the same time, the labor services required of arrendires continued undiminished; in fact, throughout this decade, Puga increased the number of arrendires on the hacienda, both to

7. Chambeu and Gorget (1975, 24) report that a criollo ox was worth S/. 50 at that time. This figure seems very low compared to Silva Santisteban's (1945, 125) data for the city of Cajamarca, however; his figures have been used in the text.

extract more rent in kind and to increase the labor supply available for developing the infrastructure for dairy production.

By the 1950s, Puga had converted the low breed stock of cattle accumulated from the arrendires into a herd of some six thousand dairy cattle (Chambeu and Gorget 1975, 28). He then began expelling some peasants from the hacienda, principally those residing in areas that he wanted to convert into enclosed pastures for the bull herd. One method he reportedly used was to let the lethal fighting bulls loose in areas inhabited by the peasants. While expelling some tenants, Puga increased his demands on the remaining arrendires by converting the principal form of rental payment to labor services. Although he suppressed the payment of rent in cash or cattle, he raised the faena obligation for these peasants from twelve days a year to fifteen days a month. For at least one peasant residing in the community of Asunción, the labor services were increased from fifteen days a month to three weeks a month, although the arrendire was allowed to sharecrop his holding with other peasants (Althaus 1975).

Some arrendires were converted into sharecroppers (Arce del Campo and Lora 1974, 4–8) and given the task of opening up new lands in the area of the hacienda that was still *montaña* (semi-jungle). After several years of crop cultivation, the peasants were moved on to open up other new plots of land, and their former parcels were converted into pastures. As one peasant put it, "We were the tractors" (cited in Chambeu and Gorget 1975, 30). Puga gradually increased the number of peons, the permanent workers considered the most loyal and submissive "gente de hacienda." Until the late fifties, their principal remuneration consisted of weekly gifts of salt, grains, and, sometimes, tips. The exact level of remuneration was tied to the personal relation between each household and the landlord. Favored workers were allowed to have their own sharecroppers and to pasture horses or cattle on the hacienda's improved pastures. Not until 1958 were wages paid to the peons on the hacienda, and reportedly not until much later to the remaining hacienda work force for their faena.

Although Rafael Puga, who served as deputy and senator to the national congress from Cajamarca, developed a modern commercial enterprise, he never relied on a fully proletarian labor force of wage workers. Nor did he create the preconditions for a skilled or educated labor force, for such a group might have challenged his total authority within the hacienda. In the 1950s, the families of the Malat section of the Hacienda La Pauca hired their own private teacher for their children, only to have Puga hire away the teacher in order to close down the school. Chambeu and Gorget (1975, 27–28) interviewed this teacher in 1975, and he claimed that Puga had bribed him to leave the school, offering him an administrative job on the hacienda. Puga reportedly said, "If you teach them to read whatever book and to sign their name, just because they think they know something these cholos get uppity and leave the hacienda for

Lima, Trujillo, and the coast. If they run into me they just sit down to eat at the same table without even greeting me and no longer respect me. That is why I don't want them to learn anything; I want them to stay right here, working." Only in 1973, after the initiation of the agrarian reform, were state primary schools established on La Pauca. Ironically, the *Documentál del Perú: Cajamarca* (1967, 147) lists support for education among Puga's primary legislative interests during his 1956–1962 term in the national congress.

Puga also did his best to resist any intrusions onto the hacienda by APRA sympathizers. Reportedly, he gave orders to kill several Aprista organizers on sight, should they set foot on hacienda lands (Chambeu and Gorget 1975, 27). Clearly, the modernization of this hacienda, with the incipient development of a wage labor force, was closely intertwined with the reproduction of the ideological and political conditions of feudal class relations.

LAND REFORM BY PRIVATE INITIATIVE:
THE HACIENDA LAND SALES

A third landlord response to the new conditions of production in the province was the parceling of haciendas. Although haciendas had been purchased, sold, or subdivided in previous decades, nothing in the early part of the twentieth century could come close to the massive transfer of land that occurred during the 1950s and 1960s: it was transferred among the landed elite, from the landed elite to new capitalist farmers, and from the landed elite to the peasantry.

These land sales were an integral part of the Junker path of capitalist development in Cajamarca in this sense: by selling marginal hacienda lands to the resident peasantry, modernizing landowners were able to rid themselves of feudal obligations while consolidating a permanent wage labor force on the dairy farms. The land sales effectively undermined any potential peasant resistance to being displaced from the most productive core of the haciendas. Moreover, given the rising value of land, its sale to the peasantry and to others provided an effective means of generating the financial resources to capitalize the haciendas as dairy farms.

Although the land sales had a clear economic rationale, political factors also played a role. The 1950s and early 1960s were a period of considerable rural strife throughout highland Peru, and a national consensus was being built around the need for agrarian reform. In Cajamarca, there was no notable trend toward increased peasant militancy from 1940 to 1960, although there was a high correlation between peasant rebellion and attempts to increase peasants' rents, particularly on the haciendas belonging to church groups and public charities. Many of these properties in fact became "unmanageable" because of peasant resistance to increases in the rate of exploitation. Not surprisingly, the first land sales to the peasantry were initiated on these properties in the 1940s.

The second wave of land sales—initiated between 1950 and 1968—was based on a different set of factors: the anti-feudal and pro-capitalist struggle of the landlord class to reorganize the productive process in response to the opening up of the internal market and, during the 1960s, in response to the perceived threat of agrarian reform. Harding's (1975) analysis of how the landed oligarchy adopted a position consistent with its own self-interest is most relevant here. The more progressive landlords condemned feudalism, advocating the consolidation of wage labor on the estates and the creation of a rural proletariat; they thought underutilized estates should be divided among land-hungry peasants. Moreover, they expected that modern enterprises employing wage labor would be exempt from any state-initiated process of agrarian reform. Cajamarca appears to differ from the rest of the sierra in that the second wave of land sales there was very much a preventive move, temporarily suppressing the land question, rather than a response to peasant militancy sparked by attempted proletarianization of the work force.[8] The land sales were thus an important component of the Junker path of capitalist development in the area. The third wave of land sales (analyzed in Chapter 9), from 1968 to 1974, was the final submission of the landed oligarchy to the new agrarian social reality.

The major land sales initiated by church groups and public charities were a response to peasant struggle on particular haciendas. Peasant rebellions broke out in 1941 on the Hacienda Santa Ursula and the fundo Chamis, owned by the Madres Concepcionistas and the Beneficiencia Pública of Cajamarca, respectively; similar struggles occurred in the mid-1940s in the neighboring province of Hualgayoc on the Hacienda Llaucán of the Colegio San Juan de Chota. All three cases were prompted by arrendire attempts to increase the level of peasant rents, partly as a result of the higher rental levels for the haciendas themselves.[9] The opposition of colonos led to some of these haciendas going unleased for years at a time—clearly an unprofitable situation for these charity organizations (Chávez Aliaga 1957, 1:187).

The decision by the Beneficiencia Pública of Cajamarca to sell the Hacienda Porcón set the trend for subsequent land sales to the peasantry in the province. As discussed in chapters 1 and 2, this hacienda had witnessed years of peasant struggle against exacting landlord-arrendires, and the Beneficiencia had been unable to raise its rent on the hacienda for some twenty-six years (Gorget 1975b). In 1937 the Beneficiencia assumed direct management of the hacienda, and finally, in 1940, the board of directors voted to solicit authorization from

8. The Cajamarcan case contrasts markedly with that of Huancavelica. According to Favre (1976, 118–120), members of the Huancavelican landlord class sold their haciendas in their entirety after 1959 because of the perceived threat of agrarian reform. Moreover, they were selling the haciendas at much below their market price.

9. A major struggle broke out on the Hacienda Pallán (owned by the Madres Concepcionistas) in Celendín in 1946, although for different reasons than those mentioned above. A second period of struggle on this hacienda, from 1954 to 1961, was a result of the increase in the rent paid by the landlord-arrendire, which he attempted to pass on to the peasantry. See Gitlitz's (1975, chaps. 6 and 7) detailed account.

the government to parcel the hacienda into lots for sale to its tenants. It was not until 1950, however, that the first tract was sold—13,843 hectares of jalca land to the SCIPA as a high-altitude experiment station. In 1953 the board voted to proceed with the sale of land parcels to the 450 tenant households and to sell the rest of the jalcas in a public auction. The majority of the land sales, encompassing some 15,000 hectares, were not concluded until the late 1950s.

The 1941 tenant rebellion on the Hacienda Santa Ursula provides another example of how peasant militancy initiated a move toward the eventual parceling of the hacienda. The resolution of the conflict had led to a uniform rental contract for all peasant sub-arrendires on this hacienda and the stipulation that no labor service be unremunerated.[10] The landlord apparently considered the terms of that arrangement too unprofitable, for in 1943 Otoya Puga transferred his rental contract to Serapio Montoya Cabanillas. Montoya probably failed to meet the terms of the agreement, for peasant struggle on the hacienda continued. The peasants' demands had changed, however: they now wanted the hacienda to be subdivided and sold to them.

In 1944 the Bureau of Indian Affairs of the Ministry of Labor was forced to intervene to mediate the dispute on Santa Ursula. According to Davies (1974, 144–145), an agreement was reached whereby the tenants were to purchase the hacienda from the Madres Concepcionistas for the sum of S/. 80,000. Reportedly, the tenants sold their livestock and crops and deposited the required sum in a special account in the Banco de Credito del Perú. Apparently, at that moment, the abbess of the convent changed her mind and proposed new conditions for the sale. By this time, APRA had become a legal party, and, in November 1945, Cajamarca's Aprista senator, Felipe Alva y Alva, introduced a bill in the national congress calling for the expropriation of the hacienda and its division among the tenants.[11] After two years in committee, the bill was approved in 1947. The Madres Concepcionistas filed an appeal, however, and the hacienda was never expropriated. Three more landlords attempted to manage this hacienda before the convent finally relented and subdivided the estate among the resident peasantry in the early 1960s.[12]

10. "Proyecto de reglamentación de relaciones contractuales y de trabajo entre el conductor don Antonio Otoya Puga y los colonos sub-arrendatarios de la Hacienda Santa Ursula, 5 Junio 1942," Hacienda Santa Ursula files, Agrarian Reform Office, Ministry of Agriculture, Agrarian Zone II, Cajamarca.

11. Cotler (1978, 264) notes that in the three years during which APRA was legal in this period (1945 to 1948), its congressional activity focused on resolving individual land conflicts such as this one. Also see Saco (1946).

12. Another example of the parceling of an estate because of peasant militancy is the case of the Hacienda Llaucán, owned by the Colegio San Juan de Chota, in the province of Hualgayoc. Again, peasant opposition to rent increases made the hacienda unmanageable. The rental of the hacienda also was not producing sufficient revenue to maintain the secondary school run by the religious group that owned it. In 1950 the national congress authorized the school to parcel the hacienda and invest the funds in more lucrative urban activities. Land sales on this hacienda began in 1952 (Scott 1976, 328).

The political volatility of the land issue was not lost on the landlord class. Among the initial acts of the Association of Agriculturalists and Cattlemen in 1943 was to send a memorandum to the national government "warning of the seriousness of the social situation in the region, when peasants—the cases of the hacienda Santa Ursula and the fundo Chamis—refuse to comply with their obligations and ignore laws" (cited in Eslava 1973, 68). But in the next decade these same landowners themselves made their tenants property owners. In the early 1950s, Manuel Cacho Sousa subdivided and sold the Hacienda Cochamarca, as well as some parcels of the Hacienda Santa Teresita de La Quispa (formerly part of the Hacienda Polloc).[13] According to Chávez Aliaga (1957, 1:249), Cacho Sousa sold this land to his tenants because he owned more land than he could productively utilize; Chávez Aliaga added that "no one else would have thought of doing the same." But over the next two decades, most of Cajamarca's landed elite did follow the example of Cacho Sousa, in effect carrying out a private land reform approximately equal in scope to that of the Velasco government in the 1970s.

Some haciendas—Yanacancha, Jancos, La Laguna, and Huayanmarca, for example—had been subdivided and sold to the resident peasantry in the 1940s (Silva Santisteban 1945, 54). Whether these sales took place in response to rising land values or simply because the owners lacked heirs interested in managing the haciendas is not known. These sales differ from those carried out in the following decade, however, in that they were not associated with developing dairy farms on the most productive core of hacienda lands. Moreover, these earlier sales were generally limited to hacienda tenants.

The case of the Hacienda Combayo illustrates how the later land sales of the 1950s were initially undertaken in order to capitalize the hacienda core and were then continued because of the initiation of the 1964 agrarian reform. These developments eventually led to the parceling of almost the entire hacienda. Recall from Chapter 2 that after the death of the innovating landowner, the mining engineer Eloy Santolalla, this hacienda reverted to absentee management, and its mining and agricultural production declined. In the mid-1940s, sheep raising was its principal economic activity; the hacienda owned a herd of approximately 2,200 sheep. Four mitayos were employed on a quarterly rotating basis to care for the herd. The only full-time worker was a puntero who cared for the hacienda's herd of cattle (averaging around 175 head), suggesting that dairy activities still had not been developed on the hacienda.[14]

---

13. Chávez Aliaga (1957, 1:249) refers to Cacho Sousa's hacienda as the Hacienda Cochabamba, but no hacienda of this name is listed in the 1940 census. Moreover, it is known that Manuel Cacho Sousa was the owner of Cochamarca in the 1950s, during the time he was senator from Cajamarca (Díaz S. 1971, 17).

14. Data on the number of workers employed from 1944 to 1947 and on the size of herds were drawn from the debt book found on the Hacienda Combayo (files of Gonzalo Pajares, Cajamarca).

In 1947 Nicolás Santolalla Bernal, the author of the 1918 monograph on Combayo, and his sister, Rosalia Santolalla Bernal, purchased the hacienda from their mother and siblings and began to develop a dairy enterprise. Butter and cheese processing at the casa hacienda resumed, and several of the resident peons were hired as full-time wage workers to run the operation. The first land sales to arrendires coincided with the construction of the feeder road from La Encañada to Yanacancha. Completed in 1956, it allowed the Santolallas to become milk suppliers to PERULAC. By this time, they had constructed a new irrigation system and had increased the number of hectares in improved pastures significantly, all through the use of faena labor. The funds generated from the sale of land were reinvested in improved dairy cattle.

Nicolás Santolalla died only a few years later, in 1959, and his heirs decided to subdivide and sell the bulk of this vast hacienda, keeping only the most productive, irrigated core, the 863 hectares surrounding the casa hacienda. The land sales to the peasantry thus continued, but a land invasion by peasants from the neighboring Community of La Encañada forced the Santolallas to resort to the newly created Instituto de Reforma Agraria y Colonización for assistance in carrying out the sales. This institute had been created by the Prado government as a result of the growing momentum for land reform in Peru. It was responsible only for administering a colonization program, but it also served as facilitator for the parceling of haciendas by private initiative. Landowners went to the institute of their own volition for technical assistance in carrying out subdivisions or for assistance in settling border disputes with neighboring communities. The landowners, however, were required to accept the terms of sale, including the per hectare price, recommended by the institute.

The official subdivision of the Hacienda Combayo was still in progress in 1966, for at this point the hacienda had fallen under the jurisdiction of the 1964 Agrarian Reform Law. The Santolallas were required to prove that the hacienda was not characterized by feudal class relations and, moreover, that the land claims of the neighboring community were invalid. The final subdivision of the estate was approved in 1967, but by this time the Santolallas were ready to withdraw from the hacienda completely. In 1969 they sold the core of the hacienda, the dairy farm, to Gonzalo Pajares.

Throughout the 1950s, a number of haciendas were sold almost intact either to other members of the landed elite or to newcomers on the Cajamarcan agrarian scene. The sellers were usually absentee landowners taking advantage

---

The information on the Hacienda Combayo that follows is drawn from material found in the Hacienda Combayo files, Agrarian Reform Office, Ministry of Agriculture, Agrarian Zone II, Cajamarca: "Memoria Descriptiva, 31 Julio 1961"; "Informe Legal No. 6 sobre Fundo Combayo, 1965"; "Expediente No. 978-3 (15–DAC), Instituto de Reforma y Promoción Agraria, 1966"; and "Resolución No. 80/67, Instituto de Reforma y Promoción Agraria, Consejo Nacional Agrario, Mayo, 1967." The archival material was supplemented by my interviews on this hacienda in July 1976, and December 1981.

of the rising value of land. Sometimes these haciendas were resold within a short period. For example, the Villanueva property, the Hacienda Purhuay, was willed to six heirs in 1942; subsequently, half of the hacienda was purchased by the Negociación Agricola Ganadera and the other half consolidated by Barreto Saavedra in 1944. By 1945 the Negociación Agrícola Ganadera had already sold its half to Angulo Herrera. Then, in 1951, Wenceslao Valera Villacorta managed to consolidate the full hacienda, purchasing both halves. He paid S/. 33 per hectare in 1951; he resold the hacienda two years later to Gonzalo Pajares at S/. 40 per hectare.[15]

In the process of this rapid turnover, some peasants also managed to buy hacienda land. For example, in the early 1950s, some of the arrendires on the Hacienda Chaquil were given the opportunity to buy fairly large tracts of grazing land before this hacienda was sold by the Requejo family to Felipe Ganoza, who resold it to the Cerro de Pasco Corporation in 1953.[16] A year later, the Cerro de Pasco Corporation sold out to Gonzalo Pajares. Between 1957 and 1965, Pajares subdivided and sold parcels of this hacienda to peasants and others; he did likewise with the haciendas Purhuay and Huacataz. (The full story of his entrepreneurship is discussed in the next section.)

In the land sales of the 1960s, landowners clearly were motivated to terminate feudal obligations. As landlords scrambled to reduce the size of their estates, they also rid themselves of peasants who could claim *feudatario* status (and thus preferential rights to land) under the impending agrarian reform. Although it was never clear that the Belaunde government would go beyond a selective application of the 1964 reform law, estate subdivisions were a good insurance policy.

The land sales continued at an accelerating pace over this decade. The properties of the Cacho family (haciendas La Quispa, Polloquito, and Hotel Polloc) and of the Buenos (Hacienda Sondor, formerly; at this time known as Casablanca and Vista Alegre) were extensively subdivided, both among family members and through sales to the peasantry. Even Rafael Puga sold 5,117 hectares of the southern portion of the Hacienda La Pauca in 1960, primarily to peasants, although the largest block, some 1,600 hectares, was sold to Pedro Pajares, who subsequently parceled it at a significant profit (Chambeu and Gorget 1975, 30).

The various church groups and public charities rid themselves of their remaining properties. The Asilo de Ancianos Desámparados in the mid-1960s sold parcels of the fundo Cristo Rey to the peasantry and, in 1970, sold the bulk

15. Drawn from Notaría Pública de Ernesto Velarde Aizcote, Lima, "Testimonio de Escritura de Venta, 1951"; and Notaría de Luis Vergara, Cajamarca, "Protocolo del Bieno 1953–54, No. 983, Fojas 1078, 1955"; both in Pajares files.

16. Drawn from Notaría Pública de Luis Vergara, "Segundo Testimonio, No. 1965, Fs. 2214, 1953"; and Notaría Pública y de Hacienda de Alfonso Rodriguez, "Primer Testimonio, No. 3368, Fs. 3374, 1956"; both in Pajares files.

of the fundo itself (Burga Posito et al. 1980, 14). The Madres Concepcionistas finally parceled not only the haciendas Santa Ursula and Pallán but also Chotén and Yana Yacu (Valderrama 1974, 4).

The actual magnitude and dates of the hacienda sales are difficult to estimate. Working through the property register of the department, Mariano Valderrama (1974, table 1) enumerated entries corresponding to the parceling of thirty-seven haciendas registered between 1962 and 1970. His estimates of the size of these haciendas suggest that about 400,000 hectares were sold, equivalent to approximately one-third of the total lands reported in use in the 1961 census. Few of the land purchases by the peasantry were actually registered in the department's land registry, however. For example, the parceling of the section of the Hacienda Combayo known as Santa Rosa was completed by 1968; this section, 8,906 hectares, was subdivided into 129 lots with the assistance of the Instituto de Reforma Agraria y Colonización. But as of December 1981, only fifty-four sales, totaling 3,145 hectares, had been officially registered by the new owners.[17]

Most sales were conducted on the basis of either oral contracts or handwritten sales slips; at best, they were notarized legally if not officially registered. Of a sample of 433 peasants who had purchased land on the Hacienda Porcón, for example, only 45 percent had legal property titles, and few of these sales were recorded in the public registry (Bazán 1972, 9). Scott (1976, 329) reported that some eighty thousand property owners in Cajamarca showed up to register their properties under the provisions of the 1964 reform and that fewer than 10 percent held legal titles to their land. This would prove to be a major problem in the 1970s.

The data presented in Table 17, for six haciendas, illustrate some other characteristics of the process. The average size of the parcels sold varied significantly on different haciendas. This variation partly reflects the relative importance of natural pastures in the composition of lands sold and other land quality considerations. On the Hacienda Combayo, for example, most sales included a significant amount of natural pastures. The average size of purchase also varied with the social position of the buyer. Some haciendas were largely subdivided among the resident peasantry, whereas others were carved up into medium-sized farms. The sales on the Hacienda La Quispa followed this latter trend. Table 17 also demonstrates how the average price per hectare varied on different estates, again a function of the amount of pasture land included in the sale, the size of the purchase, and the social position of the buyer (see Chapter 7). Because the price data reflect the year in which the sale was agreed upon—a date not known with precision—and not the year in which the sale was registered, it is difficult to draw any definitive conclusions from these

17. These sales were recorded in Registros Públicos de Cajamarca, Registro de la Propiedad, city of Cajamarca (RPC) (2: 235).

TABLE 17. Registered Land Sales on Selected Haciendas

Hacienda	Years in Which Sales were Registered	Number of Sales	Total Hectares Sold	Average Sale (Hectares)	Total Value of Sales (Current Peruvian Soles)	Average Price per Hectare (Current Peruvian Soles)
Combayo	1969–1980	51	3,145	61.7	1,834,160	583
Santa Ursula	1962–1979	38	652	17.2	445,798	684
Sondor	1963–1980	38	281	7.4	233,950	833
Vista Alegre	1964–1980	20	753	37.6	425,394	565
La Quispa	1955–1977	14	2,820	201.4	748,400	265
Polloquito	1960–1977	29	615	21.2	425,200	692

SOURCES: Registros Públicos de Cajamarca, Registro de la Propiedad, city of Cajamarca (2:235; 8:108; 183:351; 144:295; 95:329–331; 165:309).
NOTE: The table includes only sales for which complete data on the number of hectares and the price were reported. Approximately 5 percent more sales were registered than are shown here, but they were recorded with incomplete information.

data, for the 1960s saw continual inflation. With this caveat, the data on the total value of registered sales at least suggest the importance of these sales as a source of capitalization for the dairy farms.

The data in Table 17 exclude those land sales that represent partitions of haciendas among family members. The Hacienda Santa Teresita de La Quispa (made up of one-third of the former Hacienda Polloc, the Hacienda Polloquito, and several other annexes) was inscribed in the public land registry by Manuel Cacho Sousa in 1939 as consisting of 7,500 hectares.[18] Manuel's son, Carlos Cacho Sousa Castro, took over the management of the core of the hacienda in 1954, officially renting La Quispa for ten years for a monthly rental fee of S/. 5,000. In 1958 the section of the hacienda known as Polloquito (3,136 hectares) was sold to another son, Luis. Carlos purchased the hacienda core, 200 hectares, for S/. 100,000 in 1962; and in 1965 a daughter, Delia, purchased 1,000 hectares for the same amount. The Hotel Polloc section was purchased by a relative, Gonzalo Saenz Cacho. By 1965, as a result of the partition of the hacienda among family members, as well as land sales, Manuel Cacho Sousa owned only 500 hectares of the former estate. The Cacho Sousas thus expected their properties to be exempt from the possible implementation of the 1964 agrarian reform.

THE FARMER PATH IN CAJAMARCA

Until the 1940s, most landlords who rented properties of the church and public charities were concerned only with maximizing their accumulation of surplus through the collection of feudal rents. The growing market opportunities of the 1940s attracted a new breed of arrendire, however, one interested in reorganizing the productive process. But there were often structural impediments to what members of this modernizing group could do with their rental properties, for the landowners sometimes controlled key conditions of the exploitation of labor. On the church-owned Hacienda Santa Ursula and the fundo Cristo Rey, for example, arrendires were explicitly prevented from expelling peasants, and the number of peasant households they could bring onto the hacienda was restricted (Burga Posito et al. 1980, 24). Rental contracts sometimes stipulated that at the end of the rental period the owner would not compensate the arrendire for any improvements (Hacienda Santa Ursula; fundo Miraflores, in Burga Posito et al. 1980, 16).

Of those who attempted to develop dairy activities on their rental properties, despite the obstacles, Juan Miguel Rossell was one of the most

18. Notaría Pública y de Hacienda de Dr. Alfonso Rodríguez, "Minuta de Segundo Testimonio, No. 68, Fs. 83, 1949," Pajares files. In 1939 two-thirds of the former Hacienda Polloc, principally the jalca section, had been sold by Manuel Cacho Gálvez to Ricardo Knoch Hempell. Knoch made some sales of land to the peasantry of the community of Tambomayo and perhaps others in the 1940s (Chambeu 1975f).

successful. Through a process of both feudal and capitalist accumulation, he generated the resources to purchase and develop one of the exemplary dairy farms of the province, the Hacienda Tres Molinos. Rossell rented his first property, the Hacienda Huayobamba, in the district of San Marcos, in 1942. This hacienda had recently been purchased by Augusto Gil, who subsequently donated it to the Beneficiencia Pública of Celendín in 1949 (Mejía and Correa 1979, 7). Rossell rented this 1,775-hectare hacienda until 1957 for an annual sum of S/. 12,000. Over a fifteen-year period, he succeeded in forming a small labor force of wage workers on the hacienda and developed one of the better dairy herds in the province. The arrendire who preceded Rossell, Miguel Zevallos, had already introduced dairy cattle to the hacienda, bringing some fifty Brown Swiss from Sunchubamba; but his activities had been confined to butter production for the San Marcos market. Rossell considerably expanded the irrigated and improved pastures of the hacienda after the road from Cajamarca to San Marcos was completed in 1945 and the PERULAC plant installed. By the early 1950s, he had a herd of some eight hundred cattle, producing 1,000 liters of milk daily (Chávez Aliaga 1957, 1:247).

In the late 1940s, this hacienda had about 280 hectares of irrigated land, of which Rossell reserved 120 hectares for his dairy activities. The remaining irrigated land was in the hands of the approximately eighty-five sharecropper households residing on the hacienda. Rossell continued to sharecrop with these tenants and rented out the remaining pasture lands to peasants from nearby communities. According to interviews on this hacienda, Rossell maintained the same regime of labor obligations as his predecessor: the sharecroppers provided only one day a month of unpaid faena labor. But he introduced the payment of wages for a new obligation—an additional week of labor per year for the development of the hacienda's infrastructure.[19] He began to assemble a skilled, permanent work force on the hacienda by training some young men as specialists in the care of dairy cattle; others were trained as tractor drivers or mechanics. Their wives were trained as milkmaids.

In the late 1940s, Rossell rented two other haciendas: Cochamarca, from Manuel Cacho Sousa; and Casa Blanca, from Olga Bueno. He pursued dairy farming on both of these rentals while continuing to sharecrop with the resident peasantry. According to advertisements in *El Rodeo* (1948, no. 9), he was marketing significant quantities of wheat, barley, potatoes, and corn— produced by his sharecroppers—as well as specializing in the sale of improved cattle breeds.

19. My interviews on this hacienda in October 1976 confirm the data on labor services in the 1940s reported by Rivera (1974, 4). A later report on this hacienda (Mejía and Correa 1979) does not specifically mention the administration of Rossell but notes that in 1942 the labor services on the hacienda increased to one week per month. According to my interviews, it was the arrendires who followed Rossell—Julio de la Puente and Abraham Noriega—who tried to increase the labor services of the sharecroppers and rid themselves of many of the arrendires.

In 1950 Rossell made his first purchase of land in the valley of Cajamarca, buying the small fundo El Triunfo. He dropped the rental of the Hacienda Cochamarca and increasingly concentrated his best herd in the valley. In these years, he had some 450 head of dairy cattle on the 84-hectare spread in the valley, another 250 on Casa Blanca, and 800 head on Huayobamba. Rossell purchased what was to become the center of his dairy activities in the valley, the Hacienda Tres Molinos, in 1952 for 1 million soles.[20] At the same time, he purchased the smaller, neighboring fundo La Merced, thus consolidating approximately 260 hectares of land in the northern corner of the valley. As he purchased these haciendas, he moved the sharecroppers who had remained on the valley bottom land to the higher elevations of the Hacienda Tres Molinos and, as noted earlier, sold small parcels of land to these peasants, thus ending all obligations to them. In the mid-1950s, Juan Rossell used only wage labor for his increasingly capitalized dairy production. In addition to operating a modern butter factory on Tres Molinos, Rossell supplied milk to PERULAC and to Vásquez's manjar blanco factory.

In the 1950s, capitalist land rentals were much more common in the valley of Cajamarca than on the larger haciendas. During this period, more than half of the forty-four major dairy entrepreneurs (each producing more than 60 liters of milk a day) were renting their farms (Chávez Aliaga 1957, 1:246–247), and most relied on a small, permanent wage labor force. Over the next fifteen years, many of these capitalist-arrendires purchased land, forming capitalist dairy farms on the basis of private property. The partition of the haciendas offered the opportunity; the heavy investment in infrastructure required by dairy farming provided the incentive. At times, they had no choice: they were forced to buy their farms because absentee landowners were no longer willing to rent, given the potential threat of state expropriation. This particular situation is what turned Rafael Gómez Sánchez into a property owner.

Gómez Sánchez was a specialist in dairy husbandry, trained at the National Agrarian University, La Molina, in Lima.[21] As a young man, he was hired by PERULAC to assist in developing the Cajamarcan dairy industry. He had been charged with PERULAC's promotional activities, providing technical assistance to the valley dairy farmers in animal health, adaptation of new dairy breeds, and artificial insemination. He had also been involved in developing improved pasture varieties and for a while managed the tractor pool run by the firm. In the early 1950s, he was charged with developing the new milk collection routes in the province. Gómez Sánchez worked for PERULAC for seven and a half years before deciding to go into dairy farming for himself.

In 1956 he rented the fundo Argentina in the valley and proceeded to build

20. According to Becerra Bazán et al. (1981, 14), Rossell paid S/. 333,400 for the land; the S/. 1 million includes the valuation of the cattle and eucalyptus on the property.

21. I interviewed Rafael Gómez Sánchez in Cajamarca in September 1976 and again in December 1981.

one of the prize dairy herds of the province. His was a model capitalist operation, relying exclusively on a wage labor force that he carefully trained. In 1961, when the potentially more productve fundo Cristo Rey was available, he rented the 102-hectare core of this fundo from the Asilo de Ancianos Desámparados. Because land values were continually rising, he was to pay progressively increasing annual rents, beginning at S/. 120,000 in the first year; by 1971, at the end of his ten-year contract, he was to have paid S/. 168,000 per year. In addition, throughout the rental period, he was to provide 40 liters of milk daily to the Asilo for its charity activities.[22]

Gómez Sánchez had no real interest in buying property and considered it a useless way to tie up capital. It seemed much more productive to invest in high-quality dairy cattle, of which he had 180 head, and to specialize in breeding improved bulls and cows, while supplying milk to PERULAC as a complementary activity. National political events, however, forced him to buy land. After the promulgation of the 1969 Agrarian Reform Law, the Asilo decided to sell the fundo Cristo Rey. Gómez Sánchez purchased the 102 hectares in 1970 at a cost of S/. 40,000 per hectare. The Asilo itself financed the operation, providing Gómez Sánchez with a S/. 5 million mortgage on the propety for ten years (Burga Posita et al. 1980, 14). In this manner, the Asilo protected itself from being classified as an absentee landowner during the upcoming reform.

The farmer way of capitalist development in Cajamarca thus involved both capitalist renting and the purchase of land to establish capitalist dairy farms. Social origins were what primarily distinguished this farmer group from the agrarian bourgeoisie who followed the Junker path of capitalist development. Whereas those on the Junker path had generally been born into the Cajamarcan landed oligarchy, most of those pursuing the farmer way were new entrants to the Cajamarcan elite and, often, to the agricultural sector. Some were technicians, such as Gómez Sánchez, or state employees and functionaries. Others were doctors, lawyers, teachers, and housewives. Many came from the ranks of the rural petty bourgeoisie, including small shopkeepers and former mill operators, as well as cattle traders and merchants. A few were wage workers. All took advantage of the booming land market to rent or purchase potential dairy farms.

The Potential for Upward Mobility

One of the most remarkable entrepreneurial stories of the period is that of Gonzalo Pajares Goicochea.[23] Born into the rural petty bourgeoisie, he formed his original capital through cattle trading in the 1940s; by the late 1950s, he

---

22. RPC (8:331); cited in Burga Posita et al. (1980, 13–14).

23. The following entrepreneurial history is based on interviews with Gonzalo Pajares; his wife, Beatríz Velázquez de Pajares; and their children, Adolfo, Elsy, and Napoleón Pajares Velázquez, in Cajamarca, December 1981. The oral history is complemented by archival materials from Pajares's personal files cited elsewhere.

owned six haciendas and a number of smaller properties in the provinces of Cajamarca and Cajabamba. In the 1960s, through the use of the labor services of the resident peasantry, as well as funds generated through the parceling of these haciendas, he formed an impressive set of dairy enterprises in the valley of Condebamba.

Pajares was born in 1919, in the pueblo of Namora, into a family of eight children. His father owned some 10 hectares of land, but his main occupation was the operation of the local grain mill. Pajares grew up alternating schooling with work for his father in the mill and on the family property. He finished the eighth grade and then took his first job, as an employee of the Franciscan monks.

The Franciscans had received a donation of a 10-hectare farm, which had been carved out of the Hacienda Tartar in the Cajamarca Valley in the early 1940s, and Pajares was hired to raise dairy cattle on the property. He was initially paid S/. 30 a month. He was newly married, and his wife, Beatríz Velázquez, took charge of the daily milking activities while he cared for the cattle and transported the milk to the monastery each day. According to don Gonzalo, the only way to get ahead during these years was to trade in cattle. Because he had access to the pastures of the farm, he began purchasing cattle in the jalcas and bringing them to the valley to fatten, later reselling them to the cattle merchants from the coast. In the early years, his half-brothers, Anuario and Absalón Pajares, who were also cattle traders, financed his trading operations. Because the trips to purchase cattle often took him away from the valley for weeks at a time, Pajares hired a peon to take care of his responsibilities to the Franciscans. He recalls that they were not especially pleased with his trading, but because he worked hard to improve the pastures and because milk production increased steadily, they tolerated his entrepreneurial activity.

In order to expand his cattle-fattening and trading operations, Pajares rented several small fundos in the valley in the late 1940s: Huacariz, from Isabel de Casteñada; La Redonda and Florestal, belonging to María de Arredondo; and the fundo Belempampa, from the Beneficiencia of Celendín. His main interest in managing these fundos was cultivating pasture as feed for his cattle operation. But by the early 1950s, Pajares was investing in dairy cattle as well and supplying milk to PERULAC. He had some 240 head of dairy cattle in production on the fundos Belempampa and Ajoscancha, having purchased the latter with his half-brother Absalón (Chávez Aliaga 1957, 1:247). He also purchased the fundo Santa Elena, near the city of Cajamarca, and moved his growing family there. By now, he had resigned his position with the Franciscans and could no longer reside on that property.

In 1949 Pajares also made his first purchase of land outside the valley of Cajamarca. He joined with eight partners to purchase the jalcas of Polloc from Ricardo Knoch. He was interested in this property primarily for its huge expanses of natural pastures suitable for grazing cattle. In 1953, at the age of thirty-four, Gonzalo Pajares purchased his own large hacienda, buying the 5,000-hectare Hacienda Purhuay for S/. 200,000. An indication of the wealth he had acquired is that he purchased this hacienda with a down payment of S/. 80,000 and paid off the remainder in ten months without relying on credit. That same year, he purchased the 2,700-hectare Hacienda Chaquil for the sum of S/. 650,000, paying S/. 350,000 of this in cash.

The haciendas Purhuay and Chaquil were located in the highlands of the district of La Encañada and did not have good sources of water for irrigation. Pajares intended to use these properties mainly to fatten cattle during the rainy season. But the haciendas also had a relatively good-sized labor force and were good agricultural investments, producing potatoes and other tubers, wheat, and barley through sharecropping arrangements. According to don Gonzalo, he maintained the same labor arrangements that had prevailed earlier on the estates. He gave the tenants seed and access to land, and the sharecroppers provided the labor; the crop was later divided in equal shares. In addition, the sharecroppers were obligated to provide fifteen days a year of faena. He successfully introduced the practice of paying off the faena outside the estate, and the Pajares home in Cajamarca was built with this faena labor.

In 1957 Pajares purchased his first estate outside the province of Cajamarca, in the valley of Condebamba. This valley is at a lower elevation than the valley of Cajamarca, and the prevailing wisdom was that once developed, the dairy industry would be even more productive in the valley of Condebamba than in Cajamarca. Therefore, he began disposing of his rentals in the Cajamarca Valley—several were passed on to his brothers and sisters—and concentrating his energies and wealth on developing the Hacienda Amarucho in the

TABLE 18.   Purchases of Haciendas by Gonzalo Pajares

Year of Purchase	*Hacienda*	*Hectares*	*Price*	*Previous Owner*
1949	Polloc (jalcas)	4,271	S/. 53,750	Ricardo Knoch
1953	Purhuay	5,000	200,000	Wenceslao Valera Villacorta
1953	Chaquil	2,700	600,000	Cerro de Pasco Corp.
1956	Chaquil	a	50,000	Requejo Zevallos family
1957	Amarucho	860	1,000,000	Segundo Ibañez
1958	Huacataz	8,196	500,000	Victor Burga Saavedra
1962	Pampa La Culebra	294	200,000	Madres Concepcionistas
1963	El Huayo	800	exchange	Negociación Agrícola El Huayo
1969	Combayo (core)	410	a	Rosalía Santolalla Bernal

SOURCE: "Escrituras de Compra-Venta," files of Gonzalo Pajares, Cajamarca.
aNo data available.

Condebamba. Doing so required considerable investment, for a road had to be built, a canal system developed, and flood control introduced. His main problem was obtaining the labor needed to carry out his plans.

Pajares solved the labor problem by mobilizing the resident tenants on his Cajamarcan estates. Every fifteen days, a truck would be sent to the haciendas Purhuay and Chaquil to bring the resident peasants to work in the Conde-bamba Valley, on a rotating basis. The tenants were first required to pay off their faena obligations, which, according to Pajares, were remunerated, and could then work for higher wages. During this period, Pajares continued to purchase and rent other haciendas in the Cajamarcan highlands in order to secure sufficient labor for developing the Condebamba hacienda.

In 1957 he rented the Hacienda Santa Ursula from the Madres Concepcio-nistas. This hacienda had more than eighty-eight resident households (Peru 1940, vol. 2, table 34). Subsequently, he purchased the Hacienda Huacataz, which had nearly one hundred fifty resident households. By the late 1950s, Gonzalo Pajares owned a string of contiguous haciendas on the eastern highlands of the valley of Cajamarca, spanning approximately 20,000 hectares (see Table 18). The resident labor force on which he could draw to develop the Condebamba estates consisted of more than five hundred households.

The majority of Pajares's land purchases in the 1960s were in the Condebamba Valley. He acquired the 800-hectare fundo El Huayo in the Condebamba as a trade for a 235-hectare section of the Hacienda Huacataz. He also bought a number of smaller properties (including the fundos El Algarrobo, Mangallana, and Cholocal) that surrounded his two larger fundos, joining an entire section of the Condebamba Valley under his ownership. El Huayo at this time was totally undeveloped, without access to irrigation; thus Pajares proceeded to build a 27.5-kilometer canal to bring water to the hacienda. In order to secure workers for this undertaking, as well as to generate the funds to capitalize the Condebamba estates, Pajares moved to subdivide and sell most of his highland haciendas. It proved to be a brilliant strategy of labor recruitment.

As Pajares says, "I carried out a legal, private land reform." He commenced sales on the Hacienda Chaquil in 1957, following with sales on the haciendas Purhuay and Huacataz. Most peasants purchased their usufruct parcels by migrating to the Condebamba Valley to work off their debt over the next ten years. At the prevailing wage of S/. 3 per day plus food, the average peasant had to work approximately three hundred days for each hectare of land purchased (see Table 19).[24] Pajares's own records register only a fraction of the

24. According to Manrique and Valderrama's (1974) interviews on the Hacienda Huacataz, Pajares increased the faena on this hacienda to six days of labor per month. Peasant households were required to send a migrant to Condebamba for fifteen days a month, but only one week would be remunerated, because the first week consisted of the faena obligation, which, according to these interviews, remained unpaid. This of course would have significantly increased the total amount of labor time required to purchase a land parcel.

TABLE 19.   Land Sales by Gonzalo Pajares to the Resident Peasantry on
Three Haciendas

Hacienda	Years of Sales	Number of Sales	Total Hectares Sold	Total Value of Sales	Average Size of Parcel	Average Price per Hectare
Chaquil	1957–1965	34	297.9	S/. 261,370	7.45	S/. 877
Purhuay	1958–1968	40	158.9	157,920	4.68	994
Huacataz	1958–1965	110	882.4	732,438	8.02	830

SOURCE: "Escrituras de Compra-Venta de Fracciones de Terreno, 1969," Notario Público Mario Silva Rocha, files of Gonzalo Pajares, Cajamarca.

total land sales made during this period. Even fewer sales are officially registered in the public land registry of Cajamarca.[25] Most were concluded only with spoken agreements or handwritten receipts. Also, many peasants never finished paying off their debt and thus were not included in the declarations of sale summarized in Table 19. According to a 1965 account of his assets, Pajares was owed some S/. 400,000 by hacienda peasants for land sales. By then, he had sold off all of the Hacienda Chaquil and had only 150 hectares left on the Hacienda Purhuay, as well as the jalcas of Polloc and those of Huacataz.

Many of the land sales were made not to the resident peasantry but rather to the Cajamarcan petty bourgeoisie, which was eager to purchase land. A number of medium-sized properties were carved out of the haciendas. For example, the core of the Hacienda Chaquil, 221 hectares, was sold to Adolfo Bueno León. On the Hacienda Huacataz, 100 hectares were sold to the cattle trader Pedro Ruiz Soto, and 123 hectares, including the casa hacienda, to Victoriano Muñoz. At least another three large sections were sold to town residents in the subsequent years. Even the civil guard became involved, buying smaller 10-hectare farms (Manrique and Valderrama 1974). According to Pajares, these sales were always made on the "lands of the hacienda," those that had traditionally been part of the hacienda's demesne. Nonetheless, considerable conflict was to be generated on these haciendas in later years over these land sales. If they had access to water, the new farms of the petty bourgeoisie were dedicated to dairy production; otherwise, they were used to fatten cattle.

For his part, Gonzalo Pajares invested the funds generated from the sales of land, as well as the hours that the sales represented in labor time, in the Condebamba Valley. In 1965 the Hacienda Amarcucho was worth S/. 2.2 million, and El Huayo was worth S/. 2.0 million. He carried out some land sales in this valley as well, selling some thirty-seven blocks of property for S/. 1.3

25. For example, Manrique and Valderrama (1974) reported only seventy-five registered sales for the Hacienda Huacataz over the period from 1961 to 1971 and only a handful for the Hacienda Purhuay.

million over a five-year period. In 1965 Pajares's total assets were on the order of S/. 10 million.

More typical of the farmer path of capitalist development in Cajamarca than Pajares's merchant/landlord/farmer route was the trajectory of Abelardo Rojas, at one time a wage worker on the plantation Casa Grande.[26] As an employee of a dairy farm, he was able to accumulate the initial capital to purchase land and invest in a dairy herd. The scale of his eventual dairy farm— 57 hectares, with eighty dairy cattle—is also more representative of the dairy industry in Cajamarca.

Abelardo Rojas's family, like that of Pajares, was from the rural petty bourgeoisie, positioned socially between the rich peasantry and the lower urban middle class. His father had migrated from Spain in the late nineteenth century, marrying a peasant woman from the district of Jesús and going to work as an employee of the haciendas Sexemayo and Huacraruco. Abelardo and his siblings, however, grew up in the city of Cajamarca. After finishing primary school, Rojas migrated to the coast on his own volition at the age of twelve. For the next ten years, from 1934 to 1944, he was a wage worker on the plantation Casa Grande. He returned to the sierra after his father died, to help his mother cultivate the 6 hectares of land they had purchased in the community of Yanamarca, in Jesús. There, he married Rita Alcalde, the daughter of relatively well-to-do peasants, and shortly thereafter began his career as a technician and administrator of a dairy farm in the valley.

He first worked on the fundo Shultín for Enrique Dobbertin, who trained him in veterinary techniques. The next year, in 1945, he became the administrator of the 153-hectare fundo Tartar Grande, the property of Susana Miranda and her husband, Ing. Emilio Alzamora. Over the next twenty years, Rojas developed this as a prosperous dairy farm. As he recalls, he constructed the stables and canals, improved the pastures, and built up the Alzamoras' herd to approximately 1,200 by the early 1950s. According to don Abelardo, when he first went to work for Alzamora he earned S/. 50 per month, which he considered a good salary; peons earned only S/. 1 per day. Moreover, his agreement with Alzamora was that he would be entitled to 20 percent of the hacienda's profits. That payment never materialized, however, and instead he was given permission to pasture his own cattle on the improved pastures of the hacienda. In addition, he received one dairy calf a year in lieu of vacations.

Rojas purchased his first piece of property, from his uncle, in the late 1940s with a loan from his employer. This small farm was contiguous with his own inheritance in Yanamarca. Over the next decade, he continued to purchase lands in Yanamarca, mostly by buying out the heirs of his wife's family, and by 1958 he had accumulated 57 hectares of land. Throughout the 1950s, his wife oversaw the sharecropping of this land with neighboring peasant households.

26. I interviewed Abelardo Rojas in Cajamarca in December 1981.

In 1959 they invested in a tractor and began putting in improved pastures. When Rojas resigned from his job on the fundo Tartar Grande in 1962, he had accumulated a herd of eighty dairy cattle. These were subsequently moved to the emerging dairy farm in Yanamarca, which now had 30 irrigated hectares of pasture. He employed three or four wage workers, although only the two milkmaids were permanent employees. Rojas continued to work the dairy farm himself, aided by one of his daughters.[27]

These examples of entrepreneurial activity illustrate the dynamic growth resulting from the development of the dairy industry in Cajamarca. The farmer way was spurred both by the possibility of profitable milk production and by the expansion of the land market, a product of the changes in the dominant class relations occurring in the province.

CONCLUSION

The transformation of the dominant class relations on the Cajamarcan haciendas from feudal to capitalist took approximately thirty years. The process was uneven and contradictory, with feudal class relations often the basis for the process of accumulation that engendered capitalist dairy farms. The development of the dairy industry also contributed to dissolving the conditions of existence of feudal class relations, both by its effect on the land market and as a result of its particular labor requirements.

Another factor supporting the change in class relations and the switch from food production to dairy farming (besides the relative profitability of the two activities) was the shifting national political current, which made agrarian reform increasingly inevitable. This, along with the rising value of land and the capitalization requirements of the dairy enterprises, accelerated the parceling of the haciendas and the expansion of petty production among the peasantry. It also engendered the partial dispossession of the peasantry and the consolidation of a small wage labor force on the dairy farms. The land sales also contributed to making medium-sized farms employing a minimal number of permanent wage workers the basis for the Cajamarcan dairy industry. As a result, the new agrarian capitalist class was most heterogeneous. Not only did feudal landlords and landlord-arrendires change class positions; merchants, employees, and even wage workers became capitalist extractors of surplus value while often occupying multiple class positions.

27. The entrepreneurial history of Abelardo Rojas suggests that the capitalized family farm, employing small amounts of wage labor, was indeed compatible with what Lehmann has termed the "involuted path" of agrarian estate development. See Lehmann (1982) on two paths of agrarian development in Latin America.

SEVEN

The Peasant Household in the Transition

Commenting on the fact that the population of the province was one-third Indian, Luis Amorín, president of the Association of Agriculturalists and Cattlemen of Cajamarca, considered the indigenous people of Cajamarca to be "a negative factor," for they neither produced nor consumed. "Their life oscillates between laziness and vices, best expressed by their absurd religiosity...seen in the innumerable fiestas commemorating a church saint, a sterile activity that must absorb three-quarters of their time during the year." Amorín also complained of the Indians' "lack of racial pride, their spiritual hollowness and negative temperament," in contrast to the mestizos of the province who were "clearly intelligent and hard-working" (Amorín 1948, 1).

But even as Amorín was writing, the "Indios" of the Cajamarcan haciendas were becoming the skilled labor force of the new dairy farms. Moreover, the Junker path of development in Cajamarca, based on the subdivision and sale of hacienda lands, created a precondition for the expansion of petty production and the social reproduction of an independent peasantry. Peasant producers—Indian, mestizo, and white—were to provide an increasing share of Cajamarca's foodstuffs. A significant number would also become dairy producers. And, after the 1940s, the peasantry of Cajamarca also became increasingly literate, a result of their demands that the state expand schooling.[1]

The development of capitalism in agriculture, however, produced quite heterogeneous results. Some peasant households accumulated means of production and employed wage labor. Most offered their labor power for sale. The process of social differentiation, based on multiple class positions and

1. Data on twenty-six peasant communities reveal that in 1972–1973, twenty-one had schools. The earliest had been built in 1934 in La Laimina, Jesús. Approximately half the schools were set up in the 1940s, with the remainder built more recently (Chambeu, Garay, and Samaniego 1975, table 4).

differing positions within the capitalist class process, was partially related to the unequal access to means of production that resulted from the land sales, itself a product of feudal differentiation on the haciendas. The rapid monetization of the rural economy, spurred by the development of the land market, which integrated petty producers even more tightly into product and labor markets, also contributed to social differentiation and gradually eroded some of those "sterile activities" that the cattleman Luis Amorín disdained.

THE CREATION OF A WAGE LABOR FORCE ON THE ESTATES

The switch from agricultural production to dairy farming on the haciendas created a small and relatively skilled wage labor force that included both men and women. But the process of conversion to new class relations placed different demands on men and women, demands that affected their roles within the household unit.

The initial investment in infrastructure for dairy production relied almost exclusively on male labor services. Large numbers of men were required to build irrigation systems and enclosures and to improve pastures. On most haciendas—including La Pauca, Combayo, and Polloc—this period of estate development brought about an increase in the surplus labor time appropriated from men.

The increased demand for male labor services often required women to take on greater responsibility for the household subsistence plot. This was particularly true when men were forced to emigrate, for example, to the Condebamba Valley from Gonzalo Pajares's haciendas to perform the required labor services. But as agricultural production on the haciendas' demesnes declined, the agricultural processing that had required so much female labor in the past declined. The female mingas were slowly eliminated, as landowners dedicated more and more land to cattle production and parceled the remaining hacienda lands.

As landlords invested in improved cattle breeds, the skill requirements of the labor force also increased. According to the dairy entrepreneurs, greater responsibility was now required of workers, and the management of cattle could no longer be entrusted to women or children. Only men were recruited and trained as full-time cattle hands (punteros). Men replaced women not only in animal raising but also in the tasks associated with butter and cheese production, previously carried out by peasant women in their homes. As the scale of milk production increased, landowners invested in modern butter- and cheese-making equipment and trained men in this new and highly skilled occupation. Capitalizing the productive process and upgrading the skill level of the labor force thus brought about a change in the traditional gender division of labor.

Although these two activities that had traditionally been defined as female became male occupations when the skill level increased, one task, milking, remained within the female domain. According to the dairy entrepreneurs, women were uniquely qualified for this job because they had the greater physical agility necessary for stooping beside the cows for hours at a time and the greater dexterity and attentiveness needed to ensure that all the milk was extracted from the cows' udders.[2] In addition, milking was compatible with women's domestic role: because it is usually done in two shifts, in the early morning and the late afternoon, a skilled labor force could be created that did not need to be employed for a full workday.

Milking was also the last occupation in the emerging dairy enterprises to be remunerated. When women finally received regular payments for this work, the rate of remuneration was considerably less than what men received for a comparable hour of work. For example, when dairy cattle were introduced on the Hacienda Huacariz de San Antonio in the early 1940s, the male sharecroppers trained as punteros and as workers in the processing factory were paid between S/.0.50 and S/.1.00 daily (see Table 16). By the mid-1940s, milking had become a specialized activity carried out by a group of five women, but they received only tips for their labor, on the order of S/.1.00 per month.

On the Hacienda Huayobamba in San Marcos, wages were paid regularly to both male and female workers by the late 1940s. But whereas men were remunerated at the rate of S/.1.00 for an eight- to ten-hour working day, the dairy maids earned only S/.3.00 per month, or S/.0.10 for a four- to five-hour working day. The hourly wage gap was about five to one. Wages in the valley of Cajamarca were considerably higher, but the gap persisted. On the Hacienda Tres Molinos, the dairy maids earned S/.10 per month in 1948, or S/.0.33 per day; in those years, male workers in the valley dairy enterprises earned S/.3 to S/.4 per day.

By the late 1950s, male wages in the dairy industry were becoming fairly standardized, but female wages varied tremendously, depending largely on the predilection of different landowners. As Table 20 shows, the wages of milkmaids on the Hacienda Huacariz de San Antonio lagged considerably behind those paid by the more thoroughly capitalistic and less paternalistic Juan Miguel Rossell of the Hacienda Tres Molinos.

On the Hacienda Huacariz de San Antonio, women's servile obligations to the landlord also continued, even as women became part of the specialized wage labor force. The milkmaids on this dairy farm were always subject to overtime work at no extra pay. Because milking is done in two shifts per day, the labor process lends itself to abuse. Between shifts, José Velgara frequently used

2. At least one dairy entrepreneur was aware of how taxing the work of milking actually was. In an article in *El Rodeo* (1949, 15), Enrique Dobbertin, the owner of the Hacienda Shultín Grande, explained that milking 8 to 9 liters of milk required some eight hundred hand motions. He estimated that milking ten cows twice a day required the same energy expenditure as lifting 80 quintales of grain 1 meter high.

TABLE 20.   Observations on Monthly Wages of Milkmaids on Provincial Dairy Farms, 1942–1976
(in Current Peruvian Soles)

	Huacariz de San Antonio	Tres Molinos	Other Farms
1942	1		
1948		10	3[a]
1952	10		
1955		50	
1956		92	
1958	50		
1959			50
1964		400	
1965	60		348[b]
1967	100		
1970			540[b]
1971		600	558[c]
1973		690	
1974	350		
1975		840	1,095[b]
1976	1,200[d]	869[d]	1,380[b]

SOURCES: Information on Huacariz de San Antonio and Tres Molinos is based on the
author's interviews with milkmaids during January and February 1976 (using the
most frequent response for each year, wages net of benefits). Data for Tres Molinos
for 1971 and 1973, and for both enterprises for 1976, were corroborated by
information in the Planillas de Trabajo at the office of the Ministry of Labor in
Cajamarca. Information on the Hacienda Huayobamba is based on the author's
interviews with milkmaids on the CAP Huayobamba in October 1976. Information
for 1959 is from *Boletín* (1960, no. 1). Information on the fundo Cristo Rey is based
on "Informe de Empadronamiento y Verificación, Fundo Cristo Rey, Septiembre
1973," fundo Cristo Rey file, Agrarian Reform Office, Ministry of Agriculture,
Agrarian Zone II, Cajamarca.
[a] Hacienda Huayobamba, San Marcos.
[b] The legal minimum wage (estimate based on four hours of work per day, thirty days
of work per month), not including social security and other deductions.
[c] Fundo Cristo Rey, Cajamarca.
[d] In 1976 Huacariz de San Antonio was a production cooperative; Tres Molinos
remained a private enterprise.

the unpaid labor of his female workers for such traditionally female tasks as
processing grains and cooking for the male field hands. When asked why they
complied, the milkmaids responded that they were intimidated by the landlord,
who thought nothing of beating them. Moreover, if they did not comply, there
were plenty of other women willing to take their places, even under such
oppressive conditions.

By the 1960s, the semanera duty had also been transformed. Perhaps
because of the greater availability of "free" female labor, full-time domestic

servants had largely replaced the unpaid labor services of women and children in the landlord's house. Rainbird and Taylor (1976, 14) note that on the Hacienda La Colpa, "in recent years, the only regular obligation was that of preparing the mid-day food ration for the workers." In other words, as feudal exactions from the peasantry disappeared, women's unpaid labor—in this case, that of the male workers' wives—was the last labor service to go. Nevertheless, the process of developing dairy enterprises on the haciendas primarily increased the rate of exploitation of male labor, while female labor services were greatly reduced in number. Women, were, however, required to dedicate more of their time to subsistence production in order to ensure household reproduction.

Once the wage labor force on the dairy enterprise was in place, the rate of exploitation of women workers exceeded that of men because of the differences in the level of remuneration. The gender wage gap narrowed over the years, especially after the passage of Peru's first national minimum-wage legislation in 1962, which established the same minimum wage for men and women. Not until the 1970s, however, and the threat of land expropriation for noncompliance with labor legislation under the agrarian reform were men and women remunerated equally per hour worked.

The creation of a permanent wage labor force on the Cajamarcan dairy farms had two other special features: this labor force generally consisted of a small number of domestic or kin groups; and, although these workers were employed full-time, they often still had access to land. The general pattern in the province was that as landlords developed a specialized dairy work force, they tended to recruit their most loyal and trusted workers, drawing on the personalized and paternalistic features of feudal class relations. It was generally the wives or daughters of these male workers who were trained as milkmaids. This partially explains both how milking could develop as a skilled and specialized but unremunerated activity on many haciendas and the wide differential in the hourly return to male and female workers when this labor was finally remunerated.

Feudal class relations were contractual relations between men, and, not surprisingly, the development of the wage relation on the haciendas followed a similar pattern. The male head of the household was contracted as the wage worker, although implicit in the contract was that male labor came with an "appendage," a woman. Even when women were remunerated for their labor, their secondary status in the dairy labor force was reinforced by the common practice of paying their wages to their male kin. For the dairy maids of Cajamarca, the capital-labor relation did little to reduce their subordination. But in material terms, they and their households were quite well off. Milking was the highest-paid occupation available to women in the province, and households with two wage-earners—especially in the 1960s, when minimum-wage standards began to be enforced—were much better off than other rural households.

Because the formation of Cajamarca's dairy labor force was accompanied by the parceling of the haciendas, many of these wage workers, particularly those residing on the haciendas at the higher elevations, were also able to purchase land. Moreover, because they were the most trusted hacienda employees, they were sometimes able to purchase good-sized parcels of quality land. On the haciendas Hotel Polloc and Chuchún, managed in the early 1970s by Gonzalo Saenz Cacho as one dairy farm, nine of the twenty-six permanent wage workers purchased land when the hacienda was subdivided in the 1960s.[3] Four of these worker-landowners worked parcels less than 2.5 hectares in size, but the remainder owned plots that were between 8.9 and 18.1 hectares. Sometimes, they sharecropped these larger parcels with other peasants, continuing the practice that had been common on the haciendas. But it often fell to the women and children to generate the household's subsistence production when the husbands were full-time wage workers.

In the valley of Cajamarca, it was more common for the dairy labor force to be fully proletarian. Nonetheless, some wage workers in the valley had managed to purchase small parcels of land. The majority of the milkmaids on the Hacienda Tres Molinos, for example, belonged to households that had purchased such parcels.[4] Dairy maids who were wives were often responsible for agricultural production on these plots, because their husbands worked full-time and their own occupation was compatible with both domestic labor and petty production. The very small size and poor quality of these parcels meant that petty production served, at most, as a small complement to the wage in terms of meeting household reproduction requirements.

With the dissolution of the hacienda system, most Cajamarcan rural households were to experience changes in the gender division of labor that were quite different from those noted above, for the actual magnitude of employment generated by the dairy industry was small (see Chapter 8). Much more important for the majority of former hacienda households was the role of the land sales in enabling them to become independent petty producers.

THE LAND SALES AND THE EXPANSION OF PETTY PRODUCTION

A salient feature of the development of agrarian capitalism in Cajamarca via the Junker road was that thousands of hacienda peasant households became

3. "Informe de Empadronamiento y Verificación No. 20–E1–L, No. 4, URAC, Junio 8, 1973," Hacienda Hotel Polloc files, Agrarian Reform Office, Ministry of Agriculture, Agrarian Zone II, Cajamarca.

4. Six of the eleven milkmaids interviewed in January 1976 belonged to households that had purchased land from Rossell in the caserio Tres Molinos. One other had purchased land with her husband from Enrique Dobbertin in the caserío Santa Bárbara. Four milkmaids were from landless households. Six of the milkmaids were wives, mothers, or daughters of male employees.

landowners for the first time, while many households within the independent peasant communities managed to expand their private holdings. According to the 1976 Peasant Family Survey, 18 percent of the peasant households in the province directly purchased hacienda lands. Another 46 percent were constituted as units of production through land purchases from other peasants, reflecting the subsequent subdivision of hacienda land parcels as well as the growing commodification of land within the independent peasant communities. Only 34 percent were constituted as units of production primarily through inheritance: 14 percent through female inheritance, 11 percent through male inheritance, and 9 percent through approximately equal male and female inheritances.[5]

Although the parceling of the haciendas provided a precondition for the expansion of petty production, the amount of land that different households could buy was very unequal, as illustrated in Table 21 for a sample of nine haciendas. The overall effect of the land sales was to provide the material base for a middle and a rich peasantry. Nonetheless, on some haciendas such as Purhuay and Chaquil, the majority of peasants bought land parcels too small to reproduce the new owners as petty producers.[6] The unequal size of the land purchases was related to the previous process of feudal differentiation within the haciendas and the unequal ability of different households to generate sufficient resources to purchase land. It was also related to the particular way the different haciendas were parceled and sold.

Peasant holdings on the haciendas had certainly not been equal in size. As I have stressed, the amount and quality of land to which a household had access depended on the personalized landlord-peasant relationship. This played a role in the land sales, too, with favored hacienda tenants given the opportunity to buy larger and better quality parcels at better terms of purchase. Moreover, favored tenants usually had larger herds of animals and thus greater resources at their disposal to buy land when it was offered for sale.

When resident households were unable to generate the necessary cash to purchase their parcels, the land was sometimes offered for sale to the upper peasant strata of the hacienda as well as to outsiders, including peasants from nearby communities and the rural petty bourgeoisie. Peasants from neighboring communities who had arrendire arrangements on the hacienda came from both the land-hungry poor peasant strata and the upper peasant strata. The latter group usually had large animal herds grazing on the hacienda and thus, when the chance arose, they had the potential liquidity to enable them to buy

5. The remaining 2 percent of the households were agrarian reform beneficiaries by 1976. The data refer to the predominant form of land acquisition.

6. This tendency was even more pronounced on the Hacienda Porcón. Of the 923 households that purchased land on this hacienda, 32 percent bought parcels smaller than 1 hectare, and 42 percent purchased parcels of between 1 and 3 hectares. Only thirty-six households, 4 percent of the buyers, were able to purchase parcels of 10 hectares or more (Gorget 1975b, chap. 3).

TABLE 21.   Distribution of Land Purchases by Size on Selected Haciendas

Hacienda	3.5 Hectares or Less (%)	3.51 to 11.0 Hectares (%)	11.01 to 30.0 Hectares (%)	More than 30.0 Hectares (%)	Total
Combayo	2.0	15.7	21.5	60.8	100% N = 51
Santa Ursula	10.6	52.6	34.2	2.6	100% N = 38
Sondor	36.8	39.5	21.1	2.6	100% N = 38
Vista Alegre	15.0	25.0	30.0	30.0	100% N = 20
Polloc	7.1	21.4	42.9	28.6	100% N = 14
Polloquito	17.3	31.0	31.0	20.7	100% N = 29
Huacataz	35.4	54.6	5.4	4.6	100% N = 110
Purhuay	52.9	38.3	8.8	—	100% N = 34
Chaquil	60.0	32.5	2.5	5.0	100% N = 40

SOURCES: Compiled from Registros Públicos de Cajamarca, Registro de la Propiedad, city of Cajamarca (2:235; 8:108; 183:351; 144:295; 95:329–331; 165:309); and, for haciendas Huacataz, Purhuay, and Chaquil, from "Escrituras de Compra-Venta de Fracciones de Terreno, 1969," Notario Público Mario Silva Rocha, files of Gonzalo Pajares, Cajamarca.

rather large land parcels (Hacienda Santa Ursula).[7] When these large parcels were subsequently subdivided and resold to other peasants it was at much higher prices. This practice was exacerbated when landowners relied on the petty bourgeoisie to carry out the subdivision and sale. For example, Rafael Puga sold 1,600 hectares of the Hacienda La Pauca to Pedro Pajares (brother of Gonzalo Pajares) in 1960 for S/. 1,000 per hectare. Over the next seven years, Pajares parceled this property, selling lots at prices between S/. 3,000 and S/. 12,000 per hectare. The majority of the buyers were non-hacienda residents—rich peasants from the communities of Paucamarca, Las Huaylas, La Laguna, Huayanay, and as far away as San Marcos. The resident peasants on this section of the hacienda who were unable to raise the money to purchase land were forced to emigrate (Chambeu and Gorget 1975, 30).

7. Garay (1975a), in her case study of Chilacat, Namora, reports that when the Hacienda Casa Blanca was subdivided and sold, many of the buyers were non-hacienda residents. Also see Chambeu (1975f) on land sales of the Hacienda Santa Teresita de La Quispa.

TABLE 22.   Price per Hectare, Land Sales on Selected Haciendas
(in Current Peruvian Soles)

Hacienda	Range	Mean	Mode	Median	Small Parcels[a]	Large Parcels[b]
Combayo	184–1,732	583	621	699	1,731	549
Santa Ursula	359–1,830	684	700	700	961	678
Sondor	227–2,000	833	1,000	1,000	1,235	829
Vista Alegre	351–3,000	565	1,000	978	1,587	470
Polloc	207–1,600	656	500	640	1,000	247
Polloquito	100–8,000	692	200	313	1,140	237
Huacataz	407–1,633	830	1,000	1,000	1,003	615
Purhuay	177–2,500	994	1,000	1,200	1,391	547
Chaquil	455–4,000	877	1,000	1,250	1,420	536

SOURCES: Compiled from Registros Públicos de Cajamarca, Registro de la Propiedad, city of Cajamarca (2:235; 8:108; 183:351; 144:295; 95:329–331; 165:309); and, for haciendas Huacataz, Purhuay, and Chaquil, from "Escrituras de Compra-Venta de Fracciones de Terreno, 1969," Notario Público Mario Silva Rocha, files of Gonzalo Pajares, Cajamarca.

[a] Mean price per hectare for parcels of 3.5 hectares or less.
[b] Mean price per hectare for parcels of 30.0 hectares or more.

The social differentiation resulting from the hacienda land sales was overdetermined by feudal differentiation in yet another way. The amount of land peasant households could buy was a function of the price of land, and this price was again partly determined by the personal relationship between tenant and landlord. As Table 22 shows, peasants who bought small parcels of land uniformly paid more per hectare than did those purchasing large tracts. Larger parcels could include significant extensions of natural pastures, worth much less than cultivable land. Nonetheless, the disparity in the price per hectare for small and large purchases is not explained by differing land quality alone. Because one of the objectives of the land sales was to recoup the most productive and easily irrigated lands for dairy production, peasants were often offered only the more marginal hacienda lands. The higher price paid for small land parcels was thus not directly related to land quality.

Moreover, the available data on the prices paid by the petty bourgeoisie for potential dairy farms support the argument that land prices were determined by the relative bargaining position of different social actors. For example, the 123-hectare core of the Hacienda Huacataz was sold for S/. 407 per hectare in 1962.[8] The average small parcel on this hacienda sold for S/.1,003 per hectare (see Table 22). The peasantry paid dearly for its access to private property, and, not surprisingly, the land sales triggered a liquidity crisis in the peasant economy.

8. Derived from "Escrituras de Compra-Venta," files of Gonzalo Pajares, Cajamarca.

Coming Up with the Cash: Decapitalization and Migration

When the land sales began on a hacienda, peasant households were given very little time to raise at least a down payment, if not the full payment. A typical contract on the Hacienda Santa Ursula, for the sale of 10.87 hectares, required the household to pay S/. 2,086 immediately and then S/. 655 per year for five years.[9] In the 1960s, peasants on one sector of the Hacienda Combayo were given only fifteen days to raise the cash to purchase their parcels (Manrique 1974, 6–8).

To raise cash, hacienda households could pursue one of three alternatives: they could sell their animal stocks, they could go into debt, or the male members of the family could migrate to the coast to earn wage income. Animal stocks have traditionally represented the peasant household's accumulated wealth. Moreover, in periods of high inflation, such as the 1940s, there was an even greater tendency for any peasant surplus to be invested immediately in sheep, cattle, and work animals. In lean years or in emergencies, the animals were then sold. The land sales provoked such an emergency and brought about a tremendous decapitalization among the great mass of hacienda tenants, as well as in the independent communities.[10] Table 23 illustrates the magnitude of the average land purchase in terms of the equivalent sale of animal stocks or days of local wage labor.[11]

If the peasant household did not have a sufficiently large stock of animals to sell to meet the down payment, or in some cases the full payment, then its principal alternative was to go into debt. Some households turned to their wealthier compadres on the hacienda or in the pueblos, as they did on the Hacienda Porcón (Bazán 1972, 11). More frequently, however, peasants probably turned to the enganche system, taking cash advances they could later repay by wage labor on the coastal sugar plantations. According to Rosario Mosqueira, the labor contractor for the plantation Casa Grande in the town of Jesús, the main reason peasants came to him for advances in the 1950s was to buy land.[12] The usual advance was between S/. 1,000 and S/. 2,000. Most

9. "Contrato de Promesa de Venta, Hacienda Santa Ursula, 1962–1964," Hacienda Santa Ursula files, Agrarian Reform Office, Ministry of Agriculture, Agrarian Zone II, Cajamarca.

10. Also see Althaus (1975) for land purchases by peasants in the community of Asunción from the Hacienda La Pauca; Flecha (1975) for purchases by the community of Quebrada de San Francisco from the Hacienda Polloquito; Bazán (1972) on the Hacienda Porcón; and Chambeu (1975f) on the haciendas Polloc and Santa Teresita de La Quispa.

11. The price data used to calculate the equivalencies in Table 23 have been taken from the 1950s; interviews on these haciendas reveal that most of the terms of sale were agreed to during that decade. The main exception is the Hacienda Combayo, where the terms of sale were agreed to in a valuation of land undertaken by the Instituto de Reforma Agraria y Colonización in 1961; the terms of equivalency in this case are overstated. Inflation was very high during the 1960s, and inflation would have worked in the peasantry's favor if the terms of the original promises of sale were maintained as peasants paid off their debts.

12. I interviewed Rosario Mosqueira in December 1981 in the city of Cajamarca. He was the Casa Grande labor recruiter in Jesús from 1944 until the office was finally closed in 1968.

TABLE 23.   Average Value of Land Purchase and Equivalency in Animal
Stocks and Wage Labor on Selected Haciendas

Hacienda	Average Value of Purchase (Current Peruvian Soles)	Equivalent Number of Cattle	Equivalent Number of Sheep	Equivalent Number of Days of Local Wage Labor
Combayo	35,948	40	514	4,494
Santa Ursula	11,731	13	168	1,466
Sondor	6,156	7	88	770
Vista Alegre	21,261	24	304	2,658
La Quispa	8,495	9	121	1,062
Polloquito	14,663	16	209	1,833
Huacataz	6,657	7	95	832
Purhuay	4,652	5	66	582
Chaquil	6,534	7	93	817

SOURCES: Average monetary value (in current Peruvian soles) calculated from data found in Registros
Públicos de Cajamarca, Registro de la Propiedad, city of Cajamarca (2:235; 8:108; 183:351; 144:295;
95:329–331; 165:309), and in "Escrituras de Compra-Venta de Fracciones de Terreno, 1969," Notario
Público Mario Silva Rocha, files of Gonzalo Pajares, Cajamarca; see also tables 17 and 19, above. Numbers of
cattle and sheep calculated based on Chávez Aliaga's (1957, 1:242) price estimates for the mid-1950s of S/. 900
per head of cattle and S/. 70 per head of sheep. Labor equivalency calculated based on an estimated provincial
rural wage rate for 1959 of S/. 8 per day, taken from *Boletín* (1960, no. 1).

peasants repaid the advance in three to four months. Others, if they were
"*muy borracho*" (drunks), might have to stay a full year on the coast, Mosqueira
said.

   The impact of the land sales on the peasantry's need for liquidity was not lost
on the coastal plantations that were competing for highland labor during this
period. When the Hacienda Llaucán in Bambamarca was to be subdivided and
sold in the early 1950s, the Casa Grande agency in Cajamarca reported in a
letter to the plantation administration: "Not all the tenants have sufficient cash
to buy their parcels of land. This will produce a demand for money by the
peasants in Bambamarca which will largely be supplied by the haciendas
Pomalca, Tumán, and Cayalti in the form of advances and socorros to the
peons. *This is the time to obtain labour from Bambamarca.* Llaucán has 1,000
tenants" (cited in Scott 1976, 328; my emphasis).

   In the 1950s, Casa Grande was still trying to increase the number of
permanent workers on the plantation and reduce the turnover of its work force.
In 1956 only one-third of the field workers were permanent (Scott 1976,
334–335), but by the end of the decade, Casa Grande was taking on few
additional permanent workers. Its demand for highland seasonal migrants was
largely limited to the cane harvest, given the growing mechanization of
planting and weeding that characterized the 1950s. By the mid-1960s, the use of

mechanical harvesters on all of the Chicama plantations reduced the demand for temporary workers dramatically.[13]

For the Cajamarcan peasantry, the short-run implication of these developments was that the enganchadores were not an important source of credit for the land sales that took place during the 1960s. According to Mosqueira, orders from the main agency in Cajamarca to recruit workers came less and less frequently during that decade, and in 1968 the Jesús office was closed completely.

The end of the enganche system did not begin to stem the tide of temporary coastal migrants until the next decade. The ongoing process of hacienda parceling, as well as the now-institutionalized need of the near-landless to earn wage income, meant that peasants continued to migrate on their own volition. A former tenant of the Hacienda Santa Ursula, who migrated to the coast for the first time in 1962 when this hacienda was finally parceled, recounted the decision-making process: "The Madrecitas had given us five years to pay for the land, but we had to pay half the price first in cash. I was going to sell all of my sheep when Arturo—he lives up there on the hill—came down and told me I was foolish, that we should go to Casa Grande. He had already gone once with the enganchadores before he got married, and he knew where to go. So I sold only four of my sheep and begged the Madrecitas to wait until November when I could bring back the money from the coast. About six of us went together."[14]

The significant wage gap between coast and sierra—coastal wages were three to seven times higher, depending on whether or not one includes social benefits—explains why temporary migration continued to be an attractive proposition for the Cajamarcan peasantry even when the length of coastal employment was reduced. Moreover, although a labor surplus was developing on the coast—partly because of increased permanent migration from the sierra—wages continued to rise more rapidly on the coast than in the sierra as a result of the more effective application of minimum-wage laws and the growing strength of the plantation unions.[15]

Not all of the temporary migrants succeeded in saving enough during their stay on the coast to purchase land during these years (Samaniego 1975a, 19). My interviews reveal, however, that the great majority of the households who

13. When the plantation Cartavio mechanized its cane harvest in 1961, its demand for temporary workers was reduced from six hundred workers per 2,000 tons of cut cane to fifteen workers (Róquez 1979). Fortunately for Cajamarcan households, the process of mechanization of the cane harvest was uneven among the coastal plantations.

14. This quotation is drawn from a life history I compiled in October 1976. This former hacienda tenant was at that time residing in the caserío Sarín.

15. From 1960 to 1965, highland wages increased at most 50 percent in nominal terms (from around S/. 10 to S/. 15), whereas wages on the plantation Cartavio, from 1961 to 1965 alone, increased 68 percent (from S/. 26.09 to S/. 43.86). The data for Cartavio do not include the value of bonuses, overtime, rations, or the subsidized sale of products. The full wage in 1965 was estimated as the equivalent of S/. 133.59 (Róquez 1979, 50).

did manage to buy hacienda lands or subsequently replenish their depleted animal stocks had at least partially relied on savings from temporary coastal migration.[16] Participation in capitalist class relations as wage workers thus allowed the reproduction of peasant households as petty producers and the expansion in their numbers.

Changing Access to Resources and Household Reproduction

The subdivision and sale of hacienda lands provided a unique opportunity for female tenants. Under feudal class relations, women had been excluded from direct usufruct rights to land; only men entered into rental arrangements with the landlord class. Earlier, I argued that women in the independent communities had more options and autonomy than women who resided on haciendas because inheritance of land in the communities was bilateral. Hacienda women were apparently aware of the advantages that land ownership offered them, and they took advantage of the land sales to buy land in their own names. As Table 24 shows, in the sample of land transactions on nine haciendas, 25 percent of the sales were made to women. Another 24 percent were registered in the names of both husband and wife. Fourteen percent of the sales were made to a group of peasants, usually kin, which often included a widowed woman and her married or unmarried children. Only 37 percent of the sales were made exclusively to men. The large share of land sales in which women were at least included suggests that peasant women understood the importance of owning land.

Gonzalo Pajares, who conducted the land sales on the haciendas Huacataz, Purhuay, and Chaquil, noted in our 1981 interview that it was often peasant women who convinced their husbands to migrate to the Condebamba Valley in order to earn money to purchase land parcels. He also speculated that there were relatively more female buyers for land on his haciendas because men were away so much in those years, earning wage income. Moreover, it was often the women who came up with the final payment for the land parcel, because the households' animal stocks were under their care and often subject to their decisions.

Whether peasant women were able to buy land in their own names or jointly with their husbands, however, did not depend only on their desires and capabilities. The whims and prejudices of the landowning class were also important here, as suggested by the contrasting patterns of sales on the different haciendas. For example, the lowest relative share of female buyers is found on the two haciendas owned and subdivided by the Bueno family, Vista Alegre and Sondor. Peasant family structure also played a role in determining how land ownership was defined. On the Hacienda Combayo, long characterized

16. 1976 Peasant Family Survey and household case studies in La Succha, Jesús, and La Laguna, San Marcos. Also see Chambeu (1975c, 1975f).

TABLE 24.   Distribution of Land Purchases on Selected Haciendas According to Registered Owner

	Registered Owner				
Hacienda	Male (%)	Female (%)	Couple (%)	Group (%)	Total
Combayo	21.6	7.8	31.4	39.2	100 N = 51
Santa Ursula	34.2	23.7	31.6	10.5	100% N = 38
Sondor	44.7	7.9	23.7	23.7	100% N = 38
Vista Alegre	55.0	5.0	20.0	20.0	100% N = 20
Polloc	64.3	28.6	7.1	—	100% N = 14
Polloquito	75.9	20.7	—	3.4	100% N = 29
Huacataz	40.0	32.7	22.7	4.6	100% N = 110
Purhuay	8.8	41.2	41.2	8.8	100% N = 34
Chaquil	22.5	37.5	25.0	15.0	100% N = 40
Total	37.2	24.6	24.3	13.9	100% N = 374

SOURCES: Compiled from Registros Públicos de Cajamarca, Registro de la Propiedad, city of Cajamarca (2:235; 8:108; 183:351; 144:295; 95:329–331; 165:309); for haciendas Huacataz, Purhuay, and Chaquil, from "Escrituras de Compra-Venta de Fracciones de Terreno, 1969," Notario Público Mario Silva Rocha, files of Gonzalo Pajares, Cajamarca.

by the prevalence of extended families, 39 percent of the sales were to one extended family group.

In all except the case of the Hacienda Purhuay, men bought significantly larger parcels, on average, than did women. On the Hacienda Huacataz, where an important share of the sales were made to women, women purchased an average of 3.9 hectares, whereas men purchased 13.1 hectares. On most haciendas, the average amount of land purchased by men was also greater than the average amount purchased by couples. This statistic suggests that patriarchal decision making was much more prevalent among the rich peasant strata on the haciendas, a pattern reinforced by men's role in the land purchases.

Women not only purchased smaller quantities of land; they also paid a higher price per hectare, a pattern conforming to the inverse relation between parcel size and per hectare price noted earlier. In five of the nine haciendas studied, women paid more per hectare than any other group of buyers. The highest per hectare price in the sample, S/. 3,000, was paid for a 1-hectare plot in 1962 by the only female buyer on the Hacienda Vista Alegre. This sum was almost six times the mean price of land sold on this hacienda. Women's disadvantage reflects their weaker bargaining power vis-à-vis the landlord under feudal class relations, as compared to peasant men.

Whether the majority of women who purchased land were single heads of households or married women whose husbands were temporarily away is impossible to determine from the available data. But it seems likely that most of these women were in fact married, given that the hacienda system so strongly discouraged female heads of households. Moreover, as illustrated in Table 23, it probably would have been difficult for a woman to buy land solely on the basis of selling animal stocks; wage work was crucial in raising the cash to purchase land. Female heads of households would have been at a tremendous disadvantage in earning wage income, for few wage employment opportunities in the province were available to women. Few women had the chance to become dairy maids, and other available jobs, such as domestic service in the city of Cajamarca, were remunerated at a much lower rate than comparable male wage employment.

Throughout this period, the overwhelming majority of temporary migrants to the coast were men. Although only men were employed on the sugar plantations, the rice plantations did hire women, particularly for the labor-intensive transplanting.[17] But most women employed on the rice plantations of the Jequetepeque Valley were coastal residents. In my interviews, I found that women from only one community, El Azufre in San Marcos (noted for its poor lands and relative poverty), had migrated temporarily to find wage work on the coastal rice plantations. The great majority of rural women considered it impossible for women to become temporary migrants because of their responsibility for child care and animal care. As many responded, "Who can abandon one's children and animals and go to the coast?"

Consequently, perhaps somewhat ironically, the gender division of labor, in which seasonal wage migration was a male endeavor, made male absence an important prerequisite for women on the haciendas to buy land, either in their own names or along with their husbands. Thus the constitution of households of independent petty producers that resulted from the partition of the haciendas

17. Hunt (1977, table 8) notes that in 1931 there were 8,000 female wage workers among the 32,433 workers employed on the rice plantations but that this number declined to 2,000 by 1934, although total employment had expanded to 48,210. Hunt writes that female employment remained at this lower level thereafter. My interviews in the Jequetepeque Valley in 1976 indicate, however, that female employment expanded considerably in the 1950s with the introduction of the more labor-intensive rice-transplanting technique.

took place under terms more favorable for gender equality than those governing household relations under feudal class relations.

The new class relations in which these households would engage were closely related to the quantity and quality of land they were able to purchase. On the one hand, those who bought sufficiently large segments—the middle and rich peasantry—did quite well, and they became increasingly integrated into the expanding commodity market for both agricultural and animal products. On the other hand, those households that purchased parcels barely sufficient to fulfill their subsistence requirements found that the reproduction of household labor power from petty production alone was an increasingly tenuous proposition.

The hacienda had been an all-encompassing socioeconomic system. The landlord provided the peasant household with access to a wide range of resources, as well as social security. In lean years, the landlord provided food and seed for planting. The landlord also extended credit if a peasant needed to buy a work animal or to sponsor the celebration of a saint's day. Now, as independent producers, the peasantry had no ready credit system upon which to rely. If the crops were lost, or if there was no seed left to plant, the landlord was no longer there to meet emergencies. By the end of the 1960s, the enganchadores from the coastal plantations were also gone. Merchants and rich peasants increasingly replaced the landlord class and the enganche system as the primary sources of credit, but at even less favorable terms. The new trend was for merchants to give advances to peasants on market days, which the peasants paid back with their crops during the harvest, at below market prices (Garay 1975e, 26).

An unexpected result for many former tenant households was that, once the haciendas were parceled, they no longer had access to the haciendas' natural resources. Hacienda residents had always been able to collect wood for fuel and to use the forests and streams for hunting, gathering, and fishing and other natural resources for construction and artisan production. Moreover, they either had access to common pasture for grazing or could obtain it for a fee. Now, as independent producers, they had use rights only over their own private plots. What had served as common pasture was someone else's private property.

The lack of access to sufficient resources had important consequences for household productive activity and domestic labor. With limited access to grazing lands, animal raising became more difficult. This situation primarily affected peasant women, who had traditionally been charged with the care of the household's sheep and cattle. Now, the peasant woman and her children had to spend more time searching for pastures on which to graze a reduced flock of sheep. It also became increasingly common for peasant households to own no large animals at all.[18] As wood became scarcer, women also had to spend more

18. For example, in the community of Jocos in Matara, Chambeu (1975c, 15) found that few households owned cattle, because of the lack of pastures after the Hacienda Lajas was subdivided and sold. Only two families owned a herd of sheep of fifteen to twenty head.

time searching the hillsides for firewood, or else someone in the household had to find new sources of cash income to purchase wood or coal. Lack of access to water sources meant that carrying water for daily consumption also absorbed increased amounts of family labor time. For these former hacienda tenants, the hours once appropriated by the landlord class as surplus labor time were now employed as increased necessary labor time to reproduce familial labor power.

Cash income had initially been necessary to buy land; but, for these former hacienda households now constituted as smallholders, cash income also became increasingly necessary to meet part of household consumption requirements. For these households, as well as for smallholders in the independent peasant communities, the post-1940s were characterized by a growing reliance on the sale of labor power (see Chapter 8). Both men and women felt the detrimental effects. Men migrated temporarily to the coast and to other areas of the department to seek wage employment. Women were left behind to tend the fields, the animals, and the homestead, taking over what would become the household's secondary activity, petty production.

The fate of those households who had managed to purchase sufficient land was quite different. With access to pastures, animal raising continued to be an important household economic activity, one that remained in the female domain. Many of the rich peasants were also able to develop dairy farms during the subsequent decades, becoming milk suppliers to PERULAC. When households had enough land to become both commercial agricultural producers and dairy farmers, women often became the managers of the dairy operations. This situation, however, did not necessarily lead to greater female economic autonomy, for men tended to control the household's relation with PERULAC and, most important, the income from the sale of milk.[19]

With the opening of the intraprovincial roads in the 1950s, peasant commercial agricultural production also flourished, especially in the district of San Marcos. In the late 1950s, at least fifty trucks were arriving there from Cajamarca and the coast each weekend to participate in the pueblo market, returning laden with eggs and chickens for Lima and cereals, potatoes, lard, and fruit for coastal markets. Another sixty vendors from throughout the province sold their wares in the pueblo market (Díaz S. 1971).

---

19. This finding is corroborated by the fact that few women were included on PERULAC's list of milk suppliers in the mid-1970s. Those who were tended to be larger suppliers, suggesting that they were capitalist dairy farmers rather than from the upper peasant strata. In my case study of the communities of Quinoamayo and Michiquillay, I observed that many of the middle and rich peasants who provided milk to PERULAC did not provide enough milk daily (1 *porongo*) to be official suppliers. They thus pooled their milk to meet this critical minimum, with one peasant man serving as *cabeza de porongo*. He would receive the weekly check from PERULAC and distribute the proceeds to each contributing household. Although women generally took care of the dairy cattle, did the milking, and delivered the milk to the cabeza de porongo's house, the proceeds of the sale were almost always distributed among the male household heads.

The basis of this flourishing trade was the increased peasant production, particularly by the middle and rich peasant strata resulting from the partition of the haciendas (Acevedo 1976). This trade may also have had unintended consequences, spurring peasant social differentiation. Not only would the rich peasant strata come to be a major source of credit for the poorer peasantry, but also, over time, these wealthy strata would increasingly rely on the wage labor of other peasants. As discussed in the next chapter, the growing monetization of the rural economy gradually led to the replacement of traditional forms of labor recruitment, such as the minga, by the payment of cash wages.

The parceling of the haciendas also had profound political consequences for the Cajamarcan peasantry. Rich peasants, particularly those who became dairy farmers, identified strongly with the landlord class. In the 1960s, with agrarian reform in the wind, the Cattlemen's Association reportedly did its best to cultivate the political allegiance of the peasant dairy farmers by extending the services of FONGAL (Fondo de Desarollo de la Ganadería Lechera de Cajamarca), the Cajamarcan dairy industry's development fund, to such farmers.

Peasant struggle over land in Cajamarca was also considerably mitigated by the land sales. Many of the longstanding community-hacienda conflicts over land were diluted as some community members became owners of what had been hacienda land. The Community of Hualqui, for example, had for decades struggled with the Hacienda Lacas for the return of usurped lands. But when this hacienda was parceled, between 1956 and 1968, a number of rich peasants from the community managed to purchase good-sized land parcels and subsequently retreated from the collective claim to hacienda land (Chambeu 1975b, 10). A similar process happened in two communities in the district of Namora—Adacucho, which had long struggled against the Hacienda Adacucho; and Chilacat, which had been in conflict with the Hacienda Casa Blanca (Chambeu 1975a; Garay 1975a).

Although the land sales had profound economic and political implications in terms of bolstering petty production in the province, the process was clearly a part of the generalized development of agrarian capitalism in Peru's social formation. In fact, as we have seen, the expansion and reproduction of petty production might not have been possible without peasant participation in capitalist class relations as temporary wage workers. Morover, the land sales did little to reverse the other main trend in this period—increased permanent migration from the highlands, which contributed to creating a relative surplus population for capitalist development on the Peruvian coast.

SIERRA-COAST MIGRATION

Growing land pressure within the independent peasant communities in the first half of the century explains why seasonal wage migration was an attractive complement to petty production. Not until the 1950s, however, was pressure on the land sufficiently acute to drive significant numbers of peasants into permanent migration to the coast. An important group among the permanent migrants must have included peasants expelled from the haciendas, such as those from the Cajamarca Valley, who had no alternative but to seek permanent wage employment. Some migrated only as far as the city of Cajamarca, which experienced a substantial population increase. But the majority migrated directly to the northern Peruvian coast and in growing numbers to Lima, the Amazon, and the northernmost provinces of the department of Cajamarca.

At the time of the 1940 census, 11 percent of the persons born in the department of Cajamarca were residing either permanently or temporarily in other Peruvian departments. Of the 61,624 migrants, 42 percent lived in the department of La Libertad and another 29 percent in Lambayeque. Only 18 percent were located in the department of Lima, with the remainder (11 percent) distributed among all other departments (Peru 1940, various volumes, table 19).

By the time of the 1961 census, a total of 138,095 people, or 16 percent of those born in Cajamarca, had migrated either permanently or temporarily from the department. The department of Lima had increasingly become the focus of migration: by 1961, 30 percent of all Cajamarcan migrants were located there, compared with 51 percent in La Libertad and Lambayeque, and 9 percent in the department of Amazonas (Peru 1961c, vol. 1, table 27; Peru 1961a, various volumes, table 8).

In the eleven years between 1961 and 1972, as many Cajamarcans left the department as had left in the previous twenty-one years; by 1972, 33 percent of the persons born in Cajamarca had emigrated permanently. Migration to the Amazon region was especially pronounced, tripling during this period; the department of Amazonas claimed 16 percent of the total Cajamarcan migrants by 1972 (Peru 1972a, vol. [1], table 5).[20] Thirty-one percent of the migrants resided in the department of Lima, 43 percent in the departments of Lambayeque and La Libertad.

Disaggregated data for 1972 show that the province of Cajamarca was the primary source of migrants from the department of Cajamarca to the departments of La Libertad (35 percent of the total), Ancash (31 percent), and Lima (28 percent). In contrast, the province contributed only 5 percent of the permanent migrants from Cajamarca to Lambayeque; 42 percent of the Cajamarcan migrants to that department were from the province of Chota (Peru 1972a, vol. [1], table 5).

---

20. For the 1972 and 1981 censuses, the twenty-four departmental volumes are unnumbered in the original. Volume numbers given in brackets here are those assigned by libraries for cataloging purposes.

The changing pattern of migration is well documented in community case studies (Garay 1975a, 1975b; Chambeu 1975a, 1975b, 1975c; Samaniego 1975a). Even in those districts—Jesús, Namora, Matara—that had sent the largest proportion of temporary and permanent migrants to the plantation Casa Grande in La Libertad before 1940, the migrant stream by the end of the 1960s consisted of permanent migrants to Lima and, secondarily, to other coastal cities.

The major change in the 1970s was the growing attraction of the department of San Martín in the Amazonian region to permanent migrants from Cajamarca. Whereas only 2,318 Cajamarquinos were counted in the census there in 1972, by 1981 this figure had increased tenfold, to 25,800 (Peru 1972a, vol. [1], table 5; Peru 1981, vol. [1], table 8). Hence, in 1981 the two departments located in the northern jungle of Peru—Amazonas and San

TABLE 25.   Estimated Average Annual Migration from the Department of Cajamarca to Selected Areas of Peru, 1952–1981

	Destination (Department)					Total Migration to Five Principal Destinations
	Lamba- yeque	La Libertad	Ancash	Amazonas	Lima	
Permanent migrants						
1952 to 1956	984	1,492	186	435	1,640	4,737
1957 to 1960	1,476	2,165	367	1,142	2,148	7,298
1968 to 1972	2,211	2,386	304	2,770	3,045	10,716
1977 to 1981	2,814	2,667	299	2,579	3,908	12,267
Temporary migrants						
1961	1,628	2,462	232	2,568	1,615	8,505
1972	1,301	1,820	199	1,499	1,997	6,816

SOURCES: Compiled from census data (Peru 1961a, vols. 1, 2, 12, 18, and 28, table 8 in each volume; Peru 1972a, vols. [1, 2, 13, 14, and 15], tables 7 and 8 in each volume; Peru 1981 national vol. [1], table 7).

NOTE: The annual rates of permanent migration for the periods 1952 to 1956 and 1957 to 1960 were calculated by dividing the number of people who had migrated during each period by the relevant number of years (five and four, respectively). Numbers were limited to those persons born in the department of Cajamarca but residing at the time of the 1961 census in one of the five major destinations of migration. The figures for 1968 to 1972 represent the number of people born in Cajamarca who resided in one of the specific departments above at the time of the 1972 census but had lived in Cajamarca in 1967, divided by the five years of that period. The estimate for 1977 to 1981 was similarly derived, based on migrants who had resided in Cajamarca in 1976.

The flow of temporary migrants in 1961 was estimated by subtracting the average annual flow of permanent migrants (based on the four preceding years) from the number of migrants who in 1961 had resided in the specific department less than one year. This assumes that the annual permanent migration rate did not change, thus probably overstating the number of temporary migrants in this period. Data on temporary migrants were reported directly in the 1972 census, where they were defined as those counted in a given department who usually reside in another department. Such information was not reported in the 1981 census.

Martín—accounted for 21 percent of the permanent migrants from the department (see Map 1). Thirty percent of the permanent migrants resided in Lima, 40 percent in the departments of Lambayeque and La Libertad.

Table 25 presents estimates of the average annual rates of temporary and permanent migration from the department of Cajamarca to other regions. From 1952 to 1956, the years when peasant sharecroppers were being dispossessed from the smaller haciendas and fundos of the Cajamarca Valley, some 2,476 permanent migrants were leaving the department annually for the coastal departments of La Libertad and Lambayeque, with 4,737 migrants leaving Cajamarca annually for all five major destinations. By the late 1950s, the average annual flow of permanent migrants to the coastal departments increased to 3,641, with 7,298 Cajamarcans departing annually for these major destinations. The rate of migration from the department increased steadily throughout the 1960s; by the end of the decade, more than 10,000 permanent migrants were leaving the department annually.

By the late 1960s, the average annual number of permanent migrants exceeded that of temporary migrants. The temporary migration captured in census statistics actually decreased between 1961 and 1972, as Table 25 shows. Only the number of temporary migrants to Lima increased, but this increase was dwarfed by the permanent migration to the nation's capital. The reduction of temporary migration to the northern coast conforms with the previously noted analysis of the changing coastal labor market in the 1960s. In the 1970s, seasonal wage migration was increasingly limited to the rice harvests in the Jequetepeque Valley and in the province of Jaén.

The changing pattern of migration reflects not only the changes in the demand for seasonal highland labor but also different generational migration strategies. As long as peasant households had access to some land from which they could produce part of their subsistence, seasonal migration may have been a more attractive proposition than permanent migration. Temporary wage employment in this case allowed the reproduction of peasant households as units of production. But, for the children, especially when their inheritance promised to be inconsequential, permanent migration became their most attractive opportunity, particularly when combined with the possibility of obtaining secondary education on the coast. The majority of permanent migrants from Cajamarca, like those from the Peruvian highlands as a whole, tended to be between fifteen and twenty-four years old, with men outnumbering women (ONEC 1974, 36).

The increased rate of permanent migration did little to relieve land pressure within the highlands, given the high rate of population growth. But permanent migrants did provide a new source of income for sierra households: migrant remittances. Moreover, the periodic return of permanent migrants to the highlands served to tie the villages of the province even more tightly to the changing national economic and political currents.

CONCLUSION

In the period following the 1940s, the transformation in both class and household relations among the peasantry was profound. As this chapter has demonstrated, the process of agrarian capitalist development spurred the social differentiation of peasant producers. This certainly was not a linear process but rather was based on complex multiple class relations and changing class positions. For the majority of hacienda residents, the primary change in class position was from feudal peasant to petty producer. The possibility of purchasing land and replacing a depleted animal stock, however, often required participation in capitalist class relations as a wage worker. For a smaller group, the primary change was from feudal peasant to capitalist wage worker, either through employment on the dairy estates or through permanent migration from the highlands after being dispossessed of one's lands. A significant group of the permanent wage workers on the dairy farms were able to purchase land, placing these households in at least two fundamental class relations, capitalist and petty. A group of rich peasants was also consolidated who participated increasingly in both petty and capitalist production, employing wage labor.

The multiple class positions of peasant households were often based on the gender division of labor, with women taking on more responsibility for petty production and men taking on wage work. But individuals, such as the dairy maids who tended the household's subsistence plot between milking shifts, often occupied more than one fundamental class position.

The dissolution of feudal class relations on the estates had contradictory effects for different groups of rural women. All women who had resided on haciendas gained by the gradual reduction in the surplus labor time that had been appropriated by the landlord class. Often, however, the increase in the surplus labor appropriated from men required women to provide more of the necessary labor time to reproduce household labor power. This demand placed on women became even stronger as men became the primary temporary wage workers. Women's increased participation in agricultural production (because of male absence) also contributed to a growing role in agricultural decision making. With the opportunity to purchase land, moreover, many women gained the potential for economic autonomy. During this period, however, petty production increasingly became a secondary activity, complementing the wage income earned by men.

Rich peasant households were much more patriarchal than those of the poor peasantry, a pattern reinforced through land sales and the development of the dairy industry. Women often took responsibility for dairy farming, but this responsibility did not necessarily provide an independent income source or the basis for female autonomy. Women who found employment on the dairy enterprises were certainly among the better-off women in the province, but, as we have seen, the development of a female labor force did little to change female subordination. Rather, women's subordination, to men and to capital, was transformed and reproduced in new ways.

One of the most interesting aspects of Cajamarca's land reform by private initiative was that it reduced the potential for class struggle in the fundamental feudal class relation as the haciendas underwent a process of Junker transformation. The feudal peasants rather easily accepted their transformation into petty producers, although the land sales often required that in the process they themselves be subject to a higher rate of feudal exploitation. The land sales also required that they join the semi-proletarian migrants to the coast, occupying the class position of worker in capitalist production in order to achieve the goal of becoming an independent petty producer. Nonetheless, one factor came to link poor, middle, and rich peasants, as well as the farmer and Junker capitalist class in the 1970s: the defense of private property.

EIGHT

Structural Changes in the Provincial Economy

In the 1961 national agricultural census, the department of Cajamarca was second only to the department of Lima in the total volume of milk produced, and it was first in the production of butter and lard (Peru 1961b, table 35). The transformations that produced these results included changes in land use, reflecting the relative profitability of dairy versus foodstuff production; changes in the distribution of farm size, as a result of parceling the haciendas; and changes in land tenure, brought about by the dissolution of feudal class relations.

The development of the province as a dairy region had little effect on the sectoral composition of the labor force, given the dominant role of the agricultural sector in Cajamarca's growth after 1940. At the same time, however, significant changes had taken place in the principal economic activities of rural men and women. By the 1970s, the majority of peasant households participated in the wage labor market of the province. The dairy industry, despite its growth, had not created large-scale rural employment opportunities, and the primary employers of peasant labor in rural areas in fact were other peasants.

As the 1969 agrarian reform approached, the particular regional pattern of capitalist development largely determined the focus of class struggle. Neither feudal class relations nor even community-hacienda struggles over land were the primary sources of conflict; rather, the tension in the province centered on the relationships among dairy producers (both small and large), multinational capital, and the state. Within the independent communities, with households variously linked to dairy, foodstuff, and labor markets, the main sources of tension were the conditions under which labor was provided and obtained.

THE DAIRY INDUSTRY AND THE TRANSFORMATION OF
LAND USE, TENURE, AND PROPERTY

The changes in land use were most pronounced in the valley of Cajamarca. Before the 1940s, the valley had specialized in foodstuff production, particularly wheat, barley, and corn. By the 1950s, the very best lands, those with access to irrigation, had been turned over to improved pastures of clover, rye grass, and alfalfa. By the 1970s, foodstuff production in the valley had all but disappeared.

Unfortunately, census data do not allow even a poor approximation of the changes in land use in the province. Data on crop cultivation in the Peruvian highlands before the 1961 agricultural census are available only at the departmental level and are considered highly unreliable; subsequent attempts to revise earlier estimates have been very inconsistent (Thorp and Bertram 1978, 274; Hopkins 1979). Even the more reliable census data for 1961 and 1972 do not consistently distinguish between improved, cultivated, managed, and natural pastures.[1] Perhaps the best indication of changes in land use in the province is the available data on the number of wheat mills in operation. In the early 1940s, there were sixty-four wheat mills in the province (Silva Santisteban 1945, 90); in the mid-1950s, only eighteen were counted (Chávez Aliaga 1957, 4:43).

The data on the number of cattle stocked in the province are more consistent than the estimates of land use, perhaps because the animal stock on the haciendas was subject to annual censuses (the rodeos) for the purpose of collecting rent. Between 1940 and 1961, the number of head of cattle increased by at least 50 percent.[2] In the following decade, the size of the cattle stock stabilized, as efforts to control breeding quality intensified, with 93,145 head enumerated in the 1972 census (Peru 1972b, vol. [6], table 18).

The changing size distribution of farms in the province is also difficult to quantify precisely, because data for the period before 1961 are not available. Population census data for 1940 and 1961 do capture the partial dissolution of

1. In the 1961 agricultural census (Peru 1961a, vol. 6, table 4.1), approximately half the total reported farm land in the province was dedicated to animal production, including 120,136 hectares of natural pastures and 8,438 hectares of cultivated pastures. The 1972 census figures report 139,484 hectares of natural pastures, but only 2,193 hectares of cultivated pastures (Peru 1972b, vol. [6], table 11). The decrease in cultivated pastures perhaps reflects the more refined categories of the 1972 census, in which "natural pastures" are designated as managed—that is, enclosed, rotated, irrigated, or fertilized—(8,389 hectares) or unmanaged (131,095 hectares). Managed pastures could well include improved pastures counted as "cultivated" in 1961. If the areas reported in 1972 as cultivated and managed pastures are combined, the total area of improved pastures could have increased by as much as 25 percent between 1961 and 1972.

2. The 1961 census figure is 96,652 head (Peru 1961a, vol. 6, table 14). The Ministry of Agriculture office in Cajamarca, however, apparently considered this figure too high, for it reported 92,552 head as the revised 1961 figure for the province (Zona Agraria Cajamarca, Departamento Estadístico, cited in Eslava 1973, table 31).

the hacienda system, however. In 1961, only 19 percent of the rural population of the province resided on 197 haciendas and fundos, whereas 28 percent had resided on 235 haciendas and fundos in 1940.[3]

Between 1961 and 1972, the distribution of farms by size became more equal, as a result of the parceling of the haciendas. During this period, the number of farm units increased by 37 percent, while the land area farmed increased by only 26 percent, a change reflecting the tendency toward the fragmentation of rural property. The significance of the land sales in breaking up the concentration of land ownership is especially evident with respect to farms of more than 500 hectares. In 1961 forty-six haciendas of this size held 65 percent of the province's agricultural land; by 1972 only thirty-five haciendas remained in this category, accounting for 49 percent of the agricultural land (Peru 1961a, vol. 6, table 2.1; Peru 1972b, vol. [6], table 1).

The land sales contributed to doubling the number of farms that were between 5 and 500 hectares. More detailed breakdowns are not available at the provincial level for 1961; data for the department show that the most growth occurred in the number of farms between 10 and 50 hectares (a 255 percent increase), with the absolute amount of land held by farms of this size tripling. The next greatest growth was among farms between 50 and 500 hectares (a 120 percent increase in numbers), followed by those of 5 to 10 hectares (a 114 percent increase) (Peru 1961b, table 4; Peru 1972b, vol. [6], table 1). The data suggest that the primary beneficiaries of this land reform by private initiative were the petty bourgeoisie and rich peasants who were able to consolidate commercial-size farms.

The census data also reveal that the more egalitarian distribution of land by farm size was accompanied by growing landlessness among the peasantry. Near-landlessness was already a significant phenomenon in the province in 1961. In that year, 32 percent of the provincial farm units were smaller than 1 hectare, a statistic indicative of the degree of land pressure within the independent peasant communities (Peru 1961a, vol. 6, table 2.1). Between 1961 and 1972, the number of these very small farms grew by 42 percent, whereas the total amount of land held by this group increased by only 31 percent. As a result, average farm size in this category fell from 0.38 to 0.35 hectares. At the same time, the land sales did bolster the number of peasant farms in the range of 1 to 5 hectares. Both the number of farms in this category and the amount of land held increased (by 10.8 percent and 16.7 percent, respectively); average farm size thus grew slightly, from 2.2 hectares in 1961 to 2.3 hectares in 1972 (Peru 1972b, vol. [6], table 1).

3. The decline in the resident hacienda population was both relative and absolute: 30,468 hacienda and fundo residents were counted in 1940, but only 28,349 in 1961. The percentage of the rural population living on haciendas declined in all districts. The most dramatic decline took place in the western district of Magdalena, from 47 percent in 1940 to only 9 percent in 1961 (Peru 1940, vol. 2, table 34; Peru 1961a, vol. 6, table 3.6).

The census data also point to the gradual dissolution of feudal class relations on the haciendas. In 1961, 13.5 percent of the farms in the province were worked under some form of sharecropping or colono arrangement; by 1972, the proportion had declined to 2 percent. Cash renting, which could be feudal or capitalist, also declined significantly, from 5 percent to 0.7 percent of the total number of farms.[4] In 1961, cash renting had been more prevalent on farms larger than 5 hectares than it was on smaller farms—reflecting the importance of capitalist renting among dairy farmers in this period. By 1972, the greater prevalence of cash renting on small farms, those less than 5 hectares, indicates both the decline of capitalist renting and the monetization of traditional land tenure arrangements within the independent communities.[5]

One of the more important features of the development of the dairy industry in Cajamarca was that it was based primarily on medium-sized property. In the 1972 census, as Table 26 illustrates, farms of 10–50 hectares accounted for 31 percent of the dairy cows in production and for one-third of the average daily milk production in the province. Farms in the next two categories (50–100 and 100–200 hectares) combined held 21 percent of the dairy cows and represented another one-third of the daily milk production, a reflection of their higher average productivity. The largest haciendas in the province—those of 500 hectares or more—continued to hold an important share (20 percent) of the province's cattle stock, principally beef cattle; they accounted for only 7 percent of the province's milk production. If one assumes that farms smaller than 10 hectares belonged to the peasantry, then peasant households still owned the major share of the province's cattle stock, 48 percent. They accounted for one-third of the dairy cows in production and 19 percent of milk production.[6]

Peasant producers were the main source of the rather spectacular growth in

4. The decline in feudal class relations was more abrupt in the province than in the department as a whole. In 1961, 26.1 percent of the farms in the department were characterized by sharecropping, colono, or cash rental agreements; this figure declined to 8.1 percent in 1972. By 1972 only 2.7 percent of the farms in the province of Cajamarca were so categorized (Peru 1961b, tables 7a and 7b; Peru 1972b, vol. [6], table 9).

5. Methodological inconsistencies in the censuses obscure the importance of the growth of private property from 1961 to 1972. In the 1972 census, data pertaining to land tenure were not collected for farms that did not meet the minimum criteria for an agricultural unit; as a result, information on land tenure was incomplete for 25 percent of the farms in the province and for 32.5 percent of those smaller than 5 hectares. This omission distorts one of the more significant events of the period, the expansion of private property as the basis for petty production. Nonetheless, these data attest to the precariousness of petty production among a sizable sector of the peasantry.

6. Farms between 10 and 50 hectares accounted for approximately the same relative share of the cultivated and managed (or improved) pastures (21 percent and 28 percent, respectively) in the province as the farms of the next two size categories combined (20 percent and 26 percent, respectively). Farms smaller than 10 hectares held 31 percent of the cultivated and 17 percent of the managed pastures; fewer than 17 percent of peasant households had pastures that had been improved in any way (Peru 1972b, vol. [6], table 18).

TABLE 26. Characteristics of the Dairy Industry, Province of Cajamarca, 1972

Farm Size (Number of Farms)	Number of Farms with Cattle	Number of Cattle	Number of Milk Cows in Production	Daily Milk Production (liters)	Daily Liters per Cow
Less than 1 hectare	3,628	8,023	375	1,376	3.7
(11,070)	(20.0%)	(8.6%)	(3.8%)	(2.7%)	
1–5 hectares	7,963	23,703	1,710	4,672	2.7
(14,005)	(44.0%)	(25.4%)	(17.4%)	(9.0%)	
5–10 hectares	3,261	12,869	1,118	3,655	3.3
(4,263)	(18.0%)	(13.8%)	(11.4%)	(7.1%)	
10–50 hectares	2,868	19,728	3,038	17,177	5.7
(3,337)	(15.9%)	(21.2%)	(30.9%)	(33.2%)	
50–100 hectares	212	4,003	961	8,281	8.6
(239)	(1.2%)	(4.3%)	(9.8%)	(16.0%)	
100–200 hectares	85	3,930	1,066	8,472	7.9
(97)	(0.5%)	(4.2%)	(10.8%)	(16.4%)	
200–500 hectares	40	2,559	674	4,324	6.4
(47)	(0.2%)	(2.7%)	(6.9%)	(8.4%)	
More than 500 hectares	31	18,326	880	3,735	4.2
(35)	(0.2%)	(19.7%)	(9.0%)	(7.2%)	
Total	18,088	93,141	9,822	51,692	5.3
(33,093)	(100.0%)	(100.0%)	(100.0%)	(100.0%)	

SOURCE: Peru (1972b, vol. [6], table 18).

NOTE: The total number of farms and the number of farms with cattle in the table above differ by one from the totals reported in the census because incomplete information was provided for one farm. The total number of cattle above differs by four for the same reason.

the number of milk suppliers to PERULAC in the late 1960s and through the 1970s (see Table 15). Moreover, their numbers are probably understated—producers who did not meet the minimum production level (1 porongo daily) to be a PERULAC supplier were not listed as individual suppliers but rather would group themselves under a cabeza de porongo in their dealings with the processing plant. Even so, in 1971 the vast majority of official PERULAC suppliers (76 percent) were providing fewer than 50 liters of milk daily. Only 37 farms provided more than 250 liters a day, while 135 supplied between 50 and 250 liters (Eslava 1973, 136). By the late 1970s, small producers were providing approximately 50 percent of all the milk delivered to PERULAC (Burga Bartra 1981, 29).

What most distinguished the dairy producers of different-sized farms from one another, and capitalist producers from the peasantry, were productivity levels, indicative of the unequal degree of capitalization. Farms smaller than 10 hectares averaged fewer than 4 liters of milk daily per cow, not much more than provincial averages for criollo cows in the 1940s. The use of improved dairy breeds, as well as scientific management of herds and pastures, is reflected in the average productivity levels only on farms of 50–200 hectares (see Table 26).

Productivity levels also varied according to location. In the early 1970s, the Cajamarca Valley still accounted for 53 percent of the province's milk production, and the valley dairy farms were considerably more productive than those at higher elevations. The average dairy cow in the valley produced 7.9 liters of milk daily, compared with 5 liters for cows outside the valley. Stocking ratios differed considerably, too: 0.8 cows per hectare at the higher elevations, compared with 1.6 in the valley, where there was a greater concentration of improved pastures. As a result, farms in the valley produced 14.8 liters of milk per hectare, whereas those outside the valley produced only 4.3 (Eslava 1973, table 33). Dairy farming was thus a considerably more profitable proposition in the valley of Cajamarca, where the majority of capitalist farms were located.

Another disadvantage for milk producers outside the valley was that milk suppliers bore the cost of transporting the milk to the PERULAC factory in the valley. In its early years, PERULAC had operated a fleet of trucks and assumed the cost of transportation; but by 1968, it had sold the fleet to individual truck drivers, and the cost of transportation was transferred to producers. The per kilo cost of milk transport for suppliers outside the valley was as much as five times the cost for those within the valley's 80-kilometer perimeter (Caballero and Tello 1976, 6). In addition, the price of milk varied with both its fat content and its acidity.[7] Because milk was collected outside the valley only once a day, in contrast to the two daily collections in the valley, the volume of milk

7. The maximum level of acidity accepted by PERULAC was a degree of eight. Milk above this critical level was sold to a butter factory. Producers were remunerated for this milk, but at a significantly lower price than the standard (Eslava 1973).

discarded at the factory gate because of excessive acidity was higher for nonvalley producers (Eslava 1973, table 34).

Although PERULAC is often described as a local monopoly, that description is not entirely correct. In 1971 PERULAC was purchasing 68 percent of the average monthly milk production in the province. The main alternatives to being a PERULAC supplier were to process the milk into cheese; to sell it to a butter, cheese, or manjár blanco factory; or to sell it fresh in the city of Cajamarca. In the 1960s, there were only four major milk-processing establishments in the environs of the city of Cajamarca: the Negociación Ganadera El Triunfo of Juan Miguel Rossell, which produced butter; the Cocchambul cheese factory of Serapio Montoya; and the smaller butter and manjar factories, belonging to Napoleón Gálvez and H. Apel (*Documentál del Perú: Cajamarca* 1967, 152). By the mid-1970s, there were at least another half-dozen such establishments. Whereas medium and large-scale producers in the Cajamarca Valley were more likely to sell milk to the butter and manjár factories as well as to PERULAC, smaller producers tended to be the main suppliers of fresh milk to the city of Cajamarca.

The alternatives for producers outside the valley were somewhat different. In the 1950s, some fifteen haciendas had butter factories, many located on haciendas not yet on PERULAC's milk collection routes (Chávez Aliaga 1957, 4: 94). Even after many of these haciendas became PERULAC suppliers, butter production continued as a complementary activity, given its profitability as a luxury food item. For small producers outside the valley, the principal alternative use of milk was the home production of soft white cheeses (*cuajada* or *quesillos*) for sale at the weekly pueblo markets (Eslava 1973, table 34). Given the alternative uses of raw milk, PERULAC never established a complete monopoly over Cajamarcan producers; but as the principal buyer, its pricing policies largely determined the profitability of dairy production.

Multinational Capital and Local Producers and Consumers

Although PERULAC served as the most important catalyst for the development of Cajamarca as a major dairy region, its role in the province has been a source of controversy. The primary tensions among PERULAC, the milk suppliers, the state, and the townspeople of Cajamarca have been over price policy.

Although the Association of Agriculturalists and Cattlemen of Cajamarca played a key role in bringing PERULAC to Cajamarca, and although PERULAC invested considerable resources in promoting dairy production in the region, the relationship between the association and the company was never one of simple collusion around shared interests. True, each was most dependent on the other. PERULAC needed to maximize the number of milk suppliers if it was to operate its plant at a profit and earn a return on its initial promotional activities; and although producers had some alternative markets, these markets were too small to accommodate the growing milk production capacity of the province. But both the producers and PERULAC were profit maximizers, compelled to cover their costs of production and accumulate. Not surprisingly, then, major tension between them centered on the price of milk and the actual valuation of the milk delivered to PERULAC's factory gate, a valuation based on fat content, acidity, and weight.

PERULAC used some strong-arm tactics to ensure that producers would sell it most of their milk production. In 1959, for example, it refused to raise the price of milk because five association members had begun selling milk to a competitor in Trujillo, VITALECHE. But along with the stick came the carrot, and PERULAC offered to pay S/. 0.10 more per liter to those producers who promised to sell the company all of their milk production (*Boletín* 1960, no. 1).

Although the Cattlemen's Association continually complained of low milk prices, the data suggest that the price of milk paid to PERULAC suppliers usually kept pace with the general cost-of-living index. As Table 27 indicates, in constant 1953 prices the association was generally successful in lobbying for significant price hikes in those years when the price of milk had fallen considerably in real terms, such as 1953 and 1954, 1964 and 1965, and 1971. Moreover, the price increases obtained in the late 1950s raised the real price of milk slightly above the incentive price of 1948.[8] The consumer price index for Lima is not a totally adequate measure of the potential profitability of the milk industry, however, because costs of production in the sierra, and for a specific industry, do not always follow the overall urban consumer price trend—a continual complaint of the Cattlemen's Association. The detailed analysis of costs of production carried out by the association in 1959 showed that the per liter cost of milk was S/. 1.70, whereas PERULAC was paying only S/. 1.60 per liter (*Boletín* 1960, no. 1, B–1).

Price policy, nonetheless, was not totally under PERULAC's control, for prices were negotiated with the state. From 1967 on, the state determined milk prices directly. Throughout this period, the state's main interest was in maintaining low urban consumer prices (Hopkins 1981, 90, 116). Price determination was also subject to international factors such as the price of imported dry milk and milk fat, which could supply PERULAC's Chiclayo operations just as well as Cajamarcan milk could. The price that PERULAC was willing to pay to local milk suppliers thus also depended on the degree of protection afforded its final milk-based products, particularly evaporated milk, and the tariff exemptions it obtained on inputs.

---

8. There is a discrepancy between the price data reported by PERULAC to Eslava (1973) (shown in Table 27) and the available documentation of the Association of Agriculturalists and Cattlemen of Cajamarca for the years of 1949, 1959, and 1960. For example, according to the association's *Boletín* (1960, no. 1, B–5, 6), the price of milk in 1949 was S/. 0.80 per liter, rather than the S/. 0.60 reported in Table 27.

TABLE 27. Price of Milk Paid by
PERULAC, 1944–1972
(Peruvian Soles per Liter)

	Current Soles	Constant 1953 Soles
1944	0.25	0.83
1948	0.60	1.00
1949	0.60	0.86
1950	0.80	1.03
1951	0.80	0.93
1952	0.80	0.87
1953	0.80	0.80
1954	0.80	0.76
1955	1.00	0.91
1956	1.00	0.86
1957	1.20	0.96
1958	1.40	1.04
1959	1.60	1.05
1960	1.60	0.97
1961	1.60	0.90
1962	1.80	0.96
1963	1.80	0.90
1964	1.90	0.86
1965	2.05	0.80
1966	2.40	0.85
1967	3.40	1.09
1968	3.40	0.92
1969	3.78	0.96
1970	3.78	0.92
1971	3.78	0.86
1972	4.20	0.89

SOURCES: PERULAC, cited in Eslava (1973, table 26).
The figure for 1944 is taken from Silva Santisteban
(1945). Prices in 1953 constant soles are calculated on
the basis of the Lima consumer price index, cited in
Wilkie (1974, table 1).

According to Thorp and Bertram (1978, 276), tariffs on food products were
steadily reduced during the 1950s, under the open-economy model of the
period, and by the end of the decade, the tariffs were virtually zero. Not
surprisingly, PERULAC continually tried to mobilize the Cattlemen's Association as a lobby to defend its interests at the national level. In 1952, for example,
the association sent a commission to Lima to lobby in support of raising tariffs
against final milk products; and in 1954 it wrote a request to the national

government for such tariffs.[9] PERULAC had offered to raise the price of milk if the association lobbied for the tariffs, and in fact, in 1955, PERULAC raised the price by nearly 25 percent (see Table 27). In 1960 PERULAC again asked the association to pressure the government for higher tariffs on canned milk (*Boletín* 1960, no. 9).

According to Lajo Lazo (1981a, 1981b), Nestlé and Carnation were quite successful both in obtaining high tariff protection on final milk products that might compete with their local enterprises, PERULAC and Leche Gloria, and in securing zero or low tariffs on inputs for the industry. Between 1946 and 1965, imports of dairy products represented only 1.6 percent to 2.0 percent of total imports (Thorp and Bertram 1978, table 13.12); but over time the importation of inputs for the milk-processing industry increased impressively. In 1943 imports of such inputs for the dairy industry represented the equivalent of only 3 percent of total national milk production; this figure increased to 22 percent by 1960, 35 percent by 1970, and an impressive 41 percent in 1975 (Lajo Lazo 1981b, table 4). The burden of competing internationally was increasingly onerous for Cajamarcan milk producers.

Although producer prices for milk came to be under direct state control, PERULAC still determined the price actually received by the milk suppliers at the factory gate. The price schedule presented in Table 27 is for milk with the standard 3.5 percent fat content. Milk with a higher fat content was paid a premium, and if the fat content fell below 2.5 percent, the milk was rejected. Until 1952, PERULAC was the sole judge of this important component of the price paid to the producer. The Cattlemen's Association, however, did not completely trust PERULAC's quality analysis, and in 1951 the association successfully pressured the government to establish a departmental Office for Direction and Improvement of Cattle Production, charged with overseeing PERULAC's application of standards. The following year, this office purchased its own milk-fat measuring equipment to independently verify quality standards for the cattle producers.[10] In subsequent years, most of the large dairy farmers purchased their own equipment to determine fat content and weight before shipping the milk to the factory. A recurring source of tension over the years, however, was that once the milk arrived at the factory, PERULAC still had the last word on milk quality and pricing (Burga Bartra and Huamán Ruiz 1979).

The departmental office was the first step in efforts by the Cattlemen's Association to chart a more independent course, separate from PERULAC. In

9. Association of Agriculturalists and Cattlemen of Cajamarca, minutes of meetings held on January 21, 1952, and October 20, 1954. All of the data from the minutes of the association are drawn from the summaries published (but not analyzed in any detail) in Eslava (1973).

10. Association of Agriculturalists and Cattlemen, minutes of meetings held on November 26, 1951, and January 21, 1952 (Eslava 1973).

1967 FONGAL, a development fund for the dairy industry, was established by the association to meet the financial and technical costs of further developing the industry. A common fund was set up, based on automatic deductions of S/. 0.20 per liter from PERULAC paychecks to milk suppliers. (The price of milk at this time was S/. 3.40.) Of the S/. 0.20 deduction, S/. 0.15 was to be returned to the producer directly in the form of veterinary and other services; the remainder was to go into a general fund to import improved cattle, semen, and other inputs for resale to the membership and to carry out other activities in the interests of the dairy industry (Caballero and Tello 1976, 13). By 1972 PERULAC was directly involved only in road maintenance, artificial insemination, and the annual cattle fairs (Eslava 1973, 104).

Another struggle over the price of milk pitted the consumers of the city of Cajamarca against both PERULAC and the Cattlemen's Association. From the time of the installation of the PERULAC processing plant, there had been worries that the city's fresh milk supply would be endangered by the more attractive prices offered to producers by the new company. In the inflationary period of the late 1940s, the prefect of Cajamarca attempted to enforce price ceilings on milk, butter, and beef. Moreover, an attempt was made to directly negotiate the amount of milk to be supplied to the city of Cajamarca by members of the Cattlemen's Association.[11]

Some of the ensuing struggles led to fluctuating alliances among consumers, producers, and PERULAC. Consumers in the city were concerned about both the high cost of fresh milk and the high cost of PERULAC's final products, especially evaporated milk. Although the city of Cajamarca is located in the rich milk-producing valley, a significant portion of its milk is consumed in the form of canned milk, following the national Peruvian trend (Lajo Lazo 1981a). Between 1949 and 1959, the price of a case of evaporated milk increased by 193 percent, whereas the price paid for raw milk to Cajamarcan producers increased by only 75 percent (*Boletín* 1960, no. 1, B–6).

A recurring topic of discussion in Cajamarca since at least the mid-1950s has been the potential benefits of a locally owned powdered-milk factory (Eslava 1973, 40). Powdered milk would presumably cost less to produce than evaporated milk and, hence, would reduce consumer prices; at the very least, it would not require the expensive imported tin used to make the cans for evaporated milk. Not until the late 1970s, however, was such an alternative taken seriously and placed on the agenda of demands not just in Cajamarca but nationally (Burga Bartra and Huamán Ruiz 1979, 12; Lajo Lazo 1981a, 1981b).

11. Association of Agriculturalists and Cattlemen, minutes of meetings held on January 2 and April 1, 1950 (Eslava 1973).

THE PROVINCIAL LABOR MARKET

Between 1940 and 1972, the agricultural sector remained the main source of employment in the province of Cajamarca, accounting for 68 percent of the province's economically active population (EAP) in 1972 (Peru 1972a, vol. [6], tables 24 and 25). As the governmental seat of the department and the principal site of the dairy industry, however, the province experienced somewhat greater economic diversification than did the department as a whole.[12]

The available census data on changes in the sectoral and occupational composition of the economically active population are, again, not especially helpful in analyzing the changes since the 1940s, because significant modifications have been made in the definition and measurement of the EAP.[13] In 1972 wage workers accounted for only 10 percent of the provincial EAP, and almost half of these—2,400 workers—were employed in the agricultural sector.[14] The manufacturing sector accounted for only 16 percent of the wage workers of the province. Of the 779 wage workers in manufacturing, PERULAC employed only 47 (Eslava 1973, 175). At least this many workers, if not more, were employed in the small-scale butter, cheese, and manjar factories of the province.

Fewer than one-quarter of the agricultural wage workers counted in the census were covered by Peru's labor legislation. Throughout the 1960s, an

12. In 1972, 33 percent of the EAP of the province were employed in nonagricultural occupations, compared with 24 percent for the department as a whole. In that year, the province accounted for 33 percent of the department's professional and technical workers, 44 percent of the directors and administrators, 33 percent of the commercial workers, and 37 percent of the service workers, while constituting only 21 percent of the department's EAP (Peru 1972a, vol. [6], tables 24 and 25).

13. One serious problem is that changes introduced in how the economically active population is defined significantly reduced the measured participation rates of women within the EAP, with dramatic implications for the reported EAP in the manufacturing sector in Cajamarca. In 1940, when a broad definition of economic activity was used to measure the EAP, women in the province had an economic participation rate of 39 percent. The more restrictive definition employed in 1972 resulted in a measured participation rate for women of 8.9 percent (Peru 1940, vol. 2, table 17; Peru 1972a, vol. [6], table 21, vol. [1], table 1). This decline accounts for the absolute and relative decrease in the share of the EAP in manufacturing between 1940 and 1972; the manufacturing labor force decreased from 29.5 percent of the total EAP in the province in 1940 to 7.9 percent in 1972. This decrease resulted primarily from the exclusion of female artisans, mainly spinners and weavers, from the EAP in later censuses. See Deere (1982) and Deere and León (1982) for a more extended discussion of the undernumeration of rural women in the censuses.

14. The census data actually show an absolute decrease in the number of wage workers within the EAP, but this decrease is also a result of changing census definitions of what constitutes a wage worker. In the 1940 census, peasants were grouped with wage workers in the category "obrero y campesino"; in the 1961 census, peasant heads of households were enumerated as independent workers, but peasants working on haciendas were still categorized as "obreros," whether or not they were paid a wage. In the 1972 census, the category "obrero" finally appears to capture only those who are employed as wage workers.

increasing number of favorable labor laws were passed, first under the liberal regime of Belaunde and subsequently under the Revolutionary Military Government. Since 1962, when Peru's first minimum-wage legislation was passed, employers have been required to submit signed payroll lists to the Ministry of Labor indicating compliance with the minimum wage and other social benefits, although compliance with the regulation has, predictably, been less than perfect. As Table 28 shows, the number of enterprises reporting to the ministry has increased steadily, no doubt in response to the threat of expropriation, in the early 1970s, for lack of compliance. Nevertheless, the number of enterprises complying is minimal when compared to the total number of farms that presumably use wage labor. The great majority of the enterprises complying with the labor legislation in the department are dairy farms; in 1971, 87 percent of those complying were located in the province of Cajamarca.

Although the minimum-wage legislation is designed to cover both temporary and permanent agricultural workers, social security and related labor laws apply only to permanent workers. The social security system is a most important benefit, providing almost free medical care, including two months of maternity leave with full pay. Other worker benefits include workers' compensation for accidents, a retirement system, profit sharing, and a paid one-month annual vacation.

The ample benefits to which permanent workers are entitled probably contributed to the reduced demand for permanent workers and particularly to the minimal number reported to the Ministry of Labor. Between 1965 and 1971, an average of ten workers were reported per enterprise, approximately one-third of them women. In 1971, only sixteen enterprises reported employing more than ten workers, although in the mid-1970s some forty-two enterprises in the province had at least one hundred milk cows in production. The scale of production of these forty-two enterprises implies that they were easily

TABLE 28. Agricultural Enterprises Reporting to the Ministry of Labor, Department of Cajamarca, 1965–1981

	Number of Enterprises	Total Number of Workers	Mean Number of Workers	Female Workers (%)
1965	41	427	10	35
1968	42	505	10	33
1971	63	663	10	36
1976	101	672	6	31
1981	90	948	11	30

SOURCE: Compiled from the Planillas de Trabajo, Ministry of Labor, Cajamarca office, city of Cajamarca; sample drawn from the second half of June each year.

employing ten or more permanent workers, thus hinting at the degree of noncompliance with the legislation.[15]

In any case, comparing the Ministry of Labor data with the census data suggests that women workers in particular have benefited from the labor legislation. Although they were only 9.8 percent of the agricultural wage workers counted in the census in 1972, women represented 36 percent of the wage workers receiving worker benefits in 1971. Yet few women were actually employed as agricultural wage workers in the province (215), and both the census and ministry data confirm that the dairy industry generated only minimal permanent employment, probably not more than 2,300 jobs in the early 1970s.[16] These data do not capture part-time wage employment, however, and thus are not a very good indicator of either the dynamism of the local labor market or the extent of development of capitalist class relations. But the data do illustrate why, for the growing number of landless peasants in Cajamarca, proletarianization often required permanent migration to the coast.

Wage Labor and the Peasantry

By the 1970s, both the sale and the purchase of labor power were not confined to agrarian capitalist enterprises but increasingly characterized labor relations within the peasantry. This was partly because of the high degree of social differentiation spurred by the land sales and the development of the market in milk. It was also a product of the high degree of monetization of the peasant economy. By 1973, 79 percent of peasant household income was in monetary form (Deere 1978, table 21). In addition, coastal consumption patterns increasingly permeated the farthest outposts of the province; rice, noodles processed from imported wheat flour, and even beer could be found in the small stores of most caseríos.

15. This information is based on my interview with the management of the Cooperativa de Servicios de Ganaderos (formerly the Cattlemen's Association) in December 1975 in Baños del Inca. They reported that farms with one hundred dairy cows in production would employ between twenty and thirty workers, of whom one-third to one-half would be dairy maids.

16. Eslava (1973, 174–175) estimated employment in the dairy industry at 5,160, a figure I consider much too high. His estimate assumed that the 172 farms producing more than 50 liters of milk daily in 1971 employed an average of thirty workers. According to my interviews on the dairy farms during 1976, only farms with more than one hundred cows in production could possibly employ that many workers (assuming the infrastructure for dairy production was in place) (see note 15, above). For example, in 1976 Tres Molinos had 139 cows in production, producing 1,946 liters of milk daily; they employed twenty-five workers, eleven of whom were milkmaids. A more reasonable estimate of permanent jobs on the dairy farms would be about 2,090 for 1971. This assumes that the 135 farms producing 50 to 250 liters of milk daily employed an average of ten wage workers and that the 37 farms producing more than 250 liters employed an average of twenty. The dairy farms would thus account for approximately four-fifths of the agricultural wage workers reported in the 1972 census. Probably another two hundred worked in the dairy-related processing industries, bringing total employment in this industry to around 2,300 in the early 1970s.

TABLE 29.   Participation of the Peasantry in the Sale and Purchase of Labor Power, Province of Cajamarca, 1973

Land-Size Strata	Percentage of Households Engaged in Wage Labor	Wage Labor as Percentage of Total Agricultural Labor Employed
Near-landless		
0.01–0.25 hectares	72	8
(N = 169)		
Smallholders		
0.26–3.50 hectares	55	12
(N = 605)		
Middle peasants		
3.51–11.00 hectares	39	20
(N = 170)		
Rich peasants		
11.01–30.00 hectares	35	29
(N = 74)		
Farmers		
30.01 – 100 hectares	31	29
(N = 32)		
Total	53	19
(N = 1050)		

SOURCE: Compiled from the 1973 Cajamarca Income Survey.

In 1973 the first household income survey, the Cajamarca Income Survey (see Appendix III), revealed that more than half of the peasant households in the province had at least one member participating in the labor market. The survey data suggest that the magnitude of peasant participation in the labor market has been strongly underestimated in census figures.[17] Participation in wage labor characterized all strata of the peasantry, but it was most significant among those with less access to land, as Table 29 shows. Peasant households were strongly differentiated not only according to whether they participated in capitalist class relations as wage workers but also with respect to their use of wage labor. Wage labor as a proportion of the total labor employed in agricultural field work was positively correlated with the household's access to land.[18]

17. The census questionnaire asks respondents for their *principal* occupation, regardless of any multiple economic activities in which they might engage. Even though peasant men may spend more days a year in the labor market than working their own plot of land, they consider themselves as primarily agricultural producers and are thus categorized as such in the census. This same procedure results in rural women being categorized as housewives rather than by their principal economic activity. See Deere (1982).

18. The correlation coefficient between land in usufruct and the use of wage labor was .2989, whereas the coefficient between land in usufruct and the sale of labor power was −.1571.

The primary site of wage employment for the peasantry in the 1970s was the province of Cajamarca. In 1973 only 6.6 percent of rural wage workers migrated to the coast to obtain employment, partly because of the unsettled labor market resulting from the application of the 1969 Agrarian Reform Law on the coastal sugar and rice estates (discussed in Chapter 9). The highland labor market, like the seasonal coastal labor market, was primarily a male domain, with women representing only 9 percent of the 1973 participants (Deere 1978, table 64). This fact was to have significant implications for the gender division of labor and for female economic dependence on men.

Peasant participation in the labor market in the 1970s was more than a seasonal or sporadic phenomenon. One-third of the wage workers surveyed were employed almost full-time (more than 260 days), and approximately two-thirds were employed more than 121 days a year (Deere 1978, table 59). Yet few of these workers were employed on a permanent basis, with the rights and privileges accorded permanent workers. Perhaps surprisingly, the majority of peasant wage workers were employed in nonagricultural activities; non-agricultural wage employment was particularly important among those who were employed more than 260 days a year. Most of these workers found jobs in the urban construction industry or in the service sector. Agricultural employment was most important for those who worked fewer than 120 days per year (Deere 1978, table 54).

Survey data for 1976 reveal that the primary employers of wage workers in the agricultural sector were peasants themselves. Peasants were the principal employers of 30 percent of the peasant–wage workers and of 62 percent of those who worked in the agricultural sector (Deere 1978, table 54). The average length of employment of peasants by other peasants in agricultural work was sixty days, unexpectedly long. Only 28 percent of the agricultural wage workers were primarily employed by haciendas or capitalist dairy enterprises. Another 10 percent were employed by the production cooperatives created under the 1969 agrarian reform.

The development of the wage relation among the peasantry was clearly tied to the monetization of the rural economy between 1940 and 1970 and the erosion of traditional forms of labor recruitment within peasant communities, including such noncapitalist practices as labor exchange, the minga, and work for payment in kind. Reciprocal labor exchange among households follows a rather strict day-for-day accounting, whether for agricultural work, cooking for field hands, or construction work. Households exchange labor with kin and neighbors, typically those of similar social standing, the practice being most prevalent among the poor peasantry. Reciprocal labor exchange has been by far the most stable of the noncapitalist forms of labor recruitment. In 1976 labor exchanges accounted for 15 percent of the total agricultural labor days employed on peasant units of production; wage labor accounted for 14 percent (Deere 1978, table 33). Nonetheless, many peasants complain of their neighbors' lack of interest in continuing the practice: "Everyone wants to be paid a wage; you can only count on your brothers or children—even one's compadres are reluctant." Such comments, made to me by villagers in the districts of San Marcos, Jesús, and Cajamarca, suggest that the tendency is toward the gradual monetization of reciprocal labor exchange.

The practice of intraprovincial migration to other ecological zones during the harvests has been even more eroded. In the past, it seemed as if entire villages packed up and traveled to the *jalcas* during the haciendas' potato and grain harvests. The barter of agricultural and artisan products among peasants was an important component of these migrations, but peasants also recount working for payment in kind for as long as four weeks in the 1940s in the hacienda mingas. In 1976 a household member migrated to another ecological zone in the highlands in only one-third of peasant households, averaging a five-day stay. The majority worked for payment in kind and also traded or purchased agricultural products. Twenty-two percent of those who made this migration said they did so only to purchase products (particularly potato seed), because work was not available. They described the difficulty of convincing the rich peasants to let them work for products—employers always preferred to pay in cash, if they needed such labor at all (1976 Peasant Family Survey).

One of the main changes that occurred after 1950 was in the relationship between rural wages and the price of foodstuffs, illustrated in Table 30. Whereas relative prices changed considerably, the amount of the different products to be remunerated in kind during the harvest was quite "sticky," set by tradition. These data primarily capture the effect of the generation of surplus labor, with respect to employment opportunities, in the highlands.[19] Whereas the prices of the basic grains produced in Cajamarca increased 38 (barley) to 67 (lentils) times, wages increased only elevenfold between 1944 and 1976. The data also explain why cash wages were not a generalized phenomenon at least through the 1940s. During those years, it was simply cheaper to pay for labor in kind. In the 1970s, in contrast, the payment of wages in kind, and thus the minga, was a most expensive proposition.

The change in the form of labor recruitment was an important source of tension within peasant communities in the 1970s, and it had profound implications for the well-being of most rural households and for women's ability to contribute to household income. The cheapening of labor relative to foodstuffs meant that, for poor households, daily reproduction required more

19. The best evidence of surplus labor in the northern highlands is the trend in real wages. In 1953 constant prices, the wage in 1944 was S/. 10; in 1976, it was S/. 4.2 (see Table 16). The 1944 wage figure reported by Silva Santisteban (1945) is for a permanent wage worker in the valley of Cajamarca, however; the prevailing agricultural wage in the rest of the province was probably lower. The 1976 figure above is the mean wage paid for agricultural labor by peasant households as reported in the 1976 Peasant Family Survey; it was slightly higher than the mean wage earned by peasant agricultural wage workers in the sample, S/. 33.5.

TABLE 30.   Cash Wages and the Payment of Labor in Kind, Province of
Cajamarca, 1944 and 1976

Quantity of Payment in Kind	1944 Wholesale Prices, City, August–September	1976 Harvest Prices, Countryside	1976 Wholesale Prices, City, October–November
Wheat (1/2 almud)	S/. 2.10	S/. 90	S/. 100–125
Lentils (1/2 almud)	2.60	175	255
Barley (1 arroba)	2.40	90	100–150
Potatoes (1 arroba)	2.60	110	137–150
Corn (24 ears)	1.20[a]	60	—
Cash wage (daily)	3.00[b]	34.8[c]	—
Number of days of wage labor for equivalent amount of product:			
Wheat	0.7 days	2.6 days	2.9–3.6 days
Lentils	0.9	5.0	7.3
Barley	0.8	2.6	2.9–4.3
Potatoes	0.9	3.2	3.9–4.3
Corn	0.4	1.7	—

SOURCES: All 1944 data are taken from Silva Santisteban (1945, 124–125). For 1976, the harvest price refers to
the price paid to the producer at the time of sale (1976 Peasant Family Survey); the wholesale prices are based
on the author's market observations in the city of Cajamarca and the town of San Marcos; and the wage data
are taken from the 1976 Peasant Family Survey.

NOTE: Prices are in current Peruvian soles.

[a] Retail price.

[b] Wage paid to valley cowhands.

[c] Mean wage paid for agricultural wage workers by peasant households.

and more expenditure of labor time. What could have been obtained in one
day's work in the past now required three days of wage labor. Furthermore,
whereas in the first part of the century both male and female labor could have
been deployed to procure the household's stock of grains, by working for other
peasants in the community or migrating to the jalcas at harvest time, now
generally only men were employed as wage workers. Women constituted only
5 percent of the agricultural wage workers in the 1973 Cajamarca Income
Survey and 6 percent in the 1976 Peasant Family Survey.

    In contrast, women were almost as likely to work for payment in kind as
men were (80 percent versus 89 percent), and 44 percent of women migrated
to other zones to work for products, compared to 55 percent of men. Moreover,

although women traditionally received only half of what men were paid when remunerated in kind on the haciendas, within the independent communities remuneration tended to be equal by sex. Eighty-nine percent of the households surveyed reported that women in their communities were always remunerated at the same level as men (1976 Peasant Family Survey). In contrast, women earned only 60 percent of men's agricultural wage. The monetization of the peasant economy thus served to impoverish rural households, both through reducing women's opportunities to contribute to household income and through the deterioration in the terms of labor for product exchange. The overall result was to exacerbate rural poverty and peasant social differentiation and to create new forms of female subordination.

CONCLUSION

By the time General Velasco proclaimed the Revolutionary Military Government's anti-feudal agrarian reform in 1969, the configuration of land tenure in the department had been considerably altered and rural class relations transformed. The parceling of haciendas in the previous two decades had significantly lessened the degree of concentration of land ownership, contributing to the predominance of medium-sized property as the basis of the dairy industry. The land sales also created a vast new sector of independent peasant landowners bent on preserving their right to private property and reproducing themselves as petty producers. Through the land sales, peasant dispossession, internal proletarianization, and migration, the number of peasants subject to feudal class relations on estates had been substantially reduced. And one of the main points of contention in the province in the 1970s was not a fundamental class process—rather, it was the subsumed class process underlying capitalist and petty production, the role of PERULAC in marketing milk.

The temporary stabilization and expansion of petty production through Cajamarca's land reform by private initiative did little, overall, to mitigate the problem of growing landlessness. One of the main features of the provincial labor market was that the most dynamic sector—the dairy industry—generated few full-time jobs. Even the growth of the city of Cajamarca as an important administrative center generated few permanent employment opportunities for the growing landless rural proletariat. As a result, permanent migration from the province was quantitatively more significant than the temporary seasonal migration to the coast that had characterized previous decades. Moreover, permanent migration from the highlands contributed to the creation of surplus labor on the coast and therefore reduced the probability of finding seasonal employment. This, in turn, reduced highland labor's positive opportunity cost through migration and encouraged the generalized development of capitalist class relations in the highlands. The development of wage labor in the independent peasant communities was also facilitated by the process of integration of the coast and sierra during previous decades, which had contributed to changing consumption patterns and the monetization of the rural economy. In the 1970s, the conditions of labor recruitment (remuneration in cash versus in kind) and the sources of surplus extraction by rich peasants from poor (credit, marketing, and sharecropping arrangements) were sources of tension within the independent communities that were at least equal in importance to landlord-peasant struggles over the conditions of appropriation of surplus and community-hacienda struggles over land.

NINE

The Agrarian Reform in Cajamarca: State Intervention, Capital, Labor, and the Peasantry

When the Revolutionary Military Government came to power in 1968, it was well aware of the political potency of the land issue. The army had been called in repeatedly during the 1950s and early 1960s to repress peasant land invasions in the sierra. Although rural unrest had been calmed by the selective application of the 1964 Agrarian Reform Law, the military recognized the potential revolutionary threat of the peasantry. In addition, the military was committed to national modernization through industrial development, for which it considered structural reform in the agrarian sector a prerequisite.[1]

The Peruvian agrarian sector had been stagnant for the better part of two decades (Hopkins 1979; Alvarez 1980). In the 1960s, agricultural production grew by only 2.8 percent annually, whereas population growth was on the order of 3.1 percent (Caballero 1980, 28). Food imports had thus been increasing as a share of total imports. Moreover, the distribution of land was extremely skewed. According to the 1961 census, fewer than 1 percent of the nation's farms held 76 percent of the agricultural land. In a pattern typical of Latin America, control over land had led to a concentration of wealth—and hence economic, social, and political power—in a landed oligarchy.

The 1969 agrarian reform legislation was anti-oligarchic in content and modernizing in intent. President Juan Velasco Alvarado introduced the 1969 law under the banner of "land to the tiller." The anti-feudal intent of the law was contained both in the prohibitions against "anti-social" forms of tenancy and in the restrictions on farm size. Idle lands, as well as land not worked directly by its owner, were subject to immediate expropriation; sharecropping

---

1. The literature analyzing the impetus for the military government's agrarian reform, as well as its national trajectory, is substantial. See Zaldivar (1974), Caballero (1976, 1980, 1981a, 1981b), Harding (1975), and Matos Mar and Mejía (1980).

and all forms of rental contracts, along with ownership of land by joint-stock companies, were prohibited. The maximum limit on landholdings was set at 600 hectares on the coast and 165 in the sierra. The maximum limit on irrigated land was more restrictive: 150 hectares on the coast and 15 to 50 hectares in the sierra and Amazonian basin, depending on the zone. Restrictions on grazing land were more flexible, fixing limits at the amount of land necessary for grazing 1,500 to 4,500 sheep on the coast and 500 to 15,000 sheep in the sierra ("Ley de Reforma Agraria del Perú" 1970).

Former feudatarios (peasants previously tied to haciendas under feudal class relations) were given preferential rights to the land they worked. The ideal of the family-sized farm was written into the legislation, such a farm being defined as the amount of land directly farmed by the owner and the owner's family that would fully absorb the family labor force, provide a net income adequate for the family to be self-supporting, and enable the farmer to meet the land payments. The legislation also protected, and intended to foster, medium-sized farms.[2]

As soon as the reform began to be implemented, it became apparent that these objectives were incompatible. If the existing cultivable land had been divided up among all the eligible beneficiaries, family-sized farms would not have been the result. There were an estimated 234,000 families with preferential rights to land under the feudatario provision alone. According to national averages, dividing the land into family-sized parcels for this group alone would have resulted in only one out of eight peasant families acquiring land (and only one out of eleven in the sierra) (Van de Wetering 1973). Moreover, the protection afforded medium-sized commercial farms in effect excluded the majority of the rural proletariat from being potential beneficiaries of the reform.

The reform process also raised tremendous expectations, principally among those groups not initially designated as beneficiaries: rural wage workers and smallholders with insufficient land. The government had underestimated both their reaction and, specifically, the active role the rural unions would play in ensuring that the reform would maximize the number of beneficiaries (Harding 1975, 237–243).

The government's hand was forced quite early, over the issue of private parceling. The original legislation gave landowners the prerogative of divesting themselves of their excess holdings prior to expropriation. It quickly became

---

2. Considerable flexibility was written into the agrarian reform law to protect medium-sized property and capitalist enterprises in an attempt to reconcile the law's productionist framework with the social goal of redistribution. The basic limits on property holdings could be exceeded if the landowner fulfilled certain conditions. For example, if the landholding had the installations necessary for irrigation, or if three-fourths of the cultivable land had been farmed during the past three years, the maximum allowable size was doubled. If wages were 10 percent above the minimum wage and workers were provided with health, education, and housing, and if tax payments were up-to-date, the maximum holdings were also extended.

apparent that this was a major loophole in the law, one that allowed land-owners to sell land to nonpeasants and to divide up estates among family members and fictitious owners while remaining in control of the property. Subsequent legislation stipulated that workers on the estates be given preferential rights to purchase land, that the sales be supervised by the land reform agency, and that a portion of the estate be reserved for group farming.

The legislation was not made retroactive, however, and permanent and temporary workers on the coastal estates mobilized once they realized they were being excluded from the reform. Their pressure finally resulted in the government annulling some of the private parcelings on the coast and, in 1970, prohibiting all further land sales. Moreover, the government was also forced to broaden the limits for expropriation to include properties that had initially been exempt.

By 1971 it was also apparent that the military would have to abandon its vision of a reformed countryside characterized by family and medium-sized farms. If a significant number of rural workers and peasants were to benefit, the reform had to foster collective solutions to the agrarian question. The state then began to experiment with various collective schemes, as well as with integrative planning based on larger socioeconomic units. The tendency to form centralized units of production on adjudicated land was thus a response to the need to broaden the number of beneficiaries because of pressure from the base.

By 1972 the agrarian reform had resulted in the following forms of organization of production and land tenancy within the reformed sector:

1. The CAP (Cooperativa Agraria de Producción). This was to be a fully collectivized enterprise, with ownership of land and other means of production vested in the membership. These production cooperatives were to be worker-managed, with worker participation in decision making, including decisions concerning the distribution of profits.
2. The SAIS (Sociedad Agrícola de Interés Social). This represented an attempt to preserve the existing sierra estates as production units while reconciling the varying interests of neighboring peasant communities, resident feudatarios, and the wage workers of the enterprise. The productive core of the enterprise was to remain intact and be reorganized as a production cooperative; the profits generated by the cooperative, however, were to be shared with the communities forming part of the SAIS, principally through infrastructural investment in the complex.
3. Peasant Groups (Grupos Campesinos). These were also called pre-cooperatives and were seen as a temporary solution in the face of peasant resistance on many haciendas to turning over their individual usufruct plots and forming production cooperatives.
4. Peasant Communities (Comunidades Campesinas). Officially recognized indigenous communities were guaranteed their right to communal

land. They were to be favored with the adjudication of additional land (usually grazing pastures) when they claimed it as part of historical grievances against specific haciendas.
5. Individuals. The adjudication of individual, private farms received the lowest priority. Titles to private property were guaranteed, however, as long as the lands were not in conflict with the provisions of the reform.

In 1972 the government envisioned that two-thirds of the land in Peru would be affected by the reform process, directly benefiting one-third of the rural population by the end of the reform period (Horton 1976, 78–79). Expropriations and adjudications of land proceeded rather vigorously through 1975 under the Velasco government. Subsequently, under General Morales Bermúdez, the pace of the reform slowed, and the expropriations came to a near-halt in 1979 (Mejía 1980, 15–16).

Over this ten-year period, 38.3 percent of Peru's agricultural land passed to the reformed sector (Caballero and Alvarez 1980, 20). Government officials claimed that 37 percent of Peruvian rural households had benefited from the reform. This figure is a bit deceptive, however, because it includes among the 359,600 beneficiary households those within the officially recognized Peasant Communities who had been adjudicated some collective land (generally pastures) through the reform. Households within these communities accounted for more than one-third of the total number of beneficiary households (Caballero and Alvarez 1980, 45).

Data on the composition of the beneficiaries illustrate the degree to which the reform was modified as a result of pressure from the base. As of 1979, wage workers, initially excluded in the reform law, constituted 27 percent of the beneficiaries; former feudatarios, for whom the reform had been intended, made up 25 percent. Moreover, almost two-thirds of the land adjudicated went to associative enterprises such as a CAP or SAIS; Peasant Groups received 21 percent; Peasant Communities, 11 percent; and individuals, 4 percent (Caballero and Alvarez 1980, 26).

The reelection of Fernando Belaunde Terry as president in 1980 and the subsequent passage of the Agrarian Development and Promotion Law (Ley de Promoción y Desarollo Agrario) brought the military's agrarian reform process to an end.[3] Although the Revolutionary Military Government hardly

3. The adjudication of lands continued throughout 1980 and, in fact, was quite significant in the last year of the reform. A comparison of the data reported in Caballero and Alvarez (1980, tables 3 and 6) and in Mejía (1980, 14) shows that, between September 1979 and May 1980, 1,824,829 hectares were adjudicated to 41,762 beneficiaries. These figures represent a 25 percent increase in total land adjudicated and a 12 percent increase in beneficiaries in the last year of the reform.

accomplished all its objectives with respect to the agrarian sector, a significant transformation of rural land tenancy and class relations had taken place. This is certainly evident in the Cajamarcan case.

THE REFORM PROCESS IN CAJAMARCA

Under the 1964 Agrarian Reform Law, only one hacienda had been expropriated in the province of Cajamarca, the Hacienda Huayobamba, the property of the Beneficiencia Pública of Celendín. It was expropriated in 1967, apparently only because this action did not threaten the position of the landed elite. By the 1960s, the Cajamarcan agrarian bourgeoisie may have been convinced that feudal class relations were not in its interests. A redistribution of land through the subdivision and sale of the haciendas was one thing; expropriation at the hands of the state was quite another.

Although the 1964 reform had little direct impact in Cajamarca, it did raise the expectations and heighten the political awareness of the peasantry. On several fundos, peasants initiated litigation against the landowners, protesting unpaid labor services and excessive demands for the payment of rent in kind. The 1964 law reduced rental payments from the customary 50 percent of the crop to 20 percent. The expropriation of the Hacienda Huayobamba, in fact, resulted from the arrendire's infraction of this provision of the law. Other peasants, previously expelled from haciendas that were being converted into dairy enterprises, brought claims against the landowners under another provision of the 1964 law, one guaranteeing security of tenure (Hacienda Huacariz de San Antonio). The new political climate also encouraged permanent wage workers on the dairy enterprises to begin pressing for compliance with the minimum-wage legislation and payment of other social benefits (Hacienda La Colpa).

The response of the landowning class to these new conditions was to again sell land to the peasants, and the initiation of the 1969 agrarian reform process on the north coast launched the third wave of land parceling in the province. In the four-year period that saw the passage of the legislation, the official declaration of Cajamarca as an agrarian reform zone (1971), and the installation of a zonal agrarian reform office (1973), many landowners were able to divest themselves both of excess holdings (more than the maximum allowed by the law) and of "excess" peasants who might have claimed feudatario status. Landowners began selling land parcels to friends, relatives, administrators, and favored peasants, as well as to land speculators.

For example, Castro Mendívil, the owner of the modern dairy enterprise La Colpa, attempted to consolidate his workers' support by distributing some 160 hectares of good lands among his oldest workers as gifts (Rojas 1974, 21). In 1969 he sold the fundo La Victoria to Pedro Pajares, and in 1970 he also sold other sections of his property to arrendires and sharecroppers.

Rafael Puga, owner of the Hacienda La Pauca, turned over 40,902 hectares of hacienda land voluntarily to the reform authorities. This was a surprising move in 1970, for the department had not even been declared an agrarian reform zone, and there had not been any peasant mobilization on his hacienda. Apparently, he was hoping to be allowed to retain the best sections of the hacienda, the 7,000 hectares in the Tingayoc and Amante sectors, by this voluntary show of "good will." He had already moved his improved cattle breeds and prize bulls to these areas, expelling the resident peasantry. Puga also sold the lands surrounding these sectors to rich peasants and land speculators (Arce del Campo and Lora 1974, 9–14).

These sales were legal until 1970; thereafter, they were proscribed by the revised legislation. Nevertheless, the sales continued in Cajamarca.[4] Again, the majority of land sales to the peasantry were often made without legal land titles, and this caused numerous conflicts in the subsequent reordering of land tenure in the province.

The first response of the Cajamarcan dairy entrepreneurs to the 1969 reform — ridding themselves of excess lands — represented an attempt to consolidate their position in order to qualify for certificates of exemption. Through these land sales, most of the dairy farms in the valley of Cajamarca were reduced to fewer than 100 hectares. Although the maximum amount of irrigated land permissible under the reform was to be between 15 and 50 hectares, the dairy farmers initially felt confident that the flexible exemptions provided in the legislation for modern commercial operations would exclude them from the process. Rafael Gómez Sánchez, the arrendire of the fundo Cristo Rey, was even confident enough to purchase this dairy farm in 1970. The Banco Agropecuario also thought that the reform would be anti-feudal rather than anti-capitalist, for in 1971 it assumed Gomez Sanchez's mortgage.

A few landowners nonetheless decided to pull out at this time, severely decapitalizing their haciendas. The owners of the Hacienda Negritos, for example, sold their 140 head of cattle and 2,000 sheep and abandoned the hacienda (Bazán 1972, 4). The arrendire of the Hacienda Huayobamba not only sold all the cattle and equipment but also reportedly took the tile roofing off the stable when he left. By the end of 1970, Castro Mendívil of the Hacienda La Colpa decided to withdraw as well, decapitalizing in the process (Rojas 1974, 21). According to Caballero and Tello (1976, 22), this decapitalization was repeated frequently throughout the department.

But the majority of landowners, particularly the dairy farmers, stayed on and attempted to forge a landlord-peasant alliance to ensure that the reform would not ignore its legislated goal of strengthening commercial farming. The

---

4. An often-noted case of hacienda subdivision during this period is that of the Hacienda Tres Molinos owned by Juan Miguel Rossell. In 1973 he subdivided this estate among his two sons and a son-in-law (Burga Posito et al. 1980, 58; Becerra Bazán et al. 1981, 52).

Association of Agriculturalists and Cattlemen launched a major anti-reform campaign designed to consolidate peasant support behind the asserted "common threat" to private property. The Cajamarcan landowners saw this as a necessary objective once it became clear that the reform on the coast was moving beyond its original scope. Reportedly, PERULAC was especially helpful in this endeavor. The milk collection receptacles (porongos) became a major means of disseminating anti-reform propaganda.

In May 1972, the Cattlemen's Association was abolished through a national decree (Decreto Ley 19400) that dissolved the Sociedad Nacional Agraria and all its affiliated associations. In its efforts to deal with the growing tensions at the base and the attempted landlord subversion, the Velasco government imposed a new organizational structure on rural Peru in order to better control the agrarian reform process. Agrarian leagues (Ligas Agrarias) were subsequently organized at the provincial or valley level and linked nationally through the Confederación Nacional Agraria.[5]

The dairy entrepreneurs of Cajamarca stayed on the offensive, however, organizing themselves along with the smaller dairy producers into "Small and Medium Agriculturalists and Cattlemen" committees, a phenomenon that occured across Peru. In 1974 they formed an agrarian service cooperative (CAS, Cooperativa Agraria de Servicio) and succeeded in gaining official recognition in June 1975 as the Cooperativa Agraria de Servicios de Agricultores y Ganaderos de Cajamarca, Ltda., No. 018. Their major victory was to obtain control over the money involved in FONGAL, the dairy development fund based on automatic deductions from the paychecks of PERULAC suppliers.[6]

The reform was now moving quickly in Cajamarca. By mid-1974, a year after the zonal agrarian reform agency was established, thirty-four estates were in the possession of their workers. It was also becoming increasingly clear that, because of worker pressure, the dairy enterprises would be reduced to 50 hectares, no matter how well-managed they had been. In 1976 the maximum amount of irrigated land allowed a commercial farm in the sierra was officially reduced to 30 hectares (Decreto Ley 21333).

At this point, the Cajamarcan agrarian reform agency was caught in the double bind of litigating the scores of conflicts that had been unleashed among

5. At the base level, the agrarian leagues were to be constituted by the new associative enterprises (CAP, SAIS), officially recognized Peasant Communities, service cooperatives, and newly organized committees of independent peasants and landless workers. The task of organizing this new structure fell to the government office SINAMOS (Sistema Nacional de Mobilizacion Social). See Matos Mar and Mejía (1980, chap. 5) for a good description of these rural organizations.

6. See Caballero and Tello's (1976, 13) description of the struggle over FONGAL funds between the new cooperative of the former Cattlemen's Association, the CAS, and the new official agrarian reform organization in Cajamarca, FADEC (Federación Agraria Departamental de Cajamarca), which was linked to the Confederación Nacional Agraria.

peasants, rural workers, and landowners and also trying to determine viable solutions to the organization of production in the reformed sector. On estates with a permanent wage labor force, principally the dairy farms, the labor process was already socialized, and these workers were generally amenable to forming production cooperatives. Moreover, on a good number of enterprises, as the wage workers became organized, they began to press for the full expropriation of the farm. In fact, many of the dairy farms that might have qualified under the various exemptions in the law, based on productivity and compliance with labor legislation, were eventually expropriated in their entirety as a result of worker militancy and perseverance.

On haciendas still worked by feudatarios, the situation was different. Opposition to the cooperative development plan arose quickly. These peasants wanted titles to the land they worked, as promised by the initial land reform legislation. By its own momentum, the agrarian reform went beyond what its planners had originally envisioned, and the cooperative solution had to be imposed from above on an often reluctant peasantry. These unintended consequences reflect the contradictions of state intervention in rural class relations, as well as the heterogeneous nature of peasant class relations.

In an excellent analysis of the Cajamarcan agrarian reform process, Helen Rainbird and Lewis Taylor (1976, 13) point to the various levels of political consciousness among the peasantry to explain the outcome of the agrarian reform. Different groups of peasants had very different material interests—attachment to land versus attachment to wage income—which in turn reflected different degrees of development of the labor-capital relationship. Where peasants had been divorced from the means of production and were dependent on the sale of their labor power for a wage, the socialization of the work process had produced more of a social consciousness. For these peasants, the agrarian reform provided the possibility of moving from the status of worker to that of worker-owner. Recognizing the benefits of the division of labor and of centralized management led to the collective recognition that the cooperative solution was in their individual economic interests.

In contrast, on haciendas where the permanent work force was much reduced in size and where most peasants were still entangled in feudal relations, the conflict centered on control over resources, especially land. Because access to land was what guaranteed the reproduction of peasant households as direct producers, the political consciousness of these peasants was very much geared to ensuring this essential condition of existence; thus their demands focused on acquiring property. As Rainbird and Taylor (1976) point out, on these large estates the primary contradiction was between labor and land—not labor and capital, which the cooperative solution was better equipped to resolve.

The state eventually acceded to peasant demands for individual land titles. Through 1980, however, the conflict was only internalized in the new agrarian structure as peasants with claims and in control of hacienda land were required to join Peasant Groups as part of a SAIS or sometimes a CAP. Usually, this was no solution; rather, it became a source of even greater conflict, disrupting the functioning of the cooperative enterprises.

In any case, in Cajamarca, as in the whole of Peru, the agrarian reform went beyond the initial vision of the military, becoming at least partially responsive to peasant and rural worker demands. Rather than the family-sized farms envisioned in the legislation, cooperatives and large centralized units proved to be the only workable solutions to the diverse claims on land. Rather than preserving and expanding the commercial sector of medium-sized property, the reform had to at least partly socialize its ownership to accommodate the demands of peasants and rural workers for land.

Accomplishments of the Reform in Cajamarca

The initial plans for the reform called for the expropriation of 669,047 hectares, 43 percent of the total land claimed as private property in the department. Some 20,275 rural households, representing approximately 13.4 percent of the rural households of the department, were to benefit directly. By mid-1976, more than half of the land to be expropriated under the reform had been affected. In the province of Cajamarca, which accounted for almost one-third of the department lands targeted, the expropriations were virtually complete (97 percent) by the end of 1976 (Esparza Bueno et al. 1981).

Although all land expropriations ended in 1979, adjudication of agrarian reform land continued through 1981 because of the lag in organizing the new reformed sector. As of April 1981, 14,397 families in the department, representing 9.5 percent of Cajamarcan rural households, had benefited (see Table 31). The agrarian reform process had reached 71 percent of the intended households and had redistributed 62 percent of the targeted land.

When the agrarian reform began in Cajamarca, the government planned to adjudicate the great bulk (91 percent) of the expropriated land collectively; only 9 percent was to be distributed individually, to 2,914 households.[7] As it turned out, individual peasant producers were the principal beneficiaries of the reform in Cajamarca; they were granted 46 percent of the land and constituted 58 percent of those who benefited.

These individual beneficiaries were associated in Peasant Groups, and their predominance (see Table 31) was the result of a compromise. As noted previously, feudatarios on the estates strongly resisted the cooperative structure, which they viewed as imposed from above and against their individual interests. But the state was committed to the principle of collective adjudication. The resulting compromise was collective adjudication with individual usufruct. The groups were then required to maintain a portion of the estate

7. Interviews with the Agrarian Reform Office, Ministry of Agriculture, Agrarian Zone II, Cajamarca, November 1976.

TABLE 31.   Agrarian Reform Adjudications, Province and Department of
Cajamarca, December 31, 1980

Form of Adjudication	Number of Adjudications	Families Benefited		Hectares Adjudicated	
		Number	Percentage Distribution	Amount	Percentage Distribution
Province of Cajamarca					
CAP	14[a]	1,066	25.5	44,669.8	28.5
SAIS	2	2,228	53.3	73,954.6	47.3
Community	3	220	5.3	15,814.5	10.1
Peasant Groups	15	665	15.9	22,037.1	14.1
Total		4,179	100.0	156,476.0	100.0
Department of Cajamarca					
CAP	37[a]	3,489	24.2	132,362.7	31.9
SAIS	2	2,228	15.5	73,954.6	17.8
Community	5	298	2.1	17,606.4	4.2
Peasant Groups	107	8,382	58.2	191,355.8	46.1
Total		14,397	100.0	415,279.5	100.0

SOURCE: "Adjudicaciones Asociativas al 31/12/80," Ministry of Agriculture, Agrarian Region IX, Cajamarca,
April 30, 1981, mimeo.
[a]Two other CAPs were still in the process of being officially constituted.

(usually at least part of what had been the landlord's demesne) to work
collectively in order to generate the income for paying the agrarian debt. (This
debt, which will be discussed later, represented compensation paid by the state
to landowners for expropriations; cooperative enterprises were mortgaged to
the state to help pay off the debt.) In 1981 the agrarian reform agency still
considered these Peasant Groups to be pre-cooperatives, although in only a few
cases was there any kind of collective enterprise.[8]

Table 31 also shows both how few Peasant Communities in the department
benefited through the reform and the relative lack of success in organizing
SAISs. Constituting the only two SAISs in the department, both in the
province of Cajamarca—the SAIS Atahualpa on the former Hacienda Porcón
and the SAIS La Pauca on the former hacienda of the same name—had been
most difficult because of the resistance of the Peasant Communities and the
CAPs to which they were to be associated. Joining in the SAIS scheme required
these communities to give up their historic claims to hacienda land. Few saw
any benefit in doing so. The CAPs, as potentially prosperous enterprises, also
saw little to gain from sharing profit with neighboring communities of

8. In December 1981, I was shown a July 1981 internal memo from the director of the Program
Office to the director of the Agrarian Reform Office in Cajamarca (now known as Agrarian Region
IX of Cajamarca) stating that the Peasant Groups were still obligated to form a cooperative or
constitute themselves as a Peasant Community; if they did not, the paperwork required for
exemption from the agrarian debt would not be carried out.

smallholders. In some cases, the two groups had no social or historical ties; if they did, that history was often one of animosity.

Of what had once been the 28,200-hectare Hacienda Porcón, only 3,600 hectares were finally adjudicated to the SAIS Atahualpa. The individual parcels purchased by the hacienda residents in the 1950s and 1960s were declared exempt from the agrarian reform process, and few of these small-holders were interested in joining even a service cooperative. A heated conflict broke out between the core enterprise of the SAIS (a production cooperative) and the Community of Negritos, which had been destined by reform planners to join the SAIS Atahualpa. Members of the community invaded the SAIS lands, and only military intervention dislodged them.[9]

The one community that agreed to join the SAIS La Pauca, Yonapaccha-Chuco, soon pulled out of the venture when it became clear that the community was not to be given a sector of the hacienda for its own usufruct. This SAIS was finally converted to a CAP in 1980, and the various peasant communities were allocated land as Peasant Groups. In other cases, the agrarian reform agency was forced at an earlier stage to revise its plans to form a larger integrative unit.[10]

The relatively greater importance of CAPs and the lesser predominance of Peasant Groups as beneficiaries in the province of Cajamarca (as compared with the department as a whole) reflect the greater degree of capitalist development in the province. Most of the modern dairy enterprises were concentrated here, as were the greatest number of rural proletarians. As a result, the agrarian reform in the province was more anti-capitalist than anti-feudal, and cooperative development was relatively more successful.

COOPERATIVE DEVELOPMENT AS A PRODUCT OF LAND REFORM

Constituting the production cooperatives of the province was not easy. Conflicts abounded over membership, employment, and access to resources. Once the cooperatives were legally constituted, administrative and production problems were often severe.[11]

9. The Community of Negritos was one of several organized by the Confederación Campesina del Perú (CCP) in Cajamarca. The CCP initially took a strong anti-reform stance, particularly against the SAIS structure. It was instrumental in organizing several land takeovers in the region and, as a result, suffered considerable repression at the hands of the military.

10. In 1975 the agrarian reform agency planned to join the CAP El Rescate (former hacienda La Colpa) and the CAP Huacariz de San Antonio into a SAIS that would include the neighboring communities in the district of Jesús. The resistance of the cooperative members was so strong, however, that the plan was abandoned. The contradictory nature of the SAIS has been widely noted; see Matos Mar and Mejía (1980, chap. 3).

11. The data and analysis concerning the Cajamarcan production cooperatives presented in these sections are largely drawn from my case studies of the CAP Huacariz de San Antonio (carried

To be granted membership in a cooperative, a peasant or worker had to demonstrate that he or she qualified as a beneficiary of the agrarian reform. To qualify, a person had to meet the following conditions: 1) be more than eighteen years of age; 2) be the head of a household that included dependents; 3) be exclusively involved in agriculture; 4) not own land exceeding the family agricultural unit; and 5) have worked as a feudatario on a hacienda (Decreto Ley 17776, Article 84). The actual designation of beneficiary status turned out to be rather arbitrary, however, partly because on numerous haciendas few peasants wanted to join the cooperative, whereas on others, once the cooperative was constituted, all too many came to join.

The latter situation prevailed on what had been the Hacienda Huacariz de San Antonio. On this hacienda, the struggle against the landlord had been carried on by the sharecroppers who had been thrown off the hacienda in 1964, as noted in Chapter 6. A new labor force of permanent wage workers had been recruited on the dairy farm in the intervening years. These wage workers sided with the landowner Velgara in the litigation filed by the ex-sharecroppers. When the ex-sharecroppers finally won the expropriation of the hacienda under the 1969 law, the dairy farm was adjudicated to them. But the agrarian reform agency also ruled that Velgara's wage workers were entitled to join the new cooperative. The wage workers declined to do so at that time, mindful of the landlord's resolve to regain control of the hacienda.

In 1975 the CAP Huacariz de San Antonio was constituted with some thirty members, the majority of whom were former sharecroppers. But the membership also included peasants who had been neither sharecroppers nor wage workers on the dairy enterprise. When the former wage workers finally decided that they wanted to join the CAP, the cooperative's doors had already closed to new members; it had access to only 106 hectares and could not accommodate a larger membership.

The struggle on some of the larger haciendas, such as La Pauca, was much different. This SAIS had more than enough land; the problem lay in how to attract sufficient labor for the core production cooperative of the complex. The feudatarios, who had previously served as the temporary labor reserve of the hacienda, were required by agrarian reform officials to join either the CAP or a Peasant Group within the SAIS in order to maintain access to their individual usufruct parcels. Most feudatarios not only refused to join the CAP as

out in February, April, September, and November 1976), the CAP Huayobamba (October 1976), and the production cooperative of the SAIS Atahualpa (January 1976). In each case, I interviewed the cooperative management, all the milkmaids, and a random sample of the male cooperative members. I also visited and carried out unstructured interviews during 1976 on the CAPs Cajamarca, El Rescate, El Rosario, El Milagro, and Los Ayllus. The analysis of the impact of the agrarian reform is complimented by my community case studies, by the data collected during the 1976 Peasant Family Survey, and by interviews with agrarian reform officials throughout 1976 and again in December 1981.

permanent workers but also refused to work for it as temporary laborers. With plots sufficient to ensure household reproduction, combined with the relief from rental payments, they wanted only to be left alone. Even the permanent workers on the dairy enterprise were more interested in farming their own land than in working for the cooperative, and several of them usurped parcels belonging to the enterprise.

The cooperative was left with a much reduced work force, and it had to resort to traditional forms of coercion to secure sufficient labor—for example, fining feudatarios in days of labor service for grazing animals on cooperative pastures. But nothing less than intervention by the army could have persuaded the feudatarios to work a fixed number of days per month in return for their parcels, even if they were remunerated at the minimum wage. The lack of both cooperative members and temporary workers brought the enterprise almost to a standstill. Moreover, the cooperative was saddled with paying the agrarian debt for the entire SAIS.

Although membership criteria were extremely lax on cooperatives in need of a labor force, on cooperatives where peasants vied for membership, beneficiary criteria were applied in a discriminatory fashion against women. The most discriminatory legal criterion required the beneficiaries to be heads of households (Lafosse de Vega-Centeno 1969). In Cajamarca, as throughout Latin America, if a household is constituted by an adult man and an adult woman, the man is automatically considered its head. As a result, the majority of rural women who might otherwise have qualified as beneficiaries were automatically excluded.

The discriminatory aspect of this criterion was especially apparent on the dairy cooperatives, where women made up from 30 percent to 50 percent of the permanent workers. Of the fifteen cooperatives organized in the province in 1976, only five had female members. Agrarian reform officials did not officially disaggregate cooperative membership data by gender, but my interviews with them, as well as with the leadership of the CAPs, reveal that women constituted only 2 percent of the provincial cooperative membership.[12]

Dairy maids were excluded from cooperative membership primarily because their kin relationship to a man prevented them from qualifying as heads of households. Many of the dairy maids were wives, daughters, or mothers of male

12. The only national survey of cooperatives with data on the gender composition of beneficiaries was carried out in 1971. In the eighty-three cooperatives sampled, women accounted for only 5 percent of the 724 members (Buchler 1975). As a national estimate, this figure may be high, for it excluded the coastal agro-industrial sugar cooperatives where membership was exclusively male. Fernandez (1982) found that in the two Piuran cotton cooperatives she studied women made up only 2 percent of the membership. Peasant women's participation was perhaps highest in the southern sierra. A case study of a Cuzco cooperative reveals that women initially constituted 7 percent of the membership (Chambeu 1981). See Deere (1985) for a comparative analysis of how women have been excluded from Latin American agrarian reforms.

wage workers, and their male relatives became the cooperative members, supposedly representing the household. But in some cases women were denied membership even when their husbands or fathers did not work on the farm, because they were not heads of households. Others who in fact did head their own households were excluded for not having dependent children. As a result, the only women wage workers who became cooperative members were widows or separated women not living with adult men and with children under eighteen years of age.[13] The exclusion of one group of workers on the basis of gender and kinship position served to create conditions internal to the cooperative for the exploitation of one social group by another.

Peasant women were also affected negatively when individual land titles were finally given out under the Belaunde administration. Because only the male heads of households qualified as beneficiaries of the reform, the land titles were made out in their names. This practice broke with the bilateral inheritance tradition in the area and certainly was counter to the importance that Cajamarcan peasant women placed on owning land in their own names.

By mid-1976, twelve production cooperatives (CAPs) and two SAISs had been officially constituted in the province of Cajamarca (see Table 32). On average, the CAPs had sixty members, 1,098 hectares of land, and thus a favorable person-land ratio of one member per 18.3 hectares. The two SAISs dwarfed the CAPs in terms of adjudicated land, but most of this land consisted of natural pastures, and its usufruct was to be shared with the Peasant Communities grouped in the SAIS. The person-land ratio on the SAISs in 1976 was one member per 98.1 hectares.[14] The total number of agrarian reform beneficiaries reported as members of associative enterprises in that year was 1,355.

Between 1976 and 1981, at least five more cooperatives were constituted, two of these through the partition of a CAP and a SAIS.[15] Although the total number of members in associative enterprises dropped slightly (as a result of the partition of the SAIS La Pauca), the total number of CAP members increased

13. In 1976 only one cooperative in the region, the CAP Huacariz de San Antonio, had a significant number of female members, almost 30 percent. In my case study, I discovered that most of the milkmaids had falsified their declaration forms, claiming that they were widows or abandoned women with children residing in independent households. Their male kin supported this action, fearing that the agrarian reform agency was going to force them to expand the number of cooperative members. They found it preferable to limit the cooperative to family members, even if they were women.

14. These figures assume that the data reported on the SAIS in Table 32 include the members of the Peasant Communities associated with the SAIS, although the original sources are somewhat unclear on this point.

15. At least one other CAP, Santa Teresita de La Quispa, was functioning in 1976 and was reportedly in existence in 1981, but data on it were not included in the compilations of the Agrarian Reform Office. Also, one of the previously reported cooperatives, El Milagro, was dropped from the reform office's listing in 1981. The status of these cooperatives is thus unclear, and they are not included in the figures summarized in the text.

TABLE 32. Associative Enterprises, Province of Cajamarca

Year of Official Recognition	Name	Main Properties Encompassed[a]	1976		1981	
			Hectares	Members	Hectares	Members
1972	Huayobamba	Huayobamba	1,775	86	1,775	86
1975	SAIS Atahualpa	Porcón Alto, Chamis, C.S. Revolución	14,000	88	14,220	165
1975	Cajamarca	Huayrapongo, Cochambul, Luichupucro, Carahuanga II, Quirquimayo, Otuzco-Sulluchsco	2,923	119	3,112	187
1975	El Rescate	La Colpa, Pampa Cochenera, Yanamarca, Yriarco, La Pampa, La Baraja	1,632	116	1,836	113
1975	Huacariz de San Antonio	Huacariz de San Antonio (Huacariz de Santa Lucía, de Llanos, de San Martín)	106	32	136	30
1975	Luis de la Puente Uceda	San Isidro, Chimin (Tabada I, II; Tranca I, II; El Cuyso)	1,120	63	1,818	62
1975	El Rosario	Hotel Polloc, Chuchún, Santa Clotilde	1,236	105	1,237	105
1975	El Milagro[b]	El Milagro, Capellanía	218	28	—	—

1976	Los Ayllus	Quinta Mercedes, Tartar Grande, Las Mercedes, Miraflores (Cristo Rey, El Triunfo, Tres Molinos, Santa Teresita)	730	79	847	170
1976	Francisco Bologñesi	Edelmira, Sumarriba, Pampa Colorada	1,382	21	1,106	35
1976	Tallambo	Tallambo	1,355	21	1,470	27
1976	24 de Junio	La Esperanza	408	16	250	32
1976	El Triunfo	El Tingo, El Rejo	307	32	399	35
1976	SAIS La Pauca	La Pauca	48,500	549	26,674[c]	111
1979	El Gran Chimu	San Pablo de Cumulca	—	—	988	21
1981	Tuñad	Tuñad	—	—	758	21
1981	Jesús Obrero[d]	Cristo Rey, Miraflores	—	—	88	41
n.d.	La Viña	Magdalena	—	—	3,023	62
	Totals		75,672	1,355	59,737	1,303

SOURCES: Data for 1976 based on "Empresas Constituidas al 31 Septiembre 1976 PIAR-Cajamarca, Sub-Dirección de Apoyo a las Empresas Campesinas, Z.A. II," Agrarian Reform Office, Ministry of Agriculture, Agrarian Zone II, Cajamarca, mimeo. Data for 1981 based on "Adjudicaciones Asociativas al 31/12/80," Ministry of Agriculture, Agrarian Region IX, Cajamarca, April 30, 1981, mimeo.

[a] Properties in parentheses were adjudicated to the cooperative after it was initially constituted.

[b] In 1976 this was officially reported as a CAS, although it functioned as a CAP.

[c] The CAP La Pauca was officially recognized in 1980 and adjudicated the reported hectarage. Forty-five present of the land of the SAIS was adjudicated to several Peasant Groups.

[d] The CAP Jesús Obrero resulted from the partition of the CAP Los Ayllus in 1979.

from 718 to 1,138. Significantly, more cooperatives gained than lost members in this five-year period, and the average number of members per CAP also increased, from 60 to 71.

Most CAPs in the province enjoyed favorable conditions. The great majority had been adjudicated capitalist dairy farms. In most cases, the members had been wage workers on the dairy farms and had a long history of working together. Moreover, through at least 1976, cooperative development was a state priority, and the cooperatives appeared to receive the greatest share of state agricultural resources such as technical assistance and credit. But even with favorable initial conditions, cooperative development was a difficult process.

The Problems of Cooperative Development

The cooperatives faced multiple problems in consolidating themselves as viable, self-managed enterprises. They were generally adjudicated what had been capitalist farms, but some of these had been severely decapitalized. Moreover, significant amounts of land were often being farmed individually, in a practice leading to competition between the cooperative and its own membership over resources and labor. Linked to the problem of the private use of cooperative resources was the abuse of collective resources and the corruption that plagued the initial years. Most of the cooperatives also had great difficulty in fostering member participation in decision making. The transition from the status of wage worker to that of worker-owner did not produce an automatic change in consciousness.

The role of the state in fostering cooperative development was ambivalent. On the one hand, the cooperatives were its offspring, and state commitment to their economic consolidation often meant state control. This control came at the cost of cooperative self-management and discouraged not only worker participation but also interest in the cooperative itself. On the other hand, while the state concentrated most of its resources on cooperative development, the cooperatives were also to serve as a new source of surplus accumulation for the state. Payment of the interest on the agrarian debt and new state taxes often weakened the financial viability of the cooperatives and hindered their ability to generate a profit for redistribution among the membership.

Although the agrarian reform legislation was written with the intention of respecting private property, including compensating owners in cash for cattle, equipment, and machinery, some landlords seemed bent on undermining the reform process. The illegal sale of cattle and machinery before the expropriation of an estate resulted in some CAPs receiving an empty shell. Other landowners simply stopped investing in their properties once they realized that the lands were to be expropriated. They let infrastructure such as canals and irrigation systems deteriorate, and they failed to renovate pastures or repair machinery.

The cooperatives that were adjudicated these decapitalized enterprises were immediately faced with the need to rebuild herds and invest in pasture and equipment. For most, this meant immediate indebtedness.[16] Not surprisingly, Caballero and Tello (1976, 22) found that of the cooperatives they studied in the region of San Marcos and Cajabamba, the only viable one in 1976 was the CAP Jocos—the only cooperative not to have been heavily decapitalized.

This decapitalization also created problems in generating employment. Because of the lack of productive resources, not all of the cooperative members could be employed full-time. Sometimes this problem was also related to the sizable amount of cooperative land remaining in the hands of individual members. The case of the CAP Huayobamba in the district of San Marcos illustrates both of these problems.

The majority of the members of the CAP Huayobamba had wanted the parcels they had previously worked as sharecroppers and arrendires to be adjudicated to them individually. They had, in fact, been promised as much by officials administering the 1964 agrarian reform, under whose statutes this hacienda had been expropriated.[17] But before the land parcels were adjudicated, the 1969 law came into effect, and several years passed before the regional agrarian reform office turned its attention to regulating matters on this former hacienda. By 1972 official priority had been placed on organizing associative enterprises, and the CAP Huayobamba became the first production cooperative in the department. Only twenty-five households originally agreed to join the cooperative, but once it became known that only by joining would former tenants be allowed to keep their parcels, the membership increased to eighty-six individuals.

This hacienda consisted of 280 hectares of irrigated land, out of a total extension of 1,775. Most of the hacienda lands were natural pastures, previously rented out to the tenant families and to peasants from neighboring communities. The central core of the hacienda, which had been developed as a dairy farm, was only 120 hectares of the total irrigated area. Under capitalist management, only twelve or thirteen workers had been employed full-time in the dairy enterprise. The landlord had relied on the labor services of tenants and arrendires to provide the temporary labor force required for crop cultivation on the other lands of the estate.

16. For example, the CAP Huayobamba had to take out a loan for S/. 2,156,400 from the agricultural development bank to purchase 114 head of dairy cattle and to repair installations and pastures in order to resume dairy operations.

17. The majority of peasants on the Hacienda Huayobamba had even received promissory notes from the agrarian reform agency to this effect. One woman showed me the following note in her possession: "The National Agrarian Council, representing the Agrarian Reform Financing Corporation (CORFIRA) will extend to you, once the procedures [*tramites*] established by the regulation of Title 9 of Law 15037 have been met, the definitive title of property of the parcel which you occupy and work directly...." It was dated May 9, 1965, and signed by the local agrarian reform administrator.

Because of decapitalization, the CAP employed only four permanent workers in 1976, all either technical or management personnel. It continued to rely on the previous labor rotation practice, except that now the resident work force had to be paid the minimum wage. This proved to be quite an economic challenge for the cooperative in its initial years.

For the resident work force, earning the minimum wage for what had formerly been labor services represented a significant improvement in their income levels. But for many, this wage income, combined with what they produced on their usufruct parcels, was still insufficient to guarantee household reproduction, even though they no longer paid rent. Land was distributed very unequally among the resident households; close to half of the former tenants worked parcels that were smaller than 3 hectares. In the recent past, most of these smallholders had migrated seasonally to the coast, but in the early 1970s few temporary jobs were available there. Forced to rely on what jobs were available in the province, they hoped that the constitution of the CAP could resolve their employment problems.

The management of the cooperative realized that the only way sufficient employment could be generated was for the cooperative to expand its dairy operation and diversify its agricultural production. Both required going into further debt, which the management was reluctant to do. Moreover, in the intervening years between the departure of the landlord-arrendire and the final adjudication of the cooperative, many peasants had also begun cultivating what had been part of the irrigated core of the dairy enterprise. The cooperative management found itself in a double bind. It could diversify its activities and expand employment only if it had access to the 160 hectares of irrigated land that the members currently held in usufruct. But the members were unwilling to give up their usufruct plots if they could not be guaranteed full-time employment at the minimum wage on the cooperative. And the richer peasants who controlled most of the irrigated land had no interest in working for the cooperative at all.

In the meantime, there was severe competition for work among the poorer cooperative households.[18] But sharing the available work on a rotating basis gave all members equal access to wage income, irrespective of other income. This policy exacerbated income inequalities among the membership, for the individual land parcels to which they had access were of unequal size and

18. For example, on the CAP Huayobamba, fifteen women shared the work of milking. They were divided into three groups of five, with each group working for only four months out of the year. The four women who were cooperative members (out of a total membership of eighty-six) were subject to the same employment rules as other cooperative members, even though they were widows and heads of households and the sole economic support of their families. Two of them rotated the milking duty with spouses or daughters of cooperative members and the other two were employed as cooks whenever agricultural tasks were performed.

quality, producing significant differences in the agricultural income households could earn.

Caballero and Tello (1976, 23) found that the lack of employment opportunities was also a severe problem in the other cooperatives they studied in San Marcos and in the Condebamba Valley. In the CAP Francisco Bologñesi of San Marcos, there were only 2 permanent workers out of a membership of 22; in the CAP Paso de Vencedores, only 11 of the 110 members were permanent workers; and in the CAP San Martín, only 12 out of 240. In most cooperatives, the employment problem was related to the large amount of productive resources—lands, pastures, and forests—in private rather than cooperative hands.

The problem of cooperative resources being used for individual gain, sometimes tied to privileges that workers had previously been granted under capitalist management, plagued many of the cooperatives. On the CAP Los Ayllus in the valley of Cajamarca, for example, many of the members owned significant numbers of cattle, which they pastured on cooperative lands; but most (56 percent) of the *ganado huaccho*, as the privately owned cattle were called, belonged to members who had formerly worked on the fundo Tartar. This imbalance created serious tensions within the cooperative, because these members tended to abuse other cooperative resources (veterinary supplies and so forth), and income differentials among the membership were exacerbated. It was reported that nine members earned from S/. 30,000 to S/. 45,000 each from their private sales of milk to PERULAC every month (Burga Posito et al. 1980, 63, 67). The monthly income of each of these nine was two to three times the monthly income of a member working full-time for the cooperative. Among the other abuses noted on the CAP Los Ayllus were the use of the cooperative vehicle (and gasoline) for private gain and the private sale of wood from the cooperative's reforestation program. Moreover, the vice president reportedly sold twenty head of the cooperative's dairy cattle without consulting the membership and pocketed the money from the sale (Burga Posita et al. 1980, 58, 69–70).

Such conflicts partly explain the breakup of the CAP Los Ayllus into two separate cooperatives in 1979. They also reflect another problem of cooperative development in the province, the fact that the CAPs were often constituted as large-scale units by merging a number of individual farms. The CAP Los Ayllus had been formed by merging eight properties, the excess land and animals (beyond the 30 hectares of exempt irrigated land) expropriated from eight dairy enterprises (see Table 32). This practice reflected state policy under the Morales Bermúdez government, laid out in the objectives of the rural settlement and integration program (PIAR, Programa de Integración y Asentamiento Rural). Smaller farms were to be integrated into larger-sized cooperatives, primarily for efficiency. It was thought that investment could be planned more rationally, and more employment generated, on larger-scale units.

This form of integrative planning did not take into account the difficulty of administering a landholding that was composed neither of contiguous units nor of members who had any historical or social ties among themselves. This difficulty is illustrated in the excellent case study of the CAP Los Ayllus carried out by students at the National University of Cajamarca (Burga Posito et al. 1980, 56–69). Both political power and economic power were distributed unequally among the various farms that formed the cooperative. Political power rested in the largest farm, Tartar, which had the most members (41 of the 140 total). But the most productive farms, because of better production conditions and worker discipline, were the Miraflores and Cristo Rey sections of the CAP, accounting for 39 members. Animosity soon developed between the two factions over who should be the administrator of the cooperative (each group had its own candidate), over the allocation of investment decisions, and over the management of collective resources.

The Miraflores and Cristo Rey members had been disgruntled from the beginning, for they had never been consulted about integrating the farms into one large cooperative; the consolidation had been imposed on them by the state. They began petitioning the Ministry of Agriculture for partition in 1977, but their grievances were ignored until the mismanagement of resources and corruption reached such proportions that the state was forced to intervene. In 1979 the agrarian reform officials finally acceded to the partition. The Miraflores and Cristo Rey sections were then reconstituted as the CAP Jesús Obrero.[19]

The problems of mismanagement and lack of labor discipline were also related to the cooperative members' lack of training in the principles of cooperative organization and self-management. Agrarian reform officials in Cajamarca placed little emphasis on worker participation in management, and although the principles of self-management had been officially endorsed by the Velasco government, they were never vigorously promoted at the national level (McClintock 1981, 231–232).

Both the structure and the internal functioning of the cooperatives promoted by the agrarian reform were initially determined by the state. Formally, the ultimate authority of the cooperative was the general assembly, consisting of all cooperative members. The assembly was to approve the major decisions of the cooperative and to elect a five-person administrative council charged with

19. A case study of the CAP Jesús Obrero conducted by the National University of Cajamarca suggests that the workers from these two farms lost considerably in the process of constituting and dissolving the two cooperatives (Battifora Rojas et al. 1981, 93–94). The study reports that when the first cooperative (Los Ayllus) was set up, the sections Cristo Rey and Miraflores contributed sixty and seventy head of cattle, respectively. When these workers left to form the new CAP Jesús Obrero, however, they were allotted only forty-nine head.

responsibility for day-to-day management of the enterprise. A supervisory council of three members was also to be elected as a check on the administrative council. In addition, the cooperatives were to hire a professional technician as enterprise director or administrator. Final selection of the administrator rested with the state, although the administrative council was entitled to nominate candidates.

Approximately 60 percent of the cooperatives across the nation had paid directors (McClintock 1981, 34). In Cajamarca, however, most of the CAPs resisted hiring an administrator because of the expense, preferring to elect a manager from among their own membership. The agrarian reform agency finally forced those cooperatives showing a significant net profit to hire an administrator and in the others concentrated its attention on developing the leadership capability of the elected managers. Although this was perhaps a victory for the cooperative membership over the state, it came at the expense of cooperative democracy.

The manager, whether a technician or a worker, often assumed the role of "patron." There was little worker participation in decision making, for either managers rarely called meetings or, if meetings were called, they monopolized the discussions. In those cooperatives where the general assembly did meet regularly, the meetings were often disorganized and unproductive, allowing or forcing the leadership to make the final decisions. In several cooperatives, it was clear that the workers believed that little had changed from their days on capitalist estates. As a result, the transition in consciousness from wage worker to worker-owner was slow or nonexistent.

The CAP Huacariz de San Antonio was an exception to this pattern. Its small size (thirty members) relative to the provincial average certainly favored greater member participation. But cohesiveness and involvement of the membership in the cooperative project were results of the process through which this cooperative had been formed, in a ten-year struggle from which the dispossessed sharecroppers of this farm gained considerable experience in collective action as well as mutual trust. Rather than being seen as imposed from above, the cooperative was perceived as the product of their collective struggle to gain control of this hacienda.

The ties that these cooperative members had forged with several leftist parties during their long years of struggle also explain why the collective solution was viewed as superior to independent farming. Another cohesive force was the strong kinship ties among the membership; this was also the only cooperative where female family members were granted membership, and in the initial years the dairy maids contributed substantially to the consolidation of the cooperative.[20]

20. The women members of the CAP Huacariz de San Antonio quickly began to organize themselves to resolve what they considered their fundamental economic problem, low incomes.

Finally, it is important to note that although the cooperatives theoretically had the right to determine the distribution of the profits generated by the enterprise, the state in fact largely determined this allocation. Until 1979, the cooperatives were saddled with the agrarian debt. The state had assumed compensation to the landowners for the lands and other means of production expropriated through the agrarian reform. The cooperatives, in turn, were mortgaged to the state until the debt was paid off in twenty to thirty years. After 1975, the cooperatives were also subject to a profit tax. If any profits remained, 15 percent were to be directed for capital investment, 20 percent for social security and reserve funds, 5 percent for member education, and 5 percent for cooperative development. Before the remaining profits were redistributed among the membership, another 25 percent had to be used for either social or productive investment (McClintock 1981, 224).

The degree of state direction in profit allocation certainly mitigated worker participation in this important sphere of self-management. Furthermore, as Cynthia McClintock (1981) argues, for members who were principally interested in short-term gain, it made much more sense to press for wage increases than to attempt to make the cooperative profitable. Nonetheless, in Cajamarca, members' wages—theoretically, "advances" on profit—were tied to the minimum wage of the zone. The principal expression of worker discontent was to work fewer hours and decrease the intensity of labor.

Throughout the 1970s, the payment of the agrarian debt was a major point of contention between the CAPs and the state. The cooperatives were given a five-year grace period on the payment of principal but were to begin paying interest on the debt when they were officially constituted. It was immediately apparent that interest payments alone would be a significant drain.[21] Cooperative members complained that the agrarian debt was unfair in principle and that its level often exceeded the value of the means of production that they had been adjudicated. Besides, the magnitude of the debt was staggering to many members. For example, the agrarian debt of the CAP Los Ayllus was established in 1976 as S/. 51,861,643 (Burga Posito et al. 1980, 47).

Although they earned the same hourly wage as the male members, the nature of their jobs meant that they were employed only four hours a day (for the milking), and thus their daily income was lower than that of the men. New productive activities were needed that would allow them to work a full eight-hour day, as the men did. The women therefore proposed to the membership that they diversify the cooperative's activities, beginning with an experimental garden. The project was quite successful in the early years, generating more employment and becoming a lucrative activity for the cooperative. The women had been able to solve their economic problem primarily because, as members of the cooperative, they could demand access to the cooperative's resources for a project that benefited the group as a whole.

21. McClintock (1981, 222) reports that in the three CAPs she studied debt payment ranged from 11 percent to 75 percent of gross profits in the mid-1970s.

On a per member basis, this was equivalent to the annual wage income of a cooperative member over forty-three years, assuming constant prices.

The issue of the agrarian debt was especially controversial on the SAISs, where the CAPs were supposed to generate the surplus for repaying the debt for the whole association. A similar problem emerged for the CAPs, because significant CAP resources were often in the private hands of members. Yet the debt was to be repaid from collective production, which taxed its financial base. The dilemma for many cooperatives was whether to force members to individually assume the debt for the lands they controlled; doing so would have given members the right to land titles and undermined the future development of the collective enterprise.

A related problem on some cooperatives was that members had already purchased their parcels in the private, pre-reform subdivision of the estate, but these purchases had not been taken into account in the valuation of the estate or in the calculation of the debt. Now the cooperative management was saddled with both the debt and the members' recalcitrance about parting with what they considered their own private property. As a result of these problems, as well as strong peasant political pressure, the agrarian debt was finally canceled in 1979.[22] By then, because of inflation, the value of the debt (which had been fixed in nominal terms) had ceased to be such a huge burden on the cooperatives (McClintock 1981, 47).

In 1975, when inflation started to erode the significance of the debt, the state imposed the profit tax on the cooperatives. Although the tax rate varied, on the richer coastal sugar CAPs it reached 51 percent of total gross profits (Caballero 1982, 29).[23] Predictable tension arose over allowing the cooperatives to capture their own surplus, the reinvestment of the surplus to help them become viable enterprises, and the state extraction of this surplus.

The consolidation of the cooperatives as viable, profitable enterprises was no easy task. Nonetheless, the Cajamarcan cooperative members constituted an elite among rural workers and peasants. As worker-owners, the members could earn an income far exceeding that of most rural households in Cajamarca. The guarantee of the minimum wage alone placed these cooperative households among the upper 25 percent of all rural households in terms of net annual income (see Chapter 10). Moreover, cooperative members were guaranteed

22. The role of the CCP nationally was an important factor leading to the final pardon of the agrarian debt. For an analysis of the role of the two peasant organizations, the CCP and the officially created CNA, at the national level, see Matos Mar and Mejía (1980) and McClintock (1981); for an analysis focused on the local level, see Taylor (1979).

23. Data for the CAP Los Ayllus show that in 1979 it paid 9.9 percent of its net income from milk sales in various forms of taxes. The composition of taxes was as follows, aggregated over the 1976–1979 period: 38.4 percent were direct profit taxes; 47.5 percent represented contributions to social security and workers' compensation; and 14.2 percent was a contribution to the centralized provincial fund for agrarian reform enterprises (derived from Burga Posito et al. 1980).

social benefits and were even taking the one-month paid vacation to which they were legally entitled, something previously unknown in the Cajamarcan countryside. Not surprisingly, the growing inequality among rural households generated various new tensions in the province.

CONTRADICTIONS OF THE REFORM PROCESS: BENEFICIARIES, NONBENEFICIARIES, AND THE STATE

There is little question that the agrarian reform brought about a significant redistribution of landed property in the province of Cajamarca. Thirty-four percent of the total land area of the province was adjudicated to the reformed sector; this included 20 percent of the irrigated land, 12 percent of the cultivable land, and 50 percent of the natural pastures (Esparza Bueno et al. 1981, 101). But these resources were redistributed to only 11.8 percent of the province's rural households. As a result, the agrarian reform process unleashed a variety of conflicts between beneficiaries and nonbeneficiaries, between peasants and workers and the worker-owners of the cooperatives, and between the peasantry and the state.

It is important to recall that when the agrarian reform was initiated, the mass of the peasantry was not participating in either feudal or capitalist class relations on the haciendas. As a result of the dispossessions and land parceling of the 1950s and 1960s, relatively few could claim feudatario status on a hacienda. Moreover, as a result of the reduced labor requirements of the capitalist dairy enterprises, few rural households had a member permanently employed on these estates. Nonetheless, the agrarian reform gave priority to these two groups, feudatarios and permanent wage workers, as beneficiaries. Tensions initially developed over the ability to claim beneficiary status, as described in the previous section; but perhaps of more lasting consequence were the conflicts that developed over access to resources and to wage employment.

One early problem involved the way the hacienda land sales of previous decades had been conducted. Many sales had been made without being officially registered or even documented with a bill of sale. Sometimes, this land was expropriated along with the hacienda core, because legal documentation to certify it as a peasant's private property was lacking. Once this land was adjudicated to the new associative enterprise, some CAPs tried to reclaim these parcels from their peasant owners, unleashing scores of conflicts throughout the region (haciendas Polloc, La Colpa).

The peasant owners rightfully considered this land their private property, because they had paid for it once, and the emerging struggle between them and the cooperatives fueled rumors throughout the department that all private property would be expropriated by the reform. The agrarian reform agency was besieged by peasant proprietors' requests for certificates of exemption and by cooperatives' claims over title to marginal pieces of land.

The peasants of the community of La Succha, for example, considered the agrarian reform a calamity. Because of the uncertainty surrounding the "land to the tiller" pronouncement, peasants stopped sharecropping land with one another. No one trusted their neighbors, and even the intentions of family members were suspect. This situation presented quite a hardship for peasants who depended on renting or sharecropping land in order to reproduce themselves as petty producers. Fears of being expropriated for not working one's property directly did open up the land market in the independent communities, however. Permanent coastal migrants, in particular, began to sell their inheritance shares in the sierra to relatives and neighbors.

By 1976, however, things were returning to normal. It was apparent that under Morales Bermúdez a radical reform would not even be considered. The Sangay family of La Succha nevertheless did not relax until several years had passed. The agrarian reform office claimed that the land sales on the Hacienda Miche had been conducted illegally, and consequently it had initiated the expropriation of the hacienda. In order to keep their property, the Sangays were then told that they had to pay a fine of S/. 2,500. They considered this unjust, for they had already purchased the land once. Rumors that the agrarian reform would require them to farm their land collectively worried them even more. They did not trust the former colonos of the hacienda and thought that surely they would lose their land. By the late 1970s, when it was clear that the reform process was dead, the Sangays finally felt secure.

Another conflict between the CAPs and their neighboring communities focused on access to the natural resources of the former haciendas. The cooperative management was sometimes even more exacting than the capitalist entrepreneurs or the landlord class had been in enclosing natural pastures and enforcing the payment of rent for grazing rights or the right to collect wood on the enterprise's land. On some cooperatives, the management's decision not to rent resources at all caused increased resentment and conflict. The peasants of the caseríos of Agocucho and Agopampa, for example, complained bitterly over the CAP El Rescate's decision to proscribe the leasing of grazing pastures. Heated conflicts also developed over water rights. As a woman in the community of La Laimina, Jesús, complained to me concerning the SAIS José Carlos Mariátegui, "Yes, the agrarian reform has made us worse off [nos han acabado de joder], because in the days of the hacienda they would let us take out wood, and now the cooperative won't let us, and they fenced in everything."

In the general climate of peasant militancy that arose in the 1970s—partly as a result of the military's own lofty promises to the peasantry—many peasant communities began organizing for the first time to demand their rights to pasture, water, and even state services such as credit and technical assistance. The great majority of poor peasants had always been outside the scope of governmental technical assistance or credit programs. State services in the past had been directed to the commercial farms or, at best, to the large and medium-sized peasant holdings. In the mid-1970s, these services were being channeled toward the reformed enterprises.[24] The cooperatives were increasingly perceived as the privileged beneficiaries of the military. This inequality was further exacerbated by struggles over employment and the generalized effect of the agrarian reform on both the local and coastal labor markets.

Given the reliance of most Cajamarcan rural households on wage employment, the ultimate effect of the agrarian reform on the majority of peasants depended on the reformed sector's ability to generate employment opportunities, even temporary work. But, in the short run, the immediate effect of the reform was to restrict temporary employment possibilities both on the coast and in the sierra. The initiation of the reform on the north coast of Peru in 1969 was felt by Cajamarcan peasants as a reduction in the seasonal, temporary work available on the newly constituted sugar and rice cooperatives in the departments of La Libertad and Lambayeque. Initially, the coastal cooperative members appeared to prefer to do most of the agricultural work themselves. Those migrants who did find work complained that the length of employment was much reduced. According to one seasonal migrant from Pariamarca, a three-month migration to the coast now resulted only in three to four weeks of steady work.

Caballero and Tello's (1976, 39) data on eight CAPs of the Jequetepeque Valley suggest that in 1972–1973 a significant number of temporary workers were being hired by the rice cooperatives. The average length of employment of these workers, however, was greatly reduced. The eight CAPs hired a total of 16,653 temporary workers over that agricultural year, but each worker averaged only thirty days of employment. In all, temporary workers provided 51 percent of the labor required by these cooperatives, a statistic suggesting that, at least at this point in the reform, the CAPs were an important source of temporary employment. This later led to the criticism that coastal cooperative members preferred to hire cheaper temporary workers than to do the agricultural work themselves.[25]

As the employment situation relaxed somewhat on the coast, it became tighter in the sierra when the agrarian reform process went into effect. Again, the first reaction of the newly constituted cooperatives was the "shut door" policy. Burdened with the agrarian debt, the cooperatives turned inward, preferring to have members work longer hours themselves, to give first

24. The available data suggest that the commonly held perception that the cooperatives were receiving the lion's share of credit was incorrect. In 1975 the agrarian reform enterprises received 65.5 percent of the credit extended nationally by the Banco Agrario. In Cajamarca, however, associative enterprises received only 17.2 percent of the total credit extended in the department. By 1980 both figures had dropped, to 56.6 percent at the national level and to 6 percent in Cajamarca (Burga Bartra 1981, 16).

25. The labor market for temporary, casual workers on the coast is further analyzed in Caballero (1982) and Scott (1981).

preference in temporary employment to family members, and generally to rely much less on temporary labor than the estates had under capitalist management. Also, cooperatives members feared that if they employed peasants from neighboring communities, these peasants would then have a claim on beneficiary status. Although some cooperatives suffered from too small a membership, many had reached their capacity, as we have seen, being unable to generate full-time employment for the full membership.

The "shut door" policy did favor the families of the cooperative membership, and particularly female family members. They were given first priority in the assignment of temporary work. This policy worked especially in favor of those few women who were cooperative members, because they had first claim on cooperative jobs. Thus, in some cases, women were hired to do jobs that in the past had been done only by male temporary workers.[26]

The 1976 Peasant Family Survey, because it was a follow-up survey of 105 households initially surveyed in 1973, allows quantitative analysis of the changes that took place in peasant participation in the labor market during the initial period of the agrarian reform in Cajamarca. In this period, there were important changes in the rate of labor market participation, in the length of employment, and in rural wage levels. The total number of participants in the labor market increased appreciably, by 25 percent, between 1973 and 1976. The greatest increase, 35 percent, was reported by smallholder households. This greater number of participants appears to reflect changing familial labor deployment strategies in the face of a contracting labor market. If wage labor opportunities are contracting, a rational response for households dependent on wage labor is to place all available family members on the labor market, even for shorter periods of time.

Between 1973 and 1976, the average length of employment decreased significantly, by 46 days. In 1973 only 7.5 percent of those in the labor market worked 30 days or less; in 1976 one-third found only sporadic employment. In 1973 the mode of the sample was in the range of 121 to 260 days; in 1976 it was in the 30- to 120-day range. Although Cajamarcan peasants were certainly working less in 1976, the data could simply reflect a static labor market in the face of an increasing supply of labor. A more detailed examination of employment patterns suggests that a decreased demand for labor contributed to the reduction in the length of employment.

The number of permanently employed wage workers in the agricultural sector decreased substantially during this three-year period. Of the ten full-time

26. Family members who worked for the cooperative but who did not have membership status certainly did not benefit equally from the cooperative, however. Moreover, in at least one case, the exclusion of women workers from membership was detrimental to the cooperative's overall profitability: a change in the working conditions of the milkmaids, which was not taken into account by the cooperative management and membership, caused a steady decrease in the productivity of the milk cows. See Deere (1977).

agricultural wage workers in the 1976 sub-sample of the 1973 survey, only one was still employed full-time in agriculture (Deere 1978, table 62). Half the workers in this group had lost their jobs as a result of the reform. In several cases, their employers had reduced the size of the estate labor force before being affected by the reform, hoping for exemption from full expropriation by complying with the labor legislation (social security benefits, minimum wage) for a reduced work force. In another case, the agricultural worker had been ruled ineligible as a beneficiary by the agrarian reform authorities, and hence ineligible for cooperative membership, because he had not been a feudatario of the hacienda; he was unemployed in 1976. In one other case, the dairy farm worker had quit his job when the cooperative was constituted, trusting the landowner's intention to regain the farm. One-third of those who had been employed as full-time agricultural wage workers in 1973 found themselves in the ranks of temporary agricultural workers in 1976. This shift contributed to the 94 percent increase in the number of part-time workers in the agricultural sector between the two surveys.

Data on seasonal migration support the argument that the coastal agricultural labor market expanded in the mid-1970s, just as it was contracting in the highlands. In 1973 only 3 percent of the households in this sub-sample reported a temporary coastal migrant. The number of households sending a migrant to the coast tripled in 1976. Seventy percent of these were employed in the coastal agricultural sector.

Another important indicator of changes in labor market conditions is provided by wage data presented in Table 33. The average wage hardly kept pace with either the rate of increase in the minimum wage or the rising cost of living.[27] Between 1973 and 1976, the consumer price index rose by 93 percent; in contrast, the highest reported nominal wage increase, for nonagricultural full-time workers, was only 40 percent. Full-time agricultural wage workers fared much worse, with a 22 percent increase, whereas the going wage rate for temporary agricultural workers remained essentially static, with a 3 percent increase in nominal terms. It is clear that during the implementation of the agrarian reform in Cajamarca, the real wage fell.

In summary, between 1973 and 1976, the supply of peasants seeking wage employment considerably exceeded the demand for workers, which had been considerably reduced. Peasant households reacted by sending out more members into the labor market, leading to a decrease in the average length of employment as well as in the real wage for temporary work. The decreasing

27. In May 1975, the minimum wage was increased by 63 percent and 70 percent, respectively, for nonagricultural and agricultural employment in the district of Cajamarca, as compared with the rates that had been in effect since August 1972. Because the consumer price index increased by only 54 percent in the same period, this represented an increase in the legislated real wage. Prices continued to rise, however, by 33.5 percent in 1975–1976 alone, and the gain was subsequently eroded.

TABLE 33. Daily Wages Earned by Full-Time and Part-Time Wage Workers, Province of Cajamarca, 1973 and 1976 (in Current Peruvian Soles)

	Agricultural Sector	Nonagricultural Sector
1973		
Full-time workers	26.9 (N = 10)	45.8 (N = 12)
Men	28.6	49.1
Women	20.0	10.0
Part-time workers	32.6 (N = 18)	40.9 (N = 28)
Men	32.6	43.0
Women	—	23.3
Minimum wage		
Districts of Cajamarca and Jesús	43.0	49.0
District of La Encañada	40.0	44.0
1976		
Full-time workers	30.7 (N = 4)	64.2 (N = 15)
Men	38.2	77.3
Women	23.3	12.2
Part-time workers	33.5 (N = 13)	42.8 (N = 25)
Men	33.5	46.6
Women	—	22.8
Minimum wage		
Districts of Cajamarca and Jesús	73.0	81.0
District of La Encañada	63.0	73.0

SOURCES: Compiled from the 1973 Cajamarca Income Survey (sub-sample of 105 households) and the 1976 Peasant Family Survey.

NOTE: Full-time includes all those who worked more than 240 days per year, even if they were not permanent employees of an enterprise; part-time includes all those working fewer than 240 days. School teachers have been excluded from the sample in order not to bias the results upward.

number of full-time agricultural wage workers indicates the probable effect of the agrarian reform in reducing the number of wage workers on the enterprises. The minimal amount of employment offered by the Cajamarcan cooperative sector to nonbeneficiaries of the reform process spurred interregional migration once again.

It also heightened the animositites between beneficiaries and nonbeneficiaries of the agrarian reform. Cooperative members were resented on three counts: for their access to permanent employment, for their ability to exploit the resources of former haciendas for private gain, and for their higher wages. In the mid-1970s, the wage issue was an especially sore point. By being guaranteed the minimum wage, cooperative members were earning twice the local wage rate. Peasants in the nearby communities were acutely aware of this wage difference, for, if they were hired as temporary help by the cooperatives, they received only the market wage. Moreover, they were also aware of the differences this meant in terms of total wage income, given the disparity in days worked between the two groups.

In the words of Juan, a landless peasant of Pariamarca, only the cooperative members had it easy: "They have preference; the members eat and dress well; there is work to be had, but they don't give it out." The available data support peasant perceptions. The agrarian reform, while redistributing resources from capital to labor, increased income disparities among rural households.

CONCLUSION

State intervention in the Cajamarcan countryside through agrarian reform dealt the death blow to the hacienda system that had shaped the distribution of economic and political power in the province over the previous century. It also greatly circumscribed the budding agrarian capitalist development that on its own had undermined feudal class relations in the province. Moreover, state intervention in land redistribution took place under conditions more unfavorable to women than those of the hacienda land sales of previous decades.

Two groups were particularly favored in the process: the remaining feudatarios on the haciendas and the permanent wage labor force of the dairy enterprises.[28] The agrarian reform changed the dominant class process and position of each. Feudatarios secured a condition of existence, private property in land, for the expansion of petty production. Most were probably able to secure quite large extensions of former hacienda land, and the subsequent landtitling process of the early 1980s created the material base for middle and rich peasant households rather than for smallholders. But given that most remaining feudatarios were on the more distant and inaccessible haciendas—generally not on the PERULAC milk supply routes—their primary activity in coming years would remain sheep and cattle raising, combined with agricultural production.

The potentially most productive resources of the province were transferred from Cajamarca's capitalist class to its wage workers, the new worker-owners of the production cooperatives. This group saw its position transformed from capitalist producers of surplus value to communal producers and capitalist extractors. As collective owners of means of production, participating in a collective labor process, theoretically they now participated in a communal

---

28. See Matos Mar and Mejía (1980, 296–301) for an analysis of the broader issue of which social groups gained from the Peruvian agrarian reform on a national level.

class process in which they themselves appropriated and distributed their own surplus labor. But in the early years of the reform process, the appropriation and distribution of this surplus were largely determined by the state; even the degree of worker control over the labor process was minimal. The cancelation of the agrarian debt did remove one of the conditions for direct state control of cooperative development, but whether this resulted in greater financial autonomy and the fostering of a more communal labor process requires further research.

The period of the late 1970s was one of attempted consolidation of a communal class process on the cooperatives, based on a reordering of state-cooperative relations, relegating the state to a subsumed class position. But the consolidation of the communal class process on the cooperatives also depended on the cooperatives' ability to reduce the participation of their membership in petty production on usurped cooperative resources. In the general climate of 1981, it was not at all clear whether petty or communal production would become the dominant class relation within this reformed sector.

Another subsumed class process that became a source of increasing tension was the relation between the new cooperatives and PERULAC. The consolidation of the cooperatives as dairy producers depended greatly on milk pricing policy and so placed the cooperatives as new allies of Cajamarca's remaining capitalist dairy farmers in the continuing struggle over the conditions of milk marketing.

Perhaps somewhat surprisingly, if the cooperatives were to have some beneficial spill-over effect for the majority of peasant households in the province, this effect depended considerably on the cooperatives' ability not only to consolidate the communal class process internally but also to engage in capitalist class relations, hiring significant numbers of temporary wage workers. As we have seen, the ability to earn wage income was crucial to the reproduction of most households of petty producers. Their welfare depended on the possibilities for expanded employment on the cooperatives, which in turn were related to the possibilities for economic diversification of the cooperatives, their ability to control cooperative resources effectively, and continued state support, particularly in the area of credit, another subsumed class process linking the cooperatives and the state.

The agrarian reform brought about a fundamental change in the Cajamarcan agrarian structure, making rural class relations even more complex. But for all its effects, state intervention did little to change the dominant tendency of the post-1940 period: the need of most households of petty producers to participate in wage labor in order to reproduce themselves as peasant households.

PART THREE

The Class Analytics of Peasant Household Reproduction and Differentiation

TEN

The Generation of Household Income and Peasant Household Reproduction

In the aftermath of the campesinista/descampesinista debate over the fate of the Latin American peasantry, there is growing consensus on several issues. First, the sale of labor power is by itself insufficient to indicate a process of proletarianization (Warman 1980a, 169–184; Roseberry 1983, 173; Long 1984, 6–7). As Marielle Martínez and Teresa Rendón (1978) emphasize, it is crucial to distinguish between that seasonal participation in wage work which complements petty production, augmenting household income, and that which is critical for reproduction of the household. David Lehmann (1982, 138) also notes that selling labor power for a few days, particularly in the context of labor exchange or patron-client relations, is quite different from selling it as the primary means of satisfying consumption requirements. Similarly, it is necessary to distinguish between situations in which wage labor is marginal, a complement to family labor, and those in which it is central and the basis for surplus production and extraction.

The considerations have prompted reexamination of the criteria used in analyzing peasant social differentiation. The recent literature assigns priority to levels of household reproduction, although there are important differences in how household reproduction is conceived. The main point of contention is whether it is defined by the level of farm production (Schejtman 1980; Llambi 1981; Carter 1984) or the level of total household income (Martínez and Rendón 1978).

Alexander Schejtman's (1980, 294) conception typifies the former analysis. He differentiates between 1) "poor peasants"—those household units that depend on off-farm income to attain minimum subsistence incomes; 2) "average peasants"—those whose farm product is sufficient to cover family consumption and replace the means of production (what is usually termed "simple reproduction"); and 3) surplus-producing or "rich peasants"—those who systematically generate a surplus greater than simple reproduction requirements. Schejtman's framework provides a more substantive basis for analyzing peasant social differentiation than does the more limited criterion of participation in the purchase or sale of labor power. Nevertheless, its narrow focus on the productive unit and the unit's productive potential limits its usefulness in analyzing the persistence of the peasantry. It is crucial to take into account that participation in other income-generating activities besides petty production may allow the reproduction of peasant households as units of production and consumption.

A CONCEPTUAL MODEL OF PEASANT HOUSEHOLD REPRODUCTION AND DIFFERENTIATION

By definition, access to means of production is a necessary condition for a peasant household to be a unit of production. Access to means of production, however, does not guarantee that the peasant household will be reproduced as a unit of production over time. This depends on the outcome of the heterogeneous class and nonclass processes in which household members engage. The level of household reproduction, and the success of the household in reproducing itself as a unit of production, is contingent on the levels of surplus extraction and transference implied in each class relation and on their net effect on total household income. In the schematic model developed here, peasant social differentiation may be produced or forestalled by the participation of household members in multiple class relations, resulting in three possible outcomes or contingencies: simple reproduction; the possibility of accumulation; or the disintegration of the household as a unit of production and reproduction.

For simplicity of exposition, let us first consider the situation of a household that engages exclusively in petty agricultural production and that owns sufficient means of production to generate a level of household income that will reproduce the means of production and the labor power of all household members at some moral and historically defined standard of consumption. Within my framework, in order for the household to attain simple reproduction it must also secure the conditions of existence (economic, political, and cultural) of the fundamental class relation of petty production. Simple reproduction thus requires that the surplus product produced and appropriated by the direct producers be sufficient to meet all of the subsumed class payments required to reproduce the conditions of existence of petty production.

For example, petty producers may have to pay a land tax to the state to guarantee their right to private property. The tax constitutes a subsumed class payment for a political condition of existence of petty production. If these petty producers engage in petty commodity production, they may also be subject to a subsumed class payment to merchants in order to secure access to commodity markets. These subsumed class payments constitute surplus transfers out of the household that reduce the level of net household income.

If net household income is not sufficient to ensure simple reproduction once these payments are taken into account, the peasant household—as originally constituted—could disintegrate in several ways. The inability to guarantee normal levels of consumption might result in declining nutrition or lowered health standards of household members; the lowered quality of labor power reproduction might subsequently affect the productive capacity of the household in the next cycle. The household could also expel one or more of its members. Reducing household size through permanent migration directly lowers total household consumption requirements, perhaps allowing simple reproduction in the reconstituted household. In addition, permanent migration could also represent a household strategy for generating income if these migrants were obligated to send remittances to their household of origin. These remittances might represent a subsumed class payment to the peasant household if they are related to the provision of a condition of existence for another fundamental class process, for example, unemployment insurance for a worker participating in a capitalist class process. Otherwise, they constitute a nonclass payment. In either case, remittances raise household income in the parental household, perhaps allowing it to attain simple reproduction.

The peasant household unable to generate simple reproduction requirements might also disintegrate as a result of a decision to sell or rent all of its means of production. If the household ceased to be a unit of production, it would no longer constitute a peasant household by the definition employed here. Renting means of production, however, generates a surplus transfer into the household, and this rental income could guarantee that the household will continue as the principal site of labor power reproduction.

Peasant households may also forestall their disintegration by engaging in other subsumed class processes, such as borrowing money or renting additional means of production themselves. For example, the household may be able to reproduce itself as petty producers for another productive cycle through acquiring credit from moneylenders to purchase means of subsistence or means of production such as seed or fertilizer. Moneylenders, by providing a condition of existence for petty production, would be entitled to a subsumed class payment in the form of interest. Although the subsumed class payment lowers net household income directly, it may enhance the level of gross petty production. Similarly, a household with insufficient access to means of production might rent oxen or land or might engage in sharecropping. These activities would enhance the level of gross petty production but require a subsumed class payment (rent) to the owner of the means of production. In either case, the household would be engaging in multiple class relations to reproduce itself—the fundamental class relation of petty production and the subsumed class processes of moneylending or rental of means of production.

The net household income generated in petty production may also exceed the level required for the simple reproduction of the peasant household. This net surplus could be consumed, enhancing the quality of reproduction of labor power of all or a few household members, or it could be accumulated as expanded means of production. If the petty producers accumulate the surplus—buying more land or work animals, for example—they might also be in the position to hire wage workers. If, in the subsequent productive cycle, these petty producers were able to extract a surplus from their wage workers, they would be engaging in the fundamental capitalist class process. These petty producers would now be differentiated from petty producers who attain only simple reproduction by their ability to participate in two fundamental class relations: in petty production as performers and extractors of surplus labor, and in capitalist relations as surplus extractors.

Other subsumed class payments may involve the redistribution of surplus within the household. The provision of housekeeping and child-rearing services by nonproducers or part-time petty producers may require a redistribution of surplus to ensure daily and generational reproduction, both economic conditions of existence of petty production. In addition, surplus may be transferred to other household members, such as elderly parents, to guarantee their consumption levels. Such a transfer might be regarded as a subsumed class payment if the household is constituted as a unit of production through inheritance, but it might also represent a nonclass payment based on kinship relations.

The redistribution of surplus within the household need not result in equality of consumption among all household members. That depends on the other cultural and ideological practices encompassed in household relations (see Introduction). Simple reproduction based on income pooling requires only that the transfer of surplus from producers to nonproducers be sufficient to reproduce the labor power of nonproducers at socially defined levels of consumption.

It has thus far been assumed that the force compelling social differentiation is whether or not households attain simple reproduction based on the level of net household income generated in petty production. This assumption has allowed me to demonstrate how attaining simple reproduction from petty production may be contingent on the reproduction of the conditions of existence of this class relation, that is, engaging in subsumed class processes. Whether net household income is in fact sufficient for simple reproduction depends both on the size of the surplus appropriated by petty producers and on the number and size of transfer payments that must be made to secure the economic, political, and cultural conditions of existence of this fundamental class relation. Moreover, the participation of petty producers in subsumed class processes results not only in surplus transfers out of the household, as subsumed class payments, but also in petty producers being recipients of such payments. Conventional household income accounting simply summarizes the net effect of these class processes.

The differentiation of the peasantry within the framework that I am proposing, however, is not a simple linear process based on a bipolar continuum between the need for proletarianization and the possibility for accumulation defined in relation to simple reproduction. Rather, it is based on the outcome of a more complex interaction between fundamental and subsumed class relations. The income-generating activities in which peasant households engage are conditioned not only by the households' access to means of production and their labor composition but also by external factors, such as the broader political economy and social milieu. Peasant households are inscribed within social formations, and their logic and functioning cannot be analyzed independent of the predominant class relations and their conditions of existence. For example, the degree of development of commodity markets will influence the degree of monetization and the division of labor within the peasant economy. These variables, in turn, determine the possibility of peasant households being petty commodity producers, specializing in agriculture, animal raising, or artisan production. The development of markets also opens up a new occupation, that of the merchant. The degree of development of local, regional, and extra-regional labor markets also conditions the possibility that peasant household members will participate in wage labor.

The interaction of all these factors will influence the particular set of class relations in which household members participate. Whether peasant households with insufficient access to means of production are compelled into capitalist class relations as wage workers will depend on, among other things, the available economic opportunities. Households unable to secure simple reproduction from agricultural production alone could specialize in artisan production or send out one household member as a trader. The social valuation of male, female, and child labor in the labor market and the gender and age composition of the household labor force will also influence the class relations in which households engage.

In this framework, reliance on temporary wage employment need not automatically signal "incomplete reproduction" or household disintegration. Rather, wage income may be a precondition for the household to engage in petty production, for example, allowing renewal of its means of production. In a similar fashion, the possibility for expanded reproduction need not depend on the outcome of petty production alone. Income earned by household members in various occupations, whether through wage work, trading, or remittances, can serve as the basis for the household to accumulate means of production. In fact, the ability of the household members to accumulate their own surplus as petty producers may be closely related to their participation in other class relations, with income from wage work, for example, giving the household more flexibility in when and to whom it sells commodities, lowering the volume of subsumed class payments to merchants.

The array of fundamental and subsumed class relations in which peasant households in the province of Cajamarca could participate between 1900 and 1980 is summarized in Table 34. The probable effect of these class relations on household income is noted in the last column. Gross household income in this schematic model is determined by the sum of the income earned in the various

TABLE 34.   The Class Analytics of the Composition of Peasant Household Income

Fundamental Class Relation	*Form of Appropriation*	*Source of Income*	*Effect of Appropriation on Household Income*
Petty Capitalist	Self-appropriation	Gross product	Higher
Performer	Surplus value	Wage income	Lower
Extractor	Surplus value	Gross product	Higher
Feudal			
Performer	Labor services	Net product	Lower
		Gross income	Higher
Collective	Collective appropriation	Gross product	Higher

Subsumed Class Relation	*Form of Surplus Transference*	*Source of Income*	*Effect of Transfer on Household Income*
Commerce	Prices		
Producer		Net monetary income	Lower
Merchant		Commerce income	Higher
Financing	Interest		
Producer		Gross product	Higher
		Net monetary income	Lower
Moneylender		Interest income	Higher
Renting	Rent		
Producer		Gross product	Higher
		Net monetary income	Lower
Owner		Rental income	Higher
State	Taxes		
Producer		Net monetary income	Lower
Remittances	Payment	Remittance income	Higher
Domestic labor	Payment	Income pooling	Higher

fundamental and subsumed class processes plus nonclass payments. The level of net household income is contingent on the levels of surplus extraction and transference in all of the class processes in which household members engage. The three contingencies of social differentiation noted earlier—simple reproduction, the possibility of accumulation, or the disintegration of the household—depend on the mutually interactive effect of multiple class relations.

The strength of this approach is that it provides a theoretical framework that lends itself to the empirical analysis of peasantries and the observed participation of peasant household members in multiple income-generating activities. This framework also rids the analysis of social differentiation of any notion of inevitability. And although the multiple class relations in which household members engage may be considered household reproduction strategies, they are not voluntaristic. Each class relation is a potential relation of struggle. The outcome, whether or not peasant households are reproduced, is never predetermined. In some cases, economic, political, and cultural conditions of existence for petty production might be secured that reproduce the household as a unit of production. In other cases, the struggle over conditions of existence of a fundamental class relation might lead to lower or higher levels of household reproduction and changes in the multiple class relations in which households engage.

This approach is fruitful because it moves the issue of the fate of the peasantry to a broader dimension. Attempts to construct a peasant or simple commodity mode or form of production focused too narrowly on the farm unit. As a result, the demise of peasant agricultural production and increased reliance on wage work led to premature predictions regarding the disappearance of the peasantry and made it difficult to explain how peasant households persisted. Moreover, a focus on the peasant household and its reproductive strategies brings human agency back into the picture and provides a different understanding of how capital may be dominant without completely transforming or differentiating the peasantry out of existence.

ACCESS TO MEANS OF PRODUCTION AND THE GENERATION OF HOUSEHOLD INCOME

By 1973, when the first income survey of rural households was undertaken in the province, the majority of Cajamarcan peasant households did not have sufficient land to fulfill subsistence requirements through farm activities alone. Almost three-quarters of the rural households in the province had access to fewer than 3.5 hectares of land, the minimum—given ecological and technical conditions of production—necessary for a peasant family to be able to achieve simple reproduction on the basis of petty production.[1] Thirteen percent had access to less than one-quarter hectare of land and are thus termed the near-landless; they owned an average of 0.16 hectares. Smallholders, with access to between 0.26 and 3.5 hectares, made up 59 percent of rural households and owned an average of 1.33 hectares of land. Only about one-quarter of rural households had access to sufficient land to be potentially viable farmers: middle peasants, 17 percent of the total, owned an average of 5.83 hectares; rich peasants, 8 percent, owned an average of 15.86 hectares. Farms of between 30 and 100 hectares constituted only 3 percent of the total and were owned principally by the rural petty bourgeoisie rather than the peasantry (Deere 1978, table 16).

The highly unequal pattern of land ownership was also reflected in the unequal distribution of other means of production. The majority of peasant households did not own their own oxen, the main draft animal of the region. Even middle peasants were not totally self-sufficient in this regard, having to rely on the rich peasantry or the petty bourgeoisie for access to an ox (or in some cases a team) for plowing. But, on average, middle peasants controlled more than twice as much land, oxen, and total means of work as did smallholder households, and the value of their total assets was twice as great. Rich peasants, in turn, owned more than twice as much land and oxen as did middle peasants, and the value of their investment in means of work was significantly greater, as was the value of their total assets.[2]

Because access to means of production differed so significantly, it is not surprising that the activities in which households engaged differed as well. As Table 35 points out, the overwhelming majority of households participated in agricultural or animal production. Nevertheless, animal raising was among the three activities that most differentiated households statistically, for animal raising often depends on owning pasture land. But what differentiated rural households most strongly was their participation in wage labor. Whereas the majority of near-landless and smallholder households had at least one member participating in the labor market in 1973, only one-third of the upper strata of peasant households engaged in the sale of wage labor.[3] In contrast, for the other nonfarm activities that might have been alternatives to wage labor—artisan

1. A rigorous definition of the minimum amount of land required to reproduce the household through farming activities alone would require detailed attention to land quality (Caballero 1981a). The data from the 1973 Cajamarca Income Survey do not permit a more sophisticated calculation of land resources based on standardized hectares.

2. The correlation coefficient between land held in usufruct and number of oxen was .3496; with respect to the value of means of work, .4000; and with respect to total assets, .5522 (Deere 1978, 289).

3. The data on participation rates in wage labor by strata differ slightly from those presented in Table 29; the data in that table were stratified according to total land in property rather than usufruct.

TABLE 35. Rates of Participation in Income-Generating Activities, by Land-Size Strata, Province of Cajamarca, 1973

Land-Size Strata	Agricultural Production	Agricultural Processing	Animal Raising	Rental of Resources	Artisan Production	Wage Labor	Commerce	Remittances
Near-landless households (N = 140)	95.7%	1.4%	70.0%	4.3%	31.4%	71.4%	8.6%	13.6%
Smallholder households (N = 619)	99.0	1.0	79.5	8.4	28.6	55.7	8.6	13.9
Middle peasant households (N = 177)	99.4	1.7	85.9	13.0	32.8	41.8	9.6	6.2
Rich peasant households (N = 81)	97.5	1.2	95.1	21.0	33.3	34.6	8.6	6.2
Petty bourgeoisie (N = 33)	93.9	6.1	90.9	18.2	36.4	30.3	6.1	6.1
Total (N = 1,050)	98.4%	1.3%	80.9%	9.9%	30.4%	53.1%	8.7%	11.8%
χ^2	13.6	6.4	21.8	22.4	2.2	47.7	.49	11.9
Probability of error	< .01	n.s.	< .001	< .001	n.s	< .001	n.s.	< .02

SOURCE: Compiled from the 1973 Cajamarca Income Survey.

production and commerce—the differences in relative participation were not significant.

The rental of means of production also differentiated rural households statistically. Relatively few near-landless or smallholder households rented out land or animals, but this was a more frequent income-earning activity among middle peasants and was quite common among rich peasant households and the petty bourgeoisie, who controlled a sizable share of the oxen and other work animals in the countryside. The data on receipt of remittances from family members no longer residing within the household are also interesting, because they suggest that permanent migration did not necessarily lead to the dissolution of extra-household economic relations and familial responsibilities. Children of poor peasants contributed more frequently to their parental households once they left home than did those from the upper peasant strata, clear evidence of heterogeneous household reproduction strategies.

The survey data illustrate the multiplicity of activities in which peasant households engage.[4] They also reveal the marked variety, among households with differing access to means of production, of the composition of household income.[5] As Table 36 shows, farm activities constituted the primary source of household income only among rich peasant households and the petty bourgeoisie. But whereas agricultural production was the primary income source for rich peasant households, animal production (principally dairy production) was the main source among the petty bourgeoisie.

Middle peasant households generated slightly more than half of their household income from farm activities, with income from animal production exceeding that from agriculture. The income sources of these households were much more diversified than those of rich peasant households; wages contributed almost one-quarter of household income, and commerce and remittance income were also significant.

Wages were the primary source of income for both smallholders and near-landless households, significantly exceeding the income generated from farm activities. Agriculture and animal production were equally important income sources for smallholder households, but animal production was more important than agriculture among the near-landless, who, because of their extremely small plots of land, often specialized in pig, chicken, or *cuy* (guinea pig) production. And whereas commercial activities were relatively more important

---

4. The mean number of income-generating activities in the sample was three. The 1973 survey underestimated participation in at least two other income-generating activities, however: agricultural processing and product transformation, and artisan production. These activities are underreported largely because they are carried out by women and are often geared to autoconsumption. Because all the households resampled in 1976 were involved in these activities (see Table 39), the mean number of income-generating activities is closer to five.

5. The household income data include both estimates of the value of subsistence production (or autoconsumption) and estimates of cash income generated. See Appendix IV.

TABLE 36. Sources of Income: Composition of Net Income, by Relative Importance of Source and Land-Size Strata, Province of Cajamarca, 1973

Land-Size Strata	Agricultural Production	Agricultural Processing	All Animal Production	Rental	Subtotal All Farm Activities	Artisan Production	Wage Labor	Commerce	Remittance	Mean Net Income Total
Near-landless households (N = 140)	1.0%	0.1%	18.8%	0.4%	20.3%	9.2%	55.5%	10.3%	4.7%	100% S/. 12,733
Smallholder households (N = 619)	10.4	0.2	10.4	3.4	24.4	7.0	48.6	12.5	7.5	100% S/. 8,862
Middle peasant households (N = 177)	19.6	0.1	27.0	8.7	55.4	4.1	23.5	10.4	6.6	100% S/. 11,615
Rich peasant households (N = 81)	42.0	0.2	24.4	15.4	82.0	2.1	11.4	3.6	0.9	100% S/. 25,014
Petty bourgeoisie (N = 33)	26.1	0.1	62.1	1.3	89.6	0.7	5.7	3.3	0.7	100% S/. 56,771
Total (N = 1,050)	17.6	0.2	23.6	5.4	46.8	5.2	33.8	9.2	5.0	100% S/. 12,594

SOURCE: Compiled from the 1973 Cajamarca Income Survey.
NOTE: In 1973, U.S. $1 = S/. 43.

among smallholder households than among any other group, for near-landless households artisan production was more significant.

The diversified income sources among middle, smallholder, and near-landless households appear not to compensate for the groups' lack of access to sufficient means of production. As can be seen in Table 36, the mean net income of rich peasant households was twice as great as that of most other peasant strata. And households of the petty bourgeoisie generated more than twice the net income of rich peasant households.

Mean net household income for the sample as a whole (S/. 12,594, or U.S. $293) was substantially higher than median net income (S/. 6,721, or U.S. $156), a result of the high variance in the sample. Mean, as opposed to median, net income also accentuates the inequality in income levels among the various strata. Smallholder households earned the lowest median (S/. 5,945) and mean net income of all land-size strata. The fact that their income level was lower than that of the near-landless is partly explained by their attempt to reproduce themselves as petty agricultural producers, a riskier activity than either artisan production or wage work. Although the mean net income of near-landless households slightly exceeded that of middle peasants, because of the presence of a number of artisan households with extremely high incomes in the former group, the median income of middle peasant households (S/. 7,694) was slightly higher than that of the near-landless (S/. 7,107) (Deere 1978, table 29). The data suggest that the most important difference in income levels was between the near-landless, smallholder, and middle peasant households on the one hand and rich peasant households on the other.

THE CLASS ANALYTICS OF PEASANT HOUSEHOLD REPRODUCTION

The analysis of household income-generating activities allows a first approximation of the class relations in which peasant households participate. From the data in Table 35, two fundamental class relations (petty production and capitalist) and three subsumed class processes (commerce, rental of means of production, and remittances) can be identified. A number of other subsumed class processes are implicit, if not explicit, in the calculation of net income, including credit and financing charges, the value of marketing one's own production, and taxes. Because Table 37 summarizes only direct income-generating activities, it underestimates the full range of class relations in which rural households participate.

Only one-quarter of these Cajamarcan peasant households attempted to generate their livelihood primarily as petty producers, relying on farm activities (agricultural and animal production) or artisan production. Some of these petty producers may also have been capitalists, relying on the purchase of wage labor from which they extracted a surplus. The vast majority of Cajamarcan

TABLE 37. Household Participation in Multiple Class Relations, by Land-Size Strata, Province of Cajamarca, 1973

	One Class Relation	Two Class Relations			Three Class Relations				Total
	Petty Producer	Petty Producer, Wage Worker	Petty Producer, Merchant	Petty Producer, Remittances	Petty Producer, Wage Worker, Remittances	Petty Producer, Wage Worker, Merchant	Petty Producer, Wage Worker, Rent	Petty Producer, Remittances, Rent	
Near-landless households (N = 14)	21%	50%	7%	—	15%	7%	—	—	100%
Smallholder households (N = 67)	18	55	9	6	2	3	6	1	100%
Middle peasant households (N = 19)	42	26	11	5	5	11	—	—	100%
Rich peasant households (N = 5)	60	20	—	20	—	—	—	—	100%
Total (N = 105)	24	47	9	6	5	4	4	1	100%

SOURCE: Compiled from the 1973 Cajamarca Income Survey, for sub-sample of 105 households.

peasant households analyzed here participated in at least two class relations. The most common pattern, particularly for near-landless and smallholder households, included two fundamental processes, petty production and wage work. Fourteen percent of these rural households engaged in at least three class relations. Most participated in both petty production and wage work, combined with the subsumed class processes of commerce, remittances, or rental of means of production.

Near-landless households, followed by smallholders, were most likely to participate in multiple class relations, whereas households engaging in only one class relation were concentrated among the middle and rich peasantry. Access to means of production thus appears critical to the ability of peasant households to reproduce themselves on the basis of petty production alone.

In order to analyze whether the level of income attained by Cajamarcan households is sufficient to reproduce household labor power, some measure of the minimum "moral and historical" level of subsistence is required. In the absence of some direct measure of necessary consumption requirements in the region, I will take the legal minimum wage as a proxy. The minimum wage supposedly represents the minimum income required to purchase the socially defined wage-good basket for a family of four.[6] In 1973 the minimum daily wage for agricultural work in the province of Cajamarca was S/. 43 (U.S. $1). The mean wage paid by the 1,050 households in the 1973 survey to their agricultural wage workers was substantially lower, S/. 24.5 (U.S. $0.57) per day, what I will term the *market wage*.

Table 38 shows that few of these rural households—only 6 percent—earned incomes from farm activities alone sufficient to meet the legally defined standard of necessary consumption. Even when all petty production is included, only 11 percent earned this threshold level of income. These statistics suggest the importance of engaging in multiple class relations. Nonetheless, even when all income-generating activities are taken into account, only 26 percent attained this threshold level.

Cajamarcan peasant households were somewhat more successful at meeting simple reproduction levels defined according to the market-wage standard. Fifty-four percent of rural households met this threshold if total household income was taken into account. Even by this lower standard, few households reproduced themselves on the basis of petty production alone, and even fewer on the basis of farm activities only.

Near-landless households in this sample appear to be the most successful in meeting household reproduction requirements by either standard, largely because they allocated more household labor time to the labor market and to

6. Interview, Ministry of Labor, Cajamarca Office, September 1976. The minimum wages for different regions of Peru are determined by the national office in Lima. I was unable to obtain more precise information on how they were calculated.

TABLE 38. Levels of Household Reproduction, by Land-Size Strata, Province of Cajamarca, 1973

Land-Size Strata	Farm Income ≥ Minimum-Wage Income	Petty Production Income ≥ Minimum-Wage Income	Total Income ≥ Minimum-Wage Income	Farm Income ≥ Market-Wage Income	Petty Production Income ≥ Market-Wage Income	Total Income ≥ Market-Wage Income
Near-landless households (N = 14)	—	3 (21%)	7 (50%)	1 (7%)	4 (29%)	10 (71%)
Smallholder households (N = 67)	4 (6%)	7 (10%)	13 (19%)	9 (13%)	11 (16%)	34 (51%)
Middle peasant households (N = 19)	1 (5%)	1 (5%)	5 (26%)	4 (21%)	4 (21%)	11 (58%)
Rich peasant households (N = 5)	1 (20%)	1 (20%)	2 (40%)	2 (40%)	2 (40%)	2 (40%)
Total (N = 105)	6 (6%)	12 (11%)	27 (26%)	16 (15%)	21 (20%)	57 (54%)

SOURCE: Compiled from the 1973 Cajamarca Income Survey, for sub-sample of 105 households.
NOTE: The minimum-wage income is calculated to be S/. 12,900, based on a daily wage of S/. 43 for three hundred days. The market-wage income is calculated to be S/. 7,350, based on a daily wage of S/. 24.5 for three hundred days.

artisan activities. Smallholders were the least successful. The small number of observations on rich peasant households makes it difficult to draw any conclusions about the behavior of this group.

A closer analysis of petty production illustrates the precariousness of agricultural production. Only 72 percent of the households generated a positive net income from agricultural production in 1973.[7] This proportion was positively related to farm size. A slightly higher proportion (80 percent) of rural households generated a positive income from animal production; in this case, it was inversely related to farm size.

If the amount of family labor time dedicated to agricultural production is taken into account and valued at its opportunity cost—that is, the rural market wage of S/. 24.5—few households (34 percent) generated a net profit from agricultural activities. The ability to do so was, again, positively related to farm size. By this measure, even fewer households, some 15 percent, were able to generate a net profit from animal production, a fact partly related to the labor-intensiveness of the activity.[8] This analysis suggests that petty production is, indeed, a losing proposition in Cajamarca. Participation in other class relations is absolutely essential for peasant households to sustain themselves as units of production and reproduction.

If few households are able to generate a net profit from agriculture or animal raising when family labor is remunerated at the local agricultural wage rate, it is also likely that few are able to accumulate as petty producers, appropriating their own surplus. Households may be transferring a significant portion of their appropriated surplus as subsumed class payments to other social groups such as merchants and moneylenders. But another factor mitigating the amount of absolute surplus produced is low productivity, partly a result of the low level of technology employed and the poor quality of land.

Low productivity also reduces the possibility for petty producers to appropriate surplus value from wage workers. As noted previously, by the 1970s it was common for Cajamarcan peasant households to employ wage labor for agricultural activities; 52 percent did so for at least some agricultural task. Recall that peasants constituted the principal employers of temporary agricultural workers in the province.

One way to measure whether a surplus is being appropriated through the use

7. This statistic may simply reflect a bad agricultural year, of course. The 1972–1973 agricultural cycle was characterized by drought during the planting season, then severe rains during the harvest, which lowered yields (Franco 1976, 83). Nonetheless, the figure clearly suggests the contingency of household reproduction from petty production activities alone.

8. Family labor in animal production was valued at the mean market agricultural wage rate, which exceeds the opportunity cost for women and children. The data on labor days dedicated to agricultural and animal production are drawn from the 1976 Peasant Family Survey; data on labor days employed in animal production were not reported in the 1973 survey, and the agricultural data are more complete in the 1976 data set.

TABLE 39. Productivity and Surplus Appropriation in Agricultural
Production, Province of Cajamarca, 1973

Land-Size Strata	Average Product Negative	Average Product ≤ Wage	Use Wage Labor	Average Product ≥ Wage	Use Wage Labor
Near-landless households (N = 12)	4 (33%)	6 (50%)	3	2 (17%)	0
Smallholder households (N = 58)	21 (36%)	22 (38%)	20	15 (26%)	6
Middle peasant households (N = 18)	5 (28%)	5 (28%)	7	8 (44%)	8
Rich peasant households (N = 5)	2 (40%)	1 (20%)	3	2 (40%)	1
Total (N = 93)	32 (34%)	34 (37%)	33	27 (29%)	15

SOURCES: Compiled from the 1973 Cajamarca Income Survey. Labor utilization data from the 1976 Peasant Family Survey.
NOTE: The average product is calculated as the ratio of gross agricultural income, less nonwage costs of production, to total labor employed. Wage refers to the local market wage of S/. 24.5 per day.

of wage labor is to consider the relationship between the average agricultural product and some standard of "necessary" labor.[9] The average agricultural product is defined as the ratio of gross agricultural income, minus nonlabor costs of production, to the total labor days employed. We will assume that the market wage provides the most reasonable proxy of "necessary" labor. Thus, if the value of the average product exceeds the wage, the household is appropriating a surplus—a surplus produced either by its own members as petty producers or by wage workers, if they are employed in the productive process.

Table 39 presents the results of this exercise. The productivity of the majority of these Cajamarcan households was so low that the average product was either negative (34 percent) or less than the market wage (37 percent). Half of these sixty-six households used wage labor for some task; in effect, they were transferring the equivalent of necessary labor time from family workers to wage workers, because the value of the average product is less than the wage. In other words, these households were worse-off because they used wage labor.

Only 29 percent of the households managed to produce a surplus from agricultural activities; doing so was closely related to farm size. Fifteen of these

9. This analysis loosely follows the framework proposed by Martínez and Rendón (1978).

twenty-seven households used wage labor; thus 56 percent of the households generating a surplus were extracting surplus value. The remainder were appropriating a surplus based on their own efforts as petty producers. Overall, only 31 percent of the households employing wage labor actually extracted surplus value. As expected, middle and rich peasant households were more successful at this than were the poorer strata of the peasantry.

Besides demonstrating the low productive capacity of Cajamarcan households, this exercise illustrates how few households are able to accumulate, whether through petty production or through the use of wage labor. It also shows that the use of wage labor by peasant households is not a sufficient indicator of social differentiation; these households are not necessarily on "the farmer path" toward capitalist production. In the Cajamarcan case, the use of wage labor by peasant producers more realistically reflects the monetization of traditional labor practices. At the beginning of the century, the high demand for labor at critical moments of the agricultural cycle was met through labor exchanges between households or through the minga, but today these economic conditions of existence of petty production are mediated through the cash nexus. Wage labor that does not produce a surplus cannot really be regarded as a capitalist class relation; rather, it represents a subsumed class process for petty production.

Even if a surplus is appropriated through petty production or a capitalist class relation, it is important to note that this does not necessarily result in accumulation—the expansion of means of production. Accumulation depends on the outcome of all the class and nonclass relations in which households engage and the extent to which the household can cover the basic requirements of simple reproduction. The surplus produced in petty or capitalist production may simply be consumed, or it may be transferred as subsumed class payments to the social classes that control key conditions of existence of petty and capitalist production.

HOUSEHOLD LABOR ALLOCATION AND THE GENERATION OF HOUSEHOLD INCOME

Generating household income depends on the allocation of household labor to a series of productive and reproductive activities. Table 40 presents a summary of the prevailing household division of labor in the mid-1970s, showing the person primarily responsible for each activity. In terms of petty production, male heads of households were generally responsible for agriculture, whereas women were charged with animal care, agricultural processing, and artisan production. Participation in wage labor was most often the responsibility of men, whereas women tended to dominate in commercial activities. The tasks associated with domestic labor were overwhelmingly part of the female domain.

TABLE 40. Frequency Distribution of Activities of Peasant Households, by Principal Family Member Responsible, Province of Cajamarca, 1976

Activity	Responsibility of Mother	Responsibility of Father	Responsibility of Children	Responsibility of All Family Members[a]	Total
Petty production					
Agricultural processing (N = 105)	93.4%	—	1.9%	4.7%	100%
Animal care (N = 92)	61.9	4.4	22.9	10.8	100%
Agricultural work (N = 102)	5.7	64.5	7.6	22.2	100%
Artisan production (N = 101)	66.7	18.4	11.5	3.4	100%
Marketing					
Sale of own products (N = 35)	45.7	28.6	—	25.7	100%
Commerce (N = 28)	85.7	10.7	—	3.6	100%
Wage labor					
Part-time wage work (N = 51)	9.8	47.1	17.7	25.4	100%
Full-time wage work (N = 23)	13.0	43.5	30.4	13.1	100%
Domestic labor					
Cooking (N = 105)	93.4	—	2.8	3.8	100%
Washing clothes (N = 105)	93.3	—	4.8	1.9	100%
Hauling water (N = 105)	78.3	1.8	10.3	9.6	100%
Collecting wood (N = 105)	58.1	16.2	9.5	16.2	100%

SOURCE: 1976 Peasant Family Survey.

[a] This category includes cases in which the mother and father share responsibility for the activity, in which other family members carry out the activity, and in which parents and children share the responsibility equally.

Although most activities were gender-differentiated, a number of them required the participation of all family members. Table 40 shows the large number of households, the majority from the poor peasantry, that reported agricultural production, marketing one's own products, seasonal wage work, and wood collection as the responsibility of the entire family. In addition, even when agricultural production was regarded as part of the male domain, women's labor proved important. Women provided 25 percent of the labor days dedicated to agricultural production by family members; their participation was more significant among poor peasant households (35 percent) than among the upper peasant strata (21 percent) (Deere 1978, table 34).

Women from the upper strata participated only in what were generally considered "female" activities (placing the seed in its furrow or sweeping up the threshed grain) or in tasks that did not involve the use of implements (weeding or harvesting by hand). Women from the poorer strata participated in all agricultural tasks, with the exception of plowing. These women not only participated more in field work but also played a greater role in agricultural decision making.

In the majority of near-landless households, women took responsibility for providing agricultural inputs such as seed and fertilizer, when these were used; in smallholder households, men and women shared this activity. Among households of the middle and rich peasantry, decisions about agricultural inputs were usually made only by men. Among poorer peasant households, men and women jointly organized and coordinated the labor process; they also shared decisions about the disposition of agricultural products, such as how much of the crop would be saved for household consumption and how much would be sold. Among the upper peasantry, however, these decisions fell strictly within the male domain.

These differences in participation and decision making among the different strata of the peasantry suggest that although agricultural production was family-based, among the upper strata of the peasantry it involved a patriarchal family farming system (Deere and León 1982). Women contributed their labor to agricultural production, but men controlled the productive process. In contrast, among the poorer peasant strata a more egalitarian family farming system prevailed; both men and women contributed labor and made decisions.

Whether the farming system is egalitarian or patriarchal is closely related to the importance of agricultural production in the composition of household income. As Table 36 demonstrated, agriculture was an important source of household income only for the upper peasant strata. For the majority of these Cajamarcan peasant households, agricultural production was a secondary activity. As the importance of agricultural production in household income diminishes, women's participation and responsibility seem to correspondingly increase, contributing to a more egalitarian farming system.

Agricultural production occupied a minimal amount of time among land-poor households: near-landless households reported spending only ap-proximately one month and smallholder households four months a year in agricultural pursuits. Middle and rich peasant households, however, dedicated from seven to ten months a year to agricultural production, explaining why agriculture was viewed as an occupation only among these strata (Deere 1978, table 19).

Animal raising was the most time-intensive productive activity in which peasant households engaged, involving an average of thirty-eight hours a week (Deere 1978, table 19). The amount of time dedicated to animal care was positively related to farm size, largely reflecting the size of the sheep herd that could be maintained and the household's ability to allocate this duty full-time to one member. Although mothers were most often responsible for animal care, raising sheep usually depended on having a child at home, either to pasture the animals daily or to replace the mother in daily maintenance activities. Male participation in animal care was usually limited to caring for the work animals. Men were the principal persons charged with animal husbandry only in households with significant dairy herds, even though in these households women did the milking.

Domestic work was even more labor-intensive than animal care, demanding an average of forty-four hours per week. As Table 40 shows, rural women were almost solely responsible for cooking, washing clothes, and hauling water to meet consumption needs, aided in this last activity by their children. The only domestic task in which men commonly paticipated was wood collection, and then only when it involved a weekly trip to a distant area to fell a tree.

Given the labor-intensiveness of domestic work, it is surprising that women also participated in such a variety of income-generating activities. A number of petty production activities were, of course, complementary to women's domestic work and actually involved joint production, such as spinning while herding sheep and caring for children. When the labor time dedicated to animal care alone is added to that required for daily maintenance of the family, the working week of mothers reaches seventy-one hours. If income-generating activities outside the home are also included, the working day of a woman extends far beyond a mere ten hours.

Although the rural women of Cajamarca were active participants in the household's income-generating activities, their contribution to household income was not commensurate with the labor time they dedicated to pro-ductive activities—primarily a result of the lower social valuation of female labor. Peasant women of all strata were principally responsible for animal raising and commerce. These two activities generated approximately one-third of the mean net income of rural households in 1973 and thus serve as a minimum estimate of women's contribution to household income. But there were important differences in these contributions, depending on households' access to means of production.

Paradoxically, women's contribution was relatively greater among middle peasant households than among the poorer strata, reflecting the greater importance of animal raising and commerce among the former group. In middle peasant households, women directly contributed at least 37 percent of household income. In contrast, in near-landless households, women contributed 29 percent, and in smallholder households at least 22 percent (Deere 1978, tables 25–28). These differences appear not to be offset by the differing participation of women in agricultural production (given its small contribution to total household income among the poorer strata), artisan production, or wage work.

Women's lesser contribution to household income among poorer households reflects the greater integration of these households into the labor market and the differing social valuation of male and female labor. In the labor market, men and women did not have access to the same jobs. Although the minimum wage was legally the same for both sexes, men were much more likely to find work in jobs covered by the legislation. Moreover, men made up the majority of migrants to the coast, where agricultural wages were significantly higher than in rural Cajamarca. In addition, in temporary agricultural wage work in the region, men were paid twice as much as women. As a result of all these factors, male wage workers in 1973 earned an average of S/. 42 per day worked, whereas female wage workers averaged only S/. 16. Although the women who worked for wages did so for an average of 225 days, men worked only 176 days and earned a total wage income twice that of women (Deere 1978, table 23).

The level of remuneration in artisan production also reflects a differing social valuation of male and female activities. Male artisans, although fewer in number than female artisans, realized an average return of S/. 43 per day worked; female artisans earned only S/. 20 per day. Female artisan activities were considered an extension of women's work in the production of use values in the home. Men's artisan activities, in contrast, were considered skilled occupations and were remunerated as such. Thus tailors were able to make a significantly greater contribution to household income than were seamstresses.

The contribution of women from poorer peasant households to total income was thus lower, because in the activities crucial to poor peasant households— wage work and artisan production—the return to male labor was twice that to female labor. The lower social valuation of female labor meant that women's contribution to household income was not commensurate with the amount of time they dedicated to income-generating activities. This disparity was an important contributing factor to rural poverty.

Another consequence of the lower social valuation of female labor was that women were generally much better-off economically in households that included an adult male worker. In Cajamarca, as throughout Latin America, female-headed households, particularly those without sons of working age, were among the very poorest. Landless women had little recourse but to marry and be part of an income-pooling unit that included a man. Even women who owned land wanted to be married, because the presence of a man guaranteed not only a higher level of household income but also labor for those key "male-only" agricultural tasks (Bourque and Warren 1981).

The extent to which women were materially better-off in fully constituted households, however, depended on whether household income was in fact pooled. Important changes took place in this realm as a result of the growing monetization of the rural economy and the increased integration of rural households into the labor market. Chapter 3 described how the subsistence orientation of peasant agriculture on the haciendas guaranteed that petty agricultural production based on family labor would indeed result in an undifferentiated family labor product. The bulk of household agricultural production was stored or bartered after the harvest to provide for the family's consumption requirements throughout the year. Because women were responsible for food preparation, it generally fell to them to manage the household's store of grain.

The integration of households into the product market has meant that this family labor product has now become exchange value.[10] A number of intervening variables—who makes the decision to market, who conducts the sale, and who receives the cash income—came to influence whether the family labor product actually resulted in shared consumption. Among the upper peasant strata, men tended to dominate marketing and controlled the income generated by these sales. In contrast, among the poorer peasantry, women played a more active role in marketing the small surpluses produced by these households and in disposing of the income generated from the sales. As a result, women from the poorer peasant strata tended to have more economic autonomy than women from the upper peasant strata. They also tended to control the income generated through their own independent activities, whether artisan production, wage work, or petty trading, as well as remittances from children who had migrated. Women of the middle and rich peasant strata were more likely to run country stores and to be dairy producers, but they rarely controlled the net income generated by these activities.

Among poor peasant households, female economic autonomy was a necessary condition to guarantee shared consumption of the family labor product. Poor peasant men could walk away from a sale on market day right into a bar and drink away a month's worth of family labor. It was not unusual

10. In 1973 commodity sales represented 36 percent of gross income from agricultural production and 85 percent of that from animal production (Deere 1978, table 21). There were important differences by land-size strata, however, with near-landless households realizing only 10 percent of the value of agricultural production in monetary form; smallholder households, 26 percent; middle peasant households, 29 percent; and rich peasant households, 51 percent. A similar pattern holds for animal production, although the overall proportion of gross production sold was considerably higher.

to see a woman desperately trying to pull her husband out of a chicheria for exactly this reason. As a woman in the Community of Hualqui complained to me, if her husband took 3 arrobas of barley to market in Jesús, he would return with two bottles of aguardiente, 2 pounds of coca, and a package of cigarettes, forgetting about the basics (*"ni sal ni ají"*).

Men from the upper strata of the peasantry who considered themselves agriculturalists were less likely than poor peasant men to spend the family labor product in individualized consumption, particularly of alcohol. With a clearer aim of reproducing the household as petty producers, men of this group were more conservative as managers of the family finances and were more likely to reinvest farm cash income in means of production. Thus, although the households of middle and rich peasant farmers were more patriarchal, it was more likely that the family labor product in these households resulted in shared consumption.

Another factor that undermined income pooling among poor peasant households was that a growing share of household income was being generated on an individualized basis, the result of the independent activities carried out by men and women in the labor market or in commerce or artisan production. Torres and Hillenbrand (1978, 4) report that the individualization of income even led to situations where men and women controlled separate household budgets, taking biweekly turns buying the household necessities (salt, kerosene, noodles, matches, soap, and so on). My research suggests that, because of the unequal income-earning opportunities among men and women, the more common result was a growing inequality in consumption levels among men, on the one hand, and women and their children, on the other.

The growing integration of households into the labor market resulted in men controlling the most important source of household income. Because wage income is earned on an individual basis rather than by the family, there was a growing tendency for men to consider it their personal income, to be disposed of as they saw fit. The end of the enganche system of cash advances, which were generally spent in the sierra, also meant that seasonal coastal migration provided men with plenty of opportunity to treat wage income as "discretionary," to be spent on entertainment or on coastal-style clothing. This individualization of an income source also supported the practice of polygamy, contributing to increased household instability.

Whether males wage income was in fact pooled depended considerably on whether the woman was a landowner, on how committed the man was to petty production, and on the affective relations between the couple and between the man and his children. Women's participation in household decision making was closely associated with whether the women themselves were landowners, having contributed to constituting the unit of production through inheritance. Moreover, those few cases in which women dominated household and farm affairs tended to be households where their partner was landless.

There was also a much greater likelihood that wage income would be pooled when the household considered it complementary to petty production than when the household depended on it for reproduction requirements. That is, a commitment to reproducing the household as a unit of production and reproduction—remaining a peasant household—and the material possibilities of doing so fostered income pooling and were forces of cohesion in household relations. The comparative instability of households that were more nearly proletarian (lacking access to land and depending on wage income) reflected a tendency to disintegrate as units of production and reproduction.

HOUSEHOLD INCOME LEVELS IN
HISTORICAL PERSPECTIVE

The income profiles developed for tenant households on the Hacienda Combayo in 1917 allow a tentative discussion of the trends in the income levels of rural households over the course of the twentieth century. Converting the estimated income profile data for hacienda households presented in Table 13 to 1973 soles reveals that peon households earned S/. 9,309, punteros S/. 11,443, and arrendires S/. 13,014. Comparing these figures with 1973 survey data on median household income (S/. 6,721) reveals that well over 50 percent of rural households in the 1970s were earning incomes lower than the minimum estimated household income on the hacienda, that of peon households.

The analysis of mean, as opposed to median, household income suggests that only smallholder households were worse-off as a group: their mean income in 1973 was 4.8 percent lower than the income of a peon household in 1917 and 32 percent lower than an arrendire's (see Table 36). The mean income levels of near-landless and middle peasants were in the general range of income levels generated on the hacienda. Most interestingly, mean household incomes of the rich peasantry and the petty bourgeoisie in 1973 were significantly higher than the income levels that could have been generated on the hacienda, supporting the proposition that the effect of capitalist development has been to accentuate income inequalities.

As discussed previously, the hacienda land sales of the 1950s and 1960s, combined with the development of the market in milk, allowed the expansion of a middle and rich peasantry as well as the creation of a petty bourgeoisie dedicated to dairy farming. Although this process brought a boom to petty commodity and capitalist production, it undermined the productive base of the independent communities that had depended on the haciendas for access to grazing pastures. Table 41 illustrates this by comparing the composition of household income of smallholders in 1973 with that of peon households on the Hacienda Combayo.

In 1917 peon households generated an estimated 22 percent of net household income from raising animals. In 1973 the average smallholder household generated only 10 percent of net income from animal production, although this activity was still carried out by most of the households and consumed the most

TABLE 41. Composition of Household Income, Province of Cajamarca, 1917 and 1973

Source of Income	1917 Hacienda Household, Peon	1973 Smallholder Household
Agricultural production[a]	33.9%	10.2%
	(male 17%)	(male 7.5%)
	(female 17%)	(female 2.7%)
Animal production	22.2%	10.0%
	(female and children)	(male 0.9%)
		(female 6.6%)
		(children 2.5%)
Artisan production	—[b]	7.1%
		(male 3.3%)
		(female 3.0%)
		(children 0.8%)
Wage income	32.1%	48.6%
	(male 27.7%)	(male 46.2%)
	(female 2.5%)	(female 2.4%)
	(children 1.9%)	
Commerce	—	12.5%
		(male 1.1%)
		(female 11.4%)
Other[c]	11.8%	11.6%
Total	100.0%	100.0%
Women's contribution	41.6%	26.1%

SOURCES: Compiled from Santolalla ([1918] 1977), the 1973 Cajamarca Income Survey, and the 1976 Peasant Family Survey. Also see tables 13 and 36, above.

[a] These figures are based on the assumption that men and women on the hacienda contributed approximately equal shares of agricultural income; peon men worked nearly full-time for the landowner, and secondary data and life histories attest to women's participation. The gender contribution for smallholder households is based on the 1976 Peasant Family Survey; also see Deere (1978, table 26).

[b] Artisan production was an important activity among hacienda households, but quantitative data on this activity are unavailable. This lack results in an underestimation of total household income on the hacienda.

[c] For the 1917 data, this category refers to the imputed wage based on the value of rent of the peasant usufruct plot and the number of animals pastured. For the 1973 data, this category includes rental income and remittances.

labor time. The effect of the reduced land base of the majority of peasant households is also reflected in the data on the share of household income generated through agricultural production: whereas a peon household generated 34 percent of its income from this source, agricultural production in the 1970s constituted only 10 percent of the net income of smallholders.

Also important are the changes in women's contribution to household income. Whereas peon women generated an estimated 42 percent of household income, among smallholders in the 1970s they contributed only 26 percent. This discrepancy again reflects the decline in animal production and in the importance of agricultural production among smallholders in the 1970s. It also reflects the inability of women to earn significant amounts of wage income, the most important source of household income among smallholders in the 1970s. All told, the process of capitalist development in agriculture has increased the number of activities in which women engage while lowering the value of their contribution to household reproduction. In other words, the growing poverty of Cajamarcan households over time may reflect the fact that women are having to work more while earning less.

CONCLUSION

This chapter demonstrates one important reason why the peasantry does not decompose: the participation of household members in multiple class relations often ensures household reproduction over time. This process explains how, although petty production might be a losing proposition, households can nonetheless reproduce themselves as units of production and reproduction— that is, as peasant households. Participation in multiple class relations provides the households with a diverse set of income sources that, if pooled, can reproduce the labor power of all household members.

The participation of peasant households in multiple fundamental and subsumed class relations also explains the growing impoverishment of the peasantry in Cajamarca. Multiple sources of surplus appropriation and transfer reduce the possibility that peasant producers will accumulate their own surplus in petty production. Such transfers also reduce net household income and require income from wage work, for example, in some cases to ensure the conditions of petty production. Although the precise mechanisms of price formation and oligopolistic market structures, as well as the effect of interest, rents, and taxation in lowering peasant household income, require further research, the framework developed here allows a clearer conceptualization of how multiple class relations may be the basis of both peasant survival and impoverishment.

The analysis of household labor allocation and of the gender division of labor also provides another important explanation of peasant poverty. The low social valuation of female labor—itself a product of the subordination of women— and the decline in many of women's income-earning activities have resulted in women working more and earning less. The subordination of women certainly has very high costs for peasant women, but it also has high costs for peasant households.

ELEVEN

The Family Life Cycle and Generational Reproduction

In 1976 both doña María and doña Rosa lived in households we would characterize as smallholders. But over their lifetimes, their households had been part of the landless (Rosa), the near-landless (María), and even the middle peasant strata. They themselves had been wage workers and traders as well as petty producers. Their life histories reveal both the fluidity of the class relations in which peasant households participate and the role of multiple class relations in reproducing peasant households as petty producers. Their experiences also illustrate how familial relations mediate class relations and, thus, the inter-relationship between class and nonclass relations.

Tables 42 and 43 summarize the class positions occupied by these women and their husbands over the family life cycle, as well as their households' changing access to land. Recall that in her second union María "married up" on the social scale, marrying the son of middle peasants. Because of a dispute over her husband's family inheritance, however, the household's security rested on farming María's inheritance of 0.4 hectares of land for most of the couple's married life. Most of the land they farmed had to be obtained through sharecropping agreements. But the Aguilar-Rumay household did not attempt to reproduce itself on the basis of petty agricultural production alone. For most of its expansive phase (1935–1949), this household depended primarily on the income earned by María as a trader and secondarily on the income earned by her husband as a wage worker. In other words, this household participated in two fundamental class relations—petty production and wage labor—and the subsumed class process of trading. Another subsumed class process, obtaining land in sharecropping arrangements with family and other neighbors, was also critical to maintaining petty production.

Once the Aguilar inheritance was settled, María's household owned 1.4 hectares of land. By this time, her four daughters were all of working age, and

TABLE 42. Life History of María Rumay de Aguilar of Pariamarca

	Year	María Rumay de Aguilar Class Positions	Access to Land (hectares)
Birth	1912	Smallholder household	2.0 (maternal grandfather)
Work	1927 to 1930	Wage worker (maid)	
	1930 +	Trader	
Inheritance	1927		0.4
Marriages	1931	Juan Ocas, son of smallholders	1.0 (Ocas family)
	1933	Manuel Aguilar, son of middle peasants	4.5 (Aguilar family)

	Year	Household Phases Class Positions	Access to Land (hectares)
	1933–1934	Middle peasants Trader (f)	0.4 private property (f) 4.5 sharecropped 4.9 total
	1935–1949	Smallholders Trader (f) Wage worker (m)	0.4 private property (f) 1.0 sharecropped 1.4 total
	1950–1974	Smallholders Trader (f)	0.4 private property (f) 1.0 inheritance (m) 1.0 sharecropped 2.4 total
	1975	Dissolution of household	

	Year of Birth	Heirs Class Positions in 1976	Access to Land (hectares)
Francisca	1935	Near-landless Trader (f) Wage worker (m) Artisan (m)	0.1 inheritance (f) 0.1 inheritance (m) 0.2 total
Martina	1937	Middle peasants Store owner (f)	0.1 inheritance (f) 4.0 private property (m) 4.1 total
Simona	1945	Smallholder Trader (f) Wage worker (m)	0.1 inheritance (f) 1.5 sharecropped 1.6 total
Erlinda	1947	Smallholder	0.1 inheritance (f) 1.0 private property (m) 1.0 sharecropped 2.1 total

NOTE: Designations for male and female members of the household are indicated in parentheses.

TABLE 43. Life History of Rosa Fernández de Sangay of La Succha

	Year	*Rosa Fernández de Sangay* Class Positions	Access to Land (hectares)
Birth	1911	Rich peasant (f) Artisan producer (m)	10.0 + (maternal grandmother)
Work	1920 to 1927	Wage worker (maid)	
Inheritance	—		—
Marriage	1927	Julio Sangay, son of smallholders	3.0 (Sangay family)

	Years	*Household Phases* Class Positions	Access to Land (hectares)
	1927–1929	Smallholders	3.0 usufruct (m)
	1930–1936	Wage worker (m) (coast)	
	1937–1950	Smallholders	0.5 private property (m) 2.5 rented 3.0 total
	1951–1965	Middle peasants	0.5 private property (m) 2.5 rented 3.0 sharecropped 6.0 total
	1966–1976	Smallholders	3.0 private property (m, j) 0.5 sharecropped 3.5 total

	Year of Birth	*Heirs* Class Positions in 1976	Access to Land (hectares)
Teodoro	1933	Middle peasant	0.5 inheritance (f) 3.0 private property (j) 6.0 sharecropped 9.5 total
Lucho	1937	Smallholder Truck driver (m)	1.5 inheritance (f)
Silvestre	1940	Wage worker (coast)	
Rodolfo	1946	Wage worker (coast)	
Aladino	1951	Tailor (coast)	
Victor	1953	Smallholder (residing with parents)	Works family lands

NOTE: Designations for male and female members of the household, as well as for joint landholdings, are indicated in parentheses.

the household continued to sharecrop additional land to meet household subsistence needs. In the period from 1950 to 1974, María's husband dedicated himself full-time to petty production. Household reproduction continued to depend on María's cash income from trading.

Doña Rosa's marital household followed a different pattern of evolution. In the first two years of marriage, her husband, Julio, worked his family lands communally with his mother and brothers. When Rosa and Julio migrated to the coast, they became a fully proletarian household for six years. Although their savings were meager, they managed to accumulate some resources during this period, which they later invested in becoming petty producers. Upon their return to La Succha, Julio inherited 0.5 hectares of land. Because this plot was insufficient to reproduce their now-expanding household as petty producers, they rented land on the nearby hacienda, engaging in a subsumed class process. Rosa inherited no land, and she was always dependent on Julio for access to the resources that allowed her to raise animals and contribute to the household economy.

The most prosperous period for the Sangay-Fernández household was in the 1950s, when they had four working-age sons living at home. They took advantage of the fact that so many families from La Succha were migrating permanently to the coast and acquired even more land through sharecropping arrangements with these households. At one point in the 1950s, they owned six oxen; three teams could plow at one time, with a son behind each. Subsumed class processes involving other peasants and the landlord class thus allowed this household to engage in expanded reproduction for a time.

The dissolution of the hacienda system and the development of the land market provided the opportunity for Julio and Rosa to purchase land. When the Hacienda Miche was subdivided and sold in 1965, they were able to buy 2.5 hectares with a loan from a son. They were fortunate that in five years Silvestre had saved enough of his wage income on the coast to lend his parents the money. Thus a son's participation in capitalist class relations allowed this household to expand its private holdings in support of petty production.

As their sons left the parental household, however, Julio and Rosa were left without sufficient family labor power to continue as middle peasants. In the late 1960s, they farmed only 3.5 hectares—3 hectares were their own property, and the rest was irrigated land obtained through sharecropping.

Both households experienced their most prosperous years when their teenage children lived at home and worked with their parents. During these years, the Sangay-Fernández household acquired the maximum amount of land (6 hectares) that it was to farm as a unit of production. The Aguilar-Rumay household was not nearly so fortunate, for the family never again acquired as much land as it initially had farmed when the household was first constituted. Even so, at the point of maximum labor strength in the family life cycle this household farmed more land (2.4 hectares) than it had during the previous period of household expansion (1.4 hectares). Both households appear to conform to the pattern predicted by Chayanov's theory of demographic differentiation.

LENIN AND CHAYANOV REVISITED

Over the family life cycle, the size as well as the age and sex composition of a household vary, as additional children are born and others marry or leave home. According to Chayanov's (1966) theory of demographic differentiation, inequalities in farm size can be explained by the demographic process of changing household composition over the family life cycle. Farm size expands and contracts as the household first accumulates and then loses children. Family size—in particular, the number of workers or the family's labor strength—is the independent variable determining the household's access to means of production and the level of its economic activity.

The interpretation of inequality in the Russian countryside provided by Chayanov's theory is very different from the interpretation offered by the theory Lenin advanced. For Lenin (1974), inequalities in farm size and in the concentration of means of production were evidence of peasant social differentiation. He explained the observed positive relation between farm size and household size in a different way: access to sufficient means of production allowed rich peasant households to retain their grown children working on the farm, whereas poor peasant households were forced to expel them. For Lenin, "family cooperation" provided the basis for capitalist exploitation, because large peasant farms usually had more land than could be worked by family labor alone. Even with larger families, the rich peasant strata depended on hiring wage labor (Lenin 1974, 94, 110).

Data on Cajamarca reveal a pattern similar to the one found among the Russian peasantry, with household size positively correlated with farm size. Whereas near-landless and smallholder households averaged 5.6 members in 1973, the mean for middle peasants was 6.1, for rich peasants 6.5, and for the petty bourgeoisie 7.9 members (Deere 1978, table 16). A detailed analysis of household labor strength and economic activity reveals, however, that the Chayanovian hypothesis had little predictive power in the case of Cajamarca (Deere and de Janvry 1981). For example, of the households ranking highest in labor strength (6 to 9 productive members), 80 percent had access to less than 3.5 hectares of land.[1] Further, 21 percent of the households surveyed in 1976

1. The measure of labor strength for household productive capacity was constructed by assigning different weights to family members according to age. Male and female household members in each age category were weighted equally, because their labor is of equal importance to the household. Adults between the ages of eighteen and fifty-nine were assigned the equivalent of one point, with children and the elderly scaled relative to their labor contribution. See Deere and de Janvry (1981, table 2). The classification of households according to labor strength only loosely conforms with the family life cycle, because each category contains households in both the expanding and the descending phases.

reported farming more land than they owned. Contrary to Chayanovian expectations, those most likely to sharecrop or rent additional land were relatively weak in labor strength, with 3.0 to 3.9 productive workers, followed by those with 2.0 to 2.9 (Deere and de Janvry 1981, table 4). In general, smallholder households were the most likely to acquire additional land, suggesting that the small initial endowment of land held by this group is the more important variable explaining why households enter into sharecropping or rental arrangements.

In the Cajamarcan case, Chayanov's hypothesis does little to explain the inequality in landholdings among the peasantry or to predict which groups of households are able to expand their productive base in order to reproduce themselves as petty agricultural producers. If the expansion of petty production in response to larger family size, even with a well-developed land market, is not regarded as an alternative by most households, one might expect other income-generating activities to become increasingly important as household labor strength increases. That is in fact what the data on Cajamarca reveal.

Households with greater labor strength tend to participate relatively more in *all* income-generating activities that are alternatives to agricultural production—wage labor, artisan production, and commerce—than do other households (Deere and de Janvry 1981, table 12). This pattern suggests that household size is an important variable influencing the propensity of households to engage in multiple class relations.

What the theory of demographic differentiation does not take into account is that the stock of household labor and its composition by age and sex over the family life cycle are not strictly autonomous or independent variables. The level of household reproduction (as measured by income, wealth, and the possibility for accumulation) influences both household size and the quality of household labor power. Access to means of production and class reproductive strategies influence such demographics and social variables as fertility and mortality, the retention or expulsion of working-age children, and family structure.

The Chayanovian emphasis on the family life cycle is nonetheless important in understanding household economic activity and how it varies with changes in household composition, as illustrated in the households of María and Rosa.[2] But in Cajamarca, material factors—or the impact of class, as mediated by wealth and income, on demographic variables—largely explain the observed positive correlation between farm size and household size.

MATERIAL DETERMINANTS OF HOUSEHOLD SIZE

According to census data, household size in the sierra remained relatively stable as a result of the high rate of natural population growth. Between 1940 and

2. Other analyses based on the family life cycle have also demonstrated its importance in determining household economic activity. See Collins (1988), for example, on changing migration strategies over the family life cycle among the Aymara in Puno.

1961, there was no significant change in household size at either the departmental or the provincial level, despite the substantial highland-coastal migration. Mean household size in the province (4.8) was slightly smaller than in the department as a whole (5.1), the difference reflecting the higher rate of permanent migration from the province of Cajamarca. The 1972 census data do capture the increase in permanent migration during the late 1960s, however, showing a decrease in household size to 4.7 and 4.9 at the provincial and the departmental levels, respectively.[3]

Census data underestimate actual household size, however, by excluding temporary migrants; the above estimates include only those household members who slept at home the evening prior to the census. The 1973 Cajamarca Income Survey data included as household residents those who resided in the house for at least four months out of the year; average household size in the province by this measure, 5.9 members, is thus significantly larger than the census estimate. The census data also obscure the important differences in household size among land-size strata, as noted earlier.

In Cajamarca, larger household size among the upper peasant strata is explained by lower child mortality, by the tendency to retain fully productive children, and by the constitution of extended households when adult children marry. These indicators reflect household reproductive strategies based on accumulation of means of production and household labor power, much as Lenin presumed.

María and Rosa were typical of other women of their age group in their reproductive behavior. The strong pro-natalism of the period, fostered both by the high economic value of children and by the lack of effective birth control, meant that women were pregnant almost every third year until they reached their forties.[4] Rosa gave birth to thirteen children, María to eight. Each lost approximately half her children, but their daughters and daughters-in-law were more fortunate, for infant and child mortality decreased significantly over the twentieth century.

According to 1940 census data (Peru 1940, vol. 2, table 8), women born in the department of Cajamarca before 1890 and involved in unions during the first four decades of the century averaged 6.9 live births by the age of fifty. Those born during the following thirty years and involved in unions after the 1940s (Rosa and María's cohort) gave birth to an average of 7.6 children (Peru 1972a, vol. [6], table 11). Women fifty or more years of age in 1940 had lost 45 percent of the children to whom they had given birth, whereas the next generation, those fifty or more years of age by 1972, lost 37 percent. The decrease in infant and child mortality partly explains how relatively strong

3. Data on mean household size were derived from census statistics (Peru 1940, vol. 2, table 3; Peru 1961c, vol. 2, table 3.6; Peru 1972a, vol. [6], table 1).

4. The women interviewed were aware of natural forms of birth control, primarily abstinence or, in some cases, herbal mixtures prepared by midwives. These were judged not to be very effective.

population growth was maintained in Cajamarca, despite high rates of highland-coastal migration.

Although comparable census figures are not available for the province of Cajamarca, data from the 1976 Peasant Family Survey suggest that both fertility (9.6 live births) and child mortality (.497) were higher in the province than in the department. The higher fertility could reflect either the stronger influence of the hacienda system in the province, with its pro-natal bias, or larger family size as an adaptive strategy against increasing poverty within the independent communities. It could also reflect more accurate reporting in the survey than in the census.[5]

The survey data also provide strong evidence of the way material conditions influence household reproductive behavior. Women more than fifty years old from near-landless and smallholder households reported a child mortality rate of .564, whereas for those from middle and rich peasant households the rate was .280. This suggests a strong association between a household's access to resources and its ability to keep its children alive, and it reflects the differences in household income and wealth analyzed in the previous chapter. It also suggests that child mortality may, indeed, have been higher in the province of Cajamarca than in the department because of more acute land shortage and the greater prevalence of smallholdings.

The twentieth century was marked by an increase in fertility, primarily as a result of earlier age at first birth (Peru 1972a, vol. [6], table 11). In the early decades of the century, the majority of women in the department gave birth to their first child when they were twenty to twenty-four years old. The majority of women born after 1928 had their first child when they were between fifteen and nineteen years of age. This trend is also supported by survey data for the province. Whereas women born before 1927 had their first living child at the mean age of twenty-three, those born and forming unions in subsequent decades did so by the mean age of eighteen (1976 Peasant Family Survey).

This age difference could reflect younger age at marriage, an increase in premarital sexual relationships (especially those resulting in pregnancy), and the overall decrease in infant and child mortality. The size of the gap suggests that changes in the broader political economy of the period, such as the dissolution of the hacienda system, contributed to the first two factors through decreased patriarchal control over children.[6] Within the independent

5. The small sample of women fifty years of age and older (a total of thirty-three) in the 1976 Peasant Family Survey is, of course, a problem. The sampling qualities of this survey do give these results credibility, however (see Appendix IV). I consider the survey data on demographic characteristics more likely to be accurate than the data collected through the census, because the census questionnaire was directed primarily to heads of households, whereas the survey was directed at the principal adult woman of the household. Women are more likely to recall the exact number of pregnancies, live births, and infant deaths than are men.

6. Recall from the discussion in Chapter 3 that women on the haciendas tended to marry later (at a mean age of 24.2 years) than women within the independent peasant communities (mean age of 22.6 years).

communities, the alternative of temporary migration for wage labor continued to favor earlier age at marriage by giving young men a potential independent source of income.

Evidence of the trend toward decreasing age for marriage and first birth, as well as of the trend toward smaller household size, is offered by survey data on the age at which children left home. In 1976 two-thirds of the 229 children over eighteen years of age born to the sixty-eight households with children in this age group had left home. The mean age at which children left home was 17.9 years. Important differences were apparent among land-size strata, with children from near-landless household leaving at the earliest age, 16.6 years; children from smallholder households, at 17.7 years; and children from middle and rich peasant households, at 18.7 (Deere 1978, table 71). Overall, girls left home at an earlier age (17.7 years) than boys (18.2).

The differing mean ages at which children left home reflect different rates of retention and expulsion of working-age children and, thus, heterogeneous generational reproductive strategies among peasant strata.[7] These heterogeneous strategies are also apparent in the data on household composition and family structure. The majority of these Cajamarcan peasant households, 57 percent, were nuclear (Deere 1978, table 68). Middle and rich peasant households, however, were more likely to be composed of extended families (53 percent), compared with only 33 percent of near-landless households. Moreover, extended households composed of parents and married children with their offspring were predominantly found among middle and rich peasant households.[8] This pattern provides another crucial factor explaining the larger family size among the upper peasant strata. Together with the data on infant and child mortality and the age at which children left home, the evidence suggests that Lenin's hypothesis about the positive relationship between farm size and household size is supported by the Cajamarcan case: the process of social differentiation of the peasantry is an important determinant of household size.

7. The economic value of children is discussed in Deere (1978, chap. 8).

8. Family structure is also related to the peasant family life cycle. In cases where the head of the household was between the ages of eighteen and thirty-four, 41 percent of the families were living in extended households in which one or both parents were retired or which consisted of a nuclear family and unmarried adult siblings (Deere 1978, table 69). For the cohort group aged thirty-five to forty-four, the nuclear family form was predominant, found in 73 percent of all households. As would be expected, the number of extended households increased significantly among the group aged forty-five to fifty-four, with 30 percent of the households including married children and their offspring or grandchildren. For heads of household aged fifty-five or older, extended households were the norm, with children (and usually the children's offspring) living with parents who were close to retirement age.

HOUSEHOLD DISSOLUTION AND RECONSTITUTION

Doña María's household is unusual in that all four of her daughters remained in Pariamarca after their marriages. Doña Rosa's household followed the more common pattern: three of her six sons migrated to the northern Peruvian coast. The two households show contrasting patterns of household dissolution, reconstitution, and generational reproduction strategies, both because of their differing economic position and because of the differing gender of their children.

The Sangay-Fernández Household of La Succha

Doña Rosa had wanted all her sons to learn a trade so that they would not be dependent on farming. Teodoro, the eldest, finished the two years of schooling available in La Succha and then studied carpentry, but the trade did not suit him, and he gave it up before finishing his apprenticeship. Rosa also encouraged her second son, Lucho, to study carpentry, but he too gave it up and left for Cajamarca at the age of eighteen to become a chauffeur's assistant. In the 1950s, roads were opening up throughout the province; Lucho saw clearly the potential for transportation services and dreamed of purchasing his own truck.

Teodoro, in contrast, chose to be a farmer. He married a woman from La Succha when he was twenty, and, soon after their first child was born, he built a house of their own in the family compound. In the first years of his marriage, Teodoro continued working with his father, but when his family began to grow, it was necessary for his household to become economically independent. If Teodoro's parents had owned more land, he might have persuaded them to cede him part of his inheritance at this time, at least in a sharecropping arrangement, but for the vast majority of smallholders in the province this was not possible until the parents retired from field work or died. Teodoro began his attempt to consolidate himself as an independent petty producer by share-cropping the lands of several of his wife's relatives who had migrated to the coast. Through sharecropping and his wife's skill at animal raising, they were able to save enough to begin buying these land parcels. By the mid-1970s, they owned 3.6 hectares, which included a half hectare his wife had inherited.

Rosa's third son, Silvestre, was the first to finish primary school. Julio had expected Silvestre to stay on the farm and work with him, for by now he had lost the labor of his two eldest sons. But from the time he was a child, Silvestre had dreamed of migrating to the coast. In 1960, at the age of twenty, when he heard of the fishing boom in Chimbote, he went to the coast, disregarding his father's wishes.

After Silvestre left, Rodolfo, fourteen at the time, replaced him at his father's side in the fields. Rodolfo did not study a trade, because his father needed him for the agricultural work; 5 to 6 hectares under cultivation required the full-time attention of two adult men. But five years later, he also migrated to the coast against his father's wishes. Rodolfo went to Casa Grande, the traditional migration destination of peasants from Jesús. Through family connections, he was fortunate enough to secure a job in the sugar mill, although in 1965 few new permanent workers were being hired by most coastal sugar plantations.

With only two sons at home and Julio advancing in years, the family began to sharecrop less land, always aiming to farm just enough to meet its grain requirements and to produce a surplus for Rosa to sell in the Jesús market in order to purchase other necessities. As Julio tells it, with four sons gone, he had lost all hope of becoming a prosperous agriculturalist. Rosa continued to insist that her sons learn a trade, and the two youngest boys studied tailoring in Jesús when they completed primary school. When Aladino finished his apprenticeship, he immediately migrated to Casa Grande to join his brother and easily found work as a tailor. This time, Julio did not even complain about losing another son.

When I met the Sangay-Fernández family in 1976, only Victor was living at home. He had become the primary worker in the family economy, for Julio, in his seventies, was too old to work the fields. Julio was also going blind—he had had a cataract operation several years before, but it seemed not to have helped much. His only economic activity of significance was to water and feed the work animals twice daily.

Julio had designated the division of the family lands among his six sons several years before, although the lands would continue to be worked by Victor as long as Rosa and Julio remained alive and he cared for them. An agrarian reform official had urged Julio to divide the lands and draw up a will so as to avoid problems among the sons after his death. By tradition, all children usually inherit equal-sized plots, but if the actual partition is not agreed to before the parents' death, considerable conflict can ensue. (Recall the Aguilar family in Pariamarca.)

In the case of the Sangay-Fernández properties, the inheritances were not quite equal, because one son, Silvestre, had financed the purchase of the property on the Hacienda Miche. He thus inherited this property, and the remaining land, 0.5 hectares, was divided among the other five sons. Following tradition, Victor was also willed the family home, for, as the youngest son and the only one remaining at home, he was obligated to look after his parents in old age.

Quite commonly in Jesús, the youngest child (or the one remaining with the parents) subsequently purchases the inheritance shares of siblings who have migrated from the region, thus maintaining the farm intact. But it seemed unlikely that Victor would do so. He was eager to join his brothers on the coast. He liked farming, but he did not want to spend his whole life in La Succha. He studied tailoring to acquire a trade, in the hope that some day he would be free to migrate to the coast. Victor knew that it would break Rosa's heart if he abandoned tradition, as other young people were increasingly doing, by migrating before her death.

Victor worked approximately 3.5 hectares of land, including the family lands and another half hectare that he obtained from neighbors to sharecrop in potatoes. The income Victor earned through these sharecropping arrangements was considered his own. The product from the family plots was under Rosa's control and constituted the household fund. Most of the family land was planted in corn and barley. Only a small portion of their land had access to irrigation, and those parcels were planted in potatoes and alfalfa. With 3.5 hectares, Victor was quite busy and usually had to hire wage workers for planting and weeding. Rosa always cooked the midday meal for the workers.

Rosa's economic activities still included animal care, although in the mid-1970s she had only four sheep, two pigs, four chickens, and a half dozen cuyes. She continued to trade in the market of Jesús twice a week, usually taking an arroba of corn or an almud of barley to sell in small quantities. After she disposed of what she had taken to sell that day, she would do her own shopping, buying oil, salt, sugar, noodles, and whatever condiments or vegetables she needed for the week ahead.

The highlight of Rosa's week was meeting the bus that served the town of Jesús directly from Casa Grande; she could then pick up mail and packages from her sons. Two of the sons on the coast maintained very close ties with the family. Silvestre wrote almost every week and sent gifts once a month or so, consisting of medicines, clothing, or processed foodstuffs from the coast. Rodolfo also wrote frequently and sent Rosa S/. 500 or so monthly to buy necessities. This was Rosa's main source of discretionary cash income. The third son residing on the coast neither wrote nor sent gifts, and Rosa considered him an ingrate. Rosa herself would send a basketful of potatoes or corn to Silvestre one week, and to Rodolfo the next. The size of the basket varied over the course of the year, but it is doubtful that its value approximated that of the remittances sent by her sons. Still, Rosa was very proud that she had never failed to send her sons something on this biweekly basis. For her, such exchanges symbolized the meaning of family.

The net material transfer from the coast to the highlands explains Julio and Rosa's access to health care (Julio's cataract operation, for example) and the fact that their diet was more diversified than that of other households in the region. Most luxury items found in the countryside—radios, petromax lanterns, bicycles—are the result of gifts from children who have migrated. What was unusual in Julio and Rosa's case was that the two sons continued to send sizable remittances even after they married. Usually, children who migrate taper off their contributions once they have their own families. But both Silvestre and Rodolfo had done quite well as proletarians, both with permanent jobs, Silvestre in a fish-processing factory and Rodolfo in the sugar mill of Casa Grande. With the conversion of Casa Grande into a CAP through the agrarian reform, Rodolfo was indeed among the elite of Peruvian proletarians. Moreover, by the mid-1970s, he had left his wife and three children, a fact that also explains why he continued to transfer income to his parents.

Rosa had close relations, too, with the families of the two sons who lived in La Succha, especially with Teodoro's family, who lived next door. In 1976 Teodoro and his wife had seven children living at home, ranging from three to twenty-two years of age, and the children often helped Rosa with household tasks and animal care. Each granddaughter had taken a turn living with Rosa and Julio and thus provided Rosa with even more help. Rosa greatly appreciated this help and resented her daughter-in-law's reluctance to give up her daughters.

Rosa considered her other daughter-in-law, Lucho's wife, to be more generous, for she often sent Rosa plates of food she had cooked, and, when Rosa took ill, she looked after her. Nonetheless, Rosa had few good things to say about either of her sons' wives and complained continually about them. She greatly lamented the fact that none of her daughters had survived early childhood, for she thought that the relationship with a daughter-in-law could never be the same as with one's own daughter. And although granddaughters could help out with the work, their loyalties were to their own mothers.

The women of the three families nevertheless helped one another out in a number of important ways. If Rosa could not take her sheep out to pasture, either her daughters-in-law or granddaughters would do so. Whenever one household employed agricultural field workers, the women collaborated in cooking the midday meal. The men in the three families also exchanged labor for agricultural tasks. In fact, in this village, where almost all work was done for wages, reciprocal labor exchanges occurred only between immediate kin.

The families also shared the pigs they raised, enabling all three families to consume meat during much of the year. In a typical year, each family butchered two large pigs; thus, among the three households, they were butchering a pig every other month. Because the bulk of the meat is dried, this rotational exchange provided the households with lard and animal protein throughout the year.

The life cycle of the Sangay-Fernández household illustrates how its gradual decomposition did not imply a dissolution of familial economic relations. The loss of the sons' labor perhaps prevented Julio from consolidating his position as a middle peasant petty producer. Although he had wanted his sons to remain as part of the unit of production, he really did not attempt to impose his will, and each son (except the youngest) generally followed his own aspirations. Rosa, however, very much prepared the way for her sons to be upwardly mobile, insisting that they go to school and that they learn a trade.[9] The changing class position of the sons who migrated assured Rosa and Julio of a higher standard of living in old age than they would have had if the sons had remained in the sierra as petty producers.

The Aguilar-Rumay Household of Pariamarca

In 1955, María's oldest daughter, Francisca, left home at the age of twenty, forming a union with a Pariamarcan man. He was also from a smallholder family and stood to inherit only a tiny land parcel, less than 0.1 hectare. Both an artisan (a basket maker) and a wage worker, Francisca's husband migrated to the coast almost every year to work in the cane and rice harvests. Francisca followed her mother's trade, usually purchasing agricultural products in the village for resale on the sidewalks of Cajamarca. In addition, Francisca and her husband continually attempted to sharecrop lands in order to grow some of their basic foodstuffs. But sharecropping was a more difficult proposition in Pariamarca than in La Succha, because permanent migration from the first village was much less common.

María's second daughter, Martina, quickly assumed Francisca's role in the family, caring for the younger children and sharing the domestic work with her mother and the agricultural work with her father. But she became involved with a man seven years her senior, and María insisted that they formalize their relationship, because he had already had a daughter by another woman. Martina thus was married in the church at the age of nineteen. Her husband owned 4 hectares of land that he had purchased from the San Antonio Hacienda, and he set Martina up with her own store on the plaza of Pariamarca. But, according to María, Martina did not do well, for her husband beat her and chased other women (*"muy mujeriego"*).

In the same year that Martina married, thirteen-year-old Simona ran away from home. She saw a notice in the streets of Cajamarca recruiting maids for the capital and signed up to go to Lima without consulting her parents.[10] She simply did not return home from selling in the market one day. Her parents considered reporting her disappearance to the police, but finally a cousin in whom Simona had confided told them that the recruiters had paid her way and placed her with a family in Lima. María now says that she "hardly enjoyed Simona's labor." Simona returned after two years—she never adapted to living in Lima—and became a maid in Cajamarca.

The youngest daughter, Erlinda, left home at the age of fifteen to take a job as a maid in Cajamarca. Young girls were often placed as domestic servants in the city for the express purpose of earning cash income for their parents, but

9. In general, I found that women strongly favored education for their children, in contrast to the pattern reported by Stein (1980, 674) in the Callejón de Huaylas.

10. The phenomenon of coastal recruiters for domestic servants is also mentioned by Chambeu (1975f). This is a topic worthy of further research.

María had not wanted Erlinda to leave home. Neither did she expect remittances, for there were no other children left at home to raise, and it was sufficient that Simona and Erlinda earn their own way. But María missed their company, and now she had to attend to her husband and the domestic work by herself, as well as share in the agricultural work.

From time to time, a grandchild would come to live with María and Manuel. Erlinda had become pregnant by a high school student shortly after she moved to Cajamarca, and she now had a daughter. She was fortunate that she had been able to keep her job as a maid, for pregnant young maids are commonly dismissed at once. María agreed to raise this baby, recalling how she had been raised by her own grandmother. Five years later, Erlinda married a man from Pariamarca and returned to the village, reclaiming her daughter.

The darkest period of María's life came in 1974 when her husband abandoned her. She was then sixty-two and could not walk, having twisted her leg in a bad fall. Her husband, Manuel, claimed she was no longer useful, but María knew that Manuel had another woman. She lamented the fact that he had abandoned her for another woman in old age. But equally painful was the fact that after working to maintain the family for so many years, she was out in the cold without a blanket to her name.

María now considered it a grave mistake that she had married her husband in the church and not through the state, for she had been told that she had no legal claim to a share of their joint property.[11] During all the years that María and Manuel were together, they had purchased only a tiny strip of land, but they had constructed a solid house after their first one burned down. Moreover, the income María had earned from trading had gone into the purchase of the farm animals and agricultural equipment. Her husband even kept the household goods. Her greatest worry, however, was that Manuel would disinherit their four daughters, after all the money and trouble she had put into fighting the court case over his family inheritance. It was also rumored that he was planning to sell this inheritance.

The only property María had in her name was her own inheritance. She had already divided it up among her four daughters, and each sharecropped about 0.1 hectare with María. At first, she went to live with Francisca, but she was uncomfortable there. She spent the next several years living with one daughter after another. When I first met her in 1976, she was living with Simona and her partner, José, and Simona's two children. They all lived in a tiny one-room adobe chosita with only a straw roof.

11. For a woman to claim economic support from an estranged husband, she must be legally married; however, marriage by the church should have provided doña María the right to a share of their joint property. Today, civil marriage is a prerequisite for a church marriage. One of the main factors discouraging legal marriages is that a number of bureaucratic steps are required, such as obtaining a birth certificate and a police certification of residence and good conduct, with each step subject to a fee.

Simona and José had met in Cajamarca in 1967 while Simona was working as a maid. When Simona got pregnant by him, they decided to return to Pariamarca. José also had been raised in Pariamarca, by his single mother. His father had never recognized him as a son, and because his mother was landless, José was too. He was an agricultural wage worker by the age of fourteen, first migrating to the coastal sugar plantations in 1960.

José usually migrated to the sugar plantations in November and then to the rice harvests in the selva province of Jaén in May. He wanted to migrate to the selva permanently, but Simona refused to leave Pariamarca. She had tried it once; in 1972 they had spent eleven months in Jaén, but she could not adapt to the tropical climate. Simona also found it difficult to pursue her trading activities there, and she hated being totally dependent on José.

In 1976 José and Simona had approximately 1.5 hectares of land in usufruct. They sharecropped nearly 1 hectare with Simona's paternal uncle, a 0.5-hectare plot with a neighbor, and a small strip with Simona's sister's household. When they had nothing else to do, they made cane baskets. Simona also raised chickens, turkeys, several pigs, and about half a dozen sheep. The sheep were raised for their wool and seemed to be a lot more trouble than they were worth. Having someone stay home to watch the house and pasture the sheep created a constant problem. These tasks most often fell to María while she was living with them. María also did most of the domestic work, for Simona was often gone from home, pursuing her trading activities. Sometimes, however, María went to market with Simona, and José would stay home. He is one of the few men I ever observed cooking. José said he was used to it, having migrated on his own so many times.

With four daughters living in the community, María was assured of always having a place to live and someone to care for her, but in old age she was extremely poor. She no longer could earn much income on her own, and for most of her daughters, household reproduction was quite precarious. They could feed María, but it was difficult for them to attend to her other needs, such as medicines and clothing. Martina, the one daughter who had surpassed her parental household in economic status, was less disposed to help her than the other daughters were. María attributed this to Martina's alcoholism, a result of her husband's physical abuse.

María blamed the poverty of her old age on the fact that she had no sons to look after her. None of her male children had lived past infancy. According to her, "a male son at least protects one; at least he will give one part of his wage, something to protect us. With a daughter, it is different. It is not their fault— my daughters are good—but a son can find work, even if in the selva, and he earns more than a woman. Look in what disgrace you find me."

The majority of respondents in the 1976 Peasant Family Survey agreed with María. Both sons and daughters were important for security in old age, but males were more valuable than females. Sons were more likely than daughters

TABLE 44. Principal Activity of Children Who Have Left Home, by Sex and Land-Size Strata, Province of Cajamarca, 1976

Land-Size Strata	Farm Work	Housework	Artisan Production	School	Military Service	Wage Work	Total
Near-landless households							
Sons	1 (25%)	—	1 (25%)	2 (50%)	—	—	4 (100%)
Daughters	—	4 (80%)	—	—	—	1 (20%)	5 (100%)
Smallholder households							
Sons	15 (28%)	—	8 (15%)	2 (4%)	2 (4%)	26 (49%)	53 (100%)
Daughters	2 (5%)	26 (67%)	4 (10%)	2 (5%)	—	5 (13%)	34 (100%)
Middle and rich peasant households							
Sons	9 (41%)	—	1 (5%)	—	—	12 (54%)	22 (100%)
Daughters	—	18 (74%)	—	3 (13%)	—	3 (13%)	24 (100%)
Total							
Sons	25 (32%)	—	10 (13%)	4 (5%)	2 (2%)	38 (48%)	79 (100%)
Daughters	2 (3%)	48 (71%)	4 (6%)	5 (7%)	—	9 (13%)	68 (100%)

SOURCE: 1976 Peasant Family Survey.

to send cash remittances, because they were able to earn so much more. Daughters, however, were valued for the greater care they showed for parents who were ill or indisposed. As Table 44 shows, the main alternative for Cajamarcan men who left home was to join the ranks of the proletariat. Among the children leaving Cajamarcan households, men were much more likely than women to be wage workers. Moreover, men's wages significantly exceeded those of women. The majority of respondents considered their married daughters housewives, whether they were married to wage workers or were "farm wives" (petty producers as well). In either case, however, the smaller return from female income-generating activities, combined with women's greater tendency to pool any income they earned on their own for their children's benefit, mitigated the remittances that married daughters might make to their parental home.

Because they were more likely to inherit land, children of middle and rich peasant households were also more likely to become agriculturalists than were sons of poorer peasants. But the general case was for the sons of middle peasants to become smallholders and for the sons of smallholders to join the near-landless. Overall, the class position of the departing sons of middle and rich peasants was not much different from that of the majority of the rural poor; increasingly, the main option was to join the ranks of the landless proletariat.

THE HOUSEHOLD AS A UNIT OF REPRODUCTION

The growing impoverishment of the peasantry and the changes accompanying the increased integration of the peasantry into the labor market have profoundly affected household relations and the stability of peasant households as units of production and reproduction. Nonetheless, as the life histories of María and Rosa show, instability was already a characteristic of many peasant households in the independent communities before this region was substantially proletarianized. To what extent, then, can the contingency of the household as the site of reproduction of labor power be attributed to the changing composition of the class relations in which household members participate?

Here it is useful to return to the factors that differentiated household relations on the haciendas and within peasant communities in the early decades of the century. Recall that feudal class relations provided the material basis for patriarchal households by circumscribing women's access to land. The livelihood of a woman was guaranteed only through her kinship relationship to a man, whether father, husband, or son. Feudal class relations and the subordination of women supported relatively stable household units.

In the independent communities, in contrast, bilateral inheritance provided women with greater economic security and the material basis for contemplating divorce in case of male abuse. Although this security did not eliminate their dependence on men, given the complementarity in the gender division of labor and the few alternatives women had for generating income outside the farm, it did provide women with greater bargaining power within the household.

Growing land shortage within the independent peasant communities as the century progressed began to undermine the economic rationality of peasant households. The inability to generate simple reproduction on the basis of petty production, in the context of the growing monetization of the rural economy, compelled parents to enter multiple class relations to generate household income and reduced the economic value of children on the farm. As household income sources became increasingly individualized, cultural practices that guaranteed income pooling and shared consumption were also called into question.

As the pattern of temporary male migration became generalized in the 1940s and 1950s, even greater stresses were placed on households as units of production and reproduction. Peasants and observers alike noted the de-stabilizing effect of the lengthy absences of male heads of households (Torres and Hillenbrand 1978). The absence of men from the homestead increased the workload of women, who were now responsible not only for myriad tasks involved in daily maintenance of the children and animals but also for the care of the fields. The flexibility required in the gender division of labor also had its repercussions on the familial authority structure, with women taking on an even greater role in household decision making and in community affairs. Moreover, temporary migration sometimes led men to form a second family on the coast, making the migration permanent and contributing to female and child abandonment in the sierra. Not infrequently, women took advantage of their husbands' absence to develop extramarital relationships themselves.

In the 1972 census, 25 percent of the households in the province and 24 percent of those in the department were reported as headed by women (Peru 1972a, vol. [6], table 43). Of the female heads of household in the province, 28 percent were widows, 23 percent were single, and only 4 percent were reported as separated or divorced, whereas 43 percent were reported as married or involved in a consensual union. (No information was available for the remaining 2 percent.) One can only speculate as to whether the male partners of the married women and those in unions were temporarily away at the time of the census or whether these women were in fact the persons considered by others to be the head of the household, as required by the census criteria (Peru 1972a, xiii). I found it highly unusual for a woman to be considered the head of household if an adult male was present, unless the woman owned land and the male was landless. It is likely that the data simply capture the magnitude of temporary migration during the census month of June.

If we exclude those female heads of household who appear to have a male partner, then the percentage of households headed by a woman drops to 14 percent of the households in the province (Peru 1972a, vol. [6], table 43). The 1976 Peasant Family Survey figure for the same group was 16 percent.

The survey revealed that half of the female heads of household were single mothers either abandoned by or separated from the fathers of their children. If these households, 8 percent of the total surveyed, are added to those where a single mother resided with her parents, the incidence of instability of male-female unions is on the order of 13 percent (1976 Peasant Family Survey).

Torres and Hillenbrand (1978, 13) point out that the growing social inequality in the positions of men and women also contributed to tensions in gender relations and the breakup of households. Women have lagged considerably behind men with respect to formal schooling and literacy rates, and greater male mobility—to the city of Cajamarca, the coast, and the selva—has exposed men to new cultural patterns and tastes. Torres and Hillenbrand cite male rejection of the traditional ways of peasant women as an important reason for female abandonment. The cultural differences between men and women are most apparent in standards of dress. A peasant man visiting the city of Cajamarca on market day or filing some legal claim is dressed very much like his coastal counterparts, the only important exception being his straw hat and perhaps his rubber sandals (*yanquis*). In contrast, the dress of the peasant woman is still the *pollera* (long, full skirt) and shawl of her ancestors; her clothes are more likely to have been made at home from artisan-produced cloth. She is also less likely to wear shoes of any type.

Standards of dress have also affected standards of female beauty. Whereas among older men a beautiful woman was typically described as one who was robust and strong, who could stand the strains of bearing many children and working in the fields, for young men of today, beauty is defined in terms of cosmetic, not functional, characteristics and increasingly in terms of modern dress and hygienic standards.

Census data show, nevertheless, that since the 1940s a higher proportion of women are entering into unions (whether formal or informal) than in previous decades.[12] The reduction in the percentage of single women is likely related to the more favorable male-female ratio during this period, produced by the increasing rate of permanent female migration from the province.[13] Census data obscure serial monogamy, however, as well as polygamy, and do not provide a good indicator of household stability.

12. See the census statistics of several decades (Peru 1940, vol. 2, table 7; Peru 1961a, vol. 6, table 12; Peru 1972a, vol. [6], table 4).

13. Although data on migration rates by gender for this period are unavailable, the data for 1940 are revealing. Of the 25,795 Cajamarca-born migrants counted in the department of La Libertad, 45 percent were women, a statistic indicating a masculinity ratio (number of men to number of women) of 124.2 among migrants. Of the 18,062 Cajamarcan migrants to the department of Lambayeque, 39 percent were women, with a corresponding masculinity ratio of 154.2. The masculinity ratio for the department of Cajamarca in 1940 was 91.6 and that for the province was 86.8 (derived from Peru 1940, vol. 2, table 5 and vol. 3, table 21). By 1981 the departmental ratio had increased to 98.5 and the ratio for the province to 93.7 (Peru 1981, vol. [16], table 1).

My interviews indicate that it was not unusual for women and men to have had at least two partners over their lifetimes, whether in trial marriages when young (the case of María) or as a result of abandonment by a spouse (the cases of both Julio and María). Moreover, my interviews with the dairy maids on the capitalist farms and cooperatives suggest that multiple unions are increasingly common particularly among the young.

Ana, for example, had already had three partners by the age of twenty-three.[14] Her parents had made her marry her first lover legally, and she has been in the process of trying to obtain a divorce ever since. She had been only sixteen when she became involved with this man, a wage worker on a dairy farm. Because he was ten years older than she was, her parents insisted that he marry her, threatening to go to the legal authorities if he refused, for she was legally a minor.[15] Upon their marriage, they went to live with his family, and, according to Ana, both he and his parents treated her badly. She became pregnant but, as a result of his beatings, lost this baby in childbirth. As she tells it, he finally sent her home one day to her parents, for "he has plenty of women."

Her second husband was not much more committed to forming a permanent relationship ("*resultó bandolero también*"). Again, they lived with his parents, who treated her no better than her first in-laws had. They kept insisting that she bring her inheritance of four sheep and wanted her to file a lawsuit against her parents to obtain the sheep. Her parents were doubtful that this union would last and had not given her an inheritance, but Ana refused to file a suit. Her husband then abandoned her when she was seven months pregnant, and she returned to her parents' homestead. Her mother is now raising this son. Ana's third relationship lasted somewhat longer, three years, but this man abandoned her for another woman. As Ana summarizes her life, "Better death than youth . . . others who are prettier get involved with my men; me they disdain. I've always lived fighting with my husbands; others, after they are beaten, stay with the man."

Although Ana lamented her situation and saw herself being always abandoned by men, it was also apparent in the interviews that she was a very independent young woman. As a milkmaid, she had her own source of income and never contemplated giving up her employment on the dairy farm when she

14. Ana, whose name has been changed to protect her privacy, was a member of one of the CAPs in the Cajamarca Valley. I interviewed her repeatedly throughout 1976 and compiled life histories of her parents.

15. Torres and Hillenbrand (1978, 7) note the great number of lawsuits resulting from such amorous relationships. If the girl's parents find out about the relationship, and the man or his family is then opposed to a marriage, the parents of the girl can denounce him before a judge or the civil guard. The judge usually tries to arrange a marriage, but if he is not successful he can order the man incarcerated for as long as six years. Torres and Hillenbrand also report important differences in the frequency of this practice, depending on the province: it seems to be more common in the more Hispanic province of Celendín than it is in the province of Cajamarca.

joined in these various unions. Moreover, one of the main tensions in her relationships with men was that she always refused to give them control over her wages. In addition, as she noted, she also refused to accept being a battered wife. Thus, although male absence and female abandonment have challenged the viability of stable household units as the principal site of labor power reproduction, the changing position of women as a result of new and changed economic options must also be taken into account as a challenge to the stability of unions based on the premise of male dominance.

Over the course of the century, numerous other cultural practices have changed, undermining the reproduction possibilities of peasant households. For example, although more than half of the extended households in the province were formed by parents with adult children and grandchildren living at home—conforming to the cultural norm of a married child working the land with the parents or a widowed mother and awaiting the parents' full retirement and actual land inheritance—19 percent of the extended households consisted of parents and an unmarried adult child (the majority women) who herself had children but no spouse. Another quarter of the extended households were made up of aging parents accompanied by a grandchild ranging in age from three to twelve (1976 Peasant Family Survey). These last two forms of household structure predominated among poor peasant households and were a response to rural poverty and the social stresses experienced by peasant households.

This pattern is also apparent in the incidence of households where all of the children have migrated from the homestead. This household form, 8 percent of the nuclear households, was limited to the near-landless and smallholder strata, a fact suggesting the importance of the decline in access to resources in changing household composition and family structure. In these households, no heir seemed interested in taking over the meager landholding; the traditional mechanism of guaranteeing security in old age for parents—that is, that the youngest child remain at home—had simply been foregone or ignored. In some cases, a grandchild had been sent to live with the parents, but parents considered this only a temporary and unsatisfactory solution to the problem of their old-age security. The parents tended to stay on the land as long as they were able to work, but after one parent was widowed, it was often a point of contention among siblings who would take responsibility for the remaining parent. That parent's destination—migrating to the city of Cajamarca or the coast or remaining in the area—usually then determined whether the family lands were sharecropped out or sold.

One of the saddest sights on the streets of Cajamarca is the elderly woman who has no place to live and no means of subsistence, except for the plates of food she may be given as charity or the small tips she collects on Saturdays, traditionally "beggars' day" in the city. Most such women are landless and consider themselves to have been abandoned by both husbands and children who now live on the coast; some never had male children and consider this the source of their misfortune. But, as we have seen in the case studies of families in La Succha and Pariamarca, the more general case is for family bonds to persist and for the economic ties between parents and children to provide for the old-age security of parents, albeit sometimes through new practices (remittances based on wage income) rather than constituting extended farm households.

CONCLUSION

This chapter has illustrated how household and class relations interact to maintain peasant households as units of production and reproduction of labor power over time. The class relations in which household members participate and the outcomes of household economic activity condition the viability of petty production, as well as the stability of household forms. But class relations are also mediated by household and gender relations and by extra-household relations among kin. Peasant households may disintegrate as units of production on *either* account: the inability of household members to generate simple reproduction on the basis of multiple class relations; or gender and generational tensions—that is, challenges to traditional cultural norms regarding the rights and obligations between men and women and between children and their parents.

As I have stressed throughout this analysis, the reproduction of household and class relations must be viewed as a contingency, a process continually in flux, with multiple sources of tension and sites of struggle. At a minimum, household and class relations vary over the family life cycle, producing changes in household economic activity in response to internal variation in demographic variables. Household and class relations also vary in response to changes in the broader political economy in which rural households are circumscribed.

The external political, economic and cultural milieu and its effect within the household influence not only the class relations in which different family members engage but also the prospects of the next generation. There is little question that the long-term tendency among the Cajamarcan peasantry is toward participation in capitalist class relations as proletarians. But this is not a linear process, precisely because of the fluidity in the class relations in which peasant household members participate, both over the life cycle and at a moment in time. In the Cajamarcan case, the trend toward proletarianization has perhaps been accelerated, however, by the instability of gender and household relations, itself a product of land shortage, migration, female economic autonomy, and other social trends.

Participating in multiple class relations has nonetheless allowed a portion of the peasantry to secure the conditions of existence of petty production and to maintain their households as units of production and reproduction. No doubt this process has also been facilitated by the dissolution of other household units and the growing tendency toward permanent migration from the highlands, which has released land, a condition of existence for the reproduction and expansion of petty production among the remaining rural households.

TWELVE

Epilogue:
The Province in the 1980s

The reinauguration of Fernando Belaunde Terry as president of Peru in July 1980 brought to a close the period of military government that had begun with his overthrow in October 1968. By 1980 the Revolutionary Military Government had been discredited, and with it the far-reaching reformist attempt to transform Peruvian society. Caballero (1981, 24) sums up the balance sheet on the Peruvian experiment as follows: "There is no doubt in Peruvian opinion of all shades that the 'revolution' was a fiasco. But there is a big split between those who think that the experiment failed because it was a revolution and those who think it failed because it was not."

The Revolutionary Military Government's program had been ambitious. Agrarian reform had been only one component of its attempted restructuring of the model of accumulation.[1] The military had aimed to pursue a nationalist development path that was neither capitalist nor socialist but, rather, populist and focused on redistribution. In order to achieve the twin objectives of accelerated import-substitution industrialization and the enhanced export capacity to sustain it, the military government ended up consolidating state capitalism as the motor force of development.[2]

1. General Velasco's program also included industrial reform. The state took responsibility for basic industry and (as a result of the nationalization of foreign investments) public utilities, communications, and the petroleum and fishing sectors. A scheme for worker participation in enterprise decision making and profits (called "industrial communities") was also implemented in both the public and the private sectors in industry, mining, and fishing. The commercial and financial sectors were reorganized, with the state taking responsibility for the banking sector and all export marketing. Social policies included educational reform and reconstitution of Peruvian urban and rural organizations along corporatist lines. See Caballero (1981b) for a good summary, as well as Thorp and Bertram (1978, chap. 15) and FitzGerald (1979).

2. Most authors argue that state capitalism was not the military's original intent. Thorp and Bertram (1978, 308) consider the military government's primary aim to have been the development of a mixed economy with a strong private sector. When domestic capital failed to respond, however, the state took over the function of investment.

Although growth rates had been quite favorable (an average 5 percent) and inflation moderate (less than 10 percent) during the first phase of the military experiment under General Velasco, a crisis occurred in 1975 when the international economy went into recession.[3] In one year, exports dropped by 14 percent while imports increased by 70 percent. The measures designed to deal with this crisis in the external sector during the experiment's second phase, under General Morales Bermúdez, brought on a recession combined with inflation. Between 1974 and 1978, the gross domestic product per capita fell by 12 percent, and prices increased by 221 percent. Real wages plummeted, and the Peruvian sol was devalued 446 percent in three years. Moreover, the policies intended to achieve economic independence had just the opposite effect (Caballero 1981b, 20). Partly because the bourgeoisie failed to respond positively, and partly because other measures to tap the social surplus (such as tax reform) were not implemented, external borrowing became the main source of public investment. The external debt increased fivefold over the decade. In 1978 the military regime was forced to call on the International Monetary Fund, and, under the subsequent stabilization agreement, many populist policies such as price subsidies were dismantled. At this point, the military announced its intention to retire from the political scene, and elections were held in 1980.

The principal achievement of the Revolutionary Military Government was the agrarian reform. In one decade, the hacienda system was eliminated, and with it the power of the sierra landlord class. But, to quote Caballero, the agrarian reform "did much and accomplished little" (1981b, 46). It failed to solve the agrarian problem or bring social peace. Most analysts agree that the agrarian reform failed to solve Peru's "agrarian question" because it failed to address the fundamental structural imbalance between modern and traditional sectors, or highland and coastal agriculture (Caballero 1981b; Thorp and Bertram 1978, 307). Agricultural production grew at an annual rate of only 0.9 percent during the decade, significantly less than the rate of population growth, and the result was increased food dependency (Mejía 1980, 16). Moreover, the reforms had a rather small redistributive effect, transferring only an estimated 1.0 to 1.5 percent of national income. In the agricultural sector, this redistribution was concentrated among the elite wage workers—those permanently employed on capitalist farms. Small farmers' incomes stagnated as a result of both neglect and the unfavorable price policies toward the agricultural sector, particularly during the second phase. The limited scope of the military's agrarian reform partly explains the lack of enthusiasm for the reform and for the military among the majority of rural poor.

3. Data on the economic crisis are drawn from Caballero (1981b, 17–20). See his excellent analysis of the internal contradictions of the model that led to the crisis; also see Thorp and Bertram (1978, 313–315).

As Belaunde came to office in 1980, the central problems of the province of Cajamarca had changed only slightly since the 1960s: on the one hand, tension remained among milk producers, PERULAC, and the state; and on the other, the great majority of rural households still lacked access to sufficient land or employment.

THE DAIRY PRODUCERS, PERULAC, AND THE STATE

The agrarian reform initially had unsettling consequences for the dairy industry. Because many of the dairy farms had been severely decapitalized before their expropriation, the new cooperatives found themselves with the need to build up herds and repair infrastructure. Consequently, milk production was down in the early years of the reform.[4] But as production recovered in the mid-1970s, the new cooperatives faced the same problem that the remaining capitalist farmers and peasant dairy producers did: their profitability (and survival) was in large part determined by the price of milk and by PERULAC's willingness to buy their milk production.

By the mid-1970s, the PERULAC milk condensation plant was nearing full capacity (see Table 15). It was rumored that the company was not planning to expand in Cajamarca and was instead beginning to develop the Tarapato region in the Amazon (Caballero and Tello 1976). From PERULAC's perspective, its promotional work in the Cajamarca dairy basin was reaching the point of diminishing returns. New milk suppliers, whose presence might have justified an expansion of plant capacity, could be brought in only from the more distant areas where natural conditions were less favorable and where smallholders predominated.

Compounding the problem or, as some argue, actually causing it were Peru's import policies during this period. Even the nationalist-oriented military government had done nothing to halt the milk-processing industry's growing dependence on cheaper imported milk inputs. Imports of powdered milk and milk fat as inputs into PERULAC's and Leche Gloria's processing industries grew by 8 percent annually during this decade, whereas the purchase of fresh milk from national suppliers grew only by approximately 1 percent (Burga Bartra and Huamán Ruiz 1979, 17). As a result, by the end of the decade, nearly 70 percent of the total milk processed by these industries consisted of imported material (Lajo Lazo 1980, 114).

The problem came to a head in Cajamarca in 1979 when PERULAC imposed limits on the amount of milk it was willing to purchase from each supplier. Moreover, it announced its intention of no longer purchasing milk from cabezas de porongo (the groupings of small producers), presumably because they intermixed the milk of cows of different breeds, resulting in milk of lower quality, with varying fat content and acidity.

4. See Jelícic (1978, 190–191) and Table 15, above, on milk deliveries to PERULAC.

Cajamarcan producers were in a bind. In the short run, it is difficult for producers to curtail production, because cows have to be milked, and milk is not easily stored. The alternative for small producers was to process their milk into soft white cheeses (quesillos), a labor-intensive and low-profit activity. Large producers had an even more difficult problem disposing of their surplus milk, given the greater volumes. Moreover, the dairy cooperatives were saddled with large debts that had been incurred in building their herds. Capitalist producers were caught in no more favorable a situation—given their loss of land through the agrarian reform, the only way they could maintain profit levels was to intensify production on their remaining 30 hectares. But further investment in dairy production required that marketing channels be ensured.

The mixed reaction of the milk producers to PERULAC's new purchasing policy was reflected in the different platforms of the two slates for officers in the dairy service cooperative (the CAS) in 1979. One slate (called "La Vaca") argued that the proper response was to build their own locally controlled milk-processing plant; this was the only way to ensure a market for their milk. Morever, they proposed that the cooperative should lobby for the reduction and eventual elimination of imported milk inputs. Composed primarily of the smaller milk suppliers on the longest routes, this group clashed with the other slate ("El Porongo"), composed of the large suppliers and more modern dairy farmers of the Cajamarca Valley. This group was less interested in a nationalist solution and more inclined toward collaboration with the multinational. PERULAC reportedly exerted some strong-arm tactics in an attempt to have this latter group elected, promising larger quotas to all if the "El Porongo" slate won. It won by a large majority (Burga Bartra and Huamán Ruiz 1979, 12).

PERULAC also lobbied the state for lower producer prices and succeeded in having the price per liter set at S/.6 less in Cajamarca than in other milk-producing regions (Burga Bartra and Huamán Ruiz 1979, 16). Moreover, in the last months of the military government, the state stepped in to subsidize the purchase of local milk, paying 80 percent of the costs of PERULAC's purchase of fresh milk from local producers (Lajo Lazo 1980, 121). While the future of the dairy industry came to look increasingly unsettled, the Belaunde administration began to steer the economy toward an open-economy model, with reduced state intervention in all aspects of economic life.[5]

The stated aims of Belaunde's Agrarian Development and Promotion Law (Ley de Promoción y Desarollo Agrario) were to promote the modernization of agriculture and the colonization of the Amazon region. The intention was to maintain the agrarian reform structure but, with some modifications, to make it more efficient. Other aims, albeit not explicit, were to consolidate a private

---

5. According to Lajo Lazo (1980, 121), Belaunde ended the milk subsidy in January 1981. Mosley (1985, 444) reports that PERULAC retaliated, again by cutting its purchases of Cajamarcan milk. Peruvian milk producers were then successful in getting the milk subsidy for producers restored in September 1981.

agro-industrial sector and to return banking and commerce to the private sector (Mejía 1980, 23).

For the dairy cooperatives of the province, the most significant change was that cooperatives lost their priority both as a form of agricultural organization and with respect to credit and technical assistance. If the cooperatives failed, they could now be sold, like any other enterprise. In addition, the possibility of parceling the cooperatives was opened up by Article 80 of the new law: "Associative enterprises can freely decide on their entrepreneurial model." By 1981 a number of coastal cooperatives were being dissolved and parceled among their members, creating great uncertainty among Cajamarcan cooperative members. Nonetheless, on CAPs such as Huacariz de San Antonio and Jesús Obrero, the members seemed determined to prove that they could indeed manage their enterprises efficiently. The macroeconomic policies of the period, combined with the role of PERULAC in milk-pricing policy, were to prove most unfortunate for the cooperative sector. In 1984 the CAP Huayobamba, the first cooperative organized in the province, was dissolved and the land partitioned among its members.

MIGRATION TO THE AMAZON

Belaunde's vision of the colonization of Peru's Amazon region was in tune with the aspirations of many Cajamarcan rural households. Moreover, after three years of drought in the late 1970s, many had no alternative but to move from the highlands. During his first administration (1964–1968), Belaunde had begun the construction of what is known as the "*marginál de la selva*," the trunk road running north to south across the Amazon region. His presidential campaign in 1980 focused on the theme that the future of Peru was in the selva and *ceja de selva* (literally, the "eyebrow" of the jungle). The Agrarian Development and Promotion Law, however, substantially changed the rules of the game with respect to development in the Amazon. Foreign capital was to occupy a privileged position, and agro-forestry and mining projects were to take priority over colonization projects (Ballón 1980, 63). Colonization through the next decade, just as in the past two, would continue to be primarily spontaneous, following the expansion of the road network.

Cajamarcans had begun to migrate both seasonally and permanently to the Cajamarcan selva province of Jaén in the 1950s, and increasingly on a permanent basis to the department of Amazonas in the 1960s (see Table 25). For households in the province of Cajamarca, however, permanent migration to the selva region had been of relatively little importance until the late 1970s. The drought, which affected both highland and coastal agriculture, had severely reduced temporary wage employment possibilities and, in combination with the economic crisis of the period, had altered migration patterns considerably. One of the new characteristics was the diversity of destinations, ranging from Iquitos in the northern Amazon to the selva region of the department of Junín.

When I returned to the province in 1981 for a follow-up visit, it was evident that the area had fallen on hard times. In La Succha, abandoned houses were all around, for the drought had struck here especially severely. Even those households with access to irrigation had been unable to continue farming. As a consequence, entire households had migrated to the selva or to Lima. In Pariamarca, doña María and her daughters had given up their trading activities over the past few years. Three consecutive years of drought meant that, as Simona put it, "there was nothing left to buy in the countryside." She had become dependent on her partner's wage income.

José had migrated each year in search of wage work. In the fall of 1977, he had gone to the coast, but the drought had affected both the sugar and the rice plantings, and no work was to be found. So, with a friend, he decided to continue on to the selva region of Junín, where it was rumored that there was plenty of work. It was quite a long journey, taking them almost a week. From Trujillo, they had to go to Lima by bus and then by train to La Oroya, before catching a truck that took them to the booming selva region. José was impressed by what he found: the pay for coffee and rice harvesting was much higher than in the selva of Cajamarca, and the conditions of work were much better. With land plentiful, it also seemed relatively easy to stake a claim. When he returned to Pariamarca six months later, he tried to convince Simona to make a permanent move, but she again resisted leaving the highlands.

The next year, José went "*enganchado*" to the province of Santa Cruz. He had wanted to return to Junín, but he and Simona did not have the money to cover the costs of transportation. They were desperately short of cash, so when José saw the sign on the front of Señora Villanueva's store in the Baños del Inca, offering socorros for a rice hacienda in the province of Santa Cruz, he took an advance of S/. 3,000 and signed a contract to stay on the hacienda for at least one month, entitling him to round-trip transportation to the region. Once there, he rapidly paid off the advance, earning S/. 350 a day. As soon as the contract expired, he moved on to another hacienda, for the going wage in the region was S/. 600 per day. He stayed in Santa Cruz three months. In 1980 José migrated to Bagua in the Cajamarcan ceja de selva with his brother-in-law, whose relatives in the zone had requested that they come to work for them. He was disappointed with what he earned, however, for this region was not as dynamic as Junín. He planned to return to Junín in January, having heard that in the fall of 1981 workers were being paid S/. 2,000 per day to harvest coffee or rice. In Pariamarca, one was lucky to earn S/. 600.[6]

---

6. Locally, José found work only for several weeks in the construction of the weaving shop promoted by the National University of Cajamarca in Pariamarca. There had been a few changes in the village, because the university had chosen Pariamarca as the site of a rural development program.

José was still trying to convince Simona to go with him, for he had also heard that the Belaunde government was offering cheap loans for those who were willing to colonize, and he dreamed of being able to buy land. Simona was six months pregnant, and her dream was to have a healthy son; she was not about to be moved. But José convinced María's grandson to accompany him.

One of doña Rosa's grandsons also migrated to the selva, staking out a claim in Oaxapampa, in the ceja de selva of Lima, in 1979. Ignacio, the son of Rosa's eldest son, Teodoro, had to deceive his father to make this move. An uncle had already moved from La Succha to this area several years before, and Ignacio had dreamed of going with him. Ignacio's case differs from that of José and his relatives in Pariamarca: Ignacio's father was consolidating his position as a middle peasant, and the son could have looked forward to a relatively substantial inheritance. But it seemed to matter little to him, for he was determined to leave La Succha. When his father forbade him to leave, he went anyway.

The drought had allowed Teodoro to expand his land holdings to 4 hectares. Moreover, he had access to an additional 6 hectares in sharecropping arrangements if he wanted to farm them. Another sign that things had gone well for him, even with the drought, was that he now owned five oxen. Teodoro had managed to pass into the ranks of the middle peasantry. But just when he gained access to the largest amount of land he had held in his lifetime, his eldest son left home. The second son, Roger, was the family's intellectual, the first Sangay to graduate from high school. He had never liked agricultural work and, as the family favorite, was never forced to engage in it. He was now working in Cajamarca, attempting to save enough money to go to the university. Teodoro worked the fields with the help of three of his daughters. The daughters had always helped out, but they had begun to work much more than ever before, because there was so much land to attend to. Even with their help, Teodoro had to hire wage workers occasionally.

At this point, Teodoro and his wife owned three houses in La Succha, two of them purchased from families who had migrated from the village. When I asked him what he planned to do with the other houses, he pointed to the remaining five children at home: "If they have a house and lands in La Succha, then they don't have to move away." It was clear that he was bent on consolidating his position as a successful agriculturalist. But that meant at least holding on to the labor of his remaining son at home and finding husbands for his daughters.

Teodoro's oldest daughters were still unmarried at the ages of twenty-seven and twenty-one, an unthinkable situation only a decade before. Most young women then either married in their late teens or migrated to the city of Cajamarca or the coast to work as maids. But Teodoro had been very protective of his daughters, not even allowing them to begin preparing the customary dowry of blankets and other household wares or to attend the dances in the pueblo of Jesús. And drought had left few young men of marriageable age in the village. Teodoro confided to me that he regretted not having helped his daughters find husbands in the years before the drought, for then they might have married young men with promise as farmers.

Doña Rosa's youngest son, Victor, had finally realized his dream of migrating to the coast. He convinced his parents that, with the drought, they would not be able to survive on the land alone and that he should seek a job on the coast to support them. Another consideration was that his lover had become pregant and Victor was not convinced that the child she was carrying belonged to him. Migration provided the traditional way out of such situations, and thus Rosa was forced to agree to Victor's move to Chimbote. There, through his brother's connections, he found a job in a fish-processing factory. He was about to become a permanent worker when he heard that his mother was sick ("*se moría de la pena*"), and so he returned to the village. The drought had finally ended, and he again took over cultivating the family lands.

Victor was twenty-eight now and, rather than looking for a wife, was putting his energies into religion. Upon returning to La Succha, he had become an evangelist. Rosa had mixed feelings both about his new religiousness and about his failure to marry. On the one hand, she would have liked a daughter-in-law to help out with the domestic work. On the other hand, she had never really gotten along with her daughters-in-law, because few women seemed really good enough for her sons.

Rosa was nonetheless distressed that two other sons had separated from their wives. Silvestre, the son in Chimbote, abandoned his wife for another woman, and Lucho had been thrown out of the house by his wife earlier that year for having an adulterous affair. Rosa considered Lucho's wife to be too jealous. This daughter-in-law had brought legal charges against Lucho to claim his salary as child support for their seven children. In late 1981, the daughter-in-law was in the process of selling all of her animals and trying to sell the house in order to move to Cajamarca to join her eldest son.

As for doña María, since the fall of 1976 she had been living with her youngest daughter, Erlinda, in the house on the plaza of Pariamarca, sleeping in a little chosita next door. She had a stomach tumor and had not been feeling well for several years. Her activities were few now, and she could hardly even cook.

With great relief, María reported that her daughters had now made up with their father, Manuel, and that it appeared he would not disinherit them. Both Simona and Martina were sharecropping pieces of his land with him. Martina had been abandoned by the "wife beater," which María considered to be just as well, even though Martina was now as poor as the other daughters. The other three were still with their same partners.

María's main joy was her eleven grandchildren. Some of them would stop by to see her on their way back from school each day. She was proud that one grandson, Francisca's son, finished high school in Cajamarca. He was about to set off for Junín to claim some land at his uncle José's insistence. Not wishing to see him go, María reprimanded his father: "If a man is good, he works hard, saves, so that he can buy land for his sons so that they stay here and work." But neither her ex-husband nor any of her sons-in-law managed to accumulate any land in property beyond their own inheritances.

CONCLUSION: THE CLASS ANALYTICS OF THE DEVELOPMENT OF CAPITALISM IN AGRICULTURE

The main difference between the migration of Cajamarquinos to the Amazon in the late 1970s and early 1980s and the pattern of highland-coastal migration characterizing previous decades was that peasant men and women in this more recent wave were migrating not only as a strategy to reproduce peasant households in the sierra but also in order to constitute new units of production. For some households, permanent migration from the highlands was spurred by the calamity of the drought, which came on the heels of the agrarian reform and in concert with a severe economic crisis. But many of these new permanent migrants were young men who also had some education—some, like doña María's grandson, had even completed high school. Whereas the development of primary schooling in the province in previous decades had contributed to the formation of Peru's coastal working class, the province in the 1980s was to contribute toward the settlement of the Amazon with colonists who dreamed of becoming commercial farmers.

For many of these young men, temporary wage migration to the selva was but a phase in their pursuit of the goal of acquiring land in this region.[7] Wage employment was to play a role similar to the one it had played in the 1950s and 1960s, when coastal migration often helped generate the means for hacienda households to constitute themselves as land-owning petty producers and for households in the independent communities to expand their productive base through the opportunity provided by the subdivision and sale of hacienda lands. Nonetheless, for others in the 1980s, wage migration to the selva was still a seasonal phenomenon, part of a strategy to reproduce the highland household.

With the perspective of eight decades of history, peasant participation in wage labor might be considered part of a steady process of proletarianization. As we have seen, the majority of peasant children leaving the highlands by the mid-1970s joined the ranks of the landless proletariat.[8] But what I have tried to emphasize is the heterogeneous and changing significance of peasant household

7. See Collins's (1988) excellent analysis of the process of colonization in the department of Puno.

8. Whether Cajamarcan migrants were, in fact, permanently employed as wage workers in their new destinations or became part of the massive urban "informal sector" is a topic requiring further research.

participation in wage labor over this century. This emphasis allows the process of proletarianization to be understood not as a linear process, a cause and result of social differentiation, but rather as a complex movement of individual and household actions in concert with the broader structural changes which encompassed them and to which they contributed.

The initiation of Cajamarquinos into wage labor was perhaps unwitting, a practice forced on a skeptical peasantry by unscrupulous coastal labor recruiters. But within several decades, coastal labor recruitment in the highlands, with the practice of advances, had been internalized within the peasant economy of the independent communities as a credit system, perhaps as important a source of liquidity as that represented by landlords for hacienda households, if not more so. As the century progressed, wage income from seasonal migration became not just an extraordinary source of income to meet emergencies, but an integral part of a diversified household income-generating strategy, supported by a flexible gender division of labor within the household unit.

It is difficult to identify with precision when a significant number of Cajamarcan smallholder households entered into a different relationship with wage labor and capital—namely, primary reliance on wage income as a way to reproduce household labor power. The population density of several districts suggests that by the 1940s petty production was increasingly a secondary activity, complementary to wage labor. Recall, however, that not until the 1960s was land pressure sufficiently acute for permanent migration to be quantitatively more significant than temporary migration to the coast. By then, considerable changes had taken place in the class relations in the highlands.

From a broad perspective, the first six decades of the century might be considered a time when the highlands (and multiple noncapitalist class relations) provided an important condition of existence for the consolidation and expansion of capitalist agriculture on the coast: a steady supply of cheap wage labor. But the integration of coast and highlands through both the product market (the cattle trade and then, more significantly, the market in milk) and the labor market created crucial preconditions for the development of capitalist class relations in the highlands in subsequent decades.

For most households in the province, perhaps the second link had the most profound consequences. The growing monetization of the rural economy and the changed consumption patterns resulting from decades of highland-coastal integration contributed to the monetization of traditional labor recruitment practices. Quantitatively, participation in wage labor within the independent communities in the 1970s was a more significant phenomenon than wage employment on the capitalist dairy farms. Social differentiation within peasant communities was also a consequence of events in the product market and the conversion of the province into a dairy region. The tremendous variance in income levels among peasant households that resulted from different combinations of income-generating activities spurred capitalization and reliance on wage labor among the few and household disintegration among many.

Peasant social differentiation and the attainment of simple reproduction were not merely functions of the level of petty production or of participation in wage labor; rather, they were the more complex result of peasant participation in multiple class relations, both fundamental and subsumed, and the levels of surplus appropriation and transference implied in each. And, as we have seen, the gender division of labor often allowed households to participate in a wider array of income-generating activities, sometimes precluding male participation in wage labor and often buttressing households as petty producers.

Thus, although from a macrosystemic view these eighty years can be summarized as a time of the development of capitalism in agriculture, in concert with the consolidation of Peru as a capitalist social formation, I have tried to move the terms of debate away from the teleological "subordination of the peasantry to capital" or the functionalist problem of articulation of capitalist and noncapitalist modes or forms of production that produce the dominance of the former at the expense of the latter. The contribution of a microsystemic perspective is that the analysis of the genesis of the capital-labor relation is grounded in the multiple relations, struggles, and options that sometimes facilitate and at other times discourage peasant participation in, and reliance on, wage labor.

A focus on peasant household reproduction from a micro point of view provides a different understanding of how peasant households may survive in the face of impoverishment and proletarianization. It also opens up space for the analysis of the "subjective" forces of history—the actions of men and women in daily life, as well as the personal relations between them.

My goal in introducing the concept of household relations was twofold: first, to explore how nonclass relations intersect with class relations—that is, how the economic, cultural, and political practices contributing to the constitution and reproduction of households as units of production and reproduction of labor power overdetermine the class relations in which household members partici-pate; and, second, to examine the mechanisms that have produced the subordination of women within households and in the class and nonclass relations in which they engage. This approach has allowed me to illustrate two points. On the one hand, the subordination of women has had high costs for the well-being of rural households, as it has contributed to the reproduc-tion of peasant poverty over time. On the other hand, the tensions in gender and household relations are as important a factor in the contingency of peasant household reproduction as is the outcome of the class relations in which peasant households participate.

APPENDIX I: THE 1876 AND 1940 PERUVIAN CENSUSES

THE 1876 CENSUS

M. A. Fuentes, the principal statistician charged with revising the 1876 census results, noted in his preface to the *Resumen del Censo General* in 1878 that "it was impossible to guarantee the exactness of the general census" (Peru 1876b, viii). Nevertheless, he concluded as have subsequent scholars, that the 1876 census represents the best available approximation of Peru's nineteenth-century demographic and socioeconomic characteristics.

Among the problems faced by those who carried out the 1876 census was the lack of previous cartographic studies delineating administrative boundaries. Not until 1896 did the Sociedad Geográfica del Perú conduct a detailed study of Peru's departments, provinces, and districts to establish the basis for more rigorous accounting.

There were also serious difficulties, well described by Díaz (1974), in executing the census. It was a herculean task for Peru's weak administrative machinery. Moreover, because the primary means of transportation was by horseback or mule, it is not surprising that population estimates for many villages and haciendas were based not on an actual house-to-house count but rather on general estimates provided by secondary sources. The census takers, for example, generally relied on landlords to fill out the forms for the population residing on haciendas (Macera 1974, cl). Some districts and haciendas were not counted at all, because of either the resistance of the inhabitants or the negligence of the census takers.

Another problem is that the figures in the seven department volumes, published first, differ from those in the *Resumen del Censo General* prepared by M. A. Fuentes. Fuentes attempted to correct some of the grosser deficiencies, obtaining additional information from local authorities on haciendas that had incorrectly been classified as villages and estimates on those villages and haciendas that had been deleted.

Pablo Macera's seminar on rural history at the University of San Marcos in Lima published a monograph summarizing the differences between the two publications (Macera 1976). The number of haciendas listed in the *Resumen del Censo General* was greater by 20 percent nationally (4,403). The discrepancy between the two sets of figures for the hacienda population, however, was much smaller—4 percent—and that for the rural population was only 1.2 percent. The measured percentage of the rural population residing on haciendas varied slightly, from 27.4 percent according to the departmental volumes, to 28.2 percent in the *Resumen del Censo General* (Macera 1976, tables vi and vii).

In the case of the department of Cajamarca, the difference between the two sources with respect to the hacienda and rural population is less than 1 percent. Macera's (1976) tables should be used with caution, however, for checking these published figures against the actual census volumes revealed several errors for the province of Cajamarca, including errors of addition and a discrepancy in the reported hacienda population in the district of Cospán. These errors are

TABLE A1.   Concentration of Population on Haciendas,
Department of Cajamarca, 1876 and 1940

Province	Number of Haciendas	Population Residing on Haciendas	Rural Population	Percentage of Rural Population on Haciendas
		1876		
Cajabamba	43	6,970	16,330	42.7
Cajamarca	75	11,605	48,323	24.0
Celendín	9	1,178	13,602	8.7
Contumazá	17	1,918	11,155	17.2
Chota	60	10,306	51,081	20.2
Hualgayoc	29	11,804	47,992	24.6
Jaén	100	4,362	12,728	34.3
Total	333	48,143	201,211	23.9
		1940		
Cajabamba	105	15,728	35,756	44.0
Cajamarca	235	30,468	108,780	28.0
Celendín	52	5,317	35,880	14.8
Contumazá	160	5,157	25,706	20.1
Cutervo	99	15,325	49,311	31.1
Chota	105	16,669	92,279	18.1
Hualgayoc	68	21,287	91,996	23.1
Jaén	428	11,100	22,663	49.0
Total	1,252	121,051	462,371	26.2

SOURCES: Compiled from census data (Peru 1876b, 299–364; Peru 1940, vol. 2, table 34).
NOTE: The rural population includes all population centers of fewer than two thousand inhabitants.

why the absolute numbers reported in tables A1 and A2 for the department and province of Cajamarca differ from those published by Macera (1976).

The 1876 census utilized administrative definitions of rural and urban residence, including in the latter all population centers with a governor (the district capitals) or a lieutenant governor. This definition greatly inflates the urban population, including among other small communities, a hamlet with a population of only 158 (Cubicus, in the district of Chetilla). Also, the corresponding reduction of the size of the rural population contributes to an overestimation of the percentage of the rural population living on haciendas.

For consistency, Macera maintains the census definition of urban residence in his publications. He is also critical of it, however, noting that a better definition of an urban community would be one with a minimum population of 1,000 (Macera 1974, cl). Throughout my analysis, I have defined urban centers as those containing a minimum population of 2,000, the generally accepted international definition of urban centers. By this definition, only three provincial capitals qualified as urban in 1876: the city of Cajamarca (7,215), Cajabamba (2,838), and Contumazá (2,137). The department was, thus, 94 percent rural.

Defining population centers of fewer than 2,000 inhabitants as rural has the advantage of including in the rural population those independent peasant producers who reside in pueblos (the district capitals) rather than in the more dispersed caserios. It has the disadvantage of including in the rural population

TABLE A2.   Concentration of Population on Haciendas,
Province of Cajamarca, 1876

District	Number of Haciendas	Population Residing on Haciendas	Rural Population	Percentage of Rural Population on Haciendas
Asunción	3	98	4,243	2.3
Cajamarca	9	1,208	7,919	15.3
Cospán	4	2,316	3,304	70.1
Chetilla	6	385	1,572	24.5
La Encañada	12	1,520	2,897	52.5
Ichocán	3	701	4,728	14.8
Jesús	14	1,219	5,275	23.1
Llacanora	1	79	1,211	6.5
Magdalena	4	261	863	30.1
Matara	1	23	1,576	1.5
San Marcos	10	2,023	7,142	28.3
San Pablo	8	1,772	7,593	23.3
Total	75	11,605	48,323	24.0

SOURCE: Compiled from census data (Peru 1876b, 299–311).
NOTE: The rural population includes all population centers of fewer than two thousand inhabitants.

the petty bourgeoisie, who generally reside in the pueblos, as well as artisans, merchants, and, perhaps, landless laborers. Thus, the non-hacienda rural population cannot be assumed to be the equivalent of the population engaged in agricultural activities.

One other advantage of a restricted definition of urban residence, however, is that it yields the most conservative measure of the degree of population concentration on the haciendas. Because my argument centers on the dominance of the hacienda system in Cajamarca before 1940—and given the questionable reliability of the 1876 census—I consider it prudent to underestimate this measure of the hacienda's control over the rural population.

I have also chosen to work with the data from the *Resumen del Censo General* of the 1876 census rather than with the figures from the departmental volumes for a similar reason. First, I was able to verify that the department volume for Cajamarca (volume 3) had in fact incorrectly reported several important haciendas as caserios. The *Resumen del Censo General* caught some but not all of these errors. It thus represents a slightly more accurate approximation of the population on haciendas. Second, although the *Resumen del Censo General* data show a percentage of rural residents concentrated on haciendas for 1876 (23.9 percent for the department and 24.0 percent for the province of Cajamarca) that is slightly higher than the percentage shown in the department volume (23.6 percent and 22.6 percent, respectively), the former provide a more conservative estimate of the increase in the haciendas' control over rural labor during the period between the censuses (1876–1940).

In a more recent publication, Taylor (1986) covers similar terrain, analyzing the 1876, 1940, 1961, and 1972 census data for the five southern provinces of the department of Cajamarca. Our reported data differ because he includes the district capitals, regardless of size, in the urban population. His higher estimate of the urban population produces a lower rural population and thus a higher concentration of rural population on haciendas (29 percent for the province of Cajamarca).

THE 1940 CENSUS

Sixty-four years passed before the Peruvian government undertook another national census. For the intervening period, the only census materials available are for a number of the coastal cities (see Hunt 1977, table 2). The Sociedad Geográfica del Perú did attempt in 1906 to update the 1876 census to 1896 (the year in which it carried out the cartographic delineation), using parish lists of births and deaths for 1891. Its estimated growth rates for the department and province of Cajamarca are so high, however, 3.73 and 4.76, respectively, that the statistics seem of dubious validity (Málaga Santolalla 1906, 146–147).

The 1940 census represents the first reliable enumeration of Peruvian sociodemographic characteristics carried out on the basis of a house-to-house accounting of residents. It too suffers from a number of deficiencies with respect to estimates of the resident hacienda population, however, noted in the methodological preface to the census (Peru 1940, vol. I, xxvi–xxvii). Sometimes, subdivisions of a hacienda were classified as a caserio; at other times, the subdivision was classified as a hacienda in its own right. The first type of error would underestimate the total number of hacienda residents; the second type would accurately show the concentration but overestimate the total number of haciendas in a district. This second error could explain part of the impressive increase in the number of haciendas and fundos reported in the 1940 census for the province of Cajamarca (235), as compared with the number reported in 1876 (75). But this trend is also partly explained by the subdivision of haciendas through inheritance and sales.

In the 1940 census, the terms *fundo* and *hacienda* appear to have been used interchangeably. Throughout my analysis, I have grouped the data for fundos and haciendas in the category of haciendas. The 1940 census categories of *comunidad, estancia, parcialidad,* and *otros* have always been included among the non-hacienda rural population.

In 1940 the definition of urban centers as consisting of at least 2,000 inhabitants included Celendín, Cascas, Cutervo, Chota, and Bambamarca, as well as the towns of Cajamarca and Cajabamba. Contumazá fell below this critical minimum during the period between the censuses.

One final caution: the spelling of the names of haciendas, fundos, and caserios often varies from census to census and source to source. For consistency, I have followed the spellings provided in the most recent geographical and historical dictionary of Cajamarca, written by Burga Larrea (1983).

APPENDIX II: ESTIMATING PEASANT HOUSEHOLD INCOME ON THE HACIENDA COMBAYO

The monograph written by Nicolás Santolalla in 1918 on the Hacienda Combayo is the most complete economic analysis of a hacienda in the province of Cajamarca by a contemporary of the period. Nevertheless, because the monograph was not written for the purpose of estimating peasant household income, the data are incomplete for the task. Moreover, there are a number of inconsistencies in the monograph, as well as errors in addition, rounding off, and so forth. In this appendix, the problems encountered in estimating household income from the available data, as well as the more detailed assumptions that were made, are explained.

I. THE DISTRIBUTION OF LAND AND ANIMALS BETWEEN ARRENDIRES AND PEONS

Santolalla ([1918] 1977, 222–223) provides three pieces of information: 1) the total quantity of land and animals held by both groups; 2) the average size of landholding and number of animals of arrendire households; 3) the amount of rent owed the hacienda for land and animals held by arrendires and peons.

The third set of figures differs from the first set because of rounding off; the third set has been taken as the more precise. Because Santolalla provides data on the average size of landholding and number of animals for arrendires, one should have been able to derive easily the average holdings of peons. Two problems arose, however. First, it is unclear whether there were twenty or thirty peon households on the hacienda. Although in the census of hacienda residents Santolalla (1977, 223) reports twenty peon households, he later (224) mentions the figure of thirty when calculating the imputed wage of peons. Second, if only twenty peon households resided on the hacienda, taking the total number of hectares of land and animals that might correspond to peons and dividing by twenty gives an average plot size and number of animals equal to those of arrendires. I considered this result unreasonable, for the peons were reported to have worked for the hacienda an average of 250 days per year (Santolalla 1977, 224). Also, arrendire holdings were sufficiently large to accommodate an additional 1.85 agregados per holding (derived from Santolalla 1977, 223), whereas those of peons presumably were not. Dividing total peon holdings by thirty households thus gives a more plausible distribution of resources between the two groups.

But even this lower calculation gives peon households greater access to resources than Santolalla's calculation in terms of the value of imputed wage payments. According to Santolalla (1977, 224), the foregone rent from each peon holding was equivalent to S/. 32. In Table 12, I have assumed that this latter value is the most accurate measure of peon holdings; the amount of land held by peon households was reduced accordingly, and that of arrendires correspondingly increased. The amount of land, rather than the amount of animal holdings, was adjusted, because plot cultivation is more sensitive to household labor availability than is animal raising.

II. THE DERIVATION OF AGRICULTURAL INCOME

Santolalla (1977, 223) reports that peasants had 420 hectares under cultivation, distributed among five crops; this data was used to calculate a weighted average of gross return per hectare, reported in Table 11. In order to calculate the net return per hectare, only the cost of seed was taken into account, because Santolalla does not provide data on the cost of other inputs such as animal fertilizer or depreciation of tools and animal power. The amount and cost of seed were taken from the data on seed utilization in demesne production (Santolalla 1977, 265–267).

Santolalla (223) reports that total peasant holdings consisted of 622 hectares; thus 67.5 percent of the land surface leased to peasants was then in cultivation. This percentage was applied to the estimated distribution of land between arrendires and peons in order to arrive at the average amount of land under cultivation by each group and then to estimate the gross (Table 12) and net (Table 13) value of agricultural production. In the case of arrendires, the calculation of net agricultural income required one further adjustment, the deduction of rent payments. I assumed that arrendires paid the reported rental rate of S/. 2.5 per hectare for all land granted to them in usufruct, whether or not it was in cultivation.

III. THE DERIVATION OF INCOME FROM ANIMAL RAISING

Santolalla (1977, 222–223) provides data on total peasant animal stocks and the average holdings of arrendires. I calculated the average holdings of peons as a derivative, shown in Table 12. In order to evaluate animal stocks, it is necessary to know the animals' sex and age. Santolalla (237) provides such data only for the case of the haciendas' holdings; for lack of a better indicator, the corresponding ratios on composition and value have been applied to peasant stocks. These detailed data were not available for sheep; nonetheless, Santolalla (234) does mention the average price range for sheep, and the mid-range value of S/. 2.00 per head was utilized to value peasant stocks.

The data necessary to calculate net income from animal raising as the net change in animal stocks were unavailable. As a proxy, I have assumed that sales and autoconsumption of animals were on the order of 10 percent of the value of animal stocks. This estimate may understate the net income from animal raising, for the sale of cattle was the primary means by which arrendires generated the cash income to pay their rents.

IV. ESTIMATING WAGE INCOME

Santolalla (1977, 224) reports that men on the hacienda each worked 250 days per year and were paid S/. 0.30 per day, a figure that includes the nominal wage of S/. 0.20 and the value of meals, S/. 0.10. It is somewhat more complicated to estimate the average wage income of peon women and children. Santolalla (228–229) provides detailed data of labor utilization by gender for the hacienda's agricultural activities; in the aggregate, over all activities, men provided 80 percent of the agricultural wage labor, women 4 percent, and children 16 percent. Data on total wage payments for cultivation of the demesne were also provided; the division of labor figures calculated above were applied to this latter information to derive the total number of female (160) and child (640) labor days employed.

According to Santolalla (1977, 225), twenty-five peon women were available to work each day. Eight women appear to have had permanent jobs on the hacienda as milkmaids and mitayas; I have assumed that the remaining seventeen divided the available agricultural work and that they took turns serving as semaneras, two women serving each week. This calculation resulted in each woman working nine days a year as an agricultural laborer and six weeks a year in semanera duty. Santolalla reports that women were paid S/. 0.15 per day (a nominal wage of S/. 0.05 plus the value of meals, S/. 0.10).

The wage income earned by children was calculated in a similar fashion. It was assumed that the thirty peon households divided the available child employment equally, so that each household had one child employed for twenty-one days a year. According to Santolalla, children earned S/. 0.25 per day (nominal wage of S/. 0.15 plus the value of meals). Finally, peon household wage income was enhanced by the imputed wage represented by the household's access to land and grazing pastures, calculated by Santolalla (224) as worth S/. 32 per year.

I assumed that the wage income of arrendires included wages earned in both agricultural and mining activities. The number of days of agricultural wage labor was calculated as the residual of the hacienda's total agricultural labor requirements and labor days provided by male peons. In order to arrive at this number, it was first necessary to calculate the availability of male peons for agricultural work. Santolalla reports that of the thirty male peons, fifteen were available for the hacienda's agricultural and animal-raising activities. The others were employed in the hacienda's foundry operation. Of these fifteen, seven appear to have been permanently employed in animal raising. I thus assumed that the remaining eight worked 250 days a year, leaving 1,202 agricultural labor days to be performed by arrendires (Santolalla 1977, 225, 228, 238). Assuming the available employment was divided equally among the seventy-two arrendire households, each household provided 16.7 days of agricultural labor. According to Santolalla, arrendires earned S/. 0.40 per day (nominal wage of S/. 0.30 plus meals).

Santolalla does not analyze the mining operations of the hacienda in his thesis; thus he does not provide data on mining employment. My interviews on this hacienda revealed that arrendires or their agregados were required to work one month each year in the mines. According to the 1928 Planillas de Trabajo for the Oficina Combayo, the majority of workers in the mines were paid S/. 0.40 per day. It is unclear whether or not workers in the mines were also given their meals; I have assumed that they were and thus calculate the wage as S/. 0.50 per day. Finally, Santolalla (1977, 225) notes explicitly that women from arrendire households did not work for the hacienda; I have assumed that children, other than the agregados, also did not.

APPENDIX III: THE 1973 CAJAMARCA INCOME SURVEY

The 1973 Cajamarca Income Survey was carried out by the Socio-Economic Study Program of the Proyecto Piloto Cajamarca–La Libertad (PPCLL) under the direction of Ing. Efraín Franco. The PPCLL was a small-farmer development project designed on the basis of the Mexican "Plan Puebla" to introduce an integrated technological package to the pilot zone. The project was carried out by the Ministry of Agriculture–CRIAN (Centro Regional de Investigación Agropecuaria del Norte) with technical assistance from CIMMYT (the International Center for the Study of Wheat and Maize, located in Mexico). In 1973, by an agreement involving the Ministry of Agriculture, the Peruvian Foundation for National Development, and the Ford Foundation, the Socio-Economic Study Program was constituted to undertake a three-year analysis and diagnosis of the peasant farmers in the area that would serve as the basis for a future evaluation of the PPCLL's impact on the project zone. The 1973 Cajamarca Income Survey was conducted for this purpose.

The primary objective of the sample survey was to estimate the levels and sources of income of farmers representing different strata of the peasantry in the project zone. The area of action of the project corresponded to thirteen districts of the provinces of Cajamarca and Cajabamba: Cajamarca, Los Baños del Inca, Llacanora, La Encañada, Jesús, Namora, Matara, San Marcos, Ichocán, Condebamba, Cajabamba, Cochachi, and Sitacocha.

The population for the survey was determined on the basis of the sworn declarations required of all property owners in 1972 in conjunction with the implementation of the agrarian reform in Cajamarca. The data on property ownership by district were then aggregated according to the Ministry of Agriculture's officially defined land-strata for the area: *minifundios*, 0.01 to 3.50 hectares; small farmers, 3.41 to 11.00 hectares; medium farmers, 11.01 to 30.00 hectares; and large farmers, 30.01 to more than 100 hectares. For the purposes of the survey, farms of more than 100 hectares were excluded. The sample size within each district was chosen on the basis of the relative representation of each stratum within the district, subject to the overall budget constraint of 1,500 observations for the total survey. The 1,500 observations corresponded to 5 percent of the total number of farm units in the survey area. Once the number of observations within each cell was determined, the names of the property owners were chosen at random.

The survey was carried out in the months of October and November of 1973; the data correspond to the 1972–1973 agricultural year. The questionnaires were reviewed while the survey was in progress, then tabulated by hand during 1974. The preliminary results of the survey were published in draft form as Franco (1974).

The survey data were prepared for computer analysis by Bill Gibson in collaboration with the data-processing center at the National Agrarian University La Molina. Copies of the data tape were deposited there, as well as with the Pontificia Universidad Católica del Perú and the Ministry of Agriculture in Lima. The original questionnaires remain at the Cajamarca office of the Ministry of Agriculture.

My analysis of the data set was restricted to the 1,055 observations corresponding to the province of Cajamarca. The assumptions I employed in the estimation of peasant household income may be found in Deere (1978, appendix A).

APPENDIX IV: THE 1976 PEASANT
FAMILY SURVEY

The 1976 Peasant Family Survey was a follow-up survey, carried out by the author, of the 1973 Cajamarca Income Survey. Because a limited budget made reinterviewing all the respondents to the original survey—or even complete coverage of the nine districts included in that survey—impossible, a stratified random sample of the respondents in three districts of the province of Cajamarca was chosen.

The three districts selected, Cajamarca, Jesús, and La Encañada, were chosen because they represented distinct forms of insertion of the peasantry within the provincial economy. The district of Cajamarca, seat of the department capital and center of the dairy industry, represents the most highly proletarianized district in the province, linked to the urban labor market. The district of Jesús most closely represents an area of independent peasant communities, reduced to minifundios who rely on the wage income earned through temporary and permanent migration. La Encañada, a district once dominated by large haciendas, represents the area where the greatest number of family-sized farms are located, with peasants integrated into the product market as suppliers of foodstuffs and milk to PERULAC. The three districts account for 39 percent of the total number of farms and encompass 35 percent of the total farm area of the province.

In the 1973 survey, these three districts provided 45 percent of the total number of respondents in the province. For a population of 500, a sample of 83 was required for the sub-sample to be statistically representative of the population at a 95 percent level of confidence and a 10 percent probability of error. Thirty percent of the original respondents in the 1973 survey in these three districts were randomly selected for contact in order to allow for refusals and problems in locating the persons selected. The 105 completed interviews represent 22 percent of the sample population; the probability of error at the 95 percent confidence level was thus reduced to 6 percent.

The survey questionnaire focused on the gender division of labor in domestic labor, agricultural production, the labor market, and in other activities that generated household income. Particular attention was given to the migration experience of household members, as well as to their previous relationship to the hacienda system.

The questionnaire was pre-tested over a two-month period, and the survey itself carried out during the months of June and July 1976. I was assisted by four research assistants—two women with university training and a peasant couple. They were trained over a one-week period. An average of 1.5 interviews were completed per interviewer per day; each interview lasted approximately two hours. Most time-consuming was the process of locating the households selected for interviewing. Because this was a paired sample, the impossibility of substitution caused what often turned out to be two- or three-hour hikes made in vain. The survey thus took seven weeks to complete.

The response and completion rates for the survey were relatively high; 93 percent of the peasants drawn in the sub-sample were located and, of the 133 households located, interviews were completed in 79 percent. The 1976 Peasant Family Survey was aimed at the peasant woman, and thus households where no women resided were automatically excluded from the sample. Women were among the respondents in 88 percent of the households interviewed. In the remainder, although a woman resided in the household, she was unavailable, and a male was interviewed. The great distances involved, often traveled on foot or horseback, precluded many return visits.

The questionnaires were reviewed during the survey. The data was coded, keypunched, and processed at the University of California, Berkeley, during 1977. The data set, as well as the questionnaire, is available from the author. The majority of tables compiled from the survey data are available in Deere (1978).

BIBLIOGRAPHY

Acevedo, Nelly. 1976. "El Sistema de Comercialización en la Economía del Area de Influencia del PPCLL." Preliminary report. Cajamarca: Programa de Estudios Socio-Económicos, Proyecto Cajamarca–La Libertad.

Alayza Escardo, Luis. 1943. *Cajamarca y sus Posibilidades Ganaderas*. Lima: Rimac.

Albert, Bill. 1976. *An Essay on the Peruvian Sugar Industry, 1880–1920, and the Letters of Ronald Gordon, Administrator of the British Sugar Company in Cañete, 1914–1920*. Norfolk, England: University of East Anglia.

Alberti, Giorgio, and Enrique Mayer, eds. 1974. *Reciprocidad e Intercambio en los Andes Peruanos*. Lima: Instituto de Estudios Peruanos.

Althaus, Jaime. 1975. "Asunción." Preliminary report. Cajamarca: Programa de Estudios Socio-Económicos, Proyecto Cajamarca–La Libertad.

Althusser, Louis. 1970. *Reading Capital*. New York: Pantheon.

Alvarez, Elena. 1980. *Política Agraria y Estancamiento de la Agricultura, 1969–77*. Lima: Instituto de Estudios Peruanos.

Alvarez Saén, J. 1908. "Memoria que Presenta el Prefecto del Departamento de Cajamarca al Supremo Gobierno, Respondiente al Año de 1908." File E28. Biblioteca Nacional del Perú, Sala de Investigaciones, Lima.

Amariglio, Jack. 1984. "Forms of the Commune and Primitive Communal Class Process." Discussion Paper no. 19. Association for Social and Economic Analysis, University of Massachusetts, Amherst.

Amin, Samir. 1975. "El Capitalismo y la Renta de la Tierra." In *La Cuestión Campesina y el Capitalismo*, edited by Samir Amin and Kostas Vergopoulos, 9–58. Mexico City: Ed. Nuestro Tiempo.

Amorín, Luis. 1948. "Ensayo Monográfico Acerca del Departamento de Cajamarca." *El Rodeo*, no. 8.

Amorín Bueno, Adolfo. 1972. "Situación de la Ganadería Lechera en el Valle de Cajamarca." Thesis, Universidad Nacional Agraria La Molina, Lima.

Arce del Campo, Eduardo, and Jorge Lora. 1974. "La Reforma Agraria en la SAIS La Pauca." In *Informe del Trabajo de Campo Realizado en el Departamento de Cajamarca, 1974,* edited by Eduardo Arce del Campo and Mariano Valderrama, chap. 6. Lima: Taller de Investigación Rural, Universidad Católica del Perú.

Astori, Danilo. 1983. "La Agricultura Campesina en América Latina: Sus Relaciones con el Crecimiento Urbano y la Disponibilidad Alimentaria." *Estudios Rurales Latinoamericanos* 6(3): 109–140.

Aviles, J., et al. 1921. *Album Gráfico e Informativo de Cajamarca y Lambayeque*. Lima: International Publicity Co.

Ballón A., Francisco. 1980. "La Nueva Conquista de la Amazonia." In *Promoción Agraria: Para Quién?* edited by José Manuel Mejía, 63–83. Lima: Tiempo Presente Ed.

Banaji, Jairus. 1977. "Modes of Production in a Materialist Conception of History." *Capital and Class* (London), no. 3: 1–44.

Bartra, Roger. 1974. *Estructura Agraria y Clases Sociales en México*. Mexico City: Ed. ERA.

———. 1982. *Campesinado y Poder Político en México*. Mexico City: Ed. ERA.

Battifora Rojas, Norma, María Luisa Cotrina, Benito Delgado, Gabina Garcia and Avelino Malavér. 1981. "Evolución y Caracter de las Relaciones de Producción de la Cooperativa Agraria de Producción Jesús Obrero de 1930 a 1980." Cajamarca: Programa Académico de Sociología, Universidad Nacional de Cajamarca.

Bauer, Arnold. 1979. "Rural Workers in Spanish America: Problems of Peonage and Oppression." *Hispanic American Historical Review* 59(1): 34–63.

Bazán B., Victor. 1972. "La Tenencia de la Tierra y otros Datos sobre la Comunidad de Porcón, Cajamarca." In *Características del Campesino Minifundista en el Sector Rural de Cajamarca*, 1–20. Documento de Estudio e Investigación Social no. 12. Cajamarca: Departamento de Estudio e Investigación Social.

———. 1978. "La Comunidad Mitmae de Hualqui: Un Caso de Régimen Parcelario." Documento de Estudio e Investigación Social no. 14. Cajamarca: Departamento de Estudio e Investigación Social.

Becerra Bazán, Freddy, Leonardo M. Lopez, César Miyasato, Ramón V. Muñoz, Zacarias A. Padilla, and José A. Saavedra Castro. 1981. "La Economía Lechera Monopólica y su Implicancia en la Difenciación Campesina de Tres Molinos." Cajamarca: Trabajo de Investigación, Programa Académico de Sociología, Universidad Nacional de Cajamarca.

Bernstein, Henry. 1977. "Notes on Capital and Peasantry." *Review of African Political Economy* 18: 60–73.

———. 1979. "African Peasantries: A Theoretical Framework." *Journal of Peasant Studies* 6(4): 421–443.

Blanchard, Peter. 1979. "The Recruitment of Workers in the Peruvian Sierra at the Turn of the Century: The Enganche System." *Inter-American Economic Affairs* 33: 63–83.

Blanco, Hugo. 1972. *Tierra o Muerte: Las Luchas Campesinas en el Perú*. Mexico City: Siglo Veintiuno Eds.

Boletín Informativo de la Asociación de Agricultores y Ganaderos de Cajamarca. 1960. Publication of the Association of Agriculturalists and Cattlemen of Cajamarca. Nos. 1–9.

Bourque, Susan, and Kay B. Warren. 1981. *Women of the Andes: Patriarchy and Social Change*. Ann Arbor: University of Michigan Press.

Buchler, Peter. 1975. *Agrarian Cooperatives in Peru*. Berne: Sociological Institute, University of Berne.

Burga, Manuel. 1976. *De la Encomienda a la Hacienda Capitalista: El Valle del Jequetepeque del Siglo XVI al XX.* Lima: Instituto de Estudios Peruanos.

Burga Bartra, Eduardo. 1981. "La Problemática Rural." Paper presented to the Regional Meeting on Population Problems, AMIDEP (Asociación Multidisciplinaria de Investigación y Docencia en Poblaciones), November 20–25, Cajamarca. Mimeo.

Burga Bartra, Eduardo, and José Huamán Ruiz. 1979. "Problemática Lechera en Cajamarca." Paper presented to the Fourth National Seminar on the Agrarian Problem, Fundación Friedrich Eberth and Universidad Nacional de Cajamarca, November 21–25, Cajamarca. Mimeo.

Burga Larrea, Carlos. 1983. *Diccionario Geográfico e Histórico de Cajamarca.* Lima: Servicios de Artes Gráficos.

Burga Posito, Walter, Norvil Chalán, Rafael Florián, Luis Gonzales, Carlos Hoyos, and Lucio Huamán Escalante. 1980. "Informe Acerca del Carácter Histórico de la Dinámica de Clases en la Cooperativa Agraria de Producción 'Los Ayllus' Ltda., No. 073–B–II." Cajamarca: Programa Académico de Sociología, Universidad Nacional Técnica de Cajamarca.

Burgos C., Manuel, and Evelio Gaitán. 1980. *Los Movimientos Campesinos en Cajamarca.* Cajamarca: Centro de Investigaciones "Ichuna."

Caballero, José María. 1976. "Reforma y Reestructuración Agraria en el Perú." Working paper. Lima: Pontificia Universidad Católica del Perú, Centro de Investigaciones Sociales, Económicas, Políticas y Antropológicas.

—————. 1980. *Agricultura, Reforma Agraria y Pobreza Campesina.* Lima: Instituto de Estudios Peruanos.

—————. 1981a. *Economía Agraria de la Sierra Peruana antes de la Reforma Agraria del 1969.* Lima: Instituto de Estudios Peruanos.

—————. 1981b. "From Belaunde to Belaunde: Peru's Military Experiment in Third-Roadism." Working Paper no. 36. Centre of Latin American Studies, Cambridge University. August.

—————. 1982. "Agrarian Production Co-operatives in Coastal Peru." Centre of Latin American Studies, Cambridge University. December. Mimeo.

—————. 1984. "Unequal Pricing and Unequal Exchange Between the Peasant and Capitalist Economies." *Cambridge Journal of Economics* 8: 347–359.

Caballero, José María, and Elena Alvarez. 1980. *Aspectos Cuantitativos de la Reforma Agraria (1969–1979).* Lima: Instituto de Estudios Peruanos.

Caballero, José María, and Manuel Tello. 1976. "Problemas Post-Reforma Agraria en Cajamarca y La Libertad." Lima: Cuadernos CEPES (Centro Peruano de Estudios Sociales).

Cajamarca Income Survey. 1973. For the provinces of Cajamarca and Cajabamba. Carried out by the Programa de Estudios Socio-Económicos, Proyecto Piloto Cajamarca–La Libertad, Ministerio de Agricultura-CRIAN, Cajamarca. [See Appendix 3.]

Carter, Anthony. 1984. "Household Histories." In *Households: Comparative and Historical Studies of the Domestic Group,* edited by Robert McC. Netting, Richard P. Wilk, and Eric J. Arnould, 44–83. Berkeley and Los Angeles: University of California Press.

Chambeu, Françoise. 1975a. "Caserío Adacucho." Cajamarca: Programa de Estudios Socio-Económicos, Proyecto Cajamarca–La Libertad.

————. 1975b. "Hualqui." Preliminary report. Cajamarca: Programa de Estudios Socio-Económicos, Proyecto Cajamarca–La Libertad.

————. 1975c. "Jocos (Matara)." Cajamarca: Programa de Estudios Socio-Económicos, Proyecto Cajamarca–La Libertad.

————. 1975d. "Manzanilla." Cajamarca: Programa de Estudios Socio-Económicos, Proyecto Cajamarca–La Libertad.

————. 1975e. "Santa Barbara." Cajamarca: Programa de Estudios Socio-Económicos, Proyecto Cajamarca–La Libertad.

————. 1975f. "Tambomayo." Cajamarca: Programa de Estudios Socio-Económicos, Proyecto Cajamarca–La Libertad.

————. 1981. "Participación de la Mujer Rural en Acciones y Cambios Ideológicos en el Contexto de Reforma Agraria." Preliminary report. Lima: International Labour Organization.

Chambeu, Françoise, Gloria Garay, and Ramiro Samaniego. 1975. "Resumen de los 'Estudios de Caso.'" Cajamarca: Programa de Estudios Socio-Económicos, Proyecto Cajamarca–La Libertad.

Chambeu, Françoise, and François Gorget. 1975. "Estudio de Caso de la Hacienda-SAIS La Pauca." Preliminary report. Cajamarca: Programa de Estudios Socio-Económicos, Proyecto Piloto Cajamarca–La Libertad.

Chávez Aliaga, Nazario. 1957. *Cajamarca*. 5 vols. Lima: Talleres Gráficos Colegio Militar Leoncio Prado.

Chayanov, A. V. 1966. *The Theory of Peasant Economy*. Edited by Daniel Thorner, Basil Verblay, and R. E. F. Smith. Homewood, Ill.: Irwin.

Chevalier, Jacques. 1983. "There Is Nothing Simple About Simple Commodity Production." *Journal of Peasant Studies* 10(4): 153–186.

Collin-Delavaud, Claude. 1976. "Consecuencia de la Modernización de la Agricultura en las Haciendas de la Costa Norte del Perú." In *Hacienda, Comunidad y Campesinado en el Perú*, edited by José Matos Mar, 139–175. Lima: Instituto de Estudios Peruanos.

Collins, Jane L. 1988. *Unseasonal Migrations: Rural Labor Scarcity in Peru*. Princeton, N. J.: Princeton University Press.

Córdova Muñoz, Teofílo. 1913. "Prácticas Ganaderas de la Provincia de Cajamarca." Lic. thesis, Universidad Nacional Agraria La Molina, Lima.

Cotler, Julio. 1978. *Clases, Estado y Nación en el Perú*. Lima: Instituto de Estudios Peruanos.

Craig, Wesley W. 1969. "Peru: The Peasant Movement of La Convención." In *Latin American Peasant Movements*, edited by Henry Landsberger, 274–296. Ithaca, N.Y.: Cornell University Press.

Dammert B., José. 1974. *Cajamarca Independiente*. Cajamarca: Imprenta Diocesana.

Davies, Thomas M., Jr. 1974. *Indian Integration in Peru: A Half Century of Experience, 1900–1948*. Lincoln: University of Nebraska Press.

Deere, Carmen Diana. 1977. "Changing Social Relations of Production and Peruvian Peasant Women's Work." *Latin American Perspectives*. 4 (12–13): 58–69.

————. 1978. "The Development of Capitalism in Agriculture and the Division of Labor by Sex." Ph.D. dissertation, University of California, Berkeley.

————. 1982. "The Division of Labor by Sex in Agriculture: A Peruvian Case Study." *Economic Development and Cultural Change* 30(4): 795–811.

————. 1985. "Rural Women and State Policy: The Latin American Agrarian Reform Experience." *World Development* 13(9): 1037–1053.

————. 1987. "The Peasantry in Political Economy: Trends of the 1980s." Occasional Papers Series no. 19. Program in Latin American Studies, University of Massachusetts, Amherst.

Deere, Carmen Diana, and Alain de Janvry. 1979. "A Conceptual Framework for the Empirical Analysis of Peasants." *American Journal of Agricultural Economics* 61(4): 601–611.

————. 1981. "Demographic and Social Differentiation Among Northern Peruvian Peasants." *Journal of Peasant Studies* 8(3): 335–366.

Deere, Carmen Diana, and Magdalena León. 1982. *Women in Andean Agriculture: Peasant Production and Rural Wage Employment in Colombia and Peru.* Geneva: International Labour Organization.

Deere, Carmen Diana, and Robert Wasserstrom. 1981. "Ingreso Familiar y Trabajo no Agrícola entre los Pequeños Productores de America Latina y el Caribe." In *Producción Agropecuaria y Forestal en Zonas de Ladera de America Tropical*, edited by Andrés Novoa and Josh Posner, 151–167. Technical Report no. 11. Turrialba, Costa Rica: Centro Agronómico Tropical de Investigación y Enseñanza.

de Janvry, Alain. 1981. *The Agrarian Question and Reformism in Latin America.* Baltimore: Johns Hopkins University Press.

de Janvry, Alain, and Carlos Garramón. 1977. "The Dynamics of Rural Poverty in Latin America." *Journal of Peasant Studies* 4(3): 206–216.

de León, Edmundo. 1911. *La Ganadería en Piura, Cajamarca, Lambayeque y La Libertad.* Lima: Ministerio de Fomento, Imprenta América.

de Osma, Felipe. 1912. *Informe Sobre Las Huelgas del Norte Presentada al Gobierno su Comisionado.* Lima: Imprenta de la Casa Nacional de Moneda.

Departamento de Estudio e Investigación Social. 1972. "Panorama Estadístico de Cajamarca Alrededor de los Años de 1813 y 1838." Documento de Estudio e Investigación Social no. 11. Cajamarca: Departamento de Estudio e Investigación Social.

Díaz, Alida. 1974. "El Censo General de 1876 en el Perú." Lima: Seminario de Historia Rural Andina, Universidad Nacional Mayor de San Marcos.

Díaz Polanco, Hector. 1977. *Teoría Marxista de la Economía Campesina.* Mexico City: Juan Pablos Ed.

Díaz S., Salvador. 1971. "Estudio Monográfico del Distrito de San Marcos (1960)." Documento de Estudio e Investigación Social no. 8. Cajamarca: Departamento de Estudio e Investigación Social.

Dobyns, Henry F., and Paul L. Doughty. 1976. *Peru: A Cultural History.* New York: Oxford University Press.

Documentál del Perú: Cajamarca. 1967. No. 6. Lima: Iberia, S.A.

Edwards, Carlos Eduardo. 1912. "Memoria Administrativa, Año 1912, Prefecto del Departamento de Cajamarca." File E 688. Biblioteca Nacional del Perú, Sala de Investigaciónes, Lima.

Elespuru Bernizón, Eulogio. 1939. "La Provincia de Cajamarca." *Ensayos Geográficos* (Pontifícia Universidad Católica del Perú, Lima), 146–158.

El Rodeo. 1947–1949. Publication of the Asociación de Agricultores y Ganaderos de

Cajamarca (Association of Agriculturalists and Cattlemen of Cajamarca). Nos. 1–15.

Ennew, Judith, Paul Hirst, and Keith Tribe. 1977. "Peasantry as an Economic Category." *Journal of Peasant Studies* 4(4): 295–322.

Escalante, Elsa. 1972. *Personalización del Campesino y Trabajo Social*. Lima: Colección Servicio Social, Universidad Católica del Perú.

Eslava, José. 1973. "PERULAC: Sus Influencias Socio-Económicas en la Provincia de Cajamarca." Documento de Estudio e Investigación Social no. 10. Cajamarca: Departamento de Estudios e Investigación Social.

Esparza Bueno, Alejandro, Dolores Hernandez, Hugo Reyna, Doris Saldaña, Pedro Sánchez, and Celso Valladolid. 1981. "Clases Sociales en la Provincia de Cajamarca (1969–1979): Criterios para su Análisis." Cajamarca: Programa Académico de Sociología, Universidad Nacional de Cajamarca.

Esteva, Gustavo. 1978. "Y si los Campesinos Existen?" *Comercio Exterior* 28(6): 699–713.

Evers, Hans-Dieter, Wolfgang Clauss, and Diana Wong. 1984. "Subsistence Reproduction: A Framework for Analysis." In *Households and the World-Economy*, edited by Joan Smith, Immanuel Wallerstein, and Hans-Dieter Evers, 23–36. Beverly Hills, Calif.: Sage.

Favre, Henry. 1976. "Evolución y Situación de la Hacienda Tradicional de la Región de Huancavelica." In *Hacienda, Comunidad y Campesinado en el Perú*, edited by José Matos Mar, 105–138. Lima: Instituto de Estudios Peruanos.

Favre, Henry, Claude Collin-Delavaud, and José Matos Mar. 1967. *La Hacienda en el Perú*. Lima: Instituto de Estudios Peruanos.

Feder, Ernest. 1971. *The Rape of the Peasantry: Latin America's Landholding System*. New York: Anchor Books.

———. 1977–1978. "Campesinistas y Descampesinistas: Tres Enfoques Divergentes (no Incompatibles) sobre la Destrucción del Campesinado." *Comercio Exterior* 27(12): 1439–1446, 28(1): 42–51.

Fernández, Blanca. 1982. "Reforma Agraria y Condición Socio-Económica de la Mujer: El Caso de Dos Cooperativas Agrarias de Producción Peruanas." In *Las Trabajadoras del Agro*, edited by Magdalena León, 261–276. Bogota: Asociación Colombiana para el Estudio de la Población.

Figueroa, Adolfo. 1974. *Capitalist Development and the Peasant Economy in Peru*. Cambridge: Cambridge University Press.

FitzGerald, E. V. K. 1979. *The Political Economy of Peru, 1956–1978: Economic Development and the Restructuring of Capital*. Cambridge: Cambridge University Press.

Flecha, Jaime. 1975. "Quebrada de San Francisco." Preliminary report. Cajamarca: Programa de Estudios Socio-Económicos, Proyecto Cajamarca–La Libertad.

Foladori, Guillermo. 1981. *Polémica en Torno a las Teorías del Campesinado*. Mexico City: Instituto Nacional de Antropología e Historia.

Folbre, Nancy. 1986. "Cleaning House: New Perspectives on Households and Economic Development." *Journal of Development Economics* 22(1): 5–40.

Ford, Thomas. 1955. *Man and Land in Peru*. Gainesville: University of Florida Press.

Franco, Efraín. 1974. "Estudio de Diagnóstico Socio-Económico del Area de Influencia del Proyecto Piloto Cajamarca–La Libertad." Preliminary report. Cajamarca: Ministerio de Agricultura-CRIAN (Centro Regional de Investigación Agropecuaria del Norte), Programa de Estudios Socio-Económicos, Proyecto Piloto Cajamarca–La Libertad.

———. 1976. "Evaluación del Proyecto Cajamarca–La Libertad." Working Paper. Cajamarca: Programa de Estudios Socio-Económicos, Proyecto Cajamarca–La Libertad.

Friedman, Kathie. 1984. "Households as Income-Pooling Units." In *Households and the World-Economy*, edited by Joan Smith, Immanuel Wallerstein and Hans-Dieter Evers, 37–55. Beverly Hills, Calif.: Sage.

Friedmann, Harriet. 1980. "Household Production and the National Economy: Concepts for the Analysis of Agrarian Formations." *Journal of Peasant Studies* 7(2): 158–184.

Gaitán P., Evelie. 1972. "Notas Sobre la Formación de Haciendas al Norte del Valle de Cajamarca." *Humanidades* (Universidad Técnica de Cajamarca) 1 (January): 22–28.

———. 1975. "El Obraje de Porcón en Cajamarca." *Revista: Artes, Ciencia y Humanidades* (Universidad Nacional Técnica de Cajamarca): 9–20.

Garay, Gloria. 1975a. "Chilacát." Cajamarca: Programa de Estudios Socio-Económicos, Proyecto Cajamarca–La Libertad.

———. 1975b. "La Laguna." Preliminary report. Cajamarca: Programa de Estudios Socio-Económicos, Proyecto Cajamarca–La Libertad.

———. 1975c. "La Laimina." Cajamarca: Programa de Estudios Socio-Económicos, Proyecto Cajamarca–La Libertad.

———. 1975d. "Pariamarca." Cajamarca: Programa de Estudios Socio-Económicos, Proyecto Cajamarca–La Libertad.

———. 1975e. "San Pedro de Combayo." Cajamarca: Programa de Estudios Socio-Económicos, Proyecto Cajamarca–La Libertad.

Garland, Alejandro. 1908. *Peru in 1906*. Lima: Imprenta La Industria.

Gitlitz, John Stephen. 1975. *"Hacienda, Comunidad, and Peasant Protest in Northern Peru."* Ph.D. dissertation, University of North Carolina, Chapel Hill.

Gonzales, Michael J. 1978. "Cayalti: The Formation of a Rural Proletariat on a Peruvian Sugar Cane Plantation, 1875–1933." Ph.D. dissertation, University of California, Berkeley.

———. 1980. "Capitalist Agriculture and Labour Contracting in Northern Peru, 1880–1905." *Journal of Latin American Studies* 12(2): 291–315.

Gonzalez de Olarte, Efraín. 1984. *Economía de la Comunidad Campesina*. Lima: Instituto de Estudios Peruanos.

Goodman, David, and Michael Redclift. 1982. *From Peasant to Proletarian: Capitalist Development and Agrarian Transition*. New York: St. Martin's Press.

Gorget, François. 1975a. "Araqueda." Preliminary report. Cajamarca: Programa de Estudios Socio-Económicos, Proyecto Cajamarca–La Libertad, December.

———. 1975b. "Porcón." Preliminary report. Cajamarca: Programa de Estudios Socio-Económicos, Proyecto Cajamarca–La Libertad, December.

Hafer, Raymond Frederic. 1971. "The People up the Hill: Individual Progress Without Village Participation in Pariamarca, Cajamarca, Peru." Ph.D. dissertation, Indiana University, Bloomington.

Harding, Colin. 1975. "Land Reform and Social Conflict in Peru." In *The Peruvian*

Experiment, edited by Abraham Lowenthal, 220–253. Princeton, N.J.: Princeton University Press.

Harnecker, Marta. [1969] 1985. *Los Conceptos Elementales del Materialismo Histórico*. Mexico City: Siglo Veintiuno Eds.

Hartmann, Heidi. 1981. "The Family as the Locus of Gender, Class, and Political Struggle: The Example of Housework." *Signs: Journal of Women in Culture and Society* 6 *(Spring)*: 366–394.

Heynig, Klaus. 1982. "The Principal Schools of Thought on the Peasant Economy." *CEPAL Review*, no. 16: 113–139.

Hindess, Barry, and Paul Hirst. 1975. *Pre-Capitalist Modes of Production*. London: Routledge and Kegan Paul.

———. 1977. *Mode of Production and Social Formation*. London: Macmillan.

Hopkins, Raul. 1979. "La Producción Agropecuaria en el Perú, 1944–1969: Una Approximación Estadística." Working Paper no. 42. Lima: Pontificia Universidad Católica del Perú, Centro de Investigaciones Sociales, Económicas, Políticas y Antropológicas. November.

———. 1981. *Desarrollo Desiqual y Crisis en la Agricultura Peruana, 1944–1969*. Lima: Instituto de Estudios Peruanos.

Horton, Douglas E. 1976. "Haciendas and Cooperatives: A Study of Estate Organization, Land Reform, and New Reform Enterprises in Peru." Dissertation Series no. 67. Latin American Studies Program, Cornell University, Ithaca, N.Y.

Humphries, Jane. 1977. "Class Struggle and the Persistence of the Working-Class Family." *Cambridge Journal of Economics* 1(3): 241–258.

Hunt, Shane. 1977. "Real Wages and Economic Growth in Peru, 1900–1940." Discussion Paper Series no. 25. Center for Latin American Development Studies, Boston University.

Jelícic C., Jorge. 1978. *La Reforma Agraria y la Ganadería Lechera en el Perú*. Lima: Ed. Minerva.

Kapsoli, Wilfredo. 1977. *Los Movimientos Campesinos en el Perú: 1879–1965*. Lima: Delva Ed.

Kay, Cristóbal. 1974. "Comparative Development of the European Manorial System and the Latin American Hacienda System." *Journal of Peasant Studies* 1(2): 69–98.

Klarén, Peter F. 1976. *Formación de las Haciendas Azucareras y Orígenes del APRA*. Lima: Instituto de Estudios Peruanos.

———. 1977. "The Social and Economic Consequences of Modernization in the Peruvian Sugar Industry, 1870–1930." In *Land and Labour in Latin America*, edited by Keith Duncan and Ian Rutledge, 229–252. Cambridge: Cambridge University Press.

Kubler, George. 1952. *The Indian Caste of Peru, 1795–1940*. Publication no. 14. Washington, D.C.: Smithsonian Institution, Institute of Social Anthropology.

Lafosse de Vega-Centeno, Violeta Sara. 1969. "La Ley de Reforma Agraria y sus Implicaciones en la Estructura Familiar." Working Paper no. 3. Lima: Pontificia Universidad Católica del Perú. November.

Lajo Lazo, Manuel. 1980. "La Crisis de la Alimentación y el Papel de la Agroindustria." In *Promoción Agraria: Para Quién?* edited by José Manuel Mejía, 106–133. Lima: Tiempo Presente Ed.

———. 1981a. "Agroindustria, Transnacionales y Alimentos en el Perú." *Estudios Andinos*, no. 17/18: 139–174.

———. 1981b. "Efectos de la Agroindustria Transnacional en el Desarrollo Agrícola y Alimentario." Working Paper no. 47. Lima: Pontifícia Universidad Católica del Perú, Centro de Investigaciones Sociales, Económicas, Políticas y Antropológicas. May.

———. n.d. "Carnation y Nestlé en el Perú." Mimeo.

Lehmann, David. 1982. "After Chayanov and Lenin: New Paths of Agrarian Capitalism." *Journal of Development Economics* 11(2): 133–161.

Lenin, V. I. 1971. *Alliance of the Working Class and the Peasantry*. Moscow: Progress Publishers.

———. 1974. *The Development of Capitalism in Russia*. Moscow: Progress Publishers.

"Ley de Reforma Agraria del Perú, Decreto Ley No. 17716." 1970. *El Trimestre Económico* 37 (January): 170–211.

Llambi, Luis. 1981. "Las Unidades de Producción Campesina en el Sistema Capitalista: Un Intento de Teorización." *Estudios Rurales Latinoamericanos* 4(2): 125–154.

Llanos Aguero, José Rosario. 1972. *Monografía del Distrito de Jesús*. Cajamarca: Universidad Nacional Técnica de Cajamarca.

Long, Norman. 1984. "Introduction." In *Family and Work in Rural Societies: Perspectives on Non-Wage Labour*, edited by Norman Long, 1–29. London: Tavistock.

Long, Norman, and Bryan R. Roberts. 1978. "Peasant Cooperation and Capitalist Expansion in Peru." In *Peasant Cooperation and Capitalist Expansion in Central Peru*, edited by Norman Long and Bryan R. Roberts, 297–328. Austin: University of Texas Press.

———. 1984. *Miners, Peasants, and Entrepreneurs: Regional Development in the Central Highlands of Peru*. Cambridge: Cambridge University Press.

Loveman, Brian. 1979. "Critique of Arnold J. Bauer's 'Rural Workers in Spanish America: Problems of Peonage and Oppression.'" *Hispanic American Historical Review* 59(3): 478–485.

McClintock, Cynthia. 1981. *Peasant Cooperatives and Political Change in Peru*. Princeton, N.J.: Princeton University Press.

Macera, Pablo. 1971. "Feudalismo Colonial Americano: El Caso de las Haciendas Peruanas." *Acta Histórica* (Szeged, Hungary) 35: 3–43.

———. 1974. *Las Plantaciones Azucareras en el Perú, 1821–1875*. Lima: Biblioteca Andina.

———. 1976. "Población Rural en Haciendas, 1876." Lima: Seminario de Historia Rural Andina, Universidad Nacional Mayor de San Marcos.

———. 1977. *Trabajos de Historia*. 4 vols. Lima: Instituto Nacional de Cultura.

Málaga Santolalla, Fermín. 1906. *Departamento de Cajamarca: Monografía Geográfico-Estadístico*. Lima: Librería de San Pedro.

Maletta, Hector. 1980. "Cambios en la Demarcación Política y Dinámica de la Población del Perú: 1876–1972." Working Paper no. 7. Lima: Universidad del Pacífico. November.

Mallon, Florencia. 1983. *The Defense of Community in Peru's Central Highlands: Peasant Struggle and Capitalist Transition, 1860–1940*. Princeton, N.J.: Princeton University Press.

———. 1987. "Patriarchy and the Transition to Capitalism: Central Peru, 1860–1940." *Feminist Studies* 13(2): 379–407.

Malpica, Carlos. 1967. *Solido Norte, Boletín Especial para Cajamarca*. Lima: Ed. Cortez.

Manrique C., Manuel. 1974. "Cajamarca: La Tierra para el que la Trabaja?" In *Informe del Trabajo de Campo Realizado en el Departamento de Cajamarca, 1974*, edited by Eduardo Arce del Campo and Mariano Valderrama, chap. 4. Lima: Taller de Investigación Rural, Universidad Católica del Perú.

Manrique C., Manuel, and Mariano Valderrama. 1974. "Estudio de Algunos Casos de Fragmentación de Haciendas en el Departamento de Cajamarca." In *Informe del Trabajo de Campo Realizado en el Departamento de Cajamarca, 1974*, edited by Eduardo Arce del Campo and Mariano Valderrama, chap. 3. Lima: Taller de Investigación Rural, Universidad Católica del Perú.

Martínez, Marielle, and Teresa Rendón. 1978. "Fuerza de Trabajo y Reproducción Campesina." *Comercio Exterior* 28(6): 663–674.

Martínez Alier, Juan. 1973. *Los Huacchilleros del Perú*. Lima: Instituto de Estudios Peruanos y Ed. Ruedo Ibérico.

——. 1977. "Relations of Production in Andean Haciendas: Peru." In *Land and Labour in Latin America*, edited by Keith Duncan and Ian Routledge, 141–164. Cambridge: Cambridge University Press.

Marx, Karl. 1967. *Capital*. Vols. 1, 3. New York: International Publishers.

Matos Mar, José, and José Manuel Mejía. 1980. *La Reforma Agraria en el Perú*. Peru Problema no. 19. Lima: Instituto de Estudios Peruanos.

Means, Philip Ainsworth. 1920. "Indian Legislation in Peru." *Hispanic American Historical Review* 3: 509–534.

Mejía, José Manuel. 1974. "El Problema de la Regulación de Mano de Obra en la SAIS José Carlos Mariátegui." In *Informe del Trabajo de Campo Realizado en el Departamento de Cajamarca, 1974*, edited by Eduardo Arce del Campo and Mariano Valderrama, chap. 8. Lima: Taller de Investigación Rural, Universidad Católica del Perú.

——. 1980. "De la Reforma Agraria a la Promoción Agropecuaria: Un Análisis Crítico de la Nueva Política Agraria." In *Promoción Agraria: Para Quién?* edited by José Manuel Mejía, 10–39. Lima: Tiempo Presente Ed.

Mejía, Victor, and Humberto Correa. 1979. "Investigaciones Preliminares en la Cuenca Lechera, Caso Huayobamba." Paper presented to the Fourth National Seminar on the Agrarian Problem, Fundación Friedrich Eberth and Universidad Nacional de Cajamarca, November 21–25, Cajamarca.

Merino P., Victor. 1978. "La Acción del Estado y la Industria de Productos Lacteos: El Caso de la Leche Evaporada." Thesis, Universidad Nacional Agraria La Molina, Lima.

Meyers, Albert. 1982. "Expansión del Capitalismo, Estratégias de Reproducción y Estratificación Social en el Campesinado: Dos Casos en el Valle del Mantaro, Perú." *Estudios Rurales Latinoamericanos* 5(3): 275–306.

Miller, Solomon. 1967. "Hacienda to Plantation in Northern Peru: The Process of Proletarianization of a Tenant Farmer Society." In *Contemporary Change in Traditional Societies*, edited by Julian Steward, 133–225. Urbana: University of Illinois Press.

Ministry of Labor. 1981. "Fijación de Sueldos y Salarios Mínimos Vitales en el Perú." Lima: Dirección General de Remuneraciones, Oficina de Estudios Socio-Económicos.

Molano, Alfredo. 1978. "Capitalismo y Agricultura: Un Modelo Hipotético sobre las Relaciones de Producción y Circulación." *Estudios Rurales Latinoamericanos* 1(3): 34–67.

Montoya, Rodrigo. 1978. *A Propósito del Carácter Predominantemente Capitalista de la Economía Peruana Actual.* Lima: Mosca Azul Eds.

———. 1980. *Capitalismo y No Capitalismo en el Perú: Un Estudio Histórico de su Articulación en un Eje Regional.* Lima: Mosca Azul Eds.

———. 1982. "Class Relations in the Andean Countryside." *Latin American Perspectives* 9(3): 62–78.

Mosley, Paul. 1985. "Achievements and Contradictions of the Peruvian Agrarian Reform: A Regional Perspective." *Journal of Development Studies* 21(3): 440–448.

Netting, Robert McC., Richard R. Wilk, and Eric J. Arnould, eds. 1984. *Households: Comparative and Historical Studies of the Domestic Group.* Berkeley and Los Angeles: University of California Press.

ONEC (Oficina Nacional de Estadística y Censos). 1974. *La Población del Perú.* Lima: ONEC.

Orlove, Ben. 1977. "Inequality Among Peasants: The Forms and Uses of Reciprocal Exchange." In *Peasant Livelihood,* edited by Rhoda Halperin and James Dow, 201–214. New York: St. Martin's Press.

Pareja, Piedad. 1980. "Apuntes sobre Sindicalismo Agrario en el Perú." Informe de investigación. Serie: Movimientos Sociales no. 4. Universidad Nacional Agraria La Molina, Lima.

Paz-Soldán, Juan Pedro. 1917. *Diccionario Biográfico de Peruanos Contemporaneos.* Lima: Imprenta Gil.

Peasant Family Survey. 1976. For the province of Cajamarca. Carried out by Carmen Diana Deere. [See Appendix 4.]

Perú. 1876a. Dirección General de Estadística. *Censo General de la República del Perú Formado en 1876.* 7 vols. Lima: Imprenta del Teatro.

———. 1876b. Dirección General de Estadística. *Resumen del Censo General de Habitantes del Perú Hecho en 1876.* Lima: Imprenta del Estado.

———. 1940. Dirección Nacional de Estadística y Censos. *Censo Nacional de Población de 1940.* 9 vols. [1944–1949]. Lima: Imprenta Torres Aguirre.

———. 1961a. Dirección Nacional de Estadística y Censos. *Censos Nacional de Población, Vivienda y Agropecuario de 1961.* 28 departmental vols. [1965–1973]. Lima: Dirección Nacional de Estadística y Censos [subsequently Oficina Nacional de Estadística y Censos].

———. 1961b. Dirección Nacional de Estadística y Censos. *Primer Censo Nacional Agropecuario, 2 de Julio de 1961.* Resultados Finales de Primera Prioridad [1965]. Lima: Dirección Nacional de Estadística y Censos.

———. 1961c. Dirección Nacional de Estadística y Censos. *Sexto Censo Nacional de Población, 2 de Julio de 1961: Centros Poblados.* 4 vols. [1964–1966]. Lima: Dirección Nacional de Estadística y Censos.

———. 1972a. ONEC (Oficina Nacional de Estadística y Censos). *Censos Nacionales, VII de Población, II de Vivienda, 4 de Junio de 1972.* Two national and 24 departmental unnumbered vols. [1974–1975]. Lima: ONEC.

———. 1972b. ONEC (Oficina Nacional de Estadística y Censos). *II (Segundo) Censo Nacional Agropecuario, 4 al 24 de Septiembre, 1972.* One national and 24 departmental unnumbered vols. [1974–1976]. Lima: ONEC [subsequently, Instituto Nacional de Estadística].

———. 1981. INE (Instituto Nacional de Estadística). *Censos Nacionales, VIII de*

Población, III de Vivienda, 12 de Julio de 1981. Two national and 24 departmental unnumbered vols. [1984]. Lima: INE.

Piel, Jean. 1970. "The Place of the Peasantry in the National Life of Peru in the Nineteenth Century." *Past and Present,* no. 46: 108–133.

Pike, Frederick B. 1964. *The Modern History of Peru.* London: Weidenfeld and Nicolson.

Pinto, Honorio. 1972. "El Primer Censo Agropecuario del Perú. (1929)." Lima: Seminario de Historia Rural Andina, Universidad Nacional Mayor de San Marcos.

Puga, José Mercedes. 1916. "La Labor Parlamentaria del Diputado Propietario por la Provincia de Cajamarca, 1908–1914." Mimeo.

Rainbird, Helen, and Lewis Taylor. 1976. "Historical Process and Agrarian Reform in Cajamarca." Typescript.

Rapp, Rayna. 1978. "Family and Class in Contemporary America: Notes Toward an Understanding of Ideology." *Science and Society* 42(3): 278–300.

Reinhardt, Nola. 1988. *Our Daily Bread: Family Farming in the Colombian Andes.* Berkeley and Los Angeles: University of California Press.

Resnick, Stephen, and Richard Wolff. 1979. "The Theory of Transitional Conjunctures and the Transition from Feudalism to Capitalism in Western Europe." *Review of Radical Political Economy* 11(3): 3–22.

———. 1982. "Classes in Marxian Theory." *Review of Radical Political Economy* 13(4): 1–18.

———. 1987. *Knowledge and Class: A Marxian Critique of Political Economy.* Chicago: University of Chicago Press.

Rivera, Ricardo. 1974. "Huayobamba." In *Informe del Trabajo de Campo Realizado en el Departamento de Cajamarca, 1974,* edited by Eduardo Arce del Campo and Mariano Valderrama, chap. 10. Lima: Taller de Investigación Rural, Universidad Católica del Perú.

Rojas, Antonio. 1974. "La Reforma Agraria en el Fundo La Colpa." In *Informe del Trabajo de Campo Realizado en el Departamento de Cajamarca, 1974,* edited by Eduardo Arce del Campo and Mariano Valderrama, chap. 9. Lima: Taller de Investigación Rural, Universidad Católica del Perú.

Róquez, Gladys. 1979. "Desarrollo Capitalista y Agricultura en el Perú (Decadas de 1950 y 60): El Caso del Azucar." Serie Ensayos Generales no. 2. Taller de Estudios Andinos, Universidad Nacional Agraria La Molina, Lima.

Roseberry, William. 1983. *Coffee and Capitalism in the Venezuelan Andes.* Austin: University of Texas Press.

Saco, Alfredo. 1946. *Programa Agrario del Aprismo.* Lima: Ed. Populares.

Samaniego, Ramiro. 1975a. "Caserío Gigón." Cajamarca: Programa de Estudios Socio-Económicos, Proyecto Cajamarca–La Libertad.

———. 1975b. "Quinuanayo." Cajamarca: Programa de Estudios Socio-Económicos, Proyecto Cajamarca–La Libertad.

Santolalla, Nicolás. [1918] 1977. "Monografía de la Hacienda 'San Felipe de Combayo.'" Thesis, Universidad Nacional Agraria La Molina, Lima. Reprinted in *Agricultura en el Perú S.XX (documentos),* edited by Pablo Macera, 2: 210–293. Lima: Seminario de Historia Rural Andina, Universidad Nacional Mayor de San Marcos.

Sarachaga, Juan, Carlos Degola, and Braulio Arana. [1855] 1981. *Estadística Fisica y Política del Departamento de Cajamarca, Año de 1855.* Reprint. Cajamarca: Universidad Nacional de Cajamarca.

Schejtman, Alexander. 1980. "The Peasant Economy: Internal Logic, Articulation, and Persistence." *CEPAL Review*, no. 11: 115–134.

Schmink, Marianne. 1984. "Household Economic Strategies: A Review and Research Agenda." *Latin American Research Review* 19(3): 87–101.

Scott, D. C. 1976. "Peasants, Proletarianization, and the Articulation of Modes of Production: The Case of Sugar Cane Cutters in Northern Peru, 1940–1969." *Journal of Peasant Studies* 3(3): 321–341.

———. 1981. "Agrarian Reform and Seasonal Employment in Coastal Peruvian Agriculture." *Journal of Development Studies* 17(4): 282–306.

Silva Santisteban, Fernando. 1986. "Los Obrajes en el Corregimiento de Cajamarca." In *Siglos XVI–XVIII: Historia de Cajamarca*, edited by Fernando Silva Santisteban, Waldemar Espinoza, and Rogger Ravines, 181–191. Cajamarca: Instituto Nacional de Cultura and Corporación de Desarrollo de Cajamarca.

Silva Santisteban, Jesús. 1945. *Cajamarca: Divulgación de Temas Agro-Pecuarios de la Provincia, 1944*. Lima: Dirección General de Agricultura, Ministerio de Agricultura.

Smith, Carol. 1984. "Forms of Production in Practice: Fresh Approaches to Simple Commodity Production." *Journal of Peasant Studies* 11(4): 201–221.

Smith, Joan, Immanuel Wallerstein, and Hans-Dieter Evers. 1984. "Introduction." In *Households and the World-Economy*, edited by Joan Smith, Immanuel Wallerstein, and Hans-Dieter Evers, 7–13. Beverly Hills, Calif.: Sage.

Solano, Julio O. 1906. "Informe sobre el Fundo Huayrapongo." Thesis, Universidad Nacional Agraria La Molina, Lima.

Spalding, Karen. 1975. "Hacienda-Village Relations in Andean Society to 1830." *Latin American Perspectives* 2(1): 107–121.

Stavenhagen, Rodolfo. 1978. "Capitalism and Peasantry in Mexico." *Latin American Perspectives* 5(3): 27–37.

Stein, William W. 1980. "Familia y Desarrollo Educacional en Vicos, Perú." In *Parentesco y Matrimonio en los Andes*, edited by Enrique Mayer and Ralph Bolton, 657–680. Lima: Pontifícia Universidad Católica del Perú, Fondo Editorial.

Taylor, Lewis. 1979. "Main Trends in Agrarian Capitalist Development: Cajamarca, Peru, 1880–1976." Ph.D. dissertation, University of Liverpool.

———. 1984. "Cambios Capitalistas en las Haciendas Cajamarquinas del Perú, 1900–1935." *Estudios Rurales Latinoamericanos* 7(1): 93–129.

———. 1986. "Estates, Freeholders, and Peasant Communities in Cajamarca, 1876–1972." Working Paper no. 42. Centre of Latin American Studies, Cambridge University. August.

Thorp, Rosemary, and Geoffrey Bertram. 1978. *Peru, 1890–1977: Growth and Policy in an Open Economy*. New York: Columbia University Press.

Torres, Segunda, and Hans Hillenbrand. 1978. "Alrededor del Fogón: Algunas Observaciones Acerca de la Familia Campesina en Cajamarca." SEPARATA 15, Cajamarca. May.

Tullis, F. LaMond. 1970. *Lord and Peasant in Peru: A Paradigm of Political and Social Change*. Cambridge, Mass.: Harvard University Press.

UMSM (Universidad Mayor de San Marcos). 1917. *Descripción del Viaje a los Departamentos de La Libertad, Cajamarca y Lambayeque de la Delegación Universitaria en las Vacaciones del Año Escolar de 1916*. Lima: Librería de San Pedro.

Valderrama, Mariano. 1974. "El Proceso de Fragmentación de la Propiedad Rural en el Departamento de Cajamarca." In *Informe del Trabajo de Campo Realizado en el*

Departamento de Cajamarca, 1974, edited by Eduardo Arce del Campo and Mariano Valderrama, chap. 2. Lima: Taller de Investigación Rural, Universidad Católica del Perú.

Van de Wetering, Hylke. 1973. "The Current State of Land Reform in Peru." *Land Tenure Center Newsletter* (Madison, Wisc.), no. 40: 5–9.

Villanueva Urteaga, Horacio. 1975. *Cajamarca, Apuntes para su Historia.* Cuzco: Ed. Garcilazo.

von Werlhof, Claudia, and Hanns-Peter Neuhoff. 1982. "The Combination of Different Production Relations on the Basis of Nonproletarianization: Agrarian Production in Yaracuy, Venezuela." *Latin American Perspectives* (3): 79–103.

Wallerstein, Immanuel. 1984. "Household Structures and Labor-Force Formation in the Capitalist World-Economy." In *Households and the World-Economy,* edited by Joan Smith, Immanuel Wallerstein, and Hans-Dieter Evers, 17–22. Beverly Hills, Calif.: Sage.

Warman, Arturo. 1980a. *Ensayos sobre el Campesinado en Mexico.* Mexico City: Ed. Nueva Imagen.

———. 1980b. *"We Come to Object": The Peasants of Morelos and the National State.* Translated by Stephen K. Ault. Baltimore: Johns Hopkins University Press.

White, Benjamin. 1980. "Rural Household Studies in Anthropological Perspective." In *Rural Household Studies in Asia,* edited by Hans P. Binswanger et al., 3–25. Singapore: Singapore University Press.

Wilkie, James. 1974. *Statistics and National Policy.* Supplement 3. Los Angeles: UCLA Latin American Center.

———. 1984. *Statistical Abstract of Latin America.* 26 vols. Los Angeles: UCLA Latin American Center.

Winson, Anthony. 1982. "The 'Prussian Road' of Agrarian Development: A Reconsideration." *Economy and Society* 11(4): 381–408.

Wolff, Richard, and Stephen Resnick. 1986. "Power, Property, and Class." *Socialist Review* 86 (March–April): 97–124.

Wolpe, Harold. 1980. "Introduction." In *The Articulation of Modes of Production: Essays from "Economy and Society,"* edited by Harold Wolpe, 1–43. London: Routledge and Kegan Paul.

Yepes del Castillo, Ernesto. 1972. *Perú, 1820–1920: Un Siglo de Desarrollo Capitalista.* Lima: Instituto de Estudios Peruanos.

Zaldivar, Ramon. 1974. "Agrarian Reform and Military Reformism in Peru." In *Agrarian Reform and Agrarian Reformism,* edited by David Lehmann, 25–67. London: Faber and Faber.

Zalkin, Michael. 1986. "Peasant Response to State Grain Policy in Post-Revolutionary Nicaragua, 1979–1984." Ph.D dissertation, University of Massachusetts, Amherst.

Zamósc, León. 1979. "Notas Teóricas sobre la Subordinación de la Producción Mercantil Campesina al Capital." *Estudios Rurales Latinoamericanos* 2(3): 296–305.

INDEX

Adacucho (community), 39, 118
Adacucho (hacienda): land sales at, 204; wage labor at, 109
Agocucho (*caserío*), 255
Agopampa (*caserío*), 255
Agrarian debt, 252–53; cancellation of, 261
Agrarian Development and Promotion Law, 233, 319, 320
Agrarian leagues (Ligas Agrarias), 236
Agrarian reform, 163, 169–70, 186, 210, 230–34, 237, 316, 317; adjudications in, 239, 244–45; beneficiaries of, 240–46, 254, 260–61; and cooperative development, 240–54; and cooperative indebtedness, 239, 247–48, 252–53; and dairy industry, 318; effect on status of peasants, 231, 237, 254–61; and employment opportunities, 256–60; expropriations in, 234, 236, 238; and hacienda system, 260; and organization of reform sector, 232–33, 237–40; private initiatives in, 169–77; and the state, 246, 249–52, 254–61; and women, 242–43, 249n, 251n, 257
Agrarian Reform Financing Corporation (CORFIRA), 247n
Agrarian Reform Law (1964), 161, 167, 173–74, 230
Agrarian Reform Law (1969), 180, 225, 228, 230–34
Agrarian Reform Office (Cajamarca), 239n, 240, 241

Agregados, defined, 79–80
Agricultural production: commoditization of, 111; experimentation in, 154; gender division of labor in, 102–4, 282–85; growth of, 317; in 1929 census, 57; technological developments in, 56
Aguardiente, 55, 131, 139; tax on, 124
Aguilar-Rumay household, 134–37, 292–95, 305–7, 321–24
Alayza Escardo, Luis, 57
Albert, Bill, 43, 45
Alcalde, Rita, 185
Alcohol, consumption of, 139n, 288, 307
Alianza Popular Revolucionaria Americana (APRA), 39, 43n, 89, 161, 162, 169, 171
Althusser, Louis, 3
Alzamora, Ing. Emilio, 185
Amarcucho (hacienda), 182, 184
Amazonas (department), 205–6
Amazon region: development of, 319–20; migration to, 205–7, 320–22, 324
Amin, Samir, 9
Amorín, Luis, 148, 187
Ancash (department), 30n
Andahuaylas (department), 61n
Animal production, 52, 280, 287n; on haciendas, 85–86, 112–13, 333–34; in peasant households, 285. *See also* Cattle production; Sheep production
Apurímac (department), 24n
Arana vda. de Bernal, María, 35
Aranjuez (*caserío*), xv

Araqueda (hacienda), 27, 85n, 86n, 91n
Arrendires (landlord renters), 36–39, 94; and
    capitalist land rentals, 179–80; contracts
    of, 37–38, 177; on Hacienda Porcón, 37,
    88–89; on Hacienda Santa Ursula, 37,
    89; and land purchases, 180
Arrendires (peasant renters): class analysis of,
    91–93; definition of, 59–60; on Hacienda
    Combayo, 81; on Hacienda Porcón, 88;
    on Hacienda Santa Ursula, 63–64,
    70–71; income levels of, 115–16, 289;
    rental arrangements of, 64–65; rental
    rates, 66
Artisan production, 54, 102, 104, 115–16,
    226, 272–74, 276, 280; alternatives to,
    122; and gender division of labor in, 104,
    142, 286
Artisans, 7, 11, 54n, 127, 330; female, 286
Ascope (coastal town), 42
Asilo de Ancianos Desámparados, 174, 180
Association of Agriculturalists and Cattlemen
    of Cajamarca, 148, 149, 155, 172, 187,
    204; and dairy industry, 152; dissolution
    of, 236; and land reform, 236; and
    PERULAC, 216–20
Asunción (*caserío*), 68, 196
Asunción (district), 25, 135
Atahualpa (Inca), xiii
Atahualpa (SAIS), 239, 240, 241n, 244
Ayacucho (department), 24n

Bambamarca (province), 46n, 47
Banaji, Jairus, 9–10
Banco Agropecuario, 235
Banco Alemán Transatlántico, 54
Banco de Credito de Perú, 171
Banco de Fomento Agropecuario, 155
Banco de Perú y Londres, 54
Banco de Reserva del Perú, 53
Banco Italiano, 54
Banditry, 75n
Barley production, 50, 79, 112–13, 125
Barrantes, Oscar, 54
Barter, 54, 104, 135
Bartra, Roger, 5, 10
Bayeta (wool cloth), 55, 104
Bazán B., Victor, 126n, 196
Beggars, 313
Belaunde Terry, Fernando, 161, 233, 316,
    318; government of, 222, 243, 322
Belempampa (*fundo*), 36, 181

Benavides, Oscar, 41n; government of, 42,
    149
Beneficiencia Pública of Cajamarca, 36, 88,
    170; of Celendín, 178, 181, 234
Bernal de Gavaleta, Juan Manuel, 35
Bernizón, Elespuru, 55, 97, 130n, 134n
Bernstein, Henry, 6, 9–10
Bertram, Geoffrey, 43, 44, 147n
Bolivar, Simón, 40n
Bourgeoisie: national, 77; Cajamarcan, 148,
    180
Bourque, Susan, 142n
Bueno, Olga, 106, 178
Bueno Cacho family, 39
Bueno family, 34
Bueno León, Adolfo, 184
Burgos, Manuel, 124
Butter production, 56, 178, 188, 216; and
    exports, 50

Caballero, José María, 8n, 24, 247, 249, 256,
    317
Cabeza de porongo (coordinator of small milk
    producers), 203, 215, 318
Cacho, Mariano, 33n, 37, 100
Cacho family, 34, 37, 40
Cacho Gálvez, Manuel, 32n, 57, 105. *See also*
    Polloc (hacienda)
Cacho Sousa, Manuel, 54, 57, 150, 153, 172,
    177, 178
Cacho Sousa family, 177
Cajabamba (city), population of, 329
Cajabamba (province), xiii, 336. *see also*
    Araqueda (hacienda)
Cajamarca (city): commercial houses, 53,
    93–94; market, 52, 55, 87, 108, 127, 135,
    203; milk consumption in, 220;
    population, 32, 33, 329
Cajamarca (department): agricultural
    enterprises in, 50, 222; in 1876 census, 31;
    class relations in, 76; demographics, 44;
    economy, 23–24, 148–55; exports, 50–51;
    as food supplier, 23; Indian population,
    187; integration of market with coast,
    54–55; labor force, 23, 44–45; livestock
    production, 51; migration from, 204–9;
    milk production in, 210, 213; peasant
    militancy in, 169; population, 211; press
    in, 77n; representation in congress, 40n;
    in seventeenth and eighteenth centuries,
    24n; textile production in, 29;

transportation in, 51, 149, 153; wool production in, 29

Cajamarca (district), 87, 121, 226; judicial system, 167; in Peasant Family Survey, 338; population, 25, 33

Cajamarca (kingdom), xiii

Cajamarca (province), 336; agrarian reform in, 234–40; capitalist class in, 260; cooperatives in, 244–45; drought, 320–23; economically active population of, 221; hacienda system in, 19; population of, 30, 32; population of haciendas in, 24–25, 212, 329; roads, 137, 147, 153

Cajamarca Income Survey (1973), xiv, 224, 336–37

Cajamarca Valley: cattle production in, 57; land use in, 56, 211–20

Campesinista/descampesinista debate, 1–2, 265

CAP (Cooperative Agraria de Producción), 232, 233, 236n, 238, 239–40, 246, 254, 255; and agrarian debt, 253; membership in, 243–46; and temporary employment, 256–57

Capital (Marx), 4, 12, 164n

Capital, multinational, 216–20. *See also* Carnation (company); Nestlé

Capitalism: agrarian, 3, 148–50, 186, 187; state, 316. *See also* Class relations, capitalist

Capitalism, farmer. *See* Farmer path of capitalism

Capitalism, Junker. *See* Junker path of capitalism

Carnation (company), 151

Cartavio (plantation), 42, 49

CAS (Cooperative Agraria de Servicios de Agricultores), 236, 319

Casa Blanca (hacienda), 28 (Map 3); rental of, 178

Casa Commercial Querzola, 53n

Casa Grande (plantation), 42–43, 301; and cattle trade, 53; conversion to CAP, 304; diversification of crops, 50; family life on, 138n; recruitment of labor on, 46n, 47, 118, 126n, 131. *See also* Enganche system

Castro, Mariano, 40n

Castro family, 34, 37, 40

Castro Iglesias, Victor, 40n, 56

Castro Mendívil, Alejandro, 40n, 54, 57, 89, 150, 153, 154, 234, 235

Castro Pol, Edilberto, 37, 38n

Cattlemen's Association. *See* Association of Agriculturalists and Cattlemen of Cajamarca

Cattle production, 51–52, 55, 85, 211, 325; and breeding, 56–57; and exports, 24n, 51, 52; peasant domination of, 52, 86; technological developments in, 56. *See also* Dairy cattle

Cayalti (plantation), 46n, 47, 49n

CCP. *See* Confederación Campesina del Perú

Cebadín (*caserío*), 68, 131

Celendín (province), 52, 53, 55. *See also* Pallán (hacienda)

Census (1876), 30, 31, 327–30

Census (1940), 24, 30, 31n, 123, 330–31

Census (1961), 25, 210, 211n, 230n

Cerro de Pasco Corporation, 174, 182

Chamber of Commerce, Agriculture, and Industry (Cajamarca), 54, 149

Chambeu, Françoise, 65, 69, 84n, 305n

Chamis (hacienda), 28 (Map 3), 244; *colonos* at, 62; land disputes at, 39; ownership of, 36

Chaquil (hacienda), 28 (Map 3), 29, 85; land disputes at, 39; land sales at, 182–84; rental arrangements on, 64, 67, 72, 182

Charities, public, 36–39, 64, 87, 94. *See also* Beneficiencia Pública

Chavarri, Nicanór, 53n

Chávez Aliaga, Nazario, 36, 39

Chayanov, A. V., 4, 8, 296–97

Chevalier, Jacques, 6–7, 10

Chicama (coastal town), 42

Chicama Valley: plantations in, 42, 48, 50; sugar industry in, 41

Chicha (corn liquor), 78, 103, 108; sale of, 115, 124, 138

Chiclayo (coastal city), 42, 53

Chiclín (plantation), 42

Chilacat (cascrío), 194n, 204

Child mortality, 102, 298–99

Child rearing: in class processes, 16; on haciendas, 96, 105; in independent communities, 127–28, 132, 136

Children: abandonment of, 123, 132; activities after leaving households, 301–2, 305–6, 308–9; economic value of, 310; on haciendas, 62, 63, 108–9, 116, 334; as old

Children (*continued*)
age security, 307–9; in peasant
households, 96–99, 299–300
Chilete-Pacasmayo railroad, 51, 149
Chinchín (hacienda), 28 (Map 3); land
disputes at, 39
Chinese coolie labor, 43n, 45, 47
Chota (province), 46n; migration to, 47, 205
Chotén (hacienda), subdivision of, 175
Chumbil (hacienda), 28 (Map 3); marriages
at, 98; ownership, 36
Church, 94, 98; marriages by, 134, 306;
properties of, 36–39, 64, 87n, 174–75,
177, 180–82. *See also* Madres
Concepcionistas
Cia. Nacional de Recaudación, 124
Class analysis, 2; Marxist, 11–13
Class analytics: and development of
capitalism, 324–26; and hacienda system,
91–94; and household income, 270; in
peasant households, 276–82
Class processes, definition of, 12. *See also*
Class relations
Class processes, subsumed, 92–94, 261,
266–268, 276, 278; and reproduction of
labor power, 16, 19
Class relations: definition of, 13–14; on
haciendas, 91–94, 163–64, 186; and
household relations, 3, 17, 314–15; and
organization of production, 85; and
ownership of land, 202; transformation of,
208–9, 228–29, 260–61, 324–26
Class relations, capitalist, 14, 223, 269, 295;
and agrarian reform, 254; among former
hacienda residents, 208; compared to
feudal class relations, 75–76, 155–62; and
dairy industry, 159, 188–92; development
of, 89, 162, 324–25; in highlands, 228; in
independent peasant communities, 121,
141, 224; at national level, 93;
preconditions, 76; remuneration in, 75,
189–90; and subordination of women,
189–91, 227–28, 286
Class relations, communal, 14, 30; and
cooperatives, 260–61
Class relations, feudal, 13, 59, 228; and
agrarian reform, 231, 254, 260; compared
to capitalist class relations, 75–76,
155–62; and the church, 94; conditions
supporting, 92–94, 157; dissolution of,
155–57, 161–62, 208, 213; on haciendas,

74, 91–94, 119, 237; and household
relations, 95, 102, 110–11, 120, 202; and
household size, 102; remuneration in,
75–76, 79–80, 286; and subordination of
women, 110, 112, 117, 120, 202, 208,
309; and subsumed class payments, 92–94
Class relations, multiple, 58, 208, 267–68; on
haciendas, 92; in independent peasant
communities, 122, 310; in peasant
households, 2–3, 15, 143, 270–71,
276–78, 291, 314–15, 326
Class relations, petty, 14, 15, 92–94, 143,
208, 266–71, 276–82; and cooperatives,
261; expansion of, 163; and household
relations, 17, 141, 292, 310, 314–15, 326;
instability of, 142; and land sales, 163,
187, 192–97, 295; and subsumed class
payments, 92, 94, 270
Class struggle, 39, 119, 209; and capitalist
development, 210
Clauss, Wolfgang, 17
Coca, 78, 85, 103; export of, 50
Cocchambul (cheese factory), 216
Cochachi (district), 336
Cochamarca (hacienda), 28 (Map 3); rental
of, 178
Cochambul (hacienda), 38, 244
Coercion: economic, 69–75, 87, 117–19, 242;
into labor force, 45–47
Coffee production, 85, 321
Collins, Jane L., 11, 324n
Colonos: and agrarian reform, 255; in class
processes, 94; definition of, 59, 63; rental
arrangements of, 61–63, 67–68; wages
paid to, 78
Combayo (hacienda), xiv, 28 (Map 3), 29,
30n, 73; animal production on, 52n, 86,
112–13, 333–34; *arrendires* on, 66, 332–33;
colonos at, 61, 62, 63, 332–33; dairy
enterprise at, 173; fines levied at, 71;
foundry operations at, 80–81, 113n, 335;
income levels on, 86n, 111–19, 289,
332–35; irrigation systems on, 173;
kinship of owners, 35; labor force, 79–81;
land use at, 80, 85, 112, 333; migration
to, 33, 69; milling on, 104; mining on,
335; mobility, 73; size, 27; subdivision of,
172–73, 175; wage payments at, 78,
79–84, 89–91, 334–35
Commercial houses, 53–54, 93–94
Commoditization, 8

Compadrazco (fictive kinship), 75, 103, 196; and sharecropping arrangements, 69. *See also* Kinship

Comunidades Indígenas. *See* Indigenous communities

Condebamba Valley, 182–83

Confederación Campesina del Perú (CCP), 240n, 253n

Constitution of 1920, 41n

Consumer price index (Lima), 156n, 217, 258, 258n

Contumazá (city), population of, 329, 331

Cooperativa Agraria de Producción. *See* CAP

Cooperativa Agraria de Servicios de Agricultores. *See* CAS

Cooperativa de Servicios de Ganaderos, 223n

Cooperatives, xiv, 237, 238, 244–45; corruption in, 246; dairy, 320; decapitalization of, 247–48; and distribution of profit, 252; families in, 257n; indebtedness of, 247, 248; and land reform, 240–54; management of, 250–51; membership in, 241, 242, 258; misuse of resources, 249–50; on north coast, 256; and the state, 246; wages in, 252–53; women in, 242–43

Cooperativism, problems of, 246–54

Corn production, 56, 112–13

Cospán (district), 25

Credit: in cooperatives, 256n; and household reproduction, 267; and labor recruitment, 45–47; from landlords, 70, 72; in peasant communities, 129. *See also* Peasant indebtedness

Cristo Rey *(fundo)*, xiv, 235; rental of, 177, 180. *See also* Los Ayllus (CAP)

Currency, 52; devaluation of, 317

Cuzco (department), 24n

Dairy cattle, 56–57; breeding, 215, 220; Brown Swiss, 57, 178; Holstein, 57, 86, 148

Dairy enterprises, capitalist, xiv, 161, 179, 225, 317, 325; and agrarian reform, 254

Dairy industry, 148–50; and agrarian reform, 235; and *arrendires*, 177–80; capitalist class relations in, 162, 188–89; characteristics of, 213–14; effect on rural employment, 210; employment in, 159, 221–23, 228; impact on haciendas, 86, 159, 228; and land use, 211–20; level of productivity,

215; profitability of, 150; reasons for development, 162; role of peasantry in, 223, 234; role of PERULAC in, 215; and social differentiation, 223; and the state, 210; technological innovation in, 148, 151, 215; wage labor in, 186; women in, 188–89, 191–92, 208, 222

Davies, Thomas, 76–77

Debt peonage, 45, 76. *See also* Peasant indebtedness

Decapitalization: and dairy industry, 318; and land reform, 235

De Janvry, Alain, 6n, 9, 11

De León, Edmundo, 52, 56

Díaz, Alida, 327

Divorce, 15, 123, 309, 312; and abandonment of women, 131, 141–42, 306, 312–13, 323

Dobbertin, Enrique, 151n, 185, 189, 192

Elespuro Bernizón, Eulogio, 55, 97

El Milagro (CAP), 28 (Map 3), 241n, 244

El Rescate (CAP), 240n, 241n, 244, 255

El Rosario (CAP), 241n, 244

El Triunfo *(fundo)*, 179. *See also* Los Ayllus (CAP)

Empresa Agrícola Chicama, Ltda., 49–50, 53. *See also* Casa Grande (plantation)

Enganchadores, 45–47, 202

Enganche system, 47–48, 54, 60, 83, 102, 122, 158, 288; demise of, 50, 202

Ennew, Judith, 5

Epidemics, 44

Eslava, José, 23, 152n, 223n

FADEC (Federación Agraria Departamental de Cajamarca), 236n

Faenas: agricultural, 70; defined, 59; in rental arrangements, 66; of sharecroppers, 92; in transition to capitalism, 168, 182

Family farms, 7, 9

Farmer path of capitalism, 164, 169, 185, 209, 282; in Cajamarca, 177–86; defined, 164n

Farms, capitalist. *See* Dairy enterprises, capitalist

Fernández, Rosa, 131–34, 292, 294–95. *See also* Sangay-Fernández household

Fertilizer, guano, 154

Feudatarios (peasants formerly on haciendas), 231, 233, 237, 238, 258; and agrarian

Feudatarios (continued)
  reform, 254, 260; coercion of, 242
Fines, as economic coercion, 71–72, 87
Folbre, Nancy, 18
FONGAL (Fondo de Desarollo de
  Ganadería Lechera de Cajamarca), 204,
  220, 236
Food production: in Cajamarca Valley, 211;
  and terms of trade, 148, 162; in
  highlands, 47–48; during World War I,
  43
Forms of production, 6–9, 271
Franciscan monks, 181
Francisco Bologñesi (CAP), 244, 249
Franco, Ing. Efraín, xiii–xiv, 23, 336
Friedman, Kathie, 11n, 17
Friedmann, Harriet, 6–7, 9
Fuentes, M. A., 327
Functionalism, 6
Fundos, defined, 24
Fustán (*fundo*), 38

Gaitán, Evelio, 124
Gálvez, Napoleón, 216
García Puga, Juan, 35, 40
Garlic production, 128
Gil, Augusto, 178
Gildermeister family, 43, 48. *See also* Casa
  Grande (plantation)
Gitlitz, John Stephen, 23, 36, 65, 70n, 75n,
  85, 87n, 105n, 161, 170n
Gómez Sánchez, Rafael, 179–80, 235
Gonzales, Michael, 45–47
Gorget, François, 65, 69, 88n
Government, local, 123–24; landlord control
  over, 74
Grazing rights (*piseros*), 202; on haciendas,
  65; rental rates for, 66
Great Depression, 42, 147n; effect on
  Cajamarca, 50, 55; effect on sugar
  industry, 49

Haciendas, 28 (Map 3); boundary conflicts
  at, 38–39; cattle production at, 85–86;
  class relations on, 91–94, 110–11; control
  over labor, 24–34, 57; distance from
  market, 86–87; evictions from, 164–65;
  expansion of, 29, 33; feudal class relations
  on, 24, 91–93; harvests on, 103;
  integration into market economy, 53;
  land sales of, 169–77, 200, 289;

maintenance of infrastructure on, 67;
  migration to, 31, 33; mobility from,
  69–70, 73; organization of production on,
  84–91; ownership of, 34–36; population
  of, 25, 30, 32, 212n, 328, 329;
  profitability of, 158; purchases by
  Gonzalo Pajares, 181–83; rental
  arrangements on, 34, 36–39, 54, 60–69,
  70–71, 85–86; rental market, 36–39;
  rental rates for, 37, 156; role of children
  at, 62, 63, 80–82, 108–9, 116, 334; role of
  women at, 62, 63, 96n, 103–11, 334; self-
  sufficiency of, 53; size, 27; sources of
  income on, 31, 86n, 90–92; subdivision
  of, 174–77, 186, 202, 204, 212, 228;
  technological innovations on, 56; textile
  production on, 29; transition from feudal
  labor, 165–69; women owners, 35–36. *See
  also* Peasant indebtedness
Hacienda system, 3, 19, 74–75, 339; class
  analytics of, 91–94; dissolution of, 295,
  317; dominance of, 57; and protection of
  peasants, 74–75, 120
Harding, Colin, 161, 170
Health care, 303
Herrera, Angulo, 174
Hilbck, Kuntz and Cia., 53–54
Hillenbrand, Hans, 311, 312n
Hindess, Barry, 4
Hirst, Paul, 4, 5
Horton, Douglas, 90n
Hospitál Belemita, 36
Household relations, 208, 268; and class
  relations, 3, 17, 314–15, 326; defined,
  16–17; and division of labor, 16, 18;
  domestic labor in, 110; and feudal class
  relations, 95, 110, 120, 202; and gender
  relations, 2–3, 17–19, 326; in hacienda
  households, 141; in independent peasant
  communities, 126–41; life histories of,
  126–41; and reproduction of labor power,
  15–16, 110; stability of, 120, 122–23, 141,
  309–314; and subordination of women,
  242–43; and subsumed class processes, 18
Households, female-headed, 23n, 41, 100,
  141, 201, 310–11
Households, peasant: access to land in, 95;
  and *arrendire* arrangements with
  haciendas, 68–69; as basic unit of
  production, 9; and capitalist class
  relations, 224; and cash economy, 111; in

1940 census, 31; child rearing in, 18; children of, 31, 96–99, 299–300; class analytics of, 270; class relations in, 101–2, 309; and *colono* status, 63–64; composition of, 95–102, 313; constitution of, 95–102, 201; determinants of size, 297–300; differences between haciendas and communities, 141–42; disintegration of, 267, 271, 289, 301–9, 326; domestic work in, 285; effect of cooperatives on, 261; feudal class relations in, 120; formation of, 98; gender division of labor in, 102–11, 136–37, 142, 282–89, 309, 310, 325, 326, 334, 339; gender relations in, 18, 311; on haciendas, 68, 309, 334; income level of haciendas, 111–19, 289–90; income levels in, 274–76, 289–91, 332; income pooling among, 19, 111, 142, 287–89, 310; in independent communities, 68–69; instability in, 131, 141, 306, 310–14; integration into labor market, 210, 272, 287, 288; means of production in, 63, 187–88, 271–72; migration from, 339; and multiple class relations, 11–15; as producers of use values, 8; reconstitution of, 301–9; reproduction of, 208, 265–71; reproduction of labor power in, 15–19, 67, 95, 108, 202, 207, 237, 276–82; reproductive strategies, 121–22, 267, 271, 298, 301, 324–25; size of, 101–2, 296–97; sources of income in, 270, 272–76, 290; subsumed class processes in, 143n; subsumed class relations in, 291; surplus in, 268; as units of production, 11, 141, 271; as units of reproduction, 309–15. *See also* Class relations, petty
Housework. *See* Reproduction, daily
Huacariz de San Antonio (CAP), xiv, 240n, 241, 244, 251, 320; women members of, 243n, 251n, 252n
Huacariz de San Antonio (hacienda): permanent servants at, 62; sharecroppers at, 64, 87, 166; wage labor at, 109
Huacariz Grande (hacienda), 28 (Map 3), 33, 181
Huacataz (hacienda), 28 (Map 3), 29; land sales on, 182–84, 200; rental arrangements on, 183n
Huacraruco (hacienda), 28 (Map 3), 29, 185; *arrendires* on, 65, 68; livestock production,

52n, 53, 86; migration to, 33n; sale of, 48. *See also* José Carlos Mariátegui (SAIS)
Huagal (hacienda), 29; merger with La Pauca, 35
Hualgayoc (province), 29, 52, 53, 171n; migration to, 47
Hualqui (community), xiv, 68; effect of land sales at, 204
Huancavelica (department), 24n, 63n, 170n
Huasicamas (permanent servants), 62
Huayanmarca (hacienda), 28 (Map 3); subdivision of, 172
Huayobamba (CAP), xiv, 241n, 244, 247–48, 320
Huayobamba (hacienda), 28 (Map 3); expropriation of, 234, 235; and neighboring communities, 68, 69; rental arrangements on, 64, 71; rental of, 178–79
Huayrapongo (hacienda), 33, 244
Hunt, Shane, 201n

Ichocán (district), 25, 336
Iglesias, Miguel, 35, 40n
Iglesias family, 34, 36, 40, 85n
Incan empire, 56
Income levels: of hacienda households, 111–18; households on hacienda and community compared, 101n, 289–91; in independent communities, 118–19, 129, 272–76, 278–80; of landlords, 31, 86n, 90–92
Income pooling, 16–19; of hacienda households, 111; in independent communities, 129, 140, 142, 287–89, 310
Indebtedness. *See* Peasant indebtedness
Indian population, 30n, 161, 164, 187
Indigenismo (Indian question), 41, 77
Indigenous communities, 34; land base of, 29; livestock production in, 29. *See also* Peasant communities, independent
Industrial Promotion Law, 151n
Industrial reform, 316n
Inflation, 148, 317; effect of on land values, 156; effect of on peasant indebtedness, 159; during World War I, 48
Infrastructure: deterioration of, 246; maintenance of, 67, 124, 139, 318; requirements for dairy farming, 179, 223n
Inheritance, 16, 18, 141, 309; conflict over, 134–35, 137; on haciendas, 98, 110; in

Inheritance (*continued*)
  independent peasant communities, 122,
  129, 132, 139, 302, 323; in landlord class,
  34–36, 177; of women, 98, 122, 199, 243
Instituto de Reforma Agraria y
  Colonización, 173, 175
Irrigation, 154, 166
Iturbe de Iglesias, Paula, 36, 38n, 98

Jaén (province), migration to, 207, 307, 320
Jails, on haciendas, 73–74
Jancos (hacienda), subdivision of, 172
Jequetepeque Valley (Cajamarca), 44, 49,
  51, 207; CAPS in, 256; rice plantations
  in, 32n, 46n
Jesús (pueblo), 126, 131–34; market, 127,
  140, 203
Jesús (district), 50, 54n, 68, 121, 226, 336,
  338
Jesús Obrero (CAP), 244, 250, 320
Jocos (CAP), 247
Jocos (community), 202n
Jose Carlos Mariátegui (SAIS), 255
Junín (department), 24n, 63n; migration to,
  321
Junker path of capitalism, 163, 169, 170,
  180, 187, 209

Kapsoli, Wilfredo, 77n
Kinship: in cooperatives, 251; and economic
  ties, 140, 143, 225, 274–78, 303–4, 307,
  313; and sharecropping arrangements, 69,
  205, 301, 307, 323. See also *Compadrazco*
Klarén, Peter, 42, 43, 45
Knoch, Ricardo, 181–82

Labor: as commodity, 10; gender division of,
  xiv, 19, 102–11, 142, 201, 282–86;
  necessary and surplus, 102–11; reciprocal
  exchanges of, 103, 225–26, 282, 304, 310;
  shortages, 157, 161. See also Labor
  surplus, relative; Surplus labor; Wage
  labor
Labor contractors. See *Enganchadores*
Labor force: coercion into, 45–47; hacienda
  organization of, 80–81, 84–87;
  proletarianization of, 121–22, 223–24,
  283
Labor market, 8; provincial, 221–28, 256–60;
  regional development of, 44–50; women
  in, 286. See also Migration, temporary

Labor movement, coastal, 159
Labor power, reproduction of, 15–19, 120,
  268
Labor surplus, relative: on coast, 50, 158,
  198, 228; in highlands, 226n, 257–59
Lajas (hacienda), 28 (Map 3), 65, 202n
La Colpa (hacienda), 28 (Map 3); capitalist
  development at, 89; dairy enterprise at,
  56, 234; migration to, 33n;
  proletarianization of, 166; rental
  arrangements at, 66, 86; value of, 29;
  wages at, 78. See also El Rescate (CAP)
La Convención (Cuzco), 161
La Encañada (district), 25, 336, 338;
  population, 32
Laguna Seca (hacienda), agricultural
  experiments at, 154
Lajo Lazo, Manuel, 219, 319n
La Laguna (hacienda), subdivision of, 172
La Laguna (village), xiv
La Laimina (village), xiv, 65n, 68
La Liberated (department): economy, 42–44;
  migration to, 205, 207, 311n. See also
  Sugar industry; Sugar plantations
Lambayeque (department), 41; migration to,
  205, 207. See also Sugar industry; Sugar
  plantations
Land: adjudication of, 233, 239; changes in
  use of, 211–20; density, 31; enclosure of,
  164–65; expropriation of, 233; sales to
  peasants, 170, 174–75, 192–204, 234;
  value of, 156, 162, 180, 186
Landlessness, 165, 212
Landlord class, 34–41, 317; in Cattlemen's
  Association, 150; compensation to, 252;
  deteriorating power of, 162; and grazing
  rights, 68; intermarriage in, 34–41; land
  conflicts among families of, 39; luxury
  consumption of, 58, 94; and peasant
  labor, 31; public offices held by, 40;
  reactions to change, 163; and
  reorganization of productive process, 165,
  170, 173, 178–79; and rich peasants, 204
Landlord-peasant relationships, 60, 74, 101,
  110, 168
Landlord-peasant struggles, 39, 87–89, 229
La Pauca (hacienda), 28 (Map 3), 29;
  arrendires at, 65, 66; *colonos* at, 61; feudal
  class relations at, 74, 167; kinship of
  owners, 35; land disputes at, 39; and land
  reform, 235; land sales at, 174; land use

at, 85; livestock production, 52, 85, 86; migration to, 69; and neighboring communities, 68; size, 27. *See also* Puga Family

La Pauca (SAIS), 40, 239, 241–43, 244; as CAP, 245n

La Quispa (hacienda). *See* Santa Teresita de la Quispa (hacienda)

La Shita (*caserío*), 68, 131–32

Las Torrecitas (*fundo*), 130

La Succha (*caserío*), xiv, 68, 69, 125–26; and agrarian reform, 255; drought, 321; life histories in, 131–34, 137–41, 292, 294–95, 301–5, 322–23

La Tranca (hacienda), 28 (Map 3), 62, 64, 68. *See also* Luis de la Puenta Uceda (CAP)

La Victoria (*fundo*), 234

Leche Gloria, 219, 318

Leguía, Augusto, 41n; government of, 51, 52, 123

Lenin, V. I., 163n, 296–97

León y Ruppert (commercial house), 53

Ley de Conscripción Vial (Military Conscription Law, 1898), 51, 124, 129

Ley de Promoción y Desarollo Agrario (Agrarian Development and Promotion Law), 233, 319, 320

Ley Municipál (Municipal Law), 124

Life cycle, family, 292–315; and composition of family, 296–97, 314; and economic activity, 297n; and family structure, 300n

Lima: market, 23n; migration to, 205–7

Livestock. *See* Cattle production; Sheep production

Llacanora (district), 336

Llagadén (hacienda), 28 (Map 3), 62, 65

Llambi, Luis, 10

Llanos Aguero, José, 154n

Llaucán (hacienda), 46n, 49n, 87n, 170, 171n

Llushcapampa (hacienda), 28 (Map 3), 35n; agricultural experiments at, 154; land disputes at, 39; livestock production on, 52n; rental arrangements on, 61, 62, 65, 71

Los Ayllus (CAP), 241n, 244, 249, 250, 252–53

Los Baños del Inca (district), 336

Luis de la Puente Uceda (CAP), 244

Lurifico (rice plantation), 46n

Macera, Pablo, 31, 328–39

Madres Concepcionistas, 36, 37, 38, 73, 100, 170, 171, 175, 182

Magdalena (district), 25

Maids, 106–7, 130, 132, 305–6

Málaga, Santolalla, Fermín, 27, 34, 44, 50, 56, 59, 78, 106; career, 27n

Mallon, Florencia, 121, 123n, 125n

Manjar blanco production, 166, 179, 216, 221

Manzanilla (*caserío*), 68

Mariátegui, José Carlos (CAP), 244, 255

Market: commodity, 266–67, 269; development of, 6–7, 24, 44–50; internal, 42, 54, 58, 92, 170; and milk production, 162; and peasant consumption, 54–55; and peasant households, 287; product, 8, 50–57; regional, 24, 44–50. *See also* Labor market

Marriage, 15, 306; and constitution of households, 17; on haciendas, 97–98; infidelity in, 122; and tenancy, 99

Martínez, Marielle, 265

Martínez Alier, Juan, 91n

Marx, Karl, 3, 9; theory of class, 12

Matara (district), 25, 121, 336

McClintock, Cynthia, 250–53

Means of production, 92, 237, 252, 265; access to, 266, 267, 269, 271–76, 285; expansion of, 282; on haciendas, 119; rental of, 274, 276

Meiggs, Enrique, 51

Mejía, José Manuel, 65

Merchants, 113, 280; Chinese, 130; and commodity production, 15; petty, 11; as subsumed class, 12, 93

Mestizos, 30n, 74, 187

Miche (hacienda), 28 (Map 3), 69, 295

Michiquillay (community), xiv, 32n, 203n

Midwives, 96, 135

Migration: to Amazon, 205–7, 320–24; to coast, 46, 49, 205–7, 225, 301–2; to other elevations, 104, 135, 228; to haciendas, 69; to Lima, 205–7; of women, 134n, 201, 311

Migration, permanent, 49, 121, 255, 315; and coastal labor surplus, 158; and expulsion from haciendas, 205–6; and household reproduction, 267; and household size, 298; from independent peasant communities, 137; of women, 311

Migration, temporary, 45–48, 258; and

Migration, temporary *(continued)*
  capitalist class relations, 57; and demise
  of haciendas, 203; of former tenants, 165;
  during Great Depression, 50; and
  hacienda land sales, 196–98; from
  haciendas, 75, 93, 166; from independent
  peasant communities, 121, 133–34, 136,
  204–9; and income level, 117–19; and
  instability of households, 142–43, 288,
  310; magnitude of, 207; and rice harvest,
  201, 207; seasonality of, 121. See also
  Enganche system
Military Conscription Law, 51, 124, 129
Military service, 124, 158
Milk: acidity of, 215–16, 217; fat content of,
  215, 217, 219; importation of, 318–19;
  market for, 149, 289; powdered, 318;
  price of, 216–20, 318; processing of,
  216; tariff on, 217–19; transportation
  of, 215
Milkmaids, 165; on cooperatives, 241n, 242;
  on dairy farms, 189–91, 222, 223n; wages
  of, 190–99, 222–23
Miller, Solomon, 47, 138n, 141, 143n
Milling, 104, 107–8, 181, 211
Mingas (work parties), 78, 103, 225, 282; at
  Pariamarca, 128; of women on haciendas,
  62, 63, 107–8
Minimum wage, 159, 258n, 259, 260, 278
Mining, 79, 81–82, 91, 115; in Amazon
  region, 320; expansion of industry, 158;
  exports of, 50n; at haciendas, 80
Ministry of Agriculture (Cajamarca), xiv,
  149, 336
Ministry of Labor (Cajamarca), 171, 222,
  223
Ministry of Public Works (Cajamarca), 154n
Miraflores (hacienda), 33. *See also* Los Ayllus
  (CAP)
Miranda, Mariano, 37
Miranda, Susana, 185
Mitayos (shepherds), 62, 91, 109, 115, 172
Modes of production, 1, 9; definition of, 3–6
Monasterio de las Consabidas Descalzas. *See*
  Madres Concepcionistas
Moneylenders, 280; as subsumed class, 12
Montoya, Rodrigo, 10, 53
Montoya Cabanillas, Serapio, 37–38, 171,
  216
Morales Bermúdez, General, 233, 255, 317
Muleteers, 122

Municipal Law, 124
Muñoz, Victoriano, 184

Namora (district), 25, 121, 135, 181, 336
Negociación Agrícola Ganadera, 174
Negociación Agrícola Jequetepeque, 49–50
Negociación Ganadera El Triunfo (milk
  processor), 216
Negritos (community), 240n
Negritos (hacienda) 30n; land disputes at,
  39; and land reform, 235
Neira y Chavarri (commercial house), 53n
Nestlé, S.A., 149, 151. *See also* PERULAC
Noriega, Abraham, 178n
Noriega (hacienda), 68, 69, 109
Noriega family, 130

Office for Direction and Improvement of
  Cattle Production, 219
Orbegoso, Luis José, 85n
Otoya Puga, Antonio, 37, 38, 70, 89, 171
Otuzco *(fundo)*, 33; ownership of, 53n

Pacasmayo (coastal province), 41, 53
Pajares, Absalón, 181
Pajares, Anuario, 181
Pajares, Pedro, 174, 234
Pajares Goicochea, Gonzalo, 37, 173–74,
  180–85
Pallán (hacienda): ownership of, 36; peasant
  rebellions at, 170n; rental arrangements
  at, 65n, 85n; subdivision of, 175
Pardo administration, 76
Pariamarca (village), xiv, 125; life histories
  in, 126–31, 134–37, 292–95, 305–7,
  321–24
Paternalism in hacienda system, 60, 74–75
Patriarchy, 18, 95; in family farming system,
  284; in peasant households, 101, 288
Peasant Communities (Comunidades
  Campesinas), 29, 30; and agrarian
  reform, 232–33, 236n, 243
Peasant communities, independent, 33,
  121–43; administration of, 123; credit in,
  325; and dairy industry, 210; defined, 29;
  and hacienda conflict, 37, 87n; and
  hacienda rental arrangements, 60–65, 66,
  68–69; household relations in, 309; lack
  of resources in, 202; land pressure in, 58,
  142, 310; and monetization, 54, 55, 223;
  sharecropping in, 71; and the state,

123–26; and temporary migration, 299–300; wage labor in, 228; women in, 101–2

Peasant economy, 1; as form of production, 6–9; as mode of production, 3–11. *See also* Households, peasant; Class relations, petty

Peasant Family Survey (1976), xiv, 31, 61, 66, 96n, 102n, 164n, 226n, 227, 241n, 257, 280n, 299, 307, 310–11, 313, 338–39

Peasant Groups (Grupos Campesinos), 232, 233, 238, 239, 240, 241

Peasant indebtedness, 38, 70–73, 76–77, 91, 117–18, 202; at Hacienda Combayo, 79–84. *See also* Credit

Peasant militancy, 39, 169–72, 230, 255

Peasants: and agrarian reform, 254; and capital, 1, 9–11; education, of, 74, 96; as employers, 225; eviction from haciendas, 168, 228, 235; exploitation of, 87–91; integration into labor market, 309; landlessness of, 212, 228; land sales to, 170, 183–84; mobility of, 69–75; political consciousness of, 237; and product market, 54; resettlement of, 164; rights as citizens, 159; use of litigation, 125; and wage labor, 223–28. *See also* Social differentiation, peasant

Peasants, poor, 208, 282. *See also* Social differentiation, peasant; Smallholders

Peasants, rich, 202, 208, 282; and landlord class, 204. *See also* Social differentiation, peasant

Peasant studies, concepts in, 3–11

Peru: agrarian reform legislation, 166, 230; currencies, 52–53; economic policies, 23, 147, 162; export crops, 162; import policies, 318; labor legislation, 221, 222; social security system, 222

PERULAC (Compañia Peruana de Alimentos Lacteos, S.A.), 216; butter production, 221; and Cattlemen's Association, 216–19; cheese production, 221; and cooperatives, 261; employees of, 221; establishment of, 151; and land reform, 236; milk-pricing policy, 320; processing plant, 178, 318; promotional activities, 152, 179; purchasing policy, 319; relation with state, 318–20; suppliers, 152, 167, 179, 181, 203, 215, 219, 249, 260, 318, 338

Petty bourgeoisie, 276; income levels of, 289; and Junker path, 180; land sales to, 184; rural, 129, 185, 272, 274, 330

Petty producers, 14–15, 19, 276; and agrarian reform, 255; among former hacienda residents, 186, 208; life histories, 135; and wage labor, 261; women as, 285

Petty production, as mode of production, 5–60. *See also* Class relation, petty

Pike, Frederick, 40, 51

Pizarro, Francisco, xiii

Plantations: labor force on, 134n; labor struggles on, 47

Polloc (hacienda), xiv, 28 (Map 3), 29, 32n, 57; credit on, 72; land sales at, 172, 177, 181; livestock production, 52n, 57, 85; migration to, 33n, 69; milling at, 104; rental arrangements on, 62, 65, 67, 71, 72. *See also* El Rosario (CAP)

Polloquito (hacienda): *colonos* at, 64; land sales at, 174, 176–77

Polygamy, 288

Pomalca (plantation), 48

Porcón (hacienda), xiv, 28 (Map 3), 29, 30n; adjudication of, 240; *arrendires* of, 37, 66; *colonos* at, 62, 63–64; forced sales, 72; land disputes at, 39; land sales at, 170; ownership of, 36; peasant conflict at, 88; sheep raising on, 52n, 86, 103; wool spinning at, 107–8. *See also* Atahualpa (SAIS)

Porconcillo (hacienda), 33; land disputes at, 39

Porongos (milk collection receptacles), 236

Potato production, 79, 103, 109, 112–13, 125, 139, 226

Prado, Manuel, 147; government of, 149

Production, forms of. *See* Forms of production

Production, means of. *See* Means of production

Programa de Integración y Asentamiento Rural (PIAR), 249

Proletarianization, 89–91, 228, 265, 269, 324–25; after eviction, 165; and farming, 137–41; and instability of household relations, 309, 314; and temporary labor, 121

Proletariat, rural, 170, 240

Property, private, 15; and agrarian reform, 246, 253; and peasant owners, 254

Puente, Julio de la, 178n
Puga Chavarry, Carolina, 35
Puga Estrada, Rafael, 35, 40, 70, 86, 167–69, 174, 235
Puga family, 34, 35, 36, 38, 39, 40, 62. *See also* La Pauca (hacienda)
Puga Valera, José Mercedes, 35, 40
Puga y Puga, José Mercedes, 40
Puga y Puga, Pelayo, 40
Puga y Puga, Victor Napoleón, 35, 40
Punishment, physical, 73
Puno (department), 24n
Punteros (cattlehands), 91, 115, 172
Purhuay (hacienda), 28 (Map 3); land sales at, 182–84; technological innovations on, 56

Quechua (language), 30n, 88
Querzola, Domingo, 53n
Querzola, Luis, 54
Quilcate (hacienda), technological innovations on, 56
Quinoamayo (community), xiv, 203n

Railroad construction, 51
Rainbird, Helen, 237
Rapp, Rayna, 18
Rationalism, 6n
Registros Públicos de Cajamarca (RPC), 27n
Remittances (migrant), 143, 273–75, 303
Rendón, Teresa, 265
Rental contracts. See *Arrendires* (landlord renters); *Arrendires* (peasant renters)
Reproduction, daily, 16, 108, 136, 140, 202–3, 283, 285
Repúblicas (public projects), 67, 124; on haciendas, 67
Resnick, Stephen, 12, 13
Resumen del Censo General (1878), 327–28, 330
Revolutionary Military Government, 222, 228, 230, 233, 316–17
Rice industry, 136, 321; changes in technology, 157–58; employment in, 48; growth of, 49
Rice plantations, 46n; and Agrarian Reform Law, 225; labor recruitment, 47; women on, 201
Right to Remuneration Bill (1916), 76–77
Road Conscription Law, 51, 124, 129
Road construction, 153, 158, 173, 203, 320
El Rodeo (cattlemen's journal), 148, 150, 151n, 161, 178

Rodeos, 67, 211
Rodríguez, Leopoldo, 54
Rojas, Abelardo, 134n, 185
Rojas Rodríguez brothers, 37, 38n
Roma (plantation), 42, 49n
Ronquillo (hacienda), 63
Rossell, Juan Miguel, 151n, 165, 177–79, 189–90, 192n, 216, 235n. *See also* Tres Molinos (hacienda)
Rumay, María, 126–31, 292–93, 298. *See also* Aguilar-Rumay household
Rural economy, monetization of, 204, 225, 228–29, 269, 287, 310

Saenz Cacho, Gonzalo, 177, 192
SAIS (Sociedad Agrícola de Interés Social), 232, 233, 236n, 238, 239; and agrarian debt, 253
San Antonio (hacienda), 65, 125, 137, 305
Sangal (hacienda), 28 (Map 3), 62
Sangay-Fernández household, 137–41, 255, 294–96, 301–5, 322–23
San Marcos (district), 25, 28, 226, 336; market in, 203–4
San Miguel (province), 47, 54n. *See also* Udima (hacienda)
San Pablo (district), 25, 47
Santa Bárbara (*fundo*), 33
Santa Bárbara (*caserío*), xiv, 192n
Santa Cruz (province), 46n; migration to, 47, 321
Santa Teresita de la Quispa (hacienda), 37; land sales at, 174–77, 194n
Santa Ursula (hacienda), xiv, 28 (Map 3), 156; *arrendires* of, 37, 66, 177, 183; *colonos* at, 63–64; credit on, 72; dairy enterprise at, 89; fines levied at, 71, 73; forced sales, 72; land disputes at, 33n; land sales at, 175–76, 198; and neighboring communities, 68; ownership of, 36; peasant households on, 99–100; peasant rebellions at, 89, 170–72; rental contracts at, 37–38, 70–71, 77, 78, 89, 107, 109, 177; wage payments on, 78
Santiago de Cao (coastal town), 42
Santolalla, Nicolás, 27n, 52, 61, 64, 79, 81, 82, 85, 90–91, 148, 173, 333, 334; at National Agrarian University, 79–80
Santolalla Bernal, Rosalía, 91, 173, 182
Santolalla Iglesias, Eloy, 35, 73, 79, 84, 99, 172; death, 91; mining activities, 79

Santolalla Iglesias, Francisco, 35
Sarachaga, Juan, 24
Sarín (community), 198
Sattui and Cia., 54
Schejtman, Alexander, 6–7, 265–66
Schools: on haciendas, 74, 96; in independent communities, 128n, 187n
SCIPA (Servicio Cooperativo Interamericano de Producción de Alimentos), 153–54, 171
Selva regions, 320–21. *See also* Amazonian region
Semaneras (weekly workers), 62, 63, 75, 106–7, 109, 115, 334
Semiproletarianization, 209
Sexemayo (hacienda), 28 (Map 3), 185
Sharecropping, 115, 213; in independent peasant communities, 136; as fundamental class process, 92; on haciendas, 59, 60, 64–66, 87; between hacienda tenants and households in independent peasant communities, 71; rental arrangements in, 64–65; in transition to capitalism, 182
Shaullo (community), 33n
Sheep production, 51–52; among independent peasant communities, 140
Shultín (*fundo*), 28 (Map 3), 185; enclosures on, 164; sharecroppers at, 64, 87; wage labor at, 109
Silva Santisteban, Jesús, 23, 55, 57, 65, 78, 87, 154, 164, 226n
SINAMOS (Sistema Nacional de Mobilización Social), 236n
Sitacocha (district), 336
Smallholders, 240, 274, 276, 278
Smith, Carol, 6, 7
Social differentiation, peasant, 223–24; and access to land, 193–95, 197, 212, 271–73; in *campesinista/descampesinista* debate, 1–2, 265–66; and class relations, 276–82, 309, 314–15, 324–26; over family life cycle, 292–97; and gender division of labor, 282–85; and generation of household income, 271–76; on haciendas, 95, 96n, 101, 193; and household composition, 298–300; and household reproduction, 202–4, 266–71, 314–15; and income pooling, 287–89; in peasant communities, 121, 226–28, 325; and women's contribution to income, 285–87
Social formations, 4, 13

Sociedad Geográfica del Perú, 31n, 327, 330
Sociedad Nacional Agraria, 236
Socio-Economic Study Program of the Cajamarca–La Libertad Pilot Project (PPCLL), xiii–xiv, 121n, 122n, 336
Socorros (advances), 45, 321
Sondor (hacienda), 28 (Map 3), 29; *arrendires* on, 65; land disputes at, 39; land sales at, 176, 199; and neighboring communities, 88
Sousa, José, 37
Sousa, Vicente, 38n
Sousa family, 40
Structuralism, 6
Sub-*arrendires*, contracts, 70–71
Subsumption, 10; formal, 10n; Marx's concepts of, 9–11
Sugar cane, production in Cajamarca, 85
Sugar industry, 23; changes in technology, 157; collapse of market in, 49; employment in, 43n, 47, 48; expansion of, 41, 42, 44–45, 92; and international market, 43; prices, 48; taxation of, 124; wages in, 43, 118. See also *Enganche* system
Sugar plantations: agrarian conflicts at, 161; and Agrarian Reform Law, 225; labor requirements of, 47. *See also* Casa Grande (plantation); Cayalti (plantation)
Sunchubamba (hacienda), 28 (Map 3), 178; migration to, 33n; sale of, 48; size, 27
Surplus labor, 12–14; accumulation of by peasants, 268–71, 281–82, 291; in capitalist class relations, 14, 76; in cooperatives, 260–61; distribution of, 12, 14n, 67–68, 93–94; extraction of, 11, 280–82; in feudal class relations, 60, 76, 92, 107–10; in fundamental class relations, 12, 18; and gender division of labor, 105, 107, 109–10, 283; and rate of exploitation, 87–89, 109, 188–91. *See also* Labor; Labor surplus, relative; Wage labor

Tambos (general stores), 38, 72, 79
Tarapato region (Amazon), 318
Tariffs, 49, 217–19
Tartar Grande (*fundo*), 28 (Map 3), 164, 181, 185, 244. *See also* Los Ayllus (CAP)
Tartar de los Baños (*fundo*), ownership of, 36
Tartar de Otuzco (*fundo*), ownership of, 36
Taxation, 124–25, 291; reform, 317

Taylor, Lewis, 23, 53, 65n, 70n, 73n, 77n, 89, 237, 330
Tello, Manuel, 247, 249, 256
Textiles: export of, 24n; production of, 29, 104
Thorp, Rosemary, 43, 44, 147n
Torres, Segunda, 311, 312n
Trade: among independent peasant households, 135; barriers to, 52; with Casa Grande, 43; intraregional, 52
Transportation, 51, 137, 144, 149, 153
Treaty of Ancón, 35
Tres Molinos (*caserío*), xiv, 165
Tres Molinos (hacienda), xiv, 28 (Map 3), 87, 178; dairy enterprise at, 179; enclosures on, 164; and land reform, 235n; work force at, 165. *See also* Los Ayllus (CAP)
Trujillo (city), 42; import houses, 43
Trujillo (coastal province), 41
Tuñad (hacienda), 28 (Map 3), 244; livestock production on, 52n

Uceda, Diego, 38n
Udima (hacienda), 29, 85n, 86n; collection of rents at, 90n; ownership of, 35; sale of, 48
Unions, 77, 231
Upward mobility, 180–86
Urubamba (hacienda), 33
Usufruct rights, 166; on haciendas, 81, 117

Valderrama, Mariano, 175
Valera Villacorta, Wenceslao, 174, 182
Velasco Alvarado, General, 228, 230, 233, 236, 316n, 317
Velázquez, Beatriz, 181
Velgara, José, 166–67, 241
Velgara, María, 166
Vista Alegre (hacienda), land sales at, 176, 199
VITALECHE (milk processor), 217
Von Werlhof, Claudia, 10

Wage labor: and agrarian reform, 237; agricultural, 158, 160, 221, 225; on coast, 225; origin on haciendas, 75–84; in highlands, 225; and household reproduction, 269; and Junker path, 163; and land reform, 231, 233; male domination of, 142; and peasant indebtedness, 79–84; peasant

participation in, 1–2, 223–28; permanent, 257; and petty production, 261, 265; seasonal, 265; as subsumed class process, 282. *See also* Labor; Surplus labor
Wage rates: in city of Cajamarca, 130; on coast, 118–19, 138, 198; on dairy enterprises, 159, 185, 189; and differences by gender, 82, 109, 130n, 189–90, 227–28, 259, 286, 289–91; on haciendas, 78, 81–83; in independent communities, 129; and legal minimum wage, 159, 222, 259; and payment in kind, 79, 128, 136, 226–27; in province of Cajamarca, 119n, 158–60, 258–59, 321
Warman, Arturo, 2
War of the Pacific, 23, 35, 41n, 45, 51
Wheat: export of, 24n, 50; importation of, 44; production of, 112–13, 150
White, Ben, 17–18
Widows, on haciendas, 100–101
Wolff, Richard, 12, 13
Wolpe, Harold, 3–4
Women: abandonment of, 96, 310–12; access to land, 199–201, 309; age at marriage, 97, 300; contribution to household income, 286, 291; in cooperatives, 242–43, 257; devaluation of labor, 109–10, 116–17, 285–86, 291; economic activities of, 62–64, 143; education of, 311; on haciendas, 62–64, 96n, 103–11, 334; and labor legislation, 223; in near-landless households, 284; in peasant households, 95–97, 282–89; pregnancy rates, 298–99; remuneration of, 78, 286; single, 96, 100, 201; as single mothers, 127, 306, 311, 312–13; subordination of, 3, 112, 117, 120, 142n, 208–9, 242–43, 260, 291, 309, 326; as traders, 287, 303, 305; as wage laborers, 222–23, 227
Wong, Diana, 17
Wool spinning, 104, 107–8
World War I, 42, 43, 77
World War II, 148, 151

Yanacancha (hacienda), subdivision of, 172
Yanaconas (tenants), 77
Yanamango (community), 33n, 68
Yanamarca (*caserío*), 185–86, 244
Yana Yacu (hacienda), subdivision of, 175

Zevallos, Miguel, 178
Zevallos Palmer, Fidel, 37, 38, 63n